FINANCIAL MARKETS AND SERVICES

FINANCIAL MARKETS AND SERVICES

DR. R. MARIA INIGO

REGAL

REGAL PUBLICATIONS
New Delhi - 110 027

FINANCIAL MARKETS AND SERVICES

ISBN 978-81-8484-122-0

Typeset by
RAHUL COMPOSERS
358, Pocket-B, Phase-2, Sector-16 B, Dwarka, New Delhi - 110 075

Printed in India at
MAYUR ENTERPRISES
WZ Plot No. 3, Gujjar Market, Tihar Village, New Delhi - 110 018

Published by
REGAL PUBLICATIONS
F-159, Rajouri Garden, New Delhi - 110 027 • Phone : 45546396
E-mail : regalbookspub@yahoo.com

Contents

Preface

This book attempts to provide an exhaustive theoretical overview of financial market and the services available in India. Over the past few decades there have been lot of changes taking place in the Indian financial, economical, legal and the technological fronts. Keeping pace with these changes lot of amendments and modifications have also been brought about in the financial services industry and the financial markets were aligned for these changes. This book also provides various inputs from the practical angle and is meant to cater to the needs of students of various business courses as a handbook. Today there is need for comprehensively understanding these financial instruments, the market system and various institutions offering variety of financial products and services. This book is primarily intended for students and for all those who are directly involved in different capacities and roles in the financial sector, which today is one of the largest emerging sectors in the global economy. Aspirants of professional courses like, CAs, CSs and CWAs will also be much benefited out of this book and it will provide more insight on financial system to all kinds of readers. Hence, this book is expected to be useful to an expert as well as a novice on the financial system, market and services. Chapterization have been so designed to group similar and related areas of financial services and markets and the related legal measures in a coherent order, so that the readers will have an ease of reading.

R. MARIA INIGO

1

Financial System and Services

The growth of economy is enhanced by financial intermediation that pools funds of the small and scattered savers and allocates them for investment in an efficient manner by using their informational advantage in the loan market. They are principal mobilizers of surplus funds to finance productive activity and to the extent that they promote capital accumulation, they promote growth and accelerate the economic activity. Among the institutions in the financial markets commercial banks and non-bank intermediaries undertake the important process of financial intermediation whereby the funds or savings of the surplus sectors are channeled to deficit sectors. The financial institutions channel the funds of surplus economic units to those wanting to spend on real capital investment. Funds are transferred through the creation of financial liabilities such as bonds and equity shares. Among the financial institutions, commercial banks account for a larger portion of financial sector assets.

Financial intermediation is one whereby the funds or savings of the surplus sectors are channeled to deficit sectors by the institutions in the financial markets such as commercial banks and non-bank intermediaries. The financial institutions channel the funds of surplus economic units to those wanting to spend on real capital investment. Funds are transferred through the creation of financial liabilities such as bonds and equity shares. Among the financial institutions, commercial banks account for a larger part of the total financial sector assets. Financial intermediation can enhance growth by pooling funds of the small and scattered savers and allocating them for investment in an efficient manner by using their informational advantage in the loan market. They are principal the gatherer of surplus funds to finance productive activity and to the extent that they promote capital accumulation, they promote growth.

TRANSFORMATION FUNCTION

Intermediary services are of two kinds, brokerage function and asset transformation activity. Brokerage function as represented by the activities of brokers and market operators, processing and supplying information is a part and parcel of all intermediation by all institutions. Brokerage function brings together lenders and borrowers and reduces market imperfections such as search, information and transaction costs. The asset transformation activity is provided by institutions issuing claims against themselves which differ from the assets they acquire. Mutual funds, insurance companies, banks and depository institutions undertake size transformation by providing many depositors with a share of a large asset or issuing debt type liabilities against equity type assets. While providing asset transformation, financial firms differ in the nature of transformation undertaken and in the nature of protection or guarantees which are offered. Banks and depository institutions offer liquidity, insurance against contingent losses to assets and mutual funds against loss in value of assets.

Through their intermediary activities banks provide a package of information and risk sharing services to their customers. While doing so they take on part of their risk. Banks have to manage the risks through appropriate structuring of their activities and hedge risks through derivative contracts to maximize their profitability. Financial institutions provide three transformation services—

- Liability, asset and size transformation consisting of mobilization of funds and their allocation.
- Maturity transformation by offering the savers the relatively short-term claim or liquid deposit they prefer and providing borrowers long-term loans which are better matched to the cash flows generated by their investment.
- Risk transformation by transforming and reducing the risk involved in direct lending by acquiring more diversified portfolios than individual savers can. The expansion of the financial network or an increase in financial intermediation as denoted by the ratio of financial assets of all kinds to gross national product accompanies growth. To a certain extent, growth of savings is facilitated by the increase in the range of financial instruments and expansion of markets.

Services Rendered

- Benefits provided by financial intermediaries consist of reduction of information and transaction costs, grant long-term loans, provide liquid claims and pool risks. Financial intermediaries economize costs of borrowers and lenders. Banks are set-up to mobilize savings of many small depositors which are insured. While lending, the bank makes a single expert investigation of the credit standing of the borrower saving on several investigations of amateurs.
- Financial intermediaries make it possible for borrowers to obtain long-term loans even though the ultimate lenders are making only short-term loans. Borrowers who wish to acquire fixed assets do not want to finance them with short-term loans. Although the bank has used depositors' funds to make long-term loans it still promises its depositors that they can withdraw their deposits at any time on

the assumption that the law of large numbers will hold. Bank deposits are highly liquid and one can withdraw the deposit any time, though on some kinds of deposits the interest previously earned on it has to be foregone. Finally, banks by pooling the funds of depositors reduce the riskness of lending. Indirect finance in some reduces the information and transaction costs of lenders and borrowers, renders deposits liquid and reduces the risk of lending.

- The ability of the financial intermediaries to ensure the most efficient transformation of mobilized funds into real capital has not, however, received the attention it deserves. Institutional mechanisms to ensure end use of funds have not been efficient in their functioning, leaving the investor unprotected. Efficient financial intermediation involves reduction of the transaction cost of transferring funds from original savers to financial investors. The total cost of intermediation is influenced by financial layering which makes the individual institution's costs additive in the total cost of intermediating between savers and ultimate borrowers. The aggregate cost of financial intermediation from the original saver to ultimate investor is much higher in developing countries than in developed countries.

Financial Intermediaries

One of the important components of the financial system is the financial intermediary that makes the financial system a vibrant one. Today, their importance in the Indian financial system cannot be underestimated. These intermediaries stimulate every financial activity in India and due to their active role India has become one of the fastest growing economies of the world.

Development Finance Institutions: Development Financial Institutions play a crucial role in industrial development of India by catering to the needs of the growing industrial sectors as well as act as the agent of fostering growth of the economy. In addition to the financing of industry by these institutions in the traditional form term loans for project finance, underwriting, direct subscription, lease financing also provide working capital to the company. The present structure consist of development financial institutions such as, IDBI, IFCI, ICICI, SIDBI, and regional level institutions namely State Financial Corporations, State Industrial Development Corporations, etc.

Commercial Banks: Planned economiç development is a pre-requisite for proper economic development and due such effort and the nationalization at appropriate time a geographically wide and functionally diverse banking system has emerged in India. The growth of the banking system is very phenomenal and the lending of banks to various sectors of the economy and especially to rural and semi-urban areas is mentionable. The share of the priority sector in the total bank credit had always been as per the predetermined limit of 40% of the total bank credit. These banks has emerged as commercially viable, organizationally dynamic, vibrant and functionally tuned to the emerging economic conditions. The banks can be classified as scheduled and non-scheduled commercial banks. The scheduled commercial banks belong to the category of public sector, private sector or foreign banks.

Insurance Companies: After privatization of the insurance sector India's insurance has witnessed world-class standards. More percentage of foreign participation was allowed to attract foreign investment in this area. However, the age old Life Insurance Corporation of India (LIC) and General Life Insurance Corporation of India (GIC) which public sector institutions due to the government patronage operates a variety of schemes and has made significant progress in extending social security to weaker sections of the society through its Group Insurance Scheme. GIC along with its four subsidiaries viz., National Insurance Co. Ltd., The New India Assurance Company Ltd., Oriental Insurance Company Ltd, operates a number of insurance schemes to meet variety needs of different sectors of society. In recent years the thirteen insurance companies offer lot variety of schemes in both life and non-life insurance business.

Non-Banking Financial Companies: Except for few financial companies that swindled the money of some innocent investors during 1995 to 2002 the role played by the NBFCs was also worth mentionable. After the intervention of RBI into some scams of NBFCs, there is controlled and regulated growth of financial companies in India. They marked significant growth in terms of number, deposits, etc. and provide wide range of financial services. These are partly fund based and partly fee based. The important activities of NBFCs are equipment leasing, hire purchase finance, bill discounting, venture capital, housing finance, factoring, issue management, portfolio management, helping mergers and acquisitions and the like.

Kinds of Intermediation

Brokerage function and asset transformation activity are the two kinds intermediary services. Brokerage function as represented by the activities of brokers and market operators, processing and supplying information is a part and parcel of all intermediation by all institutions. Brokerage function brings together lenders and borrowers and reduces market imperfections such as search, information and transaction costs. The asset transformation activity is provided by institutions issuing claims against themselves which differ from the assets they acquire. Mutual funds, insurance companies, banks and depository institutions undertake size transformation by providing many depositors with a share of a large asset or issuing debt type liabilities against equity type assets. While providing asset transformation, financial firms differ in the nature of transformation undertaken and in the nature of protection or guarantees which are offered.

Commercial banks provide a package of information and risk sharing services to their customers. While doing so they take on part of their risk. Banks have to manage the risks through appropriate structuring of their activities and hedge risks through derivative contracts to maximize their profitability.

Financial Transformation

Financial institutions provide three transformation services—

1. Liability, asset and size transformation consisting of mobilization of funds and their allocation. That is by

provisioning for large loans on the basis of numerous small deposits.

2. Maturity transformation by offering the savers the relatively short-term claim or liquid deposit they prefer and providing borrowers long-term loans which are better matched to the cash flows generated by their investment.
3. Risk transformation is done by transforming and reducing the risk involved in direct lending by acquiring more diversified portfolios than individual savers can. The expansion of the financial network or an increase in financial intermediation as denoted by the ratio of financial assets of all kinds to gross national product accompanies growth. To a certain extent, growth of savings is facilitated by the increase in the range of financial instruments offered by the intermediaries.

Benefits of Financial Intermediation

Several benefits accrue to the persons dealing with the intermediary and the society at large. These consist of reduction of information and transaction costs, grant of long-term loans, provide liquid claims and pool risks. Financial intermediaries economize cost of borrowers and lenders. Banks are set-up to mobilize savings of many small depositors which are insured. While lending, the bank makes a single expert investigation of the credit standing of the borrower saving on several investigations of amateurs. Financial intermediaries make it possible for borrowers to obtain long-term loans even though the ultimate lenders are making only short-term loans. Borrowers who wish to acquire fixed assets do not want to finance them with short-term loans.

Bank uses depositors' funds to make long-term loans and at the same time it promises its depositors that they can withdraw their deposits at any time. Bank deposits are highly liquid and one can withdraw the deposit at any time, though on some kinds of deposits the interest previously earned on it has to be foregone which is a sort of penal interest for premature withdrawal.

Efficient financial intermediation involves reduction of the transaction cost of transferring funds from original savers to financial investors. The total cost of intermediation is influenced by financial layering which makes the individual institution's costs additive in the total cost of intermediating between savers and ultimate borrowers. The aggregate cost of financial intermediation from the original saver to ultimate investor is much higher in developing countries than in developed countries.

Finance Function and Integrated Settlement System

In today's banking, the payment, processing and settlement system has seen tremendous changes than in the past. Operational efficiency, speed, better accuracy and timelines of payment transactions as well as financial risks in the payment system are achieved by the establishment of network. The concept of e-banking, internet banking use of ATMs, etc., has put the banking system on fast track. Banking and financial market transactions reduce transaction costs and improve efficiency of channels for transmission of monetary policy. Integrated payment and settlement system has the benefit of paper-less electronic payment services with securities and funds transactions, across the money and capital markets both national and international through a reliable, secure and speedy communication networks.

Economic Environment

The growth of financial service sector in any country needs appropriate economic conditions. Various economic factors that contribute to such an conducive situation are:

- Proper economic planning
- Encouraging economic condition.
- Favourable economic system
- Suitable economic laws
- Often reviewed economic policies

Encouraging Eonomic Condition

Financial services industry can be perform their functions effectively only under encouraging economic conditions. Continued depression leading to poor economic conditions of closing down of production, etc. will lead to further deterioration of services provided by the financial servicing industry. Hence, under these situations financial services will not experience any growth. So, a controlled inflation with more scope for investment and production will be a very conducive for the expansion of financial services. There will be more demand for financial assistance by the business community that will enable financial services to play a dynamic role. The savings of the public could also be mopped up by the financial services by offering attractive interest rates. The return on investment will also be higher under controlled inflation. In case of recession in the economy, it is for the government to play a crucial role for the revival of the economy.

Proper Economic Planning

Proper economic planning decides on whether a country will be a developed or developing or underdeveloped. If a country decides a particular course or path for its development based on sound principles of economic planning that country will witness progress in the long-run. Planning fixes the rate of growth of the economy and accordingly, all the physical, fiscal and monetary resources to achieve the desired growth.

Economic planning in order to achieve rapid economic growth in all spheres of economic activity, proper planning is necessary. Thus, economic planning quantifies the extent of benefit the people in a country are expected to attain within a stipulated period. Financial services will play a commendable role as they provide financial support to various institutions and organizations by which not only production improves overall conditions prevailing in a country. This in turn will enable the people in the country to experience high living standards, enable more purchasing power and ultimately lead to developed state of economy.

Favourable Economic System

Services of the financial servicing industry will be required only when an economic system enables such a servicing. In a capitalistic society typically called as the private sector dominated economy there is always need for finance and financial intermediation. Financial services provide financial assistance according to the requirements of different business activities. The need for financial services will be felt only when there is more private sector participation with healthy competition through market forces of supply and demand. This is possible only under a free enterprise or a capital market, or capitalism as a part of economic system. In a government controlled economic system where, supply, demand, production and distribution is taken up by the government machinery there is very little possibility for competition and growth and hence the scope for financial intermediation will also very poor.

Suitable Economic Laws

Economic conditions keep changing and so the atmosphere for financial services will be encouraging only with the presence of economic laws suitable for proper functioning of these intermediaries. This not only regulates the private sector but enable the financial institutions to mobilize more funds and provide the same to the needy businessmen. Proper economic laws will not only check unscrupulous financial institutions but also place restrictions on the functioning of unethical business institutions. The misuse of funds and the increasing costs by the wastage of funds will be checked by proper economic laws. Raising of capital through proper markets, starting more institutions in the organized sector and allowing proper inflow of funds from foreign countries are other purposes of economic laws. Through various economic laws that are amended according to the prevailing economic conditions, a government will ensure curbing unwanted accumulation of wealth in private hands through proper taxation laws. A host of laws are enacted in India to curb tax evasion, control of foreign currency, smuggling of goods, accounting for export, accumulation of wealth and so on.

Due to the liberalized economic conditions many of the regulations and laws on fiscal and monetary system, regulation of financial intermediation and economic development has gone see changes in recent times. Some laws have been repealed and few laws have been amended extensively. A list of such laws is given below:

- Securities (Contract and Regulation) Act.
- Competition Act.
- SEBI Act.
- Industries (Development and Regulation) Act.
- Foreign Exchange Management Act.
- COFEPOSA (Conservation of Foreign Exchange and Prevention of Smuggling Activities) Act.

Often Reviewed Economic Policies

Government policies should be based on long-term objectives which have to enable the following aspects:

- Encourage production
- Promote investment for productive use
- Boost employment opportunities
- Encourage foreign trade

The policies have to be tuned suitable for the prevailing economic situations. Unless they are tuned up to the presently demanding factors, a country will face dangerous economic system which might several years for revival. Moreover, the fiscal and monetary policies adopted by the government and the central bank respectively should fall in line with the economic policies of the government often reviewed.

MACROECONOMIC FACTORS

Economic factors at the national level, influencing the economic condition of the country can be stated as macro-economic aggregates. Various macroeconomic factors which not only influence the economic condition of the country but also the working of financial services in the country can be categorized into the following:

Growth of Economy

Growth of the economy is a factor that can be taken as a yard stick to say that the country is developing. However, one cannot come to a hasty conclusion that increase in economic growth is necessarily means economic development. Because, the increased production may have been consumed by the increased an population, hence, the increase in production experienced in all the sectors of the economy namely, agriculture, industry and service that lead to increase in physical production should be sufficient not only to cater to the needs of population but also provide some surplus for the economy to grow. The role of the financial services is required to channelize the savings and investment.

Growth of Population

Population growth is not always bad to an economy. Only when there increase in population and if that 'population' is not put to use for productive purposes then the bad consequences will follow. Financial services require more human touch and it is here that a trained person in financial service contributes more to the economy. Countries where there is a huge population and have suitable employment opportunity will not find problems in making their economy grow. When human capital is suitably trained and put into use actually a country can benefit much from it. In fact, population can be an asset for such countries. Hence, population growth should also see development in the production and consumption.

Increased Percapita Income

Financial, services can increase the per capita income by providing various types of loans and encouraging self-employment schemes. They can also heir in the mobilization of the savings by providing various sources of investment. The mobilization of savings and channelising them in productive investment are bound to improve the economy and thereby the national income and per capita income. The national income of the country could be increased by enabling more production form industries and provision of services, this in turn will the benefit people by increasing their per capital income that would come to them through more employment.

Savings of the People

The problem that is common for almost all the developed countries is that the savings of the people are low compared to developed countries. Savings forms a major part investment in a country. Savings could be made only when the income level the people is higher and the people standard of living high.

Investment in Agriculture, Industry and Services

Investments can come through savings and such investments must generate more production and they should promote a balanced growth of all the sectors in the economy. In some countries, investment may be made in those sectors which have favourable factors and they will create a thrust in the economy leading to the growth in other sectors. Thus, more production in agriculture will create conditions for growth in industrial sector and service sector. Investment can be done both by public and private sectors. The government should play a role in promoting more investments by granting incentives and facilities so that more promoters and investors enter the market. A stable economic policy will also promote investment. And such a policy will promote the growth of capital market, money market; financial institutions with various financial services.

Capital Formation

Capital formation can happen through a reduction in consumption of finance. If the whole earnings are consumed, without allowing anything for reinvestment, capital formation will be nil. Financial services can play a major role by attracting the savings or the profit earned by the companies for a beneficial investment. Once investment of the savings is made then the invested money could be further used for capital formation.

Capital-output Ratio

This ratio reflects the ability of the capital invested to give an optimum output. If lesser capital is generating more output it reflects an optimum capital-output ratio. Such a ratio could be achieved when the investment in technology is high. Technology can bring in additional investment and output. A country becomes developed because it is capable of inventing new technology or it has the ability acquire new technology at an affordable cost. When technology plays dynamic role in a country's economy, that country is sure to galvanize growth and there by better capital-output ratio can be achieved.

Investment for Productive Use

The finance market acts as the propeller of the capital market activity. If the capital market is active, then sufficient capital will flow into the market and that will ensure finance for investment. An efficient system of market will provide to the industry the required amount of finance at the appropriate time adequately.

Favourable Export Conditions

Export plays a vital role in a country's economic development. Due care must be given to the export of all industries categories. Most of the countries which have developed rapidly have given due importance to foreign trade. The promotion of foreign trade requires the active support of financial services, Banks provide export finance. Various intermediaries in the financial market provide variety of services to boost export. Export credit guarantee is granted by corporations and special type of export assistance is arranged by banks and financial institutions in India to make a favourable export condition. Leasing companies provide equipment, while a merchant banker finances an exporter in foreign exchange to import capital equipment. All these aspects make conducive economic situation for making better exports.

Sufficient Reserve of Foreign Exchange

A country could keep reserve of foreign exchange only if it has a positive balance of payments position. This can result if the exports are more than imports. In other words, the payables in foreign currency should be less that the receivables in foreign currency. A country may face a reverse situation or negative balance of payments position if payments more than receipts, it may result due to heavy external borrowings and heavy imports. The financial services in the country can help the country from coming out of its adverse balance of payments situation. They can bring in more foreign currency by way of loan or savings from NRIs (non-resident Indians) or corporate bodies by way of investment. However, for this a suitable for trade policy and financial policy is required on the part of the government.

Foreign Capital

Foreign capital can be generated from investing companies, foreign mutual fund companies, overseas corporate bodies, foreign pension funds and the like. Financial services help the economy in mobilizing foreign capital either may be equity or debt. Such funds can be obtained in the global financial market at a competitive rate. If the foreign capital is utilized for unproductive purposes or is not properly invested, then the chances of the country raising fresh capital or loan in the foreign financial market may not be possible in future. Now-a-days many Indian corporate through the financial services offered by the intermediaries have generated millions of rupees. The government policy of foreign direct investment is the major cause for such foreign capital inflow.

Stable Exchange Rate

A country's strength in foreign trade can be measured how the exchange rate is maintained by a country in the exchange market. When a country continuously borrows in the foreign market, followed by heavy imports, then it will experience a decline in its currency value in relation to foreign currency. The financial services can reduce a fluctuating or declining exchange rate by reducing supply of home country's currency into the foreign exchange market; thereby push up the exchange rate in favour of home country. Another way by which exchange can be stabilized is by way of banking, insurance activities done abroad which will reduce debt burden. If exchange rate stability is not maintained, it will affect our foreign trade prospects and thereby exchange earnings. Hence all efforts should be taken to see that the exchange rate is kept stable. In India often RBI intervenes to see that the Indian rupee is stable against major currencies.

Employment Conditions

If employment opportunities are created it will lead to more production and production will lead to more consumption supplemented by more revenue in the hands enabled by more employment and the chain moves on that way. Hence, if employment condition improves it will stimulate economic activity. One of the important macroeconomic aggregates influenced by financial services is employment. With more financial services such as leasing, hire purchase, housing finance, insurance, etc., the level of employment opportunity in the country is bound to increase. To witness prosperity the employment market should be vibrant and efficient for which the financial services industry is a catalytic force.

Characteristics of Good Financial System

The financial system made commendable progress in length and breadth. Growth of financial intermediation and regulation of intermediaries became necessary later. Hence, more regulations were brought into force. The financial system should have some of the following characteristics in order to be a successful system.

- Banking activities
- Credit control by central bank
- Establishing fiscal and monetary policy
- Regulation of local and foreign currencies
- Enabling liquidity at all times
- Provision of funds for industrial and other use
- Facilitating more institutions to participate in financial intermediation
- Minimal regulatory measures at the same time control of the system not to be loosed.
- Encouraging competition among the players of financial system.

Emergence of specialized financial institutions in the Indian financial system to cater to the financial needs of sick industrial units, export finance, rural development, etc. also major reasons for the growth witnessed. These institutions include IDBI, IRBI, ICICI, SIDBI and the like. Throwing open of the insurance companies to the private sector also played a prominent role in resource mobilization and directing investments in productive area. Non-banking financial companies also have been in operation but their role in Indian financial has been streamlined after many companies vanished swindling the money on innocent and poor investors. These companies also undertake services such as hire-purchase, leasing, and investment.

Since the year 1991, the liberalized scenario there is an increase in financial deregulation and industrial liberalization, the role of the financial sector is increasing manifold. The liberalization process has triggered the setting up of several new institutions, both public and private, have appeared on the financial scene. These institutions like merchant banks, leasing companies, venture capital companies, factoring companies and mutual funds, etc. have expanded the range of financial services available to the Indian business community and the investors at large.

Functions of Financial System

- Providing banking services
- Regulation of currency
- Providing agency services and custody of currencies
- Establishing credit control
- Administering fiscal and monetary policies
- Maintaining liquidity of finance
- Enabling the supply of funds for productive use
- Management of international currencies

Reforms in Financial System

Financial system itself needed some major changes due to the influence of the global financial market situation. Developed financial markets allocate capital through a supply and demand mechanism establishing the cost of capital at the equilibrium of supply and demand for the securities. Financial reforms brought major changes by removing the centre of control and promoted free flow of funds and in innovative ways. The industrialization started to happen as many industries got a boost by way of sufficient flow of credit. Supportive policies of the successive governments enabled the process of financial reforms to take place in a smooth manner.

FINANCIAL SYSTEM V. FINANCIAL SERVICES

Financial system of a country means a set of closely linked complex of institutions, agents, practices, markets, transactions, claims and liabilities in the economy. Finance is the study of the nature, creation, behavior, regulation and administration of money and its functions. Therefore, financial system includes all those activities dealing in finance, organized into a system. The financial system consists of financial institutions, financial markets, financial instruments and the services provided by the financial institutions. The financial system comprised the financial services industry too. The financial system can be broadly classified into the following major areas:

Financial Intermediaries and Institutions

These engage in mobilizing the savings and transfer it to deficit areas. They are divided into regulatory, intermediaries, non-intermediaries and the like. They deal only in financial assets like deposits, securities, etc. They collect funds from those institutions and individuals having surplus to invest

Financial Markets

This is the place from where savings collected are transferred to areas requiring investment. There are two segments of financial market. They are money market and capital market. Money market is concerned with short-term funds. Capital market deals with those financial assets, which have maturity relatively of a longer period than the money market instruments. This capital market activity is also classified as primary and secondary markets. Primary market deals with new issues. The secondary market deals with dealing in the stock exchanges or buying from existing share/

unit holders. Primary markets by issuing new securities mobilize the savings directly. Secondary markets provide liquidity to the securities.

Financial Instruments

The products, which are traded in financial market, are financial assets or financial instruments. Requirement of lenders and borrowers are varied and so, there is a variety of securities in the financial markets to bridge the gap between the demand and supply. Year by year new variety of instruments with unique characteristics are developed by financial intermediaries. Financial assets represent claim on the repayment of principal at a future date.

Financial Services

Financial services include the services offered by intermediaries of the financial market.

FINANCIAL SERVICES

Origin

The origin of financial services sector in India can be traced backed since the introduction of the merchant banking services were introduced in 1960. Later in the in the early 1970s, The General Insurance business was nationalized gave a flip to the industry. Leasing activity took its root in the closing years of the 1970s. Leasing firms grew up faster in the market. Mutual funds had its presence felt since the onset of the Unit Trust of India. Factoring, discounting, venture capital, credit ratings have found their origin from 1980.

Indian financial system has witnessed a sea change in the recent past. The progress made can be known since the nationalization of commercial banks in 1969. This gave a new direction and adequate credit support for viable productive endeavor especially in agriculture and small sector. Along with the quantitative expansion and functional diversification of the banking system that lasted few decades witnessed a significant expansion of the activities of development of financial institutions for investments, especially in private sector. A significant fact in the operations of the institutions is that they have based on assured sources of funds, also provided credit at relatively stable lending rates. It inculcated debt culture in the corporate sector thus increasing dependence on these institutions. They also invested in equity of the private corporate sector through either conversion clause or underwriting commitments.

Prior to nationalization of banks Indian financial system was characterized by the absence of organized system of capital market, fewer financial intermediaries, very few public issues from companied, highly restricted flow of capital to industry, more dependence of industries on their internal sources of finance, unnecessary procedures for sanction of loan and so on. These problems were addressed by the financial system that came into being after nationalization. This paved way for larger network of banks, diffusion of funds for industrial use and support of individuals even in rural areas who were earlier neglected by the banking system. Besides the above, there were also high increase in the number of development financial institutions and their activities. They accounted for a major share of corporate financing.

Financial services are an important component of the financial system. In other words, there cannot be financial market without the services of the financial intermediaries. Financial institutions serve individual and institutional investors. Financial markets help the financial system to function smoothly through financial instruments. The successful functioning of the financial system is very much dependent on the range of financial services provided by the providers and the efficiency of the market to utilize it.

The industry that has grown up to persuade people to put their money into investments and which provides the facilities for doing so is called the 'Financial Services Sector.' In the last decade, the phenomenal growth in the capital market, money market and the fast pace of industrialization demanding enormous capital has brought in this whole new service sector. The financial services scenario in India in the last twenty-five years has undergone drastic changes. In the sleepy sixties we had a traditional pattern in the financial sector characterized by dearth of instruments. Most companies followed a strictly regimented debt equity pattern.

The primary capital markets remained inactive and the secondary capital market was somewhat disorganized. Financial institutions and a handful of brokers dominated the financial services scene. With the passing of the FERA in 1973 there was a spurt in public issues and the investing public was given an opportunity to invest in some of the blue chip multinational companies. This created a certain amount of investor confidence in the primary capital market and the shareholders population started growing. But a characteristic of such growth leading to expansion in financial services is that it has mostly been market driven and not planned by any centralized agency. Most of the development and innovations have come in from individual players, leading corporate organizations and market intermediaries and were not introduced in a phased manner by a process of legislation or after a considered study of market requirements.

The expansion of financial services at a very fast pace has left its impact on the financial services scenario in the country. The organized players in the financial services sector have increased significantly. This is the result of the coordinated efforts taken to reorganize and restructure the financial services industry. SEBI has been given legislative teeth to the financial service sector. Such efforts have been spearheaded by a spate of committees set-up by the Government to look into specific areas of the financial sector. Prominent among these have been the Narasimhan Committee on reforms in financial sector, the Prewani Committee on reorganization of stock exchanges, the Dave Committee on mutual funds, etc.

Financial Market

Financial markets perform an important function of mobilization of savings and channelizing them to areas that require. The components of the financial market are:

1. Capital Market
2. Money Market
3. Foreign Exchange Market
4. Debt Market

Elements of Financial Services Sector

Instruments

Include the public issue of shares, debentures, convertible debentures, fixed deposit certificates, etc.

Market Players

Include the Banks, Financial Institutions, Mutual Funds, Stock Brokers, etc. This includes not only those who are directly involved in the process but various intermediaries such as, advisers and consultants, underwriters, sponsors market makers, etc.

Regulatory Bodies and Specialized Institutions

This includes, the SEBI, Stock Exchanges, Credit Rating Services, Discount and Finance House of India, Stock Holding Corporation of India Ltd. and OTCEI of India and Venture Capital Companies.

The components of the financial services sector are:

- *Government:* The Central Government is one of the most important Constituent of the financial services sector because of its regulating powers. It has extensive powers under the Companies Act, 1956, Capital Issues (Control) Act, 1947 and the Securities Contracts (Regulation) Act, 1956.
- *Regulatory Agencies:* SEBI: Securities Exchange Board of India.
- RBI: Reserve Bank of India.
- Stock Exchanges.
- Stock Brokers.
- Financial Institutions.
- Banks.
- Consultants.
- Mutual Funds.
- Merchant Bankers.
- Portfolio Managers.
- Non-Banking Financial Institutions.

Functions of Financial Service Industry

Some of the important functions of the financial service industry can be grouped thus:

- Specialized services like credit rating, venture capital financing, lease financing, factoring, mutual funds, merchant banking, stock lending, depository, housing finance, raising money under book building, etc.
- Help institutions to raise the required funds and offer consultancy services for an efficient deployment of funds.
- They assist in deciding the appropriate financial mix.
- They extend their service up to the stage of servicing of lenders.
- They also provide services like bill discounting, factoring of debtors, parking of short-term funds in the money market, e-commerce, securitization of debts, etc. in order to ensure an efficient management of funds.

Regulatory System on Financial Services

The legislative position in India concerning the financial services sector is quite elaborate and is spread over a number of Acts, Rules, regulations, guidelines, notification, etc. The financial services in the country have to be regulated for which proper legislation is required. There are a number of legislations enacted by the government for improving the functioning of various financial institutions in the country. The issue of capital is governed by the Companies Act, 1956. The Stock Exchanges are governed by the Securities Contracts (Regulation) Rules, 1957, notifications of Stock Exchange Division, Department of Economic Affairs in the Ministry of Finance, etc.

These issues of debt instrument are governed by the Companies Act, 1956 and guidelines are issued by SEBI. Most of the players in the market like merchant bankers, mutual funds, brokers, etc. are governed by various guidelines issued by the SEBI. The finance companies in the private sector are governed by the Non-Banking Financial companies (Reserve

Bank) Directions, 1977. The issue of public deposits under Section 58-A of the Companies Act, 1956, is governed by the Companies (Acceptance of Deposits) Rules, 1975. Wide powers have been given to SEBI to regulate the capital market and money market securities. The various other laws and regulatory authorities' concerned exercising control over the financial services are:

- Reserve Bank of India Act, 1934.
- Banking Companies Act, 1949 (renamed as Banking Regulations Act, 1966).
- Industries (Development and Regulation) Act, 1951.
- Indian Companies Act, 1956.
- Securities Contracts (Regulation) Act, 1956.
- Sick Industrial (Special Provisions) Companies Act, 1985.
- Consumer Protection Act, 1986.
- Chit Funds Act, 1981.
- Negotiable Instruments Act, 1881.
- Securities and Exchanges Board of India Act (SEBI), 1992.
- Indian Contract Act, 1872.
- Transfer of Property Act, 1882.
- Income Tax Act, 1961.
- Customs Act.
- Securitization and Reconstruction of Financial Assets and Enforcement of Securities Act (SARFAESA), 2002.

Categories of Financial Services

Financial service is a customer-intensive industry. Identification of needs and wants of customer is the first step. It will help the financial service firms to design the financial strategy, which gives due respect to costs, liquidity and maturity considerations. Financial services are intangible in nature. The institutions providing the services should have a good image and confidence of the clients. They have to focus on quality and innovativeness of their services.

Financial services may be classified into non-fund-based activities and fund-based activities. Non-fund-based activities are—Merchant banking, portfolio management, industrial consultancy, portfolio investment services, bill discounting, factoring, etc. Fund-based activities are—hire purchase, consumer financing and real estate financing. The need-based financial services are getting swiftly professionalized with the public and private sector entering the field. It is not merely big companies or prosperous entrepreneurs who are desirous of need-based financial services. Even the common man is constantly on the lookout for financial services.

1. *Merchant Banking*

Merchant banking in India is of recent origin. Merchant bank is defined as a kind of financial institution that provides variety of services including investments, banking management of customer's securities, portfolios, insurance acceptance of bills, etc. It has its beginning in India in 1967, when Grindlays Bank established a division followed by Citi Bank in 1970 and the State Bank of India in 1972. Merchant banking divisions were set-up by few other banks like Syndicate Bank, Bank of India, Bank of Baroda, Chartered Bank, Mercantile Bank, etc. The merchant banks, as they have developed in our country could be broadly classified into three categories. The first category consists of the division of commercial banks the second category comprises of National and State level Financial Corporations like ICICI, etc. The third category includes leading broker firms who have extended their activities into merchant banking.

Merchant bankers act as a critical link between a fund raising institution and the investing public. They have an important role to play in capital and debt structuring of an organization. They are also involved in working capital management, loan syndication and syndication of project finance, mergers, capital restructuring and so on.

2. *Hire Purchase and Leasing*

A hire purchase contract is defined by Pearce EH and Omrod RFG as a contract on hire with an option of purchase in which the owner of goods lets them out on hire to the hirer for a fixed term at an agreed rental to be paid at intervals mutually agreed upon as installments, and the owner in addition to letting the goods out, further agrees that if the hirer keeps them for the agreed period and regularly pays the rent they shall become the hirer's property.

Hire purchase in India had its beginning after the First World War and has since established itself as a reliable supplementary source of finance for purchase of automobiles besides other consumer articles. However, it was only after the Second World War that its growth started assuring visible dimension. It is a form of credit where goods are supplied after payment of a deposit with an agreement to pay regular instalments over a period of time. At the end of the hiring period, legal title passes to the hirer on payment of a nominal sum. If during the period of hire, the hirer wishes to settle the agreement prematurely, a rebate of charges will normally be given by the finance house.

The Hire Purchase Act was enacted in 1972 which provides for regulating the various rights and obligations of the owner (financer) and the hirer under a hire purchase transaction. Commercial banks entered in the field of hire purchase not later than the private hire purchase financiers. The role of non-banking financial companies in this field in recent years is also significant.

Lease financing refers to the right to use and to have the control over the assets leased to another person on whom the rights are vested for a payment of a specific consideration for such right for a specific period agreed upon. Leasing done by financial intermediaries for clients, where the capital assets and leased by the intermediary for a lease rental. This benefits the company, where the cash resources required for acquiring such capital assets could be productively used for other business activities. The lease rental is revenue expenditure for the lessee and so it would also have the tax advantage.

3. *Housing Finance*

In the deregulated interest regime, in the recent past, housing finance was a thought to be an efficient mode of parking, securing funds and earning through it, by commercial banks and private housing finance companies. The National Housing Bank (NHB) has been set-up by the Government of India as an apex housing finance body. NHB recognized about ten housing finance companies as being eligible for refinance facilities. The Housing and Urban Development Corporation (HUDCO) and the Housing Development Finance Corporation (HDFC) have already been quite active in this area of providing finance for housing facilities.

In recent times housing finance has become a very popular and secured way of financing for banks. The period taken for sanction of loan has been very much less. The procedures for getting housing loan are also very minimal. This is enabled by the housing loan policies of the central government. Many public sector banks have set-up separate portfolio for housing finance. More beneficiaries are attracted towards housing loan for availing of tax benefit. Many salaried class people opt for housing loan especially for the above purpose. Different schemes of loan are available for borrowers such as the option between floating rate and fixed rate of interest. Insurance of life and property at a very nominal premium sometimes charged as onetime payment.

4. *Venture Capital Financing*

Rapid innovation and developments in industries associated with high technology in the sphere of electronics and the use of technological applications in every activity of business made venture capital is popular as a means of financing. It had its origin in USA and the overall success stimulated other countries to follow suite. The term 'Venture Capital' is normally considered as a synonym of high risk capital. It is also said to be the early stage financing of a new and young enterprises seeking to grow rapidly it is a combination of capital and management expertise provided by the venture capitalists for the initial risk of a new and emerging company, which has a good growth prospect in terms of products, technologies, business concerns or services with the objectives of retrieving the investment with a handsome reward at a future date.

Venture capital can be categorized as the investment in long-term equity finance, where the venture capitalist earns his return in the form of capital gains. The assumption is that the venture capitalist and the entrepreneurship through the commitment of capital and shareholding for the formation and setting up of small scale enterprises specializing in new ideas or new technologies. The venture Capitalist focuses on growth and wishes to see the new and unexploited technologies turn into a commercially viable proposition with an expectation of later returns. The capital in this form of investment involves the process of building and financing successful self-sustaining companies often from scratch. It means an active participation, blending of entrepreneurial insight, capacity to and desire, sound planning and an experienced management to enable the development of an ongoing enterprise.

5. *Portfolio Services*

A new area in which financial services are rendered is Portfolio Services, i.e., managing the portfolios of individual clients. SBI Personal Banking Centers and Vysya Bank's Investors' clubs are two good examples. There are also a few private investment advisers, who guide and help individual investors and manage their portfolios. An institution involved in portfolio management undertakes to manage the investment of a company and ensure better returns. The investment in various securities are kept as a trust and managed by such custodians. They offer consultancy services to diversify the portfolio individuals, finance companies, banks and other intermediaries.

6. *Factoring*

It is mechanism under which a financial institution called a factor, purchases the accounts receivables of a party called client and makes cash payment to the client immediately or from time to time after collecting the money from clients debtor. For the risk assumed and the services rendered the factor collects a fee known as factorage. The following services are offered by the factor. Finance providence, maintenance of accounts, collection of dues, and protection against credit shortfalls and risk associated with it.

7. *Bills Discounting*

This discounting of bills is different from factoring where the factor takes the responsibility of collecting the dues. In bill discounting it is only a system of arranging for short-term required of finance based on the bills raised on debtors. Bill Discounting services provide finance to the suppliers of goods against invoices. Many banks and finance companies discount bills of third parties and provide finance to the manufacturers. However, they do not take the responsibility for collection of dues.

8. *Credit Rating*

Initially, the credit rating agencies were formed to credit rate the debt instruments issued by the Indian corporates. Nowadays Credit rating institutions are involved in rating various financial instruments such as debentures, deposits, equity, commercial paper, etc. Even countries are rated when they go to international market. The international agencies that are well known for rating are Moody's ratings and ratings by Standard and Poor. But these institutions not only credit rate but also involved in general rating.

9. *Book-building*

One of modern method of raising finance from the public is book-building. Unlike the traditional method of issuing the shares at a par or premium which is a predetermined sum, the book-building process enables the issuer to get the best price on price band approved by SEBI. The securities price depends on the demand for the securities. The book runner may make application to any stock exchange for listing. On the closing date of the issue the price will be fixed. Usually merchant bankers take up the process of book-building.

10. *Underwriting*

Underwriting is a job of guaranteeing the sale of securities for any company and if minimum amount is not subscribed, the underwriters take up the deficient amount that has to be raised. An underwriting agreement is entered between the issuer of securities and the underwriter—normally financial institutions or banks or large finance corporations. The underwriter gets a commission on the portions subscribed by it and even fully subscribed by the public a minimum commission on that amount too. The liability of the underwriter arises only when they issued securities stand unsubscribed till the last day it is kept open or closed for subscription.

2

Money Market

Money markets are markets for short-term financial assets that are close substitutes for money usually with maturities of less than a year. The deregulation of money markets and their development are an essential component of financial sector reform. Well-functioning money markets provide a relatively safe income yielding outlet for the short-term investment of funds both for banks and firms and can also be an important source of short-term funds to banks in need of quick liquidity. Well developed money markets are an essential prerequisite for the efficacy of monetary policy in a deregulated financial environment with the central bank having to increasingly use indirect tools of monetary control such as open market operations to equilibrate the demand and supply of bank reserves. The effective use of open market operations greatly depends on an active secondary market for T-bills (treasury bills) and the linkages between the T-bill market and other key money markets, in particular the Inter-Bank call money market.

Indian money markets were fairly underdeveloped till the mid-eighties. The most prominent of money markets during this time was the Inter-Bank call money market which was a restricted market with a narrow base and a limited number of participants. The Indian money market before the 1990s was very much restricted to the play of banks and all India financial institutions. Entry into the market was strictly controlled by Reserve Bank of India. The market was witnessed with very few predominant lenders and a large number of borrowers. Bulk of transactions were undertaken in call and notice money market followed by commercial bills rediscounting. The interest rates in the money market were tightly regulated and there was a ceiling on the rate of interest in the call and notice money market.

The T-bill market was also very narrow with Reserve Bank of India holding most of the T-bills outstanding. Key money market instruments which are common in the developed markets of the advanced market economies such as certificates of deposit and commercial paper did not exist. Since the mid-eighties, however, money markets in India have undergone a great deal of change. Instrumental in this change has been the recommendations of two influential committee reports commissioned by the Reserve Bank of India in the mid-eighties, the Chakravarty Committee which submitted its report in 1985 and the Vaghul Committee which submitted its report in 1987.

The Chakravarty committee was mostly concerned with reviewing the working of the monetary system. Therefore, with respect to money markets, its attention was mostly centered around the Treasury bill market and ways to develop the latter so as to gradually use the T-bill as an important instrument of monetary policy. The objective of the Vaghul Committee, on the other hand, was to examine the entire spectrum of money markets in India and to recommend specific measures for their development. The Chakravarty and Vaghul Committees reports provided a blueprint to the Reserve Bank of India on how best to deregulate and develop Indian money markets and most of the reforms that have occurred in the latter since the mid-eighties can be seen as an outcome of the recommendations of these two reports.

The financial system of any economy can be broadly divided into two parts, namely, Capital Market and Money Market. Both these markets offer opportunity for the investors having surplus funds to invest their money. Similarly, these markets also offer opportunity to the corporates and other investing institutions to obtain the funds required by them. In the Money Markets the funds are invested for a shorter duration normally maximum upto one year whereas in the capital markets the funds are generally deployed for a longer duration.

In India, Money Market is a major segment of the organized sector regulated by the Reserve Bank of India. It plays a significant role in the organized market. Money market is a market for short-term monetary instruments and financial assets. In India the maturity of money market securities may vary from "On demand" to even "One year". The financial assets are close substitutes for money with minimum transaction cost. Money market is a market where excess short-term funds are deployed to meet the shortage of cash and other temporary obligations. The leading players in the money market are the commercial banks, RBI and other financial institutions. The main features of the money market instrument are its liquidity and safety. Money market is not one market but collection of markets such as call and notice money market, Treasury bill market, commercial bill market, commercial paper market and certificates of deposit market. These markets have close inter-relationships with each other.

As the name suggests what is traded in the Money Market is money itself. The participants buy and sell in the Money Markets nothing but money, which is represented by various instruments. The instruments do not carry any special right but represent mere entitlement to cash. The money market is a wholesale market and the amount invested by the participants is comparatively high. Thus the small investors do not enter this market. Presence of regulator is the pre-requisite for any market to be effective and in the case of Money Market the Reserve Bank of India plays this role. Further, a strong Money Market also requires a well organized banking system. Banks are the major players in the Money Market. Further, the Reserve Bank of India has prescribed strict guidelines as to the eligibility for participating in Money Market.

IMPORTANCE OF MONEY MARKET

❖ *Mobilizes funds:* The most important source of supply

of funds in the money market is from the all-India financial institutions such as Life Insurance Corporation, General Insurance Corporation and its subsidiaries. Unit Trust of India and Mutual funds are required to employ their funds in the long and investments and in the capital market. These institutions have regular flow of funds under their schemes and since they have to wait for appropriate opportunities for investment they usually park their substantial funds in the money market. Another important source of supply of funds is the co-operative banks. In view of seasonal nature of their lending operations as also due to limited opportunities available for gainful deployment of funds (mostly urban cooperative banks), they have to necessarily have to access the money market. As against this, the demand for funds in the money market is mostly from the commercial banks, although a few banks are net supplier of funds, by and large the banking system is found to be the net borrower of funds in the money market depending upon their reserve requirements.

- *Helps for the Development of economy:* It helps public sector and private. organizations, banking and financial institutions short-term working capital requirements and hence facilitates the development of the economy as a whole.
- *Control over Financial System:* The developed money market with a highly integrated structure enables the central bank to deal with most sensitive of sub-markets through its operations, thereby exercising control over the banking system.
- *Finances Government:* The money market is useful to the Government in two ways. It provides short-term accommodations by means of treasury bills, without affecting the banking and credit systems in the economy; and it gives stability to the Government security market and strengthens the credit of government by not resorting to printing and issuing

of money leading to increase in prices and hence an inflationary tendency for its deficit financing.

- *Efficient use of Funds by Banks:* The principal business of the commercial banks is to receive deposits and make loans and advances earning profits in a short period of time. A developed money market helps the commercial banks to employ their cash reserves more economically, and reconcile the conflicting principles of liquidity and profitability of their maximum benefit.
- *Fuller Utilization of Community Resources:* The mobilization and flow of funds from one sector to another serves the liquidity needs of individuals, business and government units. It is an invaluable agency for promoting flexibility, mobility and full utilization of community resources.
- *Facilitates Capital Market:* A well organized money market facilitates the working of the capital market. The conditions in the money market and short-term rates of interest prevailing their influence the conditions in the capital market as well as long-term rates of interest.
- *Creation of Loan Market:* The money market provides an investment outlet to the commercial banks for any temporarily surplus funds they may have available. When several banks operate similar types of business, they can accommodate each other by organizing a call loan market. If their business is affected by similar influence money will be easy or tight for each of them at the same time. The problem is easily resolved by the provision of special facilities at the central bank.
- *Helps Monetary Management*: A well developed money market is the basis for an effective performance of a central bank's policy of monetary management. Central banks therefore regulate the short-term money market so as to influence cost and availability, demand and supply of money.

CHARACTERISTICS OF MONEY MARKET

Control by a Central Bank: A money market cannot function properly without a central bank. A strong central bank is an essential pre-requisite for economical employment of cash as it permits banks to maintain stable or lower cash ratios. When the banking business is subjected to seasonal market fluctuations, banks can against the lodgment of security with the central bank, meet the demand for loans or cash on those occasions. The central bank also rediscounts eligible securities of banks, converting near money assets into cash in times of crises. It also undertakes open market operations wherein, it absorbs surplus cash during off-seasons and provides liquidity in times of financial stringency. Thus, in developed money market, the central bank intervenes from time to time and controls the operations of commercial banks.

Organized Banking System: Commercial banks being the principal dealers in short-term funds constitute the nucleus of the money market. In a developed money market, the commercial banks use their cash reserves more economically by stabilizing their cash ratios or accepting lower cash ratios. This consistent behaviour pattern is an important by-product of an integrated, organized and central banking structure.

Financial Instruments: A well functioning money market requires a continuous supply of many instruments like bills of exchange, treasury bills, short-term instruments such as bonds, etc. It is also essential that dealers and brokers participate in the buying and selling activities.

Sub-markets: A developed money market is organized into a number of submarket each specializing in a particular type of short-term asset. Each of it should possess adequate sources of supply of funds for dealing in particular type of short-term asset and be intimately connected to each other.

Mobility of Funds: Mobility of funds is a fundamental requirement of a developed money market. Free movement of money and monetary assets from surplus points to places of demand tends towards equality of rates for similar types of business at widely separated points in the economy. A developed money market mobilizes funds not only from the country, but from all over the World.

Uniformity of Interest Rates: a developed money market is characterized by the prevalence of uniform interest rates throughout the country.

Integrated Markets and Institutions: It is considered to be the most essential characteristic of a developed money market. All other characteristics emerge out of an appropriate degree of integration. A favourable balance of payments, large quantum of international trade, stable political conditions, price stabilization, organized stock exchange markets, responsive banks and financial institutions, characterize a well developed money market similar to that in New York or London.

Stability of Prices: An efficient money market system will ensure stability in prices of goods and services.

Competition among Market Players: Obviously competition ensures organized growth of business in a similar way developed money market has competitive players.

COMPONENTS OF MONEY MARKET

The money market is composed of several sub-markets each dealing in different types of short-term credit.

Call Money Market: Call Money Market is a market for short-term loans lent for periods not exceeding 14 days, sometimes, money is lent overnight. These loans are called call Money or call loans or overnight money since the banks recall loans at a very short notice, Commercial banks and a few financial institutions that have been permitted by RBI are the only players in call Money Market. Individual investors are not allowed to buy or sell the call money. However, the commercial banks provide loans to bill brokers or dealers in stock exchanges whose financial requirements may be for a very short period only.

The call money market has the benefits of paying on demand when needed, earns interest by lending idle cash and promotes exchange transactions. There may also be inter-bank call money market where banks can borrow from those having surplus reserve balance in order to maintain their reserve position according to statutory requirements. The business is transacted over telephone and the concerned parties generally do not meet to structure the deals. Call Money Receipt is one of the major instruments of the Indian Money Market.

Acceptance Market: This refers to the market for bankers' acceptances arising out of both domestic and foreign trade transactions. A banker's acceptance is made by way of draft drawn by firm on a bank and accepted by the bank. The bank undertakes to pay the bearer the required sum of money. It promotes the operations of discount houses.

Discount Market: A market where short dated papers are bought and sold is called a discount market. The instruments of credit used for this purpose are promissory notes, bills of exchange and treasury bills.

Loan Market: This refers to loans granted taking collateral securities like stocks and bonds are called collateral loans. These are given to brokers and dealers in securities either on call or for a very short period of time. These markets are not water tight compartments but are related to one another. The borrowers in the money market deal in bills which are discounted by them. Acceptance houses accept bills later on discounted in the discount market.

PLAYERS OF MONEY MARKET

Central Bank: The central bank of a country is the leader and the supreme authority of the money market. It is the lender of last resort and the ultimate reservoir of funds. The Central bank controls and channelizes credit facilities through various methods such as the open market operations, re-discounting of government and other first class securities. Its powers can be fully effective if a wide financial discipline is ensured through the service area approach.

Commercial Banks: Commercial banks are the most important constituent of the money market. The commercial banks use the funds obtained from deposits and other sources for providing short term loans to the money market. Major part of their income is derived from interest on advances, including discounted and bills purchased and interest on investments. Advances comprise a large portion of the total assets a bank.

Acceptance Houses: These institutions specialize in accepting bills of exchange. Generally they are merchant bankers. These are set-up to facilitate international trade and hence operate from the international money market. The acceptance houses accept and guarantee bills of traders whose financial standing is not known in order to make the bills negotiable. They act as second signatories on the bills of exchange and charge a small commission. They ensure much security for bills discounted.

Non-Banking Financial Institutions: The institutions like mutual funds, insurance companies, financial corporations, investment companies operate in the money market by lending their surplus short-term loanable funds.

Discount Houses: Discount house deal in the business of buying and selling bills of exchange and other bills. These are special institutions for rediscounting the bills of exchange. Bill brokers act as intermediaries between those who want to raise credit by selling bills, and institutions that have short-term funds available for investments on commission basis. Discount houses borrow huge funds for short periods from the commercial banks and RBI and invest them in discounting of bills.

INDIAN MONEY MARKET INSTRUMENTS

Call or Notice Money Market

The overnight inter-bank call money market, in which banks trade positions to maintain cash reserves, is the key segment of the money market in India. It is basically an 'over the counter' market without the intermediation of brokers. Participation has been gradually widened to include other financial institutions, primary/satellite dealers, mutual funds and other participants in the bills rediscounting market and corporates (through primary dealers) besides banks, LIC and UTI. While banks and primary dealers are allowed two-way operations, other non-bank entities can only participate as lenders. As per the announced policies, once the repo market develops, the call money market would be made into a pure inter-bank market, including primary dealers.

The call money market is influenced by liquidity conditions mainly governed by deposit mobilization, capital flows and the Reserve Bank's operations affecting bank's reserve requirements on the supply side and tax outflows, government borrowing programme, non-food credit off-take and seasonal fluctuations, such as, large currency drawals during the festival season on the demand side. At times of easy liquidity, call rates tend to hover around the Reserve Bank's repo rate, which provides a ready avenue for parking short-term surplus funds. During periods of tight liquidity, call rates tend to move up towards the Bank Rate and more recently the Reserve Bank's reverse repo rate (and sometimes beyond) as the Reserve Bank modulates liquidity in pursuit of monetary stability. Besides, there are other influences, such as, (a) the reserve requirement prescriptions and stipulations regarding average reserve maintenance, (b) the investment policy of non-bank participants in the call market which are among the large suppliers of funds in the call market, and (c) the asymmetries of the call money market, with few lenders and chronic borrowers.

Call Money Market offers the highest level of liquidity in the entire Money Market mechanism. Call Money Market (CMM) offers the perfect view of the liquidity conditions prevailing in the economy. In CMM what is traded is the money itself without involving any instrument (such as treasury bill, certificate of deposit, commercial papers, etc.). Hence, it is direct borrowing and lending of funds and the rate of interest is decided by the parties on the basis of the demand and supply conditions. The Reserve Bank of India (RBI) regulates the operations of CMM. RBI does not directly participate in the market but as and when required interferes with the Open Market Operations (OMO).

The funds lent are generally termed as "call loans". The funds are transferred to the borrower and returned to the lender using banker's pay orders. The duration for which money is lent in this market typically ranges from one to fourteen days. Money lent for one day is also called "overnight money". On the maturity date the borrower repays the money along with the interest. Money Market by its basic nature is a wholesale market and the volumes involved are high. Similarly, CMM is also a wholesale market and only big players participate. The CMM participants can broadly be divided in two parts viz. (1) those who can only lend in the market (2) those who can lend as well as borrow in the market.

Call Money Market Participants

- Banks
- Primary Dealers
- Financial Institutions
- Mutual Funds
- Corporates

Utility of the CMM

- The CMM offers high liquidity and is a place to obtain/park funds for a very short period. The CMM is generally utilized for the following purposes by various parties.
- Meeting short-term deficits (this deficit could for anything such as meeting advance tax liability, bridge loans, etc.).
- Parking surplus funds temporarily Meeting CRR requirements by the banks earning profits by arbitrage, etc.

REPOS

Repo is a money market instrument, which enables collateralized short-term borrowing and lending through sale/purchase operations in debt instruments. Under a repo transaction, a holder of securities sells them to an investor with an agreement to repurchase at a pre-determined date and rate. In the case of a repo, the forward clean price of the bonds is set in advance at a level which is different from the spot clean price by adjusting the difference between repo interest and coupon earned on the security. Repo is also called a ready forward transaction as it is a means of funding by selling a security held on a spot basis and repurchasing the same on a forward basis. Reverse repo is a mirror image of repo as in the case of former, securities are acquired with a simultaneous commitment to resell.

Subsequent to the irregularities in securities transactions, repos were initially allowed in the Central Government Treasury bills and dated securities created by converting some of the Treasury bills. In order to activate the repos market essentially to be an equilibrating force between the money market and the Government securities market, the Reserve Bank gradually extended repos facility to all Central Government dated securities and Treasury bills of all maturities. Recently, while the State Government securities were made eligible for repos, the Reserve Bank also allowed all non-banking entities, maintaining SGL and current account with its Mumbai office, to undertake repos including reverse repos. Furthermore, it has been decided to make PSU bonds and private corporate securities eligible for repos to broaden the repos market.

The Reserve Bank also undertakes repo/reverse repo operations with primary dealers and scheduled commercial banks, as part of its open market operations. It also provides liquidity support to secondary dealers and 100 per cent gilt mutual funds through reverse repos. There is no limit on the tenor of repos. The Reserve Bank initially conducted repo operations for a period of 14 days. Since November 1996, the Reserve Bank has been conducting 3-4 day repo auctions, synchronizing with working day and weekend liquidity conditions, in order to modulate short-term liquidity.

With the introduction of Liquidity Adjustment Facility (LAF) from the Reserve Bank has been injecting liquidity into the system through reverse repos and absorbing liquidity from the system through repos on a daily basis. These operations are conducted on all working days except on Saturdays, through uniform price auctions and are restricted to scheduled commercial banks and primary dealers. This is apart from the liquidity support extended by the Reserve Bank to primary dealers through refinance/reverse repo facility at a fixed price. Repos help to manage liquidity conditions at the short-end of the market spectrum. Repos have often been used to provide banks an avenue to park funds generated by capital inflows to provide a floor to the call money market.

During times of foreign exchange market volatility, repos have been used to prevent speculative activity as the funds tend to flow from the money market to the foreign exchange market. For Instance, a fixed rate repo auction system was instituted in November 1997 with a view to ensuring an effective floor for the short term interest rates in order to ward-off the spread of contagion during the South-East Asian crisis. The repo rates were reduced with the return of capital flows, which imparted stability to the foreign exchange market.

COMMERCIAL PAPERS

There is no statutory definition of Commercial Paper. However, the Guidelines for commercial paper issued by the Reserve Bank of India states that a commercial paper is an unsecured money market instrument issued in the form of a promissory note. Highly rated companies to meet their short-term requirements issue commercial papers. Commercial papers are issued at a discount by the issuer on the maturity date the principal is returned along with the interest amount. The minimum maturity period of a commercial paper is 15 days and the maximum maturity period is 1 year from the date of issue. Commercial papers can be issued in denomination of Rs. 5 lakh or multiple thereof. Further, the minimum amount to be invested by an investor cannot be less than Rs. 5 lakh.

The interest on the commercial paper is determined on the basis of the prevailing market forces and the issuer is as such free to issue commercial paper at any price. Commercial paper is a privately placed paper and there is no public issue of commercial papers. The market maker obtains various quotes from the potential investors and on the basis of this information the issuer decides the price at which the commercial papers should be issued. Commercial papers can be issued directly by the issuer to the investors or alternatively the issuer would take help of dealer.

In case of a direct paper the issuer decides the price at which the commercial papers are to be sold to the investors. However, in case of a dealer paper the issuer issues the entire issue to the dealer and further it is for the dealer to decide at what price it should be further sold to the investors. Commercial papers are unsecured instruments and as such attract high amount of risk. To address this problem the RBI has laid down stringent conditions, which the issuer has to satisfy before issuing commercial papers. Further, it is compulsory for the issuer to obtain credit rating for this purpose from a reputed Credit Rating Agency (CRA). Commercial papers are actively traded in the secondary market and are transferred by endorsement and delivery. Commercial papers can be issued by any company, Primary Dealer, Satellite Dealers and the all-India financial institutions (FIs).

Eligibility for Issue of Commercial Papers

- The tangible net worth of the Company, as per the latest audited balance sheet, is not less than Rs. 4 crore;
- Company has been sanctioned working capital limit by bank(s) or all-India financial institution(s).
- The borrower account of the company is classified as a Standard Asset by the financing bank(s)/ institution(s).
- Any investor can invest in commercial papers. However, the minimum amount that can be invested in commercial paper is Rs. 5 lakh (face value) and this as such keeps the small investors away from the commercial paper market.

Procedure for Issue of CPs

- The proposed issue is to be completed within a period of 2 weeks and the banker has to be intimated to reduce the working capital limit to the extent of the amount raised. The company should inform the RBI about the actual amount raised through CP within three days of completion of the issue.
- A company planning to issue a commercial paper selects a merchant banker and an Issuing and Paying Agent (IPA) and gets the CP credit rated by an approved credit rating agency. The company then approaches its principal banker with the credit rating certificate for their approval. The banker forwards the application to the RBI for intimation.

- Commercial papers cannot be underwritten. The CP holder should present the instrument to the paying agent on maturity. The agent receives brokerage charges for services rendered by him depending upon the maturity period of the CP.
- Commercial papers are open to individuals, financial institutions, corporate and Non-Resident Indians. Non-Resident Indians can only invest on a non-repatriable and non-transferable basis.
- The company can issue the paper on a single day or in parts on different dates. However, the entire issue has to be redeemed on the same day.
- If the company plans to issue a CP for six months, it can raise money with different maturity periods of one, two or three months.
- In cases where a company decides for a two month commercial paper, finance has to be raised within a period of two weeks from the date on which the proposal is taken on record by the bank.

Types of Commercial Papers

Direct Papers: A direct commercial paper is issued directly by the company to the investors without any intermediary. Companies issuing direct papers announce the current rate of commercial paper with different maturities for investors to choose the CP that suits their requirement.

Dealer Papers: A dealer or a merchant banker on behalf of a client issues these types of commercial papers. The dealer arranges for the private placement of the paper and also provides advisory services such as timing of the issue, determination of the discount rate and a suitable maturity period.

Features of Commercial Papers

- Issuing and Paying Agent as such does not directly participate in the market by issuing or investing in CPs. However, IPA is involved in any CP issue and is unique to CP market. IPA is an agent of the issuer arranging the issue, i.e. collecting amounts through investors and paying the maturity amount to the investors.

- Only Scheduled Banks can act as an IPA and it is compulsory to have an IPA for issuing CPs. In some cases IPAs also play role of merchant banker for the issuer, i.e. collecting quotes from various investors for price discovery and that of a dealer.
- It is a highly liquid instrument, which can be transferred by endorsement and delivery. CPs is backed by liquidity and earnings of the issuer and so an optimal combination of liquidity returns.

Benefits of Commercial Papers

- Commercial Papers play a very important role in the money market.
- Commercial papers offer advantages to both the parties, i.e. the lender and the borrower.
- From the lenders perspective they would earn interest, which would be more than what they can earn from investing in bank deposits.
- Commercial Papers involve less paper work.
- Companies and financial institutions tend to find alternative sources of funds whenever bank interest rates are higher than the interest rates prevailing in the market. Commercial paper is an easy, cheap and quick source of finance.
- Similarly, from the borrowers' perspective the rate of interest paid by it would be lower than what it would have otherwise paid had he borrowed from commercial banks. Thus, it is a cheaper source of finance for the borrower and at the same time it offers better returns to the lenders.
- The issuers are highly rated and issue is allowed only if the issuer satisfies the necessary conditions of RBI and so this investment is treated as a safe investment despite of being unsecured.
- Due to the high credibility of the issuer in the market it offers high liquidity to the investors.

- Commercial papers are privately placed instruments and as such does not involve much documentation work.

Forms of Commercial Papers

Master Note: This is a new financial paper, generally issued by finance companies to bank trust departments and other permanent money market investors. The investing firm, in an agreement, notifies the issuing company, the amount of paper that it wishes to purchase on a particular day. The issuing company then issues a paper on the agreed amount.

Medium-term Notes. These are unsecured obligations with a maturity period of 9-10 months. Investment grade corporations generally issue these notes at a particular rate of interest.

Asset-backed Commercial Paper: It offers credit at a lower interest rate to corporates. Asset-backed commercial paper is a combination of loans or credit receivables into packages. These packages are issued in the form of paper and the loans and receivables are removed from the issuing company's balance sheet and placed in a Special Purpose Entity. It helps to the issue of commercial paper to cover discount price while using the proceeds for the purchase of receivables. The issuing customer, after servicing the underlying receivables, collects interest and principal payments and passes the funds to special purpose entity.

CERTIFICATE OF DEPOSIT

Certificate of Deposits were introduced in the Indian financial markets on recommendation of Vaghul Committee in 1987. CDs were introduced to improve liquidity in the money markets. Certificate of Deposits are in the form of usance promissory notes transferable on endorsement and delivery, issued by the banks. Certificate of Deposits are also known as Negotiable Certificate of Deposit (NCD). Certificate of Deposits are nothing but the normal deposits placed by the account-holders with the bank converted into a special negotiable instrument. Certificate of Deposits are issued at a discount to the face value. The investor invests the money with the bank and gets a promissory note from the bank stating that the bank would pay certain amount on the specified day. The investor cannot get the amount back from the bank before the maturity date. However, he can sell the Certificate of Deposit in the secondary market and get cash. The buyer of the Certificate of Deposit can either hold it till the maturity date or may further sell it in the market. On the date of maturity the holder of the Certificate of Deposit would get the payment from the bank.

Features of Certificate of Deposits

- The Certificate of Deposits are issued at discount (the discount amount depends on the prevailing call rates in the market) and the current rate of interest. The minimum amount of a Certificate of Deposit is Rs. 5 lakh and thereafter in multiple of Rs. 1 lakh. There is no cap on the higher amount.
- All Scheduled banks are allowed to issue CDs. Besides banks financial institutions are also allowed to issue CDs.
- Investment in CDs is open for all and any person can invest or buy from secondary market.

Benefits of Certificate of Deposits

- In the case of normal demand deposit the account-holder can withdraw the amount as per his wish. The bank always keeps sufficient money to meet such demand.
- The bank cannot use such funds for long-term purposes and gives lower rate of interest to the account-holder.
- If the investor places the money in time deposit then he cannot withdraw money before the maturity date. Thus this creates need for an instrument wherein the investor earns more interest enjoys the flexibility *of* encashing the deposit at any time and the banker also gets funds for longer period.

TREASURY BILLS

Treasury bills are promissory notes of the Central Government for varying maturity periods (14 days up to one year) with a promise to pay the stated amount, i.e. the face value to the bearer of the instrument on the day of maturity. This is a short-term instrument used by the government to bridge the seasonal or temporary gap between its revenue and expenditure. There is no restriction on the type of investors who can invest in the T-bills. Individuals, companies, body corporates, provident funds, financial institutions and State Governments can make the investment. However, in reality the main investors in T-bills are scheduled banks, Non-Banking Finance Companies (NBFCs), insurance companies, provident funds, financial institutions and corporates. The smaller investors generally do not invest mainly because the money market as such is a wholesale market and further the T-bills offer lower returns as compared to other instruments.

Treasury bills are short-term promissory notes issued by Government of India at a discount generally for a period between 91 days and 364 days. Presently 91 days Treasury Bill are rediscounted by RBI but "additional early rediscounting fees" are levied for rediscounting of these bills within 14 days from the date of purchase. There is no predetermined targeted amount to be raised and reserve price. The sale of treasury bills is by auction and not by application and allotment.

The maturity of the Treasury bill for each auction, the amount accepted at the auction and the cut-off prices are decided by the RBI based on the debt management policy and the conditions in the money market. Treasury bills can be "purchased by any person residing in India except State Government Provident Funds for a minimum subscription of Rs. 1 lakh. Every fortnight, the Reserve Bank of India invites bid for sale of Treasury bills of varying maturities up to 364 days. The bids are scrutinized by a committee headed by a committee of the RBI. The Committee decides on a cut-off price and quoting equal to or higher than the cut-off price, is accepted. Other bids are rejected. The successful bidders would collect letters of acceptance and deposit the amount with RBI within 24 hours.

Features of Treasury Bills

- Treasury bills (T-bills) are issued at discount by the Central Government, i.e. Government of India (GOI) to meet its short-term requirements. T-bills are issued for varying maturities such as 14 days, 91 days, 182 days, and 364 days.
- T-bills does not carry a coupon rate but are issued at a discount. On the maturity date the bearer of the instrument gets the face value. The minimum size of a T-bill could be Rs. 25,000 and is issued in multiple of Rs. 25,000.
- The investor can obtain T-bills in physical form or alternatively it could also be obtained in scripless form by way of entries in the Subsidiary General Ledger (SGL) account maintained with the RBI.
- The RBI on behalf of the GOI auctions T-bills. For 91-days T-bills the auction is conducted every Friday for a notified amount. The investors are mainly the market players like commercial banks, etc. The rates of yield on the T-bills are market driven.
- The interest rates on T-bills are also treated as benchmark for the other money market instruments. Since, T-bills does not carry any risk of repayment the other instruments carry relatively higher rate of interest.
- The T-bills as such are issued by the Central Government, however, the RBI acts as a banker of the government and in practicality the issue is made by RBI as an agent of the government.

Benefits of Treasury Bills

1. For the Government of India it is a method of meeting short-term requirements of the funds. Further, the RBI also uses T-bills to control the money markets through its Open Market Operations (OMO).
2. No repayment default risk: Since issued by the government the T-bills are treated risk-free as the GOI cannot make default in repayment.

3. Assured returns and safety in respect of capital: The T-bills offer assured risk-free returns to the investors and there is no possibility of loss of capital invested.
4. High liquidity and eligibility for statutory requirements: Because of its risk-free nature T-bills are very easy to sell in the secondary market and as such offer very high level of liquidity. Further, investments in T-bills qualify for SLR requirements and thus the bankers find it very convenient to invest in T-bills.

BILL MARKET

A Bill of Exchange is a debt claim arising out of normal business transaction. The Negotiable Instruments Act, 1881, regulates the operations of bill of exchange. Further, the RBI also regulates the money market by deciding the bank rate, i.e. the rate at which RBI would discount Bill of Exchange. A Bill of Exchange is issued/prepared/drawn by a drawer. However, it is accepted by a drawee and one is to compare with the issuers as considered for the above instruments. Thus, a Bill of Exchange arises out of normal business transactions and is issued by the person purchasing goods, etc.

Features of Bill of Exchange

- The drawer who is to receive consideration from the issuer may be treated as an investor. Subsequently, when the Bill of Exchange is discounted the purchaser may be treated as an investor.
- A Bill of Exchange normally originates out of genuine business transaction and the initial investor, i.e. drawer is not investing in it as a money market instrument. However, the subsequent parties invest in it as a money market instrument. Investment in Bill of Exchange can be done by any person.
- Normally the bankers and other money market players use it as a part of their money market operations. Bill of Exchange as such is a debt claim and also has secondary market, and Bill of Exchange

is also a debt instrument. However, the instruments listed above are issued specifically to raise funds. Whereas Bill of Exchange arises out of a business transaction and the intention is not to raise funds.

- Bill of Exchange although a debt claim may not be treated as a security.
- Bill of Exchange arises as a part of normal business transaction. Thus, besides serving the parties (i.e. buyer and seller) it also offers liquidity to the money market.

3

International Financial Market

On the onset of liberalization in the domestic regulations and globalization of financial markets abroad, an increasing number of Indian companies are raising funds in international financial markets. Typically the operations are in Eurocurrency markets, which provide larger access at competitive cost. Eurocurrency market is an international market activity that specializes in borrowing and lending of currencies outside the country of issue. Thus, deposits in dollars with a bank in London are Eurodollars. Similarly, Japanese yen held by banks in London are yen, pound sterling held by banks in Germany are Euro, sterling and so on. The main centers of Eurocurrency are London and a few other places in Europe. The growth of the market has extended beyond these limits and now it includes a few centers of Asia too such as Singapore, Hong Kong and the like.

GROWTH OF INTERNATIONAL FINANCIAL MARKET

To prevent the dollar earnings being blocked by the USA, the Chinese Government began to disguise its dollar earnings by placing them with a Russia-owned bank in Paris. Following the outbreak of the Korean War in 1950, the USA blocked identifiable dollar balances in the USA. Fearing similar action against their holdings, the Russian banks in Paris and London began disguising their balances by placing them with banks in Western Europe instead of depositing them directly in New York. This led to the mutual claim between the Western Banks on dollar balances in the USA and on the Western Banks by Communist depositors.

Other factors contributing for the growth of international financial market was the decision taken by the British Government in late 1957 to impose a ban on new overseas loans, denominated in sterling to finance trade between countries outside the Sterling Area. During the same period, exchange control restrictions were relaxed throughout Western Europe, affording commercial banks the freedom to conduct foreign exchange business and to accept deposits in foreign currencies. The situation was utilized by the London banks to offer their restricted non-sterling area clients the alternative of financing in US dollars. The real impetus for the growth of Eurodollars came from certain developments in the USA itself. Regulation of the Federal Reserve Act provided mandatory ceilings on interest rates that could be paid on bank deposits. Under the regulations no interest was payable on bank deposits of less than 30 days' duration, while interest rates for longer terms were governed by strict ceilings.

The above caused the interest rates payable on dollar deposits in the USA to be restricted, while no such restriction was there for deposits outside the USA. By offering higher rates of interest than those prevailing in the USA, banks operating outside the USA were able to attract substantial dollar deposits from non-US residents. The higher rate of interest also resulted in transfer of some of dollar balances kept by foreign investors in New York to outside the USA. Initially, these deposits were placed with banks in London as they had a ready use of these funds in foreign exchange business and lending to non-sterling areas. Resultantly, Eurocurrency gained prominence and so UK became the financial centre.

The Federal Reserve Act regulation also required the banks to maintain certain percentage as reserves against deposits which resulted in the cost of operations lower in

Europe as compared to that in the USA. A part of this economy in operations could be passed on the customers in the form of higher rates of interest on deposits at the European centres. Except for a brief period, this regulation was not applied to deposits of European branches of US banks. Hence, it encouraged some US banks to move some of their depositor's accounts, including those of Americans to the European market. All the factors thus far mentioned encouraged the flow of funds into Eurocurrency markets. Certain other factors ensured its sustenance by creating adequate demand for the funds thus generated. One such factor was the controls and restrictions on borrowing funds in the United States for reinvestment abroad, begun as a voluntary restraint programme in 1965 and made mandatory in 1968. As a result of the restrictions, the borrowers were driven to seek loans outside the US market and naturally they resorted to the Eurocurrency market.

Interest Equalisation Tax of 1963 was enforced to discourage flow of dollar from USA. This was a tax on US residents' earnings on foreign securities. To cover the tax, the US lenders charged higher rates of interest from foreign borrowers. Routing the funds through the Eurocurrency market helped to avoid the interest equalization tax and thus enabled the lenders to offer fund at lesser rates.

Features of Euro Market

- Transactions in each currency take place outside the country of its issue.
- Even though the currency is utilized outside the country of its origin it has to be held only in the country of its issue.
- Eurocurrencies are outside the direct control of the monetary authorities of their respective countries of issue but they are subject to some form of indirect control. This is because the settlement of all transaction has to take place only in the country of issue.
- Eurocurrency market is a market in which foreign currencies are lent and borrowed as distinct from the

foreign exchange market, where they are bought and sold.

- This market consists of a pool of predominantly short-term deposits which provide the biggest single source of funds that commercial banks transform into medium and occasionally long-term international loans or Euro credits.
- The transactions in the market involve huge amounts running into millions of dollars. The large-scale financing has led to the development of syndications of loans, where a large number of banks participate in the lending operations.
- US dollar remains the leading currency traded in the Eurocurrency market, even though its share is declining. Other currencies traded in the market on large scale are Deutsche mark, Japanese Yen, Pound Sterling and Swiss Franc.
- Eurocurrency market is a highly competitive market with free access for new institutions in the market. Consequently, the margin between the interest rates on deposits and advances has narrowed down considerably.
- The rate of interest of this market is linked to a base rate, usually the London Inter-Bank Offered Rate (LIBOR). The interest on the deposit or the advance would be reviewed periodically and changed in accordance with change, if any, in LIBOR. This feature is called 'floating rates of interest'.

Factors Determining Interest Rates on Eurocurrency

- Volume of world trade transacted in the currency.
- Relative strength of the currency in the foreign exchange market.
- Domestic interest rates.
- Domestic monetary policy and reserve requirements.
- Domestic government regulation.

Primarily the domestic interest rates act as a floor to Eurocurrency rates because the funds flow into Eurocurrency market seeking higher interest. Although the Eurocurrency market operates in a number of centers around the world, interest rates for a particular currency are consistent. Any temporary variations at different markets are quickly eliminated by international arbitrage. Interest in Eurocurrency market is generally a floating rate of interest. Periodically, the interest rate will change with reference to a benchmark rate like LIBOR.

EXCHANGE RATES APPLIED IN INTERNATIONAL FINANCIAL MARKET

- *London Inter-bank Offered Rate:* It represents the rate at which banks in London will lend a currency to other banks for a specific maturity. Since London is a major Eurocurrency market, Libor is used as the basis for most Eurocurrency transactions. Libor varies for different maturities. Thus we have month Libor, 3 months Libor, 6 months Libor etc. Rates quoted by different banks may vary slightly, the bigger banks offering lower rates.
- *London Interbank Bid Rate:* This rate is the rate at which banks accept Eurocurrency deposits. Bid rates are lower than offered rates usually by 12 to 25 per cent. *LIMEAN* is the average of Libor and Libid.
- *Euro Libor:* While LIBOR is applicable for dollar transactions, Euro Libor is applicable for transactions in Euro. It is based on the rates quoted by 16 banks in London.
- *Euribor*: It is the acronym of Euro Interbank Offered Rate. This is the benchmark rate of the large euro money market that has emerged since 1999. Euribor is the rate at which euro inter-bank term deposits are offered by one prime bank to another prime bank and is published at 11.00 a.m. It is based on rates quoted by 57 banks in the Eurozone.
- *Sibor:* This represents the Singapore Inter-bank Offered Rate. Similar to Libor, it is the rate at which principal banks in Singapore offer to lend Asian dollars and other currencies to other banks. Sibor

forms the basis for interest rate on Asian dollar and syndicated loans.

- *Prime Rate:* This is the rate of interest charged by first class banks in USA on advances to their first class borrowers. For example, it may relate to an advance made to a multinational corporation with a very high credit rating. This rate is usually a couple of percentage points higher than the discount and Federal funds rate. While it follows the same trends, it is determined rate calculated from money market rates, specially from the 90 days Certificate of Deposit rate. Every bank in the USA announces independently its prime rate, but this tends to influence the rate of other banks also. Similarly, the prime rate has influence over the Eurodollar rate and is also influenced by it. A change in the prime rate is followed by a change in the Eurocurrency rate and *vice versa*.

Segments of Euro Market

- Euro credit markets, where international group of banks engage in lending for medium and long-term.
- Euro currency deposits, where banks accept deposits, mostly for short-term.
- Euro notes market, where corporates raise funds.
- Euro bond market, where banks raise funds on behalf of international borrowers by issuing bonds.

EURO CREDITS

Eurocredits are medium and long-term loans provided by international group of banks in currencies which need not be those of the lenders or borrowers. Eurocredit belongs to wholesale sector of the international capital market and normally involves large amounts. Security Eurocredits are provided mostly without any collateral security from the borrower. Most of the lending in Eurocurrency markets takes the form of Eurocredit. Greater emphasis is laid on the credit rating of the borrower rather than on any tangible security.

Providing Eurocredits as unsecured facilities also renders the job easy by avoiding complicated procedures to take charge of the security.

The period of Eurocredits extends up to 15 years. But most of the credits are for periods of 5 to 8 years. On an average about 5% of the total credits are for periods ranging from 1 to 5 years and about 10% from 10 to 15 years. Interest is fixed at a certain percentage over a reference rate, generally the interbank rate for Eurocurrency deposits. For dollar loans the reference rate is the LIBOR and for Euro it is EURIBOR. For loans in pound sterling the Paris Interbank Offered Rate is taken as the base rate. Generally interest for dollar loans is fixed at a percentage over Libor, say 1% over Libor. The interest is revised every six months, considering the changes in Libor. Thus, technically, the credit is 'rolled over' or renewed every six months. The difference between the interest charged on the loan and the Libor is the lending margin.

The lending margin is not fixed but depends upon the credit rating of the borrower and his bargaining capacity. Most of the loans raised are in dollars. Some loan agreements also provide for currency option. That is, initially the loan is raised in dollars. The borrower is given the option to roll over the loan in a different currency according to his requirement. This again is possible provided the bank can procure the required currency. The multi-currency option helps the borrower in avoiding exchange risk and also does not involve the lending bank in any risk.

Types of Euro Credit

Term Credit: This is similar to medium-term loans provided by banks. At the beginning itself both the lenders and borrowers agree on the schedule of drawing the facility.

Revolving Credit: It is similar to a cash credit facility. It is a standby facility to meet temporary but recurring financial requirements of the borrower. Interest is charged on the actual amount utilized, on the sanctioned but unutilized portion, a commitment fee may be charged. Repayment is arranged by progressively reducing the credit limit till the entire facility is thus reduced.

Loan Syndication in Eurocurrency: Each Eurocredit runs into a huge amount of a few hundred million dollars. It is not safe or possible for a single bank to undertake the entire amount. Thus few banks form a syndicate (similar to consortium lending in domestic banking) to provide funds to the borrower. The practice is also partly due to the US laws which provide limitations on loans of any single bank to any single borrower. Bank syndicates are not permanent groupings. They are formed in each case by banks willing to participate in the credit.

The following intermediaries play a major role in arranging Eurocredit.

- Managing banks appointed by the borrower to arrange the credit.
- Lead bank, providing most of the money.
- Agent bank appointed by lenders *to* look after their interests *once* the loan agreement is signed. All the functions may be rendered by a single bank.

The managing banks are appointed by the borrower to arrange the credit. They may be either the wholesale large commercial banks that arranges credit, take major share and are a force to reckon with or the retail sector small banks taking what participation they can get. The appointment of the managing bank is formalized with the award of mandate by the borrower. The managing bank helps the borrower in drawing up a statement of the borrower's financial condition and purpose of the credit and the loan agreement. It negotiates terms with other banks and assembles the syndicate. The manager's function comes to an end with the signing of the loan agreement by the borrower and the participating banks and the agent bank take over from there. But, in practice, the managing bank continues to keep in touch With the borrowers to help protect the interests of the lending syndicate.

The participants in the syndicate are entitled to participation fee. A part of the management fee received by the managing bank is passed on to the participants as the participation fee in proportion to the share of funds provided by each. Participation fee is not payable if share of a bank is less than a prescribed minimum. A situation may arise where the borrower has to pay facility fee in addition to the management fee. The facility fee is the commitment charge paid on undrawn portion of the credit to compensate the banks for keeping funds ready which is annually determined rate.

Secured Lending: Lending banks to protect their interests analyze the position of the borrower and his country's economic and political environment thoroughly before committing themselves of the loan. Even though all members of the syndicate sign a common loan agreement, each lending bank is responsible for its own decision and surveillance over the borrower. But the smaller banks may lack the desired infrastructure to undertake a detailed country risk analysis. The interests of the lending banks are protected better when there is co-financing by official international organizations like IMF and World Bank. In such cases information about international financial flows and debtor countries becomes easily available.

Several aspects are included in the loan agreement safeguarding the interest of the lending banks. Any misrepresentation by the borrower in the information furnished to the syndicate or failure to perform the covenants will be considered as default by the borrower. Default of any single lending bank will be regarded as default with all banks. The covenants include negative lien, maintenance of ratios between assets and liabilities, limitation on dividends and total debt service in relation to earnings, etc. But recourse to legal protection is rendered difficult because the credits fall outside the jurisdiction of any single authority. Further complication is the legal status of governments and international organisations as borrowers, although many countries have passed laws to waive sovereign immunity in commercial transactions. Hence, without taking legal course, proceeding with a political dialogue will settle the matter smoothly. In case of default, IMF may propose conditions for management of economies as a corrective measure. But co-financing by these institutions is confined to a very few cases. To compensate with loss that might arise on of weaker borrowers, the lending prescribe high lending margins.

EURO CURRENCY DEPOSITS

Eurocurrency market consists of all deposits of currencies

placed with banks outside their home currency. While Eurobonds represent the funds amassed by the banks on behalf of international borrowers, Eurocurrency deposits represent the funds accepted by the banks themselves. Eurocurrency time deposits are by far the most important instruments in the Euromarkets surpassing by several times the outstanding under Eurobond and foreign bond issues. The deposits are accepted in Eurocurrencies or in currencies of different countries representing a single basket.

Eurocurrency Deposits may be placed at call or for fixed periods as time deposits. Call deposits may be made for overnight. two-day or seven-day notice for US dollars, Canadian dollars, Sterling and Japanese yen and for a minimum notice of two days in other currencies. Time deposits are accepted for periods of 1.3, 6 and 12 months for all currencies. Thus, it can be seen there is a close link in the functioning of the Eurocurrency deposit market and foreign exchange markets. Deposits in US dollars and pound sterling can be placed for periods up to five years.

Certificates of Deposit

Certificates of deposits are issued payable to bearer and therefore can be traded in the secondary market. Most Certificates of deposits in Eurocurrency markets are in dollars and few in sterling and yen. A certificate of deposit resembles a time deposit with the difference that the former is negotiable while a time deposit is not. The minimum denomination is USD 50.000. Normally they are issued for periods up to one year. Certificates of deposits provide an excellent avenue for banks who would like to keep the liquidity and earn interest at the same time. Certificates of deposits evidence receipt of money by the bank and also carry the bank's guarantee for repayment of principal and interest.

Types of Certificates of Deposits

Floating Rate Certificates of Deposits: These are issued with maturities up to three years. Interest is adjusted every six months at 1/4 per cent over the prevailing Libor. They are therefore more beneficial to investors when compared with a straight certificate of deposits for six months rolled over three years. Interest is paid semi-annually.

Straight or Tap Certificates of deposits: They bear a fixed rate of interest and have a fixed maturity date of 1 to 12 months. Interest is normally fixed at 1/8 per cent below Libor at the time of issue. In individual cases the interest fixed depends upon the credit standing of the issuing bank and liquidity position in the market.

Tranche Certificates of deposits: It is issued with maturities up to five years and carry fixed rate of interest. It the characteristics of Eurobonds but maturing at short period. A tranche certificate of deposit is a share in a programme of certificate of deposits issued by a bank up to a predetermined level. Each tranche certificate of deposits carries the same rate of interest and matures on the same date. Usually, they are placed directly with investors rather than offered publicly to the market. Discount CDs are issued at a discount and are paid at maturity for their face value the difference representing the interest for the period. Interest calculation is similar to that for treasury bills or bankers' acceptances.

EURO BONDS

Eurobonds are those sold for international borrowers in several markets simultaneously by international group of banks and it is a major source of borrowing at Euromarkets. They are issued on behalf of multinational corporations, international agencies and governments. In the past borrowers were largely from industrialized countries. Of late, developing countries have entered the market on a large scale. Most of their borrowings had been balance of payments-oriented, either directly or indirectly. Eurobond should be distinguished from foreign bonds. Foreign bond is issued on behalf of a non-resident borrower as in the case of Eurobond. But a foreign bond is sold only in the domestic capital market of the issuing country by a group of banks in the market of issue. It is subject to regulations of the country of issue.

These are unsecured securities and so only borrowers of high financial standing are able to issue such bonds. When they are issued by government corporations and local bodies, they are guaranteed by the government of the country concerned. Issues by subsidiaries normally carry guarantee of the parent company. Most Eurobonds are bearer securities. The average maturity of Eurobonds is about 5 to 6 years although it is normal to find issues with maturity up to 15 years. Usually, selling of Eurobonds is done through Syndicates. The Lead Managing Bank is responsible for advising on the best size of the issue, terms and timing and for coordinating the issue. Lead managers take the help of co-managing banks. Entire issue is underwritten by the managers and a larger group of underwriting banks. In addition there are still larger groups of selling banks.

Management fee is charged by the lead bank and the underwriting banks get underwriting allowance. Hence, the cost of issue may come to 2% to 2.5% of the value of the issue. Initially the lead manager holds the entire commission, allowance, etc. The borrower gets the value of the issue less commission, etc., from the lead manager. The lead manager allocates the bonds to all members of the selling group at face value less their commission/allowance. Thereafter every member is on its own. They can sell to investors at whatever prices they can obtain. Thus no two investors in the Eurobond market need pay the same price for newly issued bonds.

Types of Euro Bonds

Fixed Rate Bonds: These are fixed interest-bearing securities, the interest normally payable at yearly intervals. Interest is payable on the basis of interest year of 360 days. Maturities range from 3 to 25 years. Maturity common is up to 15 years. But the actual life of a bond is reduced considerably by the borrower exercising the right to redemption before maturity that is included in the bond. The redemption is done by offering premium. Provision for redemption of bond may be made either through creation of a purchase fund or a sinking fund. In a purchase fund the borrower sets aside an amount to repurchase some of his outstanding bonds in the open market up to a stipulated amount in any given year of the life of the issue. But creation of purchase funds does not create any liability on the part of the borrower to redeem the bond before maturity.

For redemption the borrower may exercise his discretion when the market conditions favour such a decision. Often the fund is used to support bonds in the secondary markets, for the sake of credit standing of the borrower and to help future borrowing. A sinking fund is instituted when there is legal obligation to buy back. Otherwise it is similar to purchase fund.

The rate of interest of these bonds is fixed however the actual yield from the investment depends upon the price paid by the investor. Bond prices are influenced by the level of short-term interest rates and the degree of liquidity in the money market. Price fluctuations can produce capital gain or loss to the investor when he disposes the bond in the secondary market. Price fluctuations often lead to switch between bonds in the secondary market and between bonds and other instruments. There is no deduction of tax at source. But the investor is expected to declare the income to national tax authorities and pay tax.

Convertible Bonds: The investor has the option to convert them into the equity share of the borrowing company. The conversion will be done at a stipulated price for the shares and during a stipulated period. Thus convertible bonds are similar in nature to that of convertible debentures. The conversion price is normally kept higher than the market price for the equity shares on the date of bond issue. Therefore, the investor will exercise the option of conversion only if the market price during the option period is higher than the fixed price.

These securities too bear fixed interest but the rate of interest on convertible bonds is lower than that offered on a comparable straight bond. This is because the investor will profit from a rise in the share price. Another advantage to the borrowing company is that it will also receive cash for a phased programme of newly issued shares when the investors exercise their option of conversion.

Some of the bonds are issued in a currency other than the currency in which the shares of the company are denominated. This provides an opportunity to diversify the currency risk. Such bonds are issued with a fixed exchange rate clause specifying the rate at which the conversion into shares will be accounted. The investor's decision to convert or to hold bonds as such will depend upon the relative movement in exchange rates. The attraction of convertible bonds to the investors is that in addition to fixed income on their investment they stand to participate in the capital growth of the company.

Bonds with Warrants: Some bonds are issued with that gives the option of conversion into shares. Warrant is part of the bond but is detachable and traded separately when the conversion takes place. The value of the warrant is less than the conversion price of shares. The investor has, therefore, to surrender a part of the bond or pay cash to make up the difference. The investor can keep the bond and trade the warrant for the shares separately.

Currency Option Bonds: These are similar to straight bonds with the difference that it is issued in one currency with option to take payment of interest and principal in a second currency normally, option bonds are issued in sterling and provide option for payment in dollar or Euro. The conversion rate of such bond is the spot rate quoted in the market three business days before-each payment is due for interest and principal. Conversion takes place depends on the term of issue. Some bonds fix the rate of conversion at the time of issue itself.

Floating Rate Notes : Floating Rate Notes are like straight bonds compared to the maturity and denomination. Mostly issued by banks and in some cases banks invest in Floating Rate Notes. The speciality of the Floating Rate Notes is that the interest payable is varying in accordance with the market conditions unlike the fixed rate payable on a straight bond. Interest on Floating Rate Notes is payable at a spread over the Libor which is normally 1/4%. But in individual cases the spread can vary from a low of 1/8% to a high of 1.5%. The rate of interest is adjusted every six months depending upon the ruling Libor. Many bonds also provide for a minimum interest clause in case the Libor and the spread fall below a certain level. The advantage of Floating Rate Notes is that they provide the investors with the facility of investing for long-term and also benefit from movement in short-term rates.

EURO NOTES

Euro notes evolved as a process of disintermediation in the market whereby the borrowers are directly approaching the lenders without the intermediation of banks and financial institutions. Euro-notes constitute the instruments of borrowing issued by corporates in the Eurocurrency market with or without the underwriting support of financial intermediaries.

Types of Euro Notes

Commercial Paper: Usually Commercial Paper is issued on a discount to yield basis. Commercial Paper is promissory note of maturity less than a year issued by a corporate body. Generally the issue is not underwritten and therefore companies with high ranking issue commercial paper. Typically the period for which commercial paper is issued varies from 90 to 180 days. The investors are mainly from major fund managers such as insurance companies, banks and corporate houses.

The duration of commercial paper is short and so it suits short term financial plans. For the borrowers commercial paper provides a cheap source of finance as the interest rate is lesser than that paid on bank borrowings. It is flexible as the size of issue can be varied according to the requirements. First rated corporates may also back up their issues with lines of credit from banks from which they can draw if commercial paper is not fully subscribed. For the investors the yield is higher than that on bank deposits. These are liquid negotiable unsecured instruments.

Note Issuance Facilities: Note issuance facility is a device adopted to meet the divergent needs of the borrowers for medium-term funds with the willingness of the investors to invest in short-term. The reconciliation is achieved through the underwriting facility provided by banks. It is a medium-term commitment under which a borrower can issue short-term paper in its own name, but the underwriting banks are committed either to purchase any notes which the borrower is unable to sell or to provide standing credits.

The notes are rolled over on their maturity that is the existing notes are redeemed and fresh notes are issued. Banks underwrite that at the time of each rollover they would take up the unsold notes or provide matching credit. Depending upon slight variation in the methodology adopted for their issue, such a facility is also known as Revolving Underwriting

Facility or Standby Note Issuance Facility or Note Purchase Facility.

Medium-Term Notes: Medium-Term Notes were evolved to bridge the maturity gap between the short term commercial paper of less than one year and long term Eurobond of more than 5 years. Documentation procedures are simpler as compared to bond issue. They enjoy a highly liquid market. They represent a long-term non-underwritten and fixed interest rate source of raising finance, comparable with Eurobond issues. Whereas Eurobond is underwritten, this is not. These notes are like privately placed bonds but have great flexibility.

OF-SHORE BANKING

When banking involves non-resident foreign currency denominated assets and liabilities then it is called offshore banking. Such an activity has exclusive dealing with foreign currency operations alone. Offshore banking is an extension of the concept of Eurocurrency to East. An offshore banking centre is a place where deliberate attempt is made to attract international banking by offering many concessions in the form of taxes and levies being imposed at lower rates or not being charged. A more important relaxation is the exemption of the offshore banks from restrictions on operations. Offshore banking units in these centers can carry on their activities of deposit taking from and lending to international enterprises or investors without conflict with the domestic fiscal and monetary policy.

Offshore banking provides a link between Eurocurrency markets and the final borrowers. They are providing essential time zone links which are truly world-wide and ensure that the market operates 24 hours a day. While offshore banking is an integral part of Euro market. The need for channellising huge international money resources that 'Organization of petroleum exporting countries' came to possess following the oil crisis resulted in setting up of a number of offshore centers. These centers exist in many of the Asian countries.

Offshore banking units are branches of international banks or other subsidiaries or affiliates. They do not carry retail business, but generally provide wholesale banking services, namely, project financing, syndicated loans, issue of short-term and medium-term instruments like negotiable certificates of deposits and capital notes as well as merchant banking activities in foreign currency denominated bonds and equity shares.. The deals are mostly between banks or with large borrowers or multinational corporations. Offshore banking offers some exclusive benefits to banks such as the following:

- Unregulated interest rates.
- Relaxation in reserve requirements.
- Low or non-existent taxes and levies.
- Concession in License fees.
- Close proximity to the important loan outlets or deposit sources.
- Easy entry for large banks having international reputation.

This offshore banking provides the Multinational Corporations (MNCs) following several benefits and so this led to the growth of offshore banking:

- Avoidance of high tax incidence.
- Deferring tax by floating subsidiary units in such offshore centers.
- Freedom from exchange control.
- Maintenance of secrecy.

Indian banks have shown a significant progress in offshore banking. It is due to the sophistication achieved by Indian banks in international finance. That the response from Indian banks to offshore banking is positive reveals the development of these banks in the last few years in the field of international banking. Several Indian banks have set-up offshore banking units for deposit taking and final lending world over. The Sodhani Committee on Foreign Exchange Reforms (1996) has recommended allowing Indian banks and financial institutions to set-up offshore banking units as it would prove to be cost-effective for local institutions. These units can offer many services including managing funds raised by Indian corporates through GDR issues. Indian banks have the following advantages by entering into offshore banking:

- They would earn sizable profits as these ventures involve relatively low operating costs.
- By the use of multi-currency deposits the banks would be able to serve better the needs of their customers who have set-up joint ventures abroad in the form of foreign currency finance.
- The banks would be strengthening the balance of payments of the country through repatriation of profits from the venture.

Offshore Banking Unit

Successive government after the liberalization and globalization policies were tuned up are constantly helping for a smooth international business for Indian corporates. Now Indian corporations are functioning abroad and many corporations are granted permission to seek overseas finance and so the establishment of an offshore unit will help tap the resources easily. Financial experts are of the opinion that establishing of an offshore banking centre in India would greatly help Indian corporates. It has a vast market, technical manpower which could find employment in these centers. Despite the fact that has a stable economic and political performance, geographically too, India provides distinct advantages in attracting offshore banking units.

Benefits of Offshore Banking in India

- Country may earn revenue in the form of license fees and profit taxes imposed on the banks.
- The country can gain improved access to the international capital markets.
- It may also get the benefit of bank funds in the form of capital and liquidity requirements.
- Exporters would benefit in terms of finer margins on loans and better foreign exchange rates available through offshore banking unit.

- The benefits of multi-currency operations which, to an extent, minimize currency fluctuation risk will be an added advantage.
- It adds up to the prestige of the country.
- The domestic financial system may become more efficient through increased competition and through exposure of the domestic banks to the practices of offshore banks.
- The offshore banking centre will provide opportunities to train the local staff which will in turn contribute to a faster growth of the economy.
- Salaries paid by offshore banks and local expenditure incurred by them contribute to the welfare of the economy.
- The offshore banking units would help channelise non-resident Indian investments.
- It triggers development of more advanced communication facilities which is a must for its functioning.
- As the exporters could get cheaper finance and so the expenditure on export interest subsidy can be saved.

Problems of Offshore Banking

- Offshore banks may increase demand for domestic resources.
- The host country may have to incur heavily on these if the facilities are non-existing.
- The cost involved may not be justified for the benefits derived.
- The supervision and regulation of offshore banks may involve substantial costs.
- An offshore centre requires certain infrastructure such telecommunication, education and training facilities.
- Encouraging offshore banking may result in the diminution in autonomy of domestic monetary policy, since it is difficult to draw a line always between the offshore and onshore operations.

Offshore banking provides scope for tax evasion by residents.

- Offshore banks may prove to be deleterious competitors to the local banks and may inhibit their growth.

International Capital Markets

Funds in the international financial market could be tapped from various sources previously discussed. Since capital market activity is close related with the financial market, the funds generated by corporates in the international financial market are used for capital market activity too. Some of the internationally active capital markets are discussed below.

Hong Kong has a stock market attracting international capital as it was a British colony for a long time. Hangseng is the name of this capital market. It is able to attract funds throughout the globe. Japan's capital market is also equally attractive and it is known as Nikkei. Japanese foreign trade and multinational companies of Japan are responsible for improving capital market in Japan. U.S.A. has a stock market called Nasdaq compared to OTCEI in India and most of the multinational companies throughout the world have shares listed in the market. As the minimum volume and the value are kept high, not many Indian companies are in a position to list their securities in Nasdaq, with the exception of Infosys. FTSE is the name given for London Stock Exchange, in Germany it is called DAX and in France it is known as CAC.

Indian companies can raise capital in the international market subject to permission granted by SEBI and RBI and they can issue Global Deposit Receipts (GDR) and American Deposit Receipts (ADR) for raising foreign exchange. Indian banks are also permitted to issue deposit receipts in foreign markets. Unit Trust of India, in association with Merrilynch Company was able to raise funds through the issue of India Development Bonds.

Factors Influencing International Capital Market

Interest Rate: The varying interest among countries influences the capital movements and stock prices. As the international capital markets are active throughout the day, there is a close monitoring of prices.

Gold Price: Gold price will also influence capital market transactions. If the price of gold increases, a downward trend will be there in international capital market.

Arbitrage: The brokers in the international capital market take advantage of the price differences between two markets and earn profits which are called arbitrage.

Value of Currency: The fluctuation in the currency value of a country influences the stock prices. Increases in the local currency will attract inflow of capital and vice versa. For this the fiscal policy of the country should be tuned up to suit the international capital market activity.

Derivative Market: Derivative markets are an important component of capital market. Banks and other financial institutions invest their funds in derivative markets.

4

Foreign Exchange Market

The term foreign exchange market is used to refer to the wholesale segment of the market, where the dealings take place among the banks. The retail segment refers to the dealings take place between banks and their customers. The retail segment is situated at a large number of places. They can be considered not as foreign exchange markets, but as the counters of such markets. Foreign exchange market is described as an over the counter market, as there is no physical place where the participants meet to execute the deals, as in the case of usual stock exchange dealings. It is more an informal arrangement among the banks and brokers operating in a market where purchasing and selling of currencies take place connected to each other by a network.

The foreign exchange rate is largely dependent on the economic policies pursued by the Government because they have a great influence on the exchange rates. The major instruments of achieving the policies of the government are the monetary policies and fiscal policies adopted. These policies affect all the factors such as inflation, interest rate fluctuation and the like and so these causes an impact on the exchange rates. The policy of the government depends upon the priorities it has allotted to different economic objectives decided with the coalition partners of the government. The government policies depend on their agenda for development and it desires to contain inflation, and foster economic growth.

In India, the government may affect the exchange rate through its policy of maintaining the exchange rates through RBI's intervention. It may intervene if the market rate varies widely from the predetermined rate through appropriate techniques. Official intervention will have the effect of normalizing the rate in the disorderly market. The government may also enter into bilateral agreements with other countries, in which case much of the transactions are settled outside the exchange market. The other way of maintaining the rates is an agreement between the central banks of two countries. The present UPA government is working on the rupee to be valued against foreign currency by the market forces and not by the government intervention.

The views of the participants in the foreign exchange market affect the exchange rate if they foresee some changes in the exchange rates. Whenever there is a discrepancy between the previously held expectation of a given factor and actual outcome of, it exchange rates will usually be effected. The behaviour of the major participant in the market can affect the exchange rate. The influence may make the rate move differently from that determined by long-term economic forces. A large-scale buying or selling by the major participant would make others in the market to follow suit. The sentiments of the major players of foreign exchange influence the value of the currency.

Exchange rates are many times influenced by the speculative moves sometimes aggravating the trend set by other factors. A large-scale purchase or sale of foreign exchange by speculators with expectation of fall or rise in exchange rates further accelerates the fall or rise. The speculation may take the form of purchasing heavily expecting a rise in price or selling heavily expecting a fall in price. It may also take the form of leads and lags which means changing the time of settlement of debts with a view to getting advantage of the change in rates. Arbitrage operations undertaken by the speculators to take advantage of differences in two markets also cause movements in exchange rates.

The largest foreign exchange market is London, followed by New York, Tokyo, Zurich and Frankfurt. In India, Leading foreign exchange market is Mumbai. Other places such as Calcutta, Chennai and Delhi are accounting for bulk of the exchange dealings in India. The policy of Reserve Bank has been to decentralize exchange operations and develop more broad-based exchange markets. As a result of the efforts of Reserve Bank, Cochin, Bangalore, Ahmedabad and Goa have emerged as new centers of foreign exchange market. Foreign exchange markets were primarily developed to facilitate settlement of debts arising out of international trade. But these markets have developed on their own so much so that a turnover of about 3 days in the foreign exchange market is equivalent to the magnitude of world trade in goods and services.

The business in foreign exchange markets in India has shown a steady increase as a consequence of increase in the volume of foreign trade of the country. Improvement in the communications systems has led to the greater access to international exchange markets. Rupee is not an internationally traded currency and is not in great demand. Much of the external trade of the country is designated in leading currencies of the world, such as the, US dollar, pound-sterling, Euro, Japanese yen and Swiss franc. Incidentally, these are the currencies that are traded actively in the foreign exchange market in India.

CHARACTERISTICS OF FOREIGN EXCHANGE MARKET

Continuous Market: Foreign exchange markets are situated throughout world and are traded at different time zones of the globe in such a way that when one market is closing the other is beginning its operations. Thus at any point of time one market or the other is open. However, a specific market will function only during the business hours. Some of the banks having international network and having centralized control of funds management may keep their foreign exchange department in the key centre open throughout to keep up with developments at other centers during their normal working hours. In India, the market is open for the time the banks are open for their regular banking business.

Dynamic Market: Developments in communication have largely contributed to the efficiency of the market. The participants keep abreast of current happenings by access to such services like Dow Jones and Reuter. Any significant development in any market is almost instantaneously received by the other market situated at a far off place and thus has global impact. This makes the foreign exchange market very efficient as if the functioning under one roof.

Common Yardstick: In most markets, US dollar is the vehicle currency, viz., the currency used to denominate international transactions. Although in recent times euro, yen and pound sterling has gained good share in the foreign exchange market, yet US dollar is taken for valuing cross currencies.

Physical Markets: In few place such as like Paris and Brussels, foreign exchange business takes place at a fixed place in the local stock exchange buildings. At these physical markets, the banks meet and in the presence of the representative of the central bank and on the basis of bargains, fix rates for a number of major currencies. This practice is called fixing. The rates thus fixed are used to execute customer orders previously placed with the banks. An advantage claimed for this procedure is that exchange rate for commercial transactions will be market determined, not influenced by anyone bank.

Foreign Exchange Participants: The participants in the foreign exchange market comprise:

- Reserve Bank of India
- Commercial Banks
- Brokers
- Corporates

- *Reserve Bank of India*: In India, authorized dealers have recourse to Reserve Bank to sell or buy US dollars to the extent the latter is prepared to transact in the currency at the given point of time. Reserve Bank will not ordinarily buy/sell any other currency from/to authorized dealers. The contract can be entered into on any working day of the dealing room of Reserve Bank. No transaction is entered into on Saturdays. The value date for spot as well as forward delivery should be in conformity with the national and international practice in this regard. Reserve Bank of India does not enter into the market in the ordinary course. Where the exchange rates are moving in a detrimental way due to speculative forces, the Reserve Bank may intervene in the market either directly or through the State Bank of India. The RBI may intervene in the market to influence the exchange rate and change it from that would result only from private supplies and demands. The central bank may transact in the market on its own for the above purpose. Or, it may do so on behalf of the government when it buys or sells bonds and settles other transactions which may involve foreign exchange payments and receipts.
- *Commercial Banks:* Commercial banks are the major players in the market. They buy and sell currencies for their clients. They may also operate on their own. When a bank enters a market to correct excess or sale or purchase position in a foreign currency arising from its various deals with its customers, it is said to do a cover operation. Such transactions constitute hardly 5% of the total transactions done by a large bank. A major portion of the volume is accounted by trading in currencies indulged by the bank to gain from exchange movements. For transactions involving large volumes, banks may deal directly among themselves. For smaller transactions, the intermediation of foreign exchange brokers may be sought.

- *Brokers:* Foreign exchange brokers facilitate deal between banks. In the absence of exchange brokers, banks have to contact each other for quotes. Exchange brokers ensure that the most favourable quotation is obtained and at low cost in terms of time and money. The bank may leave with the broker the limit up to which and the rate at which it wishes to buy or sell the foreign currency concerned. From the 'intend' from other banks, the broker will be able to match the requirements of both. The names of the counter parties are revealed to the banks only when the deal is acceptable to them, till then anonymity is maintained. Exchange brokers tend to specialize in certain exotic currencies, but they also handle all major currencies. In India, banks may deal directly or through recognized exchange brokers. Accredited exchange brokers are permitted to contract exchange business on behalf of authorized dealers in foreign exchange only upon the understanding that they will conform to the rates, rules and conditions laid down by the FEDAI. All contracts must bear the clause "Subject to the Rules and Regulations of the Foreign Exchange Dealers' Association of India".
- *Corporates:* The business houses, international investors, and multinational corporations may operate in the market to meet their genuine trade or investment requirements. They may also buy or sell currencies with a view to speculate or trade in currencies to the extent permitted by the exchange control regulations. They operate by placing orders with the commercial banks. The deals between banks and their clients form the retail segment of foreign exchange market.

In India, the Foreign Exchange Management (Possession and Retention of Foreign Currency) Regulations, 2000 permits retention by a resident of foreign currency up to USD 2,000. Foreign Currency Management (Realisation, Repatriation and Surrender of Foreign Exchange) Regulations, 2000 requires a resident in India who receives foreign exchange to surrender it to an authorised dealer: *(a)* within seven days of receipt in case of receipt by way of remuneration, settlement of lawful obligations, income on assets held abroad, inheritance, settlement or gift; and *(b)* within ninety days in all other cases. Any person who acquired foreign exchange but could not use it for the purpose or for any other permitted purpose is required to surrender the unutilized foreign exchange to an authorized dealer within sixty days from the date of acquisition. In case the foreign exchange was acquired for travel abroad, the unspent foreign exchange should be surrendered within ninety days from the date of return to India when the foreign exchange is in the form of foreign currency notes and coins and within 180 days in case of travelers cheques. Similarly, if a resident required foreign exchange for an approved purpose, he should obtain from an authorized dealer.

EXCHANGE RATE SYSTEM

When countries were under gold standard the value of currency of a country was fixed as the value of gold of definite weight and fineness. The exchange rate between the currencies was determined on the relative value of gold content of currencies concerned. This rate of exchange was known as the *mint par of exchange.* Exchange rates were stable under gold standard because any deviation in the exchange rate would be set right automatically by the movement of gold between the countries that such deviation caused. When the paper currency system replaced the gold standard, the exchange rate was determined by relative purchasing power of the currencies. The stability in exchange rates gave way to fluctuations with dynamic situation prevailing all around.

Fixed Exchange Rates

Fixed exchange rates refer to the system under the gold standard where the rate of exchange tends to stabilize around the mint par value. Any large variation of the rate of exchange from the mint par value would entail flow of gold into or from the country. This would have the effect of bringing the exchange rate back to the mint par value. In present-day situation where gold standard no longer exists, fixed rates of exchange refer to maintenance of external value of the currency at a predetermined level. Whenever the exchange rate differs from this level it is corrected through official intervention. The par value system was abolished with the second amendment to the Articles of IMF in 1978. Still the system of fixed rates continues in many countries in the form of pegging their currencies to a major currency. If the exports of the country exceed imports the demand for the local currency in the exchange market will rise. This will raise the value of the currency in the market. Where the increase in value is beyond the support point, the central bank of the Country intervenes in the market to sell local currency and thus the foreign exchange reserves of the country increase. The sale of local currency in the market leads to increase in money supply in the country causing inflation. Revaluation may be resorted to allow for more imports and contain inflation.

If the country is facing balance of payments deficits due to higher imports, it would have the effect of increase in supply of local currency in the foreign exchange markets. The price of local currency may go below the support point and the central bank may have to intervene by buying local currency at a higher price. In the process, the foreign reserves of the country are depleted because the foreign currencies are exchanged in the market for buying local currency. To make up for the deficit, the country may be compelled to devalue the currency. The large scale buying of local currency will reduce the domestic money supply and may help fight inflation.

Under fixed rates, the compulsion to devalue the currency may be postponed or avoided by mopping up additional reserves. One such way is exchange of currency reserves between the central banks of countries. For instance, if India is in deficit, Reserve Bank may sell rupees to Bank of England against purchase of pound sterling. The sale will be reversed after a number of years when India has corrected its balance of payments.

Flexible Exchange Rates

Free or floating rates refer to the system where the exchange rates are determined by the conditions of demand for and supply of foreign exchange in the market. The rates are free to fluctuate according to the changes in demand and supply forces with no restrictions on buying and selling of foreign currencies in the exchange market.

Flexible rates of exchange refer to the system where the exchange rate is fixed, but is subject to frequent adjustments depending upon the market conditions. Thus, it is not a free or floating rate with cent per cent flexibility, but is any system providing for adjustments as and when required. However, in practice, often the above difference is ignored and both the terms are used interchangeably. The term 'managed float' or 'dirty float' is used to refer to the system where the central bank intervenes only where the market forces cause violent fluctuations, to bring some order in the market.

Under floating rates no par value is declared and the central bank does not intervene in the market. Any disparity in the balance of payments is adjusted through the changes in exchange rate that take place automatically in the market. Because the central bank does not intervene in the market there is no change in the exchange reserves of the country. A lively debate on the advisability of adopting fixed or floating rates of exchange has always been engaging the attention of economists. Forceful agreements have been put forward in favour of both systems.

Advantages of Fixed Rate System

- *Growth of International Trade:* Stable exchange rates encourage international trade by providing certainty and confidence. Exporters and importers know in advance how much they will receive or they will have to pay in terms of home currency. Advocates of floating rates point out that the post-war experiences do not support the view that stable exchange rates are required for smooth flow of international trade. Even under flexible rates of exchange international trade will flourish. So long as the balance of payments is at equilibrium, no change in the rate of exchange is expected. When the balance of payments is in disequilibrium, the rate of exchange will change but the change expected Can be assessed. Further, the importers and exporters can guard themselves against the changes by entering into forward contracts. The facility of forward contracts imparts the necessary certainty as far as the traders are concerned.

- *Promotes International Investment:* Stable exchange rates promote international investments which are essential for economic development and progress of the underdeveloped countries. Lenders on long-term would be prompted to invest in other countries only when the return in terms of home currency is ensured by stable exchange rates. The claim that stable exchange rates promote international investment is not borne out by facts. Even under fixed exchange rates it cannot be ensured that the rates will not change over a long period running into decades. The impending fear of the possibility of devaluation of the currency may act as a deterrent factor in international investments. On the other hand, flexible exchange rates adjust the external value of the currency and prevent recurrence of balance of payments crises more effectively.
- *Aids Long-term Planning:* Firms and the government can draw out long-range plans and work towards economic stability and prosperity easily under conditions of stable exchange rates. The stable exchange rates provide the necessary framework for drafting out such plans. Under flexible exchange rates, the frequent changes in exchange rates would render determination of the outlay of the plans difficult because with every change in exchange rates the outlay would vary. Proponents of flexible rates argue that under flexible exchange rates, the adjustment of balance of payments is done painlessly through changes in the rate of exchange without affecting the domestic prices and income. This helps planning by firms. Further, flexible rates allow freedom to the country in its monetary arrangements. Under fixed rates the monetary policy adopted

should be such as to facilitate maintenance of the fixed rates.

- *Development of Currency Areas:* Proper functioning of regional arrangements like sterling area or dollar area would be facilitated with the stable exchange rates. In such arrangements, if flexible rates prevail, especially for the major currency like pound-sterling or dollar with which the other currencies are linked, it will have serious repercussions on many other currencies.
- *Discourages Speculation:* Stable exchange rates avoid the dangerous possibilities of speculation and thus help in orderly growth of international markets.
- *Extensive Trading Economies:* It is argued that flexible rates will not work for small open economies, i.e., a country which trades extensively with others. Such economies may be depending upon imports to a large extent for many of its consumption goods. An adverse balance of payments, under flexible rates, will lead to depreciation of the currency of the country. This is supposed to stimulate exports due to reduction in the price of domestic products and thus adjust the deficit in the balance of payments. But, the depreciation of the currency will raise the price of imports. If the import is inelastic, it will raise the cost of living leading to rise in wages. The prices of domestic products increase offsetting of the benefit of depreciation. Thus the increase in exports may not realize. It would be better for such economies to fix the value of their currencies to the currency of the country which supplies most of their imports.
- *Inflation:* Under the fixed rate system, where rates are strictly on gold or dollar standard, there was need for the central bank to keep a close watch on the money supply and keep the inflation under control. Poor performance on this front was immediately reflected in the dwindling of foreign exchange reserves. This provided a good reason for taking strong remedial measures by the central bank. Under flexible exchange rates, the foreign exchange reserves are not affected and therefore no evidence of the

deterioration in the situation is available. This may allow inflation to creep in. However, it should be noted that under flexible rates, the change in exchange rate itself provides the needed evidence. Therefore, it may not be true to say that flexible rates are more inflationary than fixed rates.

- *Better exchange control:* Many countries maintain their currencies pegged through trade and exchange controls at a level higher than that would prevail in a free market. The introduction of flexible rate system would substantially deteriorate their terms of trade. The loss from deterioration of terms of trade would far exceed gain, if any, that accrues from introduction of flexible exchange rates.
- *No Competitive depreciation:* Under the flexible exchange rate system there is a possibility of countries engaging in competitive depreciation of their currencies in order to capture world markets. Such unhealthy practices are eliminated in the case of stable exchange rates.

Advantages of Flexible Rates

- *Adjustment of Balance of Payment*: Flexible exchange rates provide a smoother adjustment mechanism through changes in exchange rates. Changes in exchange rates affect only the external value of the currency but does not affect its domestic value. However, it should be noted that flexible exchange rates carry out the adjustment by ultimately reducing the real income. A depreciation in the value of the currency makes imports costlier which raises the cost of living and thereby reduces the purchasing power of given local income. Thus the effect of both fixed exchange rates and flexible exchange rates is same. The merit of flexible rates lies in the fact that the adjustment carried out averts adverse reaction from people.
- *Better Liquidity:* Flexible exchange rates do not require central banks to hold foreign exchange reserves, since

there is no need to intervene in the foreign exchange market. This means that the problem of having insufficient liquidity does not exist with truly flexible rates. Thus competitive devaluations of currencies aimed at securing a larger share of inadequate total stock of reserves will not take place.

- *Gains from Free Trade*: Under fixed rates, the balance of payments deficit can be corrected through monetary, fiscal or exchange control measures. Exchange control measures such .as restrictions on free flow of goods and capital and imposition of tariffs are often resorted to because of their immediate and visible effects. The imposition of restrictions is not conducive for the growth of multinational trade and costs the country in the form of loss of potential gains from the international trade and investments. Flexible rates avoid the need for such restrictions.
- *Better Confidence:* Any adverse balance in the country's balance of payments situation is corrected immediately and automatically under flexible rates. It thereby prevents the country from having persistent deficits and inspires confidence in the international financial system. The confidence created leads to fewer attempts by individual or central banks to readjust currency portfolios, and this gives rise to calmer foreign exchange markets.
- *Independence of Policy:* Under fixed exchange rates the country may be compelled to follow the same economic policy as its major trading partners. For example, let us suppose that rupee has parity with pound-sterling. If England increases its money supply, it will push up prices in England ultimately leading to deficit in balance of payments. Because rupee is fixed to sterling, a deficit in England is likely to bring surplus in India. In the exchange market, it will have the effect to putting up the price of rupee. Reserve Bank may have to sell rupee in the market to peg down the price. This will increase the money supply in India. Thus the economic policies of India

are closely tied to that of England. Under flexible exchange rates all that will happen is that value of sterling will decrease against other currencies. Thus the economic sovereignty of individual countries is maintained.

- *Cost-price Relationship:* Stable exchange rates do *not* reflect the present and true cost-price relationship between two countries; they are based on past rates. When countries follow different economic policies the cost-price relationship alters frequently. Flexible exchange rates take care of these. They provide automatic adjustment for the balance of payments disequilibria which in the process establishes the true cost-price relationship. Both the systems of exchange rates have their own merits and demerits.

CONVERTIBILITY OF RUPEE

Convertibility of a currency refers to its convertibility into a foreign currency as desired by its holder. The currency is fully convertible if the holder can convert it into any other currency at rates determined by the forces of demand and supply and without any interference from the government. The convertibility, therefore involves two aspects: The rate of exchange should be determined by the market and not by the regulatory authority and thus the holder does not incur any loss on conversion and there should not be any quantitative restrictions on the repatriation of the currency.

Earlier the exchange rate of rupee was subject to the condition that the rate quoted by a bank to its customer should not be worse than the rate based on RBI rate. Rupee was made partially convertible when dual exchange rate was introduced and 60% of the remittance into India was converted at the market determined rates. Now the value of rupee is fully determined by the market forces. Thus rupee now fulfils the first condition of convertibility that the exchange should be determined by market forces. A currency is converted to effect remittances, either from the country or into the country from abroad. Remittances are broadly classified into two categories those on current account and those on capital account.

Current Account Convertibility: Rupee is now fully convertible on current account fulfilling also the second condition for convertibility, namely, no quantitative ceiling on remittances abroad. Though subject to certain regulations. As a part of liberalization of foreign exchange transactions, The Reserve Bank has enhanced the discretionary powers for authorized dealers for making various remittances abroad. The limits on remittances for various purposes like travel, studies, medical treatments, gifts, services, etc have become indicative. In certain cases authorized dealers themselves can permit remittance beyond the indicated limits. In certain other cases, the requests for remittances over the limits shall be referred to Reserve Bank that will consider the request.

Capital Account Convertibility

The next logical step in the direction is the convertibility of rupee on capital account. In his Budget Speech for 1997-98, the Union Finance Minister described capital account convertibility as the cherished goal of the government. As a follow-up measure, the Reserve Bank of India appointed in February 1997 a committee on Capital Account Convertibility (CAC) under the Chairmanship of Sri S.S. Tarapore then Deputy Governor of Reserve Bank. The committee submitted its report on May 30, 1997.

Benefits of CAC

The Committee has put forward the following as the advantages flowing from CAC:

- Makes available a large capital stock to supplement domestic resources and thereby enables the economy to register higher growth, reduce the cost of capital and improve access to international financial markets.
- Allows residents to hold an internationally diversified portfolio which reduces the vulnerability of income streams and wealth to domestic stocks and lower funding costs for borrowers.
- Improves productivity.
- Provides impetus for domestic tax regimes to

rationalize tax structures. This removes inducements for domestic agents towards evasion and capital flight.

- Capital controls turn progressively ineffective, costly and even distortive. On the other hand, an open account would bring the weakness of the Indian financial system under a sharper focus. It would impose a strong discipline upon the financial system and expedite the early rectification of infirmities in the system and lead to widening/deepening of markets to enable the spreading/distribution of risks.

The following are considered important preconditions for CAC: A strong balance of payments position, strengthening of the financial system, fiscal consolidation and conduct of an appropriate exchange rate policy. In the implementation of CAC, restriction on inflows and related outflows by non-residents and residents, corporates and non-banks usually received preferential treatment, followed by banks and individuals. Some restriction on capital inflows were imposed during the transition period.

The Committee stipulated preconditions in three important areas for implementation of CAC. They are:

- *Fiscal Consolidation.* The ratio of Centre's gross fiscal deficit to gross domestic production to be reduced from a budgeted 4.5% in 1997-98 to 4% in 1998-99 and further to 3.5% in 1999-2000, accompanied by a reduction in the States deficit.
- *Mandated Inflation Rate.* The inflation for the three-year period (1997-2000) should be an average of 3-5 per cent.
- *Strengthening of Financial System.* Interest rates should be fully deregulated in 1997-98. The average effective CRR should be reduced to 8% in 1997-98, 6% in 1998-99 and further to 3% in 1999-2000. Gross non-performing assets to be brought down to 12% in 1997-98, 9% in 1998-99 and 5% in 1999-2000.

Exchange Rate Policy: The Reserve Bank should have a monitoring band of 5% around the neutral Real Effective Exchange Rate (REER). (REER) is the exchange rate for the currency adjusted for inflation rate differential.) Reserve Bank should ordinarily intervene as and when the REER is outside the band.

Adequacy of Reserves: The following four indicators should be for evaluating the adequacy of reserves:

- Reserves should not be less than six months of imports.
- Reserves should not be less than three months of imports plus 50% of debt service payments plus one month's exports and imports.
- The short-term debt and portfolio stock should be lowered to 60%.
- The net foreign exchange assets to currency ratio should be prescribed by law at not less than 40 per cent.

Merger of Banks: The weak banks should be converted into 'narrow banks' and the incremental resources of these narrow banks should be deployed only in Government securities.

Risk of Convertibility: Those who oppose convertibility offer the following arguments against its implementations:

- Credit rating institutions will play a vital role in decision making by the investors. The changed view of these institutions or changes in the interest or exchange rates may have a destabilizing effect on the portfolio flows.
- It will expose banks liabilities and assets to more price and exchange risks. The effect of increased volatility of exchange rate will be felt on the banks' open foreign currency positions.
- Banks may supplement their domestic deposit base with borrowings from off-shore markets. The volatility in interest and exchange rates can be dangerous to weak and fragile banks.

- Fluctuation in interest rate may affect the cost of borrowing for emerging markets and alter the relative attractiveness of investing in these markets. Real exchange rate volatility may cause currency and maturity mismatches, creating large losses for bank borrowers.
- Due to increased competition, the margins for the banks may be reduced.

FACTORS DETERMINING FORWARD MARGIN

Forward margin is the difference between the spot rate and forward rate of a currency making the forward currency cheaper or costlier as compared to the spot currency. The difference in the rate of interest prevailing at different financial centers is a dominant factor determining forward margin. Other factors that affect forward margin are demand and supply of currency, speculation about spot rates and exchange control regulations.

- *Rate of Interest:* The difference in the rate of interest prevailing at the home centre and the concerned foreign centre determines the forward margin. If the rate of interest at the foreign centre is higher than that prevailing at the home centre the forward margin would be at discount. Conversely, if the rate of interest at the foreign centre is lower than that at the home centre, the forward margin would be at premium.

If suitable conditions prevail in the market, the rate of interest would exert a greater influence than any other factor and the forward margin would tend to settle at a rate where the gain/loss in the interest rate differential is fully compensate by the forward margin. But in practice, it is hard to find this and the forward margin at any particular time is determined by other factors listed below:

- *Demand and Supply:* Forward margin is also determined by the demand for and the supply of foreign currency. If the demand for foreign currency is more than its supply forward rate would be at premium. If the supply exceeds the demand the forward rate would be at discount.

- *Speculation about Spot Rates:* Since the forward rates are based on spot rates, any speculation about the movement of spot rates would influence forward rates also. If the exchange dealers anticipate the spot rate to appreciate, the forward rate would be quoted at premium. If they expect the spot rate to depreciate, the forward rates would be quoted at a discount. These expectations about the spot rates are based on a number of factors which are outlined in the annexure to this chapter.
- *Exchange Regulations:* Exchange control regulations may put some conditions on the forward dealings and may obstruct the influence of the above factors on the forward margin. Such restrictions may be with respect to keeping of balances abroad, borrowing overseas, etc. Intervention in the forward market by the central bank may also be done to influence the forward margin.

FACTORS DETERMINING SPOT EXCHANGE RATES

It was seen in the text of the chapter that the forward margin is primarily based on the interest differential between the financial markets in the two countries concerned. But then what determines exchange rate in the spot market? The rate of exchange in the market is the outcome of the combined effect of a multiple of factors constantly at play. Not all the factors are equal in importance. Some factors, especially the economic factors, are better guides in the long-run. Some of the important factors that affect exchange rates:

Balance of Payments: Balance of payments represents the demand for and supply of foreign exchange which ultimately determine the value of the currency. Exports both visible and invisible represent the supply side for foreign exchange. Imports visible and invisible create demand for foreign exchange. When the balance of payments of a country is continuously at deficit, it implies that the demand for the currency of the country is lesser than its supply. Therefore, its value in the market declines. If the balance of payments is surplus continuously, it shows that the demand for the currency in the exchange market is higher than its supply and therefore the currency gains in value.

Inflation: It would increase the domestic prices of commodities. With the increase in prices of exports the prices may not be competitive. Hence, with the decrease in exports it will force the decline in the value of the currency.

National Income An increase in national income reflects increase in the income of residents of the country. This increase in the Income Increases the demand for goods in the country. If there is underutilized production capacity in the country, will lead to increase in production. There is a chance for growth in exports too. But more often it takes time for the production to adjust to the increased income. Where the production does not increase in sympathy with income rise, it leads to increased imports and increased supply of the currency of the country of the foreign exchange market. The result is similar to that of inflation.

Resource Discoveries: When the country is able to discover key resources, its currency gains value.

Interest Rates: The interest rate has a great influence on the short term movement of capital. When the interest rate at a centre rises it attracts short-term funds from other centers. This would increase the demand for the currency at the centre and hence its value. Raising of interest rate may be adopted by a country due to tight money conditions or as a deliberate attempt to attract foreign investment. Whatever is the intention, the effect of an increase in interest to strengthen the currency of the country through larger inflow of investment and reduction in the outflow of investments by the residents of the country influences the movement of capital.

Capital Movements There are many factors that influence movement of capital from one country to another. Short-term movement of capital may be influenced by the offer of higher interest in a country. If interest rate in a country rises due to increase in bank rate or otherwise there will be a flow of short-term funds into the country and the exchange rate of the currency will rise. Reverse will happen in case of fall in interest rates. Bright investment climate and political stability may encourage portfolio investments in the country. This leads to higher demand for the currency and upward trend in its rate. Poor economic outlook may mean repatriation of the investments leading to decreased demand and lower exchange value for the currency of the country. Movement of capital is also caused by external borrowing and assistance. Large scale external borrowing will increase the supply of foreign exchange in the market. This will have a favourable effect on the exchange rate of the currency of the country. When repatriation of principal and interest starts the rate may be adversely affected.

Political Factors: Political stability induces confidence in the investors and encourages capital inflow into the country. This has the effect of strengthening the Currency of the country. On the other hand, where the political situation in the country is unstable it makes the investors withdraw their investments. The outflow of capital from the country would weaken the currency. Any news about change in the government or political leadership or about the policies of the government would also have the effect of temporarily throwing out of gear the smooth functioning of exchange rate mechanism.

Money Supply: An increase in money supply in the country will affect the exchange rate through causing inflation in the country. It can also affect the exchange rate directly. An increase in money supply in the country relative to its demand will lead to large-scale spending on foreign goods and purchase of foreign investments. Thus the supply of the currency in the foreign exchange markets is increased and its value declines. The downward pressure on the external value of the currency then increases the cost of imports and so adds to inflation. The effect of money supply on exchange rate directly is more immediate than its effect through inflation. While in the long-run inflation seems to correlate exchange rate variations in a better way in the short-run exchange rates move more in sympathy with changes in money supply.

Psychological Factors and Speculation: In the short-run, the exchange rate is affected mostly by the views of the participants in the market about the likely changes in the exchange rates. These expectations are based on many of the factors listed above. Whenever there is a discrepancy between the previously held expectation of a given factor and actual outcome of it, exchange rates will usually be affected. The behaviour of the market maker in the market can affect the exchange rate. The influence may make the rate move differently from that determined by long-term economic forces. A large-scale buying or selling by the major participant would make others in the market to follow suit. This will have the effect of accentuating the trend.

Technical and Market Factors: Isolated large transactions in the market may upset the market's ability to balance the supply of and demand for the currency. Some currencies will be affected due to regular large payment.

SETTLEMENT SYSTEM IN FOREIGN EXCHANGE MARKET

Foreign exchange markets make extensive use of the latest developments in telecommunications for transmitting as well settling foreign exchange transactions. Banks use the exclusive network SWIFT to communicate messages and settle the transactions at electronic clearing houses such as CHIPS at New York.

CHIPS—stands for Clearing House Interbank Payment System. It is an electronic payment system owned by 12 private commercial banks constituting the New York Clearing House Association. CHIPS began its operations in 1971 and have grown to be the world's largest payment system. Foreign exchange and euro dollar transactions are settled through CHIPS. It provides the mechanism for settlement every day of payment and receipts of numerous dollar transactions among member-banks at New York, without the need for physical exchange of cheques/funds for each such transaction.

SWIFT is a acronym for Society for Worldwide Inter-bank financial telecommunications, a co-operative society owned by about 250 banks in Europe and registered as a co-operative society in Brussels, Belgium. Communication network for international financial market transactions has effectively more than 25,000 financial institutions throughout the world that have been allotted bank identifier codes. The messages are transmitted from country to another via central interconnected operating centers located in different locations around the globe. The member countries are connected to the through regional processors in each country. The local banks in each country reach the regional processors through the national networks.

The SWIFT system enables the member-banks to transact among themselves quickly for international payments, Statements, and other messages. Transmission of messages takes place within seconds and therefore this method is economical as well as time saving. Selected banks in India have become members of SWIFT. The regional processing center is situated at Mumbai. The SWIFT provides following advantages for the local banking community:

1. Provides a reliable (time tested) method of sending and receiving messages from a vast number of banks in a large number of locations around the world.
2. Reliability and accuracy is further enhanced by the built-in authentication facilities, which have only to be exchanged with each other party before they can be activated or further communications.
3. Message relay is instantaneous enabling the counter-party to respond immediately if not prevented by time differences.
4. Access is available to a vast number of banks globally for launching new cross-border initiatives.
5. Since communication in SWIFT is to be done using structure formats for various types of banking transactions, the matter to be conveyed will be very clear and there will not be any ambiguity of any sort for the receiver to revert for clarifications. This is mainly because the formats are used all over the world on a standardized basis for conducting all types of banking transactions. This makes the responses and execution very efficient at the

receiving bank's end thereby contributing immensely to quality service being provided to the customers of both banks (sending and receiving).

6. Usage of SWIFT structure formats for message transmission to counter-parties will entail the generation of local banks' internal records using at least minimum level of automation. This will accelerate the local banks' internal automation activities, since the maximum utilization of SWIFT a significant internal automation level is required.

5

Raising Foreign Capital

In the back drop of the looming foreign exchange crisis in India, the Government launched a number of liberalization measures aimed at globalizing the Indian economy. Included facilitation of external commercial borrowings and raising of resources by Indian companies from external markets. Many regulatory measures were liberalized and simplified to strengthen the Indian economy and to facilitate flow of investment into India. Reduction of Customs Duty, delicensing of industries and imports, gradual removal of administered pricing and distribution regulations are the major steps taken in and from 1991. This facilitated inflow of foreign investment both direct and portfolio. The Government followed Indian Companies to tap international capital market for raising funds through EURO issues under GDR/FCCB route.

Corporates can generate international funds either through External Commercial Borrowings (ECBs) or through Euro Issues. The major advantages that accrue from availing a foreign currency loan as they are available relatively at a lower interest rate compared to the domestic rate; they are free from exchange risk and they do not create any non-encumbrance on assets.

CHARACTERISTICS OF FCCB/GDRS

The FCCBs are unsecured that carry a fixed rate of interest on the borrowings and an option for conversion into a fixed number of equity shares of the issuer company. Interest and redemption price (if conversion option is not exercised) is payable in Dollars. Interest rates are very low by Indian domestic standards. FCCBs are denominated in any free convertible foreign currency. Low coupon security which defers, shareholders' dilutions for several years can be attractive to the issuer, as local debt markets are restricted with comparatively short maturities and high interest rates. FCCBs are preferred by family-owned companies they do not like a dilution in control. FCCBs are preferred also by foreign investors because of the Dollar denominated servicing, conversion option and the arbitrage opportunities during conversion at a discount on prevailing Indian market price.

Global Depository Receipt

A Global Depository Receipt is a negotiable instrument denominated in dollars that represents shares issued in a local currency. The shares of the issuing company are issued in the name of an international bank, called the depository who is located in a foreign country. The physical possession of the shares issued is with a 'custodian' in the issuing country. The shares are issued to the depository in the local currency. Based on the shares held by it, the depository issues the GDRs in US dollars. The dividend, after withholding tax, etc., is paid by the issuing company to the depositor in the local currency. The depository converts the dividend received into US dollars at the ruling exchange rate and distributes it among the GDR holders. GDRs are bearer instruments and traded freely in international markets either through stock exchange mechanism or on an 'Over the Counter' (OTC) basis. The settlements are done through international clearing systems like Euro clear (Brussels) or CEDEL (London).

GDRs offer many advantages to the issuing company. The exchange risk is borne by the investors as the payment towards dividend is made in the local currency. There is no dispersal of voting rights as right to vote is vested only with the depository and is regulated by an agreement between the company and for depository. It enables the company to broaden the capital base by tapping large foreign equity markets. But the issue is subject to country risk analysis and for companies from countries with poor credit rating; the issue may not be successful or can succeed only at higher cost. The value of GDRs depends upon the value of the shares of the company. The prospects of the company for future issues may be affected by decline in share prices in the local market which may be a market phenomenon unconnected with the performance of the company.

For the investors, it offers portfolio diversification in a freely traded instrument in a convertible currency. The investors bear exchange risk as well as risk of capital erosion. American Depository Receipt (ADR) is similar to GDR, but issued in the US dollars. It is a security issued by a bank or a depository, issued in the USA against underlying rupee shares of a company incorporated in India.

Advantages of FCCB/GDR

- The cost of raising equity funds from international market is generally lower than the cost of domestic issues.
- It implies acceptance by sophisticated western Investors which in turn would help to enhance the image of the company and its product internationally.
- It normally offers comparatively better share value.
- It will broaden the shareholder base and enhance investor quality.
- It enables the tapping of the international capital possible.
- It is listed and traded in international stock exchanges and hence are free from delivery and settlement problems.
- It is generally denominated in US Dollars and hence reduces the foreign exchange risk.
- Dividend, interest and capital gains on investment in Euro-issues instruments carry concessional tax rates.

- Market for most of the scrip's is more liquid and hence facilitates faster entry and exit.
- Investors in Euro-issues are not required to comply with complex formalities and regulations normally required for investment through domestic stock exchanges.

PROCEDURE FOR ISSUE OF FCCBS/GDRS

Approval of Board of Directors: A meeting of Board of Directors is required to be held for approving the proposal to raise money from Euro capital market. A board resolution is to be passed to approve the raising of finance by issue of GDRs/ FCCBs. The resolution should indicate therein specific purposes for which funds are required, quantum of the issue, country in which issue is to be launched, time of the issue, etc. A director/ Sub-Committee of Board of Directors is also to be authorized for seeking government approval in connection with Euro issue and signing agreements with depository, organizing road shows for fixation of price of GDRs. The Board meeting shall also decide and approve the notice of Extraordinary general meeting of shareholders at which special resolution is to be considered.

Approval of Shareholders: Proposal for making Euro issue, as proposed by Board of Directors, requires approval of shareholders. A special resolution under Section 81(1A) of the Companies Act, 1956 is required to be passed at a duly convened general meeting of the shareholders of the company. Approvals under Sections 94, 16 and 31 of the Companies Act, 1956 may also be obtained, if required. Form No. 23 along with requisite filing fee is to be filed with ROC of the State in which the registered office of the company is situated.

Approval of Ministry of Finance: Eligible issuing company has to make an application to the Government of India, Ministry of Finance, Department of Economic Affairs, New Delhi for obtaining approval. The application should set out in detail the following particulars:

- Proposed project or expansion of diversification

programme with details of cost of project and means of financing.

- Proposed security viz. GDRs or ADRs against underlying shares or FCCBs.
- In the case of Bonds, particulars of redemption period, rate of interest, time of conversion of bonds to equity shares of the company, price at which such conversion will take place.
- In the case of GDRs/ADRs, the price at which the equity shares will be issued.
- Justification for the foreign issue.
- Other details about the company such as management, financial capacity, financial results and management ratios, statutory liabilities/default in respect of interest/instalments of loans from Financial Institutions/Banks, exports and imports and salient features of the prospective corporate plans and diversification proposals with special reference to foreign exchange requirements.

The Government of India if satisfied with the company's proposals, issue an approval in-principle granting permission to the company to mobilize foreign currency resources for a specified amount. On completion of finalization of issue structure in consultation with the Lead manager to the issue, the company should obtain the final approval from the government.

Approval of Department of Company Affairs: The issuer company requires approval from Department of Company Affairs where the convertible bonds are being issued, which after such conversion, are likely to increase the subscribed capital of the company.

Approval of Reserve Bank of India: The issuer company has to obtain approvals from RBI under circumstances mentioned in the guidelines.

Stock exchanges approval for listing: The issuing company has to make a request to the domestic stock exchange for in-principle consent for listing of underlying shares which shall be lying in the custody of domestic custodian. These shares, when released by the custodian after cancellation of GDR, are traded on Indian stock exchanges like any other equity shares.

Consent of Financial Institutions: Where term loans have been obtained by the company from the financial institutions and the agreement relating to the loan contains a stipulation that the consent of the financial institutions has to be obtained, the company must obtain in-principle consent on the board terms of the proposed issue.

DOCUMENTATION REQUIRED FOR ISSUE OF GDRS, ETC.

Subscription Agreement: Subscription agreement provides that lead managers and other managers agree, severally and not jointly, with the company, subject to the satisfaction of certain conditions, to subscribe for GDRs at the offering price set forth. It may provide that obligations of managers are subject to certain conditions precedent. Subscription agreement provides, an option, to be exercisable within certain period after the date of offering circular, to the lead manager and other managers to purchase up to a certain prescribed number of additional GDRs solely to cover over-allotments.

Depository Agreement: Depository agreement lays down the detailed arrangements entered into by the company with the Depository, the forms and terms of the depository receipt which are represented by the deposited shares. It also sets forth the rights and duties of the depository in respect of the deposited shares and all other securities, cash and other property received subsequently in respect of such deposited shares. Holders of GDRs are not parties to deposit agreement and thus have no contractual rights against or obligations to the company. The depository is under no duty to enforce any of the Provisions of the deposit agreement on behalf of any holder or any other person. Holder means the person or persons registered in the books of the depository maintained for such purpose as holders. They are deemed to have notice of, be bound by and hold their rights subject to all of the provisions of the deposit agreement applicable to them. They may be required to file from time to time with depository or its nominee proof of citizenship, residence, exchange control approval, payment of all applicable taxes or other governmental charges, compliance with the applicable laws and regulations and terms of deposit agreement, or legal or beneficial ownership and nature of such interest and such other information as the depository may deem necessary or proper to enable it to perform its obligations under Deposit Agreement.

The company may agree in the deposit agreement to indemnify the depository, the custodian and certain of their respective affiliates against any loss, liability, tax or expense of any kind which may arise out of or in connection with any offer, issuance, sale, resale, transfer, deposit or withdrawal of GDRs, or any offering document. Copies of deposit agreement are to be kept at the principal office of Depository and the depository is required to make available for inspection during its normal business hours, the copies of deposit agreement and any notices, reports or communications received from the company.

Custodian Agreement: It has to observe all obligations imposed on it including those mentioned in the depository agreement. The custodian is responsible solely to the depository. In the case of the depository and the custodian being same legal entity, references to them separately in the depository agreement or otherwise may be made for convenience and the legal entity will be responsible for discharging both functions directly to the holders and the company. Whenever the depository in its discretion determines that it is in the best interests of the holders to do so, it may, after prior consultation with the company terminate, the appointment of the custodian and in such an event the depository shall promptly appoint a successor custodian, which shall, upon acceptance of such appointment, become the custodian under the depository agreement. The depository shall notify holders of such change promptly. Any successor custodian so appointed shall agree to observe all the obligations imposed on it.

Agency Agreement: In case of FCCBs, the company has to enter into an agency agreement with certain persons known as conversion agents. In terms of this agreement, these agents are required to make the principal and interest payments to the holders of FCCBs from the funds provided by the company.

They will also liaise with the company at the time of conversion/redemption option to be exercised by the investor at maturity.

Trust Deed: In respect of FCCBs the company enters into a Covenant (known as Trust Deed) with the Trustee for the holders of FCCBs. guaranteeing payment of principal and interest amount on such FCCBs and to comply with the obligations in respect of such FCCBs.

STEPS TO BE TAKEN FOR ISSUE OF FCCBS/GDRS (OTHER THAN DOCUMENTATION AND APPROVALS)

Apart from obtaining necessary approvals, appointment of various agencies and proper documentation, the following additional key actions are necessary for making the Euro-issue a success:

Constitution of a Board Sub-Committee: To launch a Euro-issue, the issuing company has to take a large number of decisions in time. These decisions normally fall within the power of Board of Directors. It is usually difficult to call Board Meetings frequently and to ensure presence of adequate Board Members. Thus, it is normally advisable to constitute a sub-committee of the Board with full delegation of powers with regard to Euro-issue. The delegation of powers to the Board sub-committee should normally include the following:

- Appointment of agencies.
- Authority to make applications for seeking various approvals.
- Authority to finalize and execute documents and agreements.
- Decisions about the timing, size and pricing the issue.
- Allotment of shares.

Selection of Syndicate Members: The success of any Euro-issue depends upon the well planned and coordinated efforts of the syndicate members and the company. The selection of the Syndicate members should be made depending upon the strength and capabilities of each member in different areas of specialization such as marketing, financial, research, distribution, etc. The lead manager may be entrusted with the work of selection of syndicate members. The lead manager while selecting the above members, in addition to their strength and capability, should also evaluate their sanding, image, reputation, infrastructure, past experience in handling Indian Euro-issue, etc.

Constitution of a Task Force: The due diligence is a process in which a team consisting of legal, technical and financial experts of the lead manager meets top executives of the company and visits the operation sites of the company in order to understand the strengths, weaknesses, problems and opportunities of the company. The team also studies and analyses the balance sheet of the company and its subsidiaries, its financial arrangement with the group, investment pattern and also the future prospects of the company. The purpose of above exercise is to draft the offering prospectus and work out marketing strategies for the Euro issue.

Listing with Overseas Stock Exchanges: One of the conditions of Euro-issues is that the securities are to be listed on one or more Overseas Stock Exchanges. The issuing company has to fulfil all the requirements particularly disclosure and documentation as prescribed by the Overseas Stock Exchanges. The company shall take the help of the listing agent in getting its Euro-issue instruments listed on the Overseas Stock Exchanges. The issuing company shall prepare the requisite documents as prescribed by the Overseas Stock Exchange authorities and submit the same along with formal application to it. The exchange authorities after scrutinizing the application shall send their observations which the company has to promptly reply. Thereafter, the formal approval shall be issued by the Overseas Stock Exchange. The underlying shares against GDRs are to be listed on one or more Indian Stock Exchange(s) on which the company existing shares are already listed. For this purpose, the company has to apply to the stock exchange authorities to get the shares represented by GDRs listed on the Indian Stock Exchanges. Trading of such shares on Indian Stock Exchanges will not commence until the period specified in the guidelines after the date of issue of the GDRs.

Prospectus: Prospectus (offering circular) is to be prepared very carefully giving true and complete information regarding the financial strength of the company, its past performance, past and envisaged research and business promotion activities, track record of promoters and the company, ability to trade the securities on Euro capital market. Unlike the prospectus for the domestic issue, the format of the Offering prospectus for a Euro-issue offering is not defined under any statute except certain requirements specified by the listing regulations of the Overseas Stock Exchange where the securities (GDR/FCCB) are proposed to be listed. A copy of the Offering Circular is required to be sent to the Registrar of Companies, the Securities Exchange Board of India and the Indian Stock Exchanges for record purposes. It is important that the Offering Circular should be very comprehensive to take care of overall interest of the prospective investor. The Offering Circular for Euro-issue offering should typically cover the following contents:

- Background of the company and its promoters including date of incorporation and objects, past performance, production, sales and distribution network, future plans, etc.
- Capital structure of the company.
- Deployment of issue proceeds.
- Financial data indicating track record of consistent profitability of the company.
- Group investment and their performance including subsidiaries, joint venture in India and abroad.
- Investment considerations.
- Description of shares.
- Terms and conditions of global depository receipt and any other instrument issued along with it.
- Economic and regulatory policies of Government of India.
- Details of Indian securities market indicating stock exchange, listing requirements, foreign investments in Indian securities.
- Market price of securities.
- Dividend and capitalization.
- Securities regulations and exchange control.
- Tax aspects indicating analysis of tax consequences under Indian law of acquisition, membership and

sale of shares, treatment of capital gains tax, etc.
- Status of approvals required to be obtained from Government of India.
- Summary of significant differences in Indian GAAP, UK GAAP and US GAAP and expert's opinion.
- Report of statutory auditor.
- Subscription and sale.
- Transfer restrictions in respect of instruments.
- Legal matters etc.
- Other general information not forming part of any of the above.

Research Papers: A team of lead manager/co-lead manager prepares research papers on the company before the issue. These papers are very important marketing tools as the international investors normally depends a lot on the information provided by the research analysts for making investment decisions. However, these papers are prohibited from circulation in USA.

Pre-marketing: Pre-marketing exercise is a tool through which the syndicate members evaluate the prospects of the issue. Research analysts along with the sales force of the syndicate members meet the prospective investors during pre-marketing road shows. This enables the syndicate members to understand the market and the probable response from the prospective investors. The pre-marketing exercise helps in assessing the depth of investors' interest in the proposed issue, their view about the valuation of the share and the geographical locations of the investors who are interested in the issue. The response received during pre-marketing provides vital information for taking important decisions relating to timing, pricing and size of the issue. This would also help the syndicate members in evolving strategies for marketing the issue.

Timing, Pricing and Size of the Issue: After pre-marketing exercise, the important decisions of timing, pricing and size of the issue are taken. The proper time of launching the issue is when the fundamentals of the company and the industry are strong and the market price of the shares is performing well at Indian Stock Exchanges. The timing should also not clash with some other major issues of the Indian as well as other country's companies.

Investor Relation Programme: The international investors expect that the issuing company maintains contact with them after the issue.

Road shows: Road shows represent meetings of issuers, analysts and potential investors. Details about the company are presented in the road shows and such details usually include the following information about the company making the issue:

- History
- Organizational structure
- Business lines
- Position of the company in Indian and international market
- Past performance of the company
- Future plans of the company
- Competitions—domestic as well as foreign
- Financial results and operating performance
- Valuation of shares
- Review of Indian stock market and economic situations

Thus at road shows, series of information presentations are organized in selected cities around the world with analysts and potential institutional investors. It is, in fact, a conference by the issuer with the prospective investors. The road show is arranged by the lead manager by sending invitation to all prospective investors.

Pricing of the Issue: The market price abroad has a strong correlation to the near future earnings, potential, fundamentals governing industry and the basic economic state of the country. Several other factors like prevalent practices, investor sentiment towards issues of a particular country, domestic market process, etc. are also considered in determination of issue price. Secretarial factors such as the credit rating of the country, interest rate and the availability of an exit route are important.

Closure of the Issue: Closing the issue normally takes place one week after the opening of the issue. Closing is essentially an activity confirming completion of all legal documentation and formalities based on which the company issues the share certificate to the depository and deposits the same with the domestic custodian. The depository issues the GDRs and the lead manager transfers issue proceeds to the bank account of the issuing company.

Allotment: Once the issue is closed and all legal formalities are over, the allotment is finalized in consultation with the Overseas Stock Exchange and the Lead Manager. Thereafter, the company issues shares in favour of the Overseas Depository Bank and deposits the same with the domestic custodian for custody. The particulars of the Overseas Depository Bank are required to be entered into the Register of Members of the company. The issuing company has also to file a return of the allotment with the Registrar of Companies.

FACTORS TO BE CONSIDERED BY BORROWERS FOR AVAILING OF FOREIGN CURRENCY LOAN

1. In raising a foreign currency loan the prospective borrower should verify that certain advantages are available to it. The foreign currency loan is offered in the international markets frequently against the guarantee from a bank in India. Therefore, the borrower should add the guarantee fee payable by it to its bank to the cost of raising the foreign currency loan. The guarantee commission and other incidental costs should aggregate to be less than the cost of funds in the domestic market.
2. The exchange loss on conversion can be avoided provided the purpose or which the loan is raised can be paid for in the currency of the loan and the source of repayment is also in the same currency. If the source of repayment is in a currency other than the currency of loan, the borrower will be facing exchange risk. Forward cover may be arranged, but this should be added to the cost of borrowing. Further hedging exposures for longer periods is costly.

3. Since specific assets are usually not charged for funds raised abroad, the borrowing capacity in the domestic company is not affected.
4. The period of repayment should synchronize with the cash accruals of the borrower. Loans for longer periods may be preferred but in any case the repayment cannot exceed 10 years.
5. The interest should be on a floating rate basis, rather than fixed throughout the period of loans. This will give him the leverage of benefiting from fall in interest rates.
6. Where the currency of loan and the currency of source of repayment are different, the loan agreement may be made to include a currency option. Even otherwise the currency option may give a chance to the borrower to take advantage of exchange rate movements.

EXTERNAL COMMERCIAL BORROWINGS

Generally the external commercial borrowings refer to borrowings by a business community from foreign sources. The Government announces the policy of ECB for the country as a part of prudent debt management. ECB are defined to include commercial bank loans, buyers' credit, and suppliers' credit, securitized instruments such as floating rate notes and fixed rate bonds, credit from official export credit agencies and commercial borrowings from the private sector window of Multilateral Financial Institutions.

Features of ECB Policy

1. *Approvals:* For proposals falling under the USD 5 million schemes or USD 10 million schemes. Approvals will be granted by RBI. Other proposals should be approved by the ECB Division, Department of Economic Affairs, and Ministry of Finance.
2. *Average Maturities:* The minimum average maturity period prescribed is as follows: for Loan amount not

exceeding USD 20 million—3 years and for Loan amount exceeding USD 20 million—(a) 100% EOU units—3 years (b) Others-5 years

Bonds and FRNs can be raised in tranches of different maturities as long as the average maturity of the different tranches within the same overall approval satisfies the maturity criteria. Corporates who have foreign exchange earnings are permitted to raise ECB up to thrice the average amount of annual exports during the previous three years subject to a maximum of USD 100 million without end use restrictions.

3. *Infrastructure Projects:* Holding companies/promoters will be permitted to raise ECB up to USD 50 million to finance equity investment in a subsidiary/joint venture company implementing infrastructure projects. The following sectors qualify as infrastructure sectors: power, telecommunication, railways, roads including bridges, ports, industrial parks, urban infrastructure—water supply, sanitation and sewage projects.
4. *Long-term Borrowers*: ECB of eight years and above of average maturity will be outside ECB ceiling, though Ministry of Finance approval would continue to be necessary. To be eligible for this purpose, the long-term debt instrument should not include any 'put' or 'call' options potentially reducing the stated maturities.
5. *Corporate Borrowers:* Development financial institutions (DFIs) can raise funds under this window in addition to their normal annual allocated covered by the cap. Borrowing under the long-term window should not be used to enhance the average maturity of borrowings under normal window. If they are combined then the entire borrowings will fall under the cap. Corporates may raise these borrowings either through FRN or Bond Issues or Syndicated loans, etc., as long as the maturity and interest spread are maintained as per the guidelines.

6. *On-Lending:* While DFIs are required to adhere to the average maturity criteria prescribed they are permitted to on-lend at different maturities. They may also on-lend for project-related Rupee expenditure. However, other financial intermediaries are required to adhere to the general ECB guidelines on maturity in their on-lending programs. All financial intermediaries including DFIs are required to on-lend their external commercial borrowings within 12 months of drawdown. DFIs are permitted to on-lend such Recycled Funds out of original ECBs only for import of goods and project-related rupee expenditure.
7. *End-use Requirements:* There is no restriction on end-use of funds except they cannot be used for investment in stock market or in real estate. Proceeds from Bonds, FRNs and Syndicated Loan the Corporate borrowers have raised through ECB for import of capital goods and services through Bonds/ FRN/Syndication loans are permitted to remit funds into India. The funds can be used for activities as per their business judgment except investment in stock market or in real estate for up to one year or till the actual import of capital goods and services takes place whichever is earlier.
8. *Entitlement for New Projects*: All infrastructure and Greenfield projects will be permitted to avail ECB to an extent of 35% of the total project cost. However, ECB limits for telecom projects are more flexible at 50% of the cost. Greater flexibility may also be allowed in case of power projects and other infrastructure projects based on merits. 100% EOUs will be permitted to have foreign currency exposure up to 60% of the project cost.
9. *Structured Obligations:* In order to enable corporates to hedge exchange rate risks and raise resources domestically. Domestic Rupee Denominating Structured obligations would be permitted to be Credit enhanced by International Banks/International

Financial Institutions/Joint Venture Partners Subject to the following conditions:

- In the event of default, foreign banks giving guarantee will make payment of defaulted amount after bringing in the equivalent amount of foreign exchange into the country.
- FEMA clearance should be obtained from RBI in advance.
- Prior clearance for bonds/debentures issue from RBI/SEBI should he obtained.
- In the event of default the default should be foreign currency equivalent of the outstanding calculated in rupee terms.
- The liability of the Indian company will always be rupee denominated and the debt servicing may be done in equivalent foreign exchange funds. Debt servicing in a post default situation may be in rupees or foreign exchange as envisaged initially in the contract document.
- The guarantee fee/commission/charges and other incidental expenses to the Indian company should be in rupee terms and not exceed 3% p.a.
- In case of default the interest rate could be coupon on the bond/or 250 bps over prevailing secondary market yield of 5 year government security whichever is higher.

10. *Terms and Conditions:* Apart from the maturity and end-user requirements the financial terms and conditions of each ECB proposal are required to be reasonable and market-related. The choice of the sourcing of ECB, currency of the loan and the interest rate basis will be left to the borrowers. In case of borrowing by public sector units the loan agreement should not contain the covenant that the Government will continue to hold at least 51% of equity.
11. *Validity of Approval:* Approvals are valid for a period of six months the executed copy of the loan agreement is required to be submitted within this period. In the case of FRNs, Bonds, etc., the same are required to be launched within this period. In case of

power projects, the validity of the approval will be for a period of one year and 9 months in the case of telecom sector project. Bonds, Debentures, FRNs and other such instruments will have additional validity period of three months for all the ECB approvals across the board. Extension will not be granted beyond the validity period.

12. *Pre-payment of ECB:* Prepayment facility would be permitted if they are met out of inflow of foreign equity or out of balances in EEFC account. In addition to ECB being prepaid out of foreign equity corporates can avail either of following two options for prepayment of their ECBs. Permission by the Government for prepayment may be undertaken to within the permitted period of all ECBs with residual maturity one year or Prepayment up to 10% of outstanding ECB to be permitted once during the life of the loan subject to the company complying with the ECB approval terms. Those companies who had already availed prepayment facility of 20% earlier would not be eligible. Validity of permission under the above two options will be either prepayment approval for ECBs other than Bonds/Debentures/FRNs will be 15 days or period up to next interest payment date whichever is later. In case of Bonds/FRNs validity of permission will not be more than 15 days.

13. *Financing the Existing Foreign Currency Loan:* Refinancing of outstanding amounts under existing loans by raising fresh loans at lower costs may also be permitted on a case-to-case basis, subject to the condition that the outstanding maturity of the original loan is maintained. Rolling over of ECB will not be permitted. A corporate borrowing overseas for financing its Rupee-related expenditure and swapping its external commercial borrowings with another corporate which requires foreign currency funds will not be permitted.

14. *Cost of Borrowing:* The all-in-ceiling for normal infrastructure and long-term ECBs are 300, 400 and

500 basis points over six month Libor for the respective currency in which the loan is being raised or applicable benchmark as the case may be.

15. *Liability Management:* Corporates can undertake liability management for hedging the interest and/or exchange rate risk on their underlying foreign currency exposure. Prior approval of this Department or RBI has been dispensed with for concluding or winding up of the transactions.

Procedure for Availing

A resident may borrow from a bank situated outside India for execution outside India of a turnkey project or civil construction contract or in connection with exports on deferred payment terms, provided the terms and conditions stipulated by the authority which has granted the approval to the project or contract or export. An importer in India may, for import of goods into India, avail of foreign currency credit for a period not exceeding six months extended by the overseas supplier of goods, provided the import is in compliance with the Export-Import Policy of the Government of India in force.

SCHEMES OF ECB

- *Short-term Loan Scheme:* Foreign currency credit extended by the overseas supplier of goods to an importer of goods for financing import of goods into India, provided the period of maturity of credit is more than six months but less than three years. Foreign currency loan/credit extended to an importer in India for financing imports into India. by any bank or financial institution outside India provided the period of maturity of loan/credit is less than three years.
- *Borrowing under US Dollar Five Million Scheme:* Borrowing in foreign exchange up to USD five million by an Indian entity for general corporate purposes at a simple minimum maturity of three years.

- *Borrowing under US Dollar Ten Million Scheme*: Borrowing in foreign exchange not exceeding USD ten million by an Indian entity for the following purposes:
  - ❖ For financing infrastructure projects provided the minimum average maturity of loan is three years. In case the loan is to be raised by more than one promoter entity for a single project the aggregate of loan by all promoters should not exceed USD 10 million.
  - ❖ Foreign currency loan raised by an Indian entity for financing infrastructure project provided that the minimum average maturity of loan is not less than three years.
  - ❖ Borrowing in foreign exchange by an exporter/foreign exchange earner up to three times of the average amount of his annual foreign exchange earnings during the previous three years subject to a maximum of USD 10 million with a minimum average maturity of three years.
  - ❖ Borrowing for general corporate purposes at the minimum average maturity of eight years.
- *Scheme for Raising Loans from NRIs on Repatriation Basis:* Borrowings not exceeding US $ 2,50,000 or its equivalent in foreign exchange by an individual resident in India from his close relatives resident outside India, subject to the conditions that the loan is free of interest, the minimum maturity period of the loan is seven years, the amount of loan is received by inward remittance in free foreign exchange through normal banking channels or by debit to the NRE/FCNR account of the non-resident lender, the loan is utilized for the borrower's personal purposes or for carrying on his normal business activity but not for carrying on agricultural plantation activities, purchase of immovable property or shares/debentures or bonds issued by companies in India or for re-lending and the borrower shall not utilize the funds borrowed under any of these

Schemes for investment in stock market or in real estate business.

- *Automatic Approval:* Any legal entity can enter into loan agreements for fresh ECB with average maturity of not less than 3 years for an amount up to USD 50 million and for refinancing an existing ECB provided it is in conformity with both the ECB guidelines framed by Ministry of Finance, and the regulations of RBI. There is no need to obtain prior approval from Government or RBI.
  - ❖ The loan should be availed from an internationally acceptable and/or recognized lender, such as export credit agencies, suppliers of equipments, foreign collaborators, foreign equity holders, international capital markets, reputed international banks and financial institutions, etc. Further, the loan should be organized through a reputed merchant banker registered with the regulatory authorities of the host country, viz., USA, Japan, EU countries, Singapore and such other countries as may be notified from time to time by the Government of India. The lenders should be recognized and registered in the host countries for the purpose of extending international finance.
  - ❖ The borrower should submit through an authorized dealer three copies of the signed loan agreement to the Reserve Bank. The Reserve Bank will acknowledge receipt of the copies of the agreement and will allot a loan identification number to such an agreement. The primary responsibility to ensure that ECBs raised are in conformity with the regulations will be that of the borrower. At a later date, if any violation is found, appropriate action will be taken by the Reserve Bank under FEMA.
  - ❖ The borrower will also be permitted to make necessary draw-downs under the automatic route without prior permission from the Reserve

Bank. A quarterly return should be submitted through the authorized dealer.

- *Prior Approval:* Borrowings, other than under automatic route, up to USD 10 million require approval of Reserve Bank. Proposals exceeding this limit require prior approval of the Central Government.

6

Capital Market and Regulation

A capital market is simply any market where a company or an institution can raise money to fund their operations and long term investment. Selling bonds and selling stock are two ways to generate capital, thus bond markets and stock markets (such as the Bombay stock exchange) are considered capital market. The capital market is an ideal environment for the creation of strategies that can result in raising long-term funds for bond issues or even mortgages. At the same time, the capital market provides the medium for short-term fund strategies as well. Essentially, any type of financial transaction that is meant to result in the buying and selling of securities and commodities for profit can rightly be considered part of the capital market.

Institutions are also part of the framework of the capital market. Stock exchanges are one of the more visible examples of established operations that give form and function to the capital market. Along with the stock exchanges, support organizations such as brokerage firms also form part of the capital market. Over the counter markets are also included in the working definition for a capital market. By providing the mechanisms that make trading possible, these outward expressions of the capital market make it possible to keep the process ethical and more easily governed according to local laws and customs.

Because of the broad structure of the capital market, investors of all types have the opportunity to participate in financial strategies that can strengthen the general economy as well create financial security. Persons who wish to focus on investment opportunities that are very stable and more or less ensure a modest return can find plenty of different offerings to choose from. At the same time, investors who tend to be more adventurous can also find a wide array of investment types that will allow them to take some additional risk and possibly realize larger returns on their investments. While the overall structure of the capital market may be broad, there are a number of checks and balances that help to keep the market on an even keel, ensuring that the capital market functions in a manner that is both ethical and legal.

Indian Stock Markets are one of the oldest in Asia. Its history dates back to nearly 200 years ago. The earliest records of security dealings in India are meagre and obscure. The East India Company was the dominant institution in those days and business in its loan securities used to be transacted towards the close of the eighteenth century. By 1830's business on corporate stocks and shares in Bank and Cotton presses took place in Bombay. Though the trading list was broader in 1839, there were only half a dozen brokers recognized by banks and merchants during 1840 and 1850. The 1850's witnessed a rapid development of commercial enterprise and brokerage business attracted many men into the field and by 1860 the number of brokers increased into 60.

TRADING IN STOCK EXCHANGES

Trading in Indian stock exchanges is limited to listed securities of public limited companies. They are broadly divided into two categories, namely, specified securities (forward list) and non-specified securities (cash list). Equity shares of dividend paying, growth-oriented companies with a paid-up capital of atleast Rs. 50 million and a market capitalization of atleast Rs. 100 million and having more than

20,000 shareholders are, normally, put in the specified group and the balance in non-specified group.

Two types of transactions can be carried out on the Indian stock exchanges: (a) spot delivery transactions "for delivery and payment within the time or on the date stipulated when entering into the contract which shall not be more than 14 days following the date of the contract"; and (b) forward transactions "delivery and payment can be extended by further period of 14 days each so that the overall period does not exceed 90 days from the date of the contract". The latter is permitted only in the case of specified shares. The brokers who carry over the out-standings pay carry over charges which are usually determined by the rates of interest prevailing.

A member broker in an stock exchange can act as an agent, buy and sell securities for his clients on a commission basis and also can act as a trader or dealer as a principal, buy and sell securities on his own account and risk, in contrast with the practice prevailing on New York and London Stock Exchanges, where a member can act as a jobber or a broker only.

NATIONAL STOCK EXCHANGE (NSE)

With the liberalization of the Indian economy, it was found inevitable to lift the Indian stock market trading system on par with the international standards. On the basis of the recommendations of high powered Pherwani Committee, the National Stock Exchange was incorporated in 1992 by Industrial Development Bank of India, Industrial Credit and Investment Corporation of India, Industrial Finance Corporation of India, all Insurance Corporations, selected commercial banks and others. Trading at NSE can be classified under two broad categories: (a) Wholesale debt market, and (b) Capital market.

Wholesale debt market operations are similar to money market operations—institutions and corporate bodies enter into high value transactions in financial instruments such as government securities, treasury bills, public sector unit bonds, commercial paper, certificate of deposit, etc. There are two kinds of players in NSE: (a) trading members and

(b) participants. Recognized members of NSE are called trading members who trade on behalf of themselves and their clients. Participants include trading members and large players like banks who take direct settlement responsibility.

Trading at NSE takes place through a fully automated screen-based trading mechanism which adopts the principle of an order-driven market. Trading members can stay at their offices and execute the trading, since they are linked through a communication network. The prices at which the buyer and seller are willing to transact will appear on the screen. When the prices match the transaction will be completed and a confirmation slip will be printed at the office of the trading member.

There are 24 stock exchanges in India, with the introduction of MCX Stock Exchange Ltd. the first being the Bombay Stock Exchange (BSE), which began formal trading in 1875, making it one of the oldest in Asia. Over the last few years, there has been a rapid change in the Indian securities market, especially in the secondary market. Advanced technology and online-based transactions have modernized the stock exchanges. In terms of the number of companies listed and total market capitalization, the Indian equity market is considered large relative to the country's stage of economic development. The debt market, however, is almost non-existent in India even though there has been a large volume of Government bonds traded. Banks and financial institutions have been holding a substantial part of these bonds as statutory liquidity requirement. The portfolio restrictions on financial institutions' statutory liquidity requirement are still in place. A primary auction market for Government securities has been created and a primary dealer system was introduced in 1995.

Since 1992, there has been intensified market reform, resulting in a big improvement in securities trading, especially in the secondary market for equity. Most stock exchanges have introduced online trading and set-up clearing houses/ corporations. Depositories has become operational for scripless trading and the regulatory structure has been overhauled with most of the powers for regulating the capital market vested with SEBI. The Indian capital market has experienced a process of structural transformation with operations conducted to standards equivalent to those in the developed markets. It was opened up for investment by foreign institutional investors (FIIs) in 1992 and Indian companies were allowed to raise resources abroad through Global Depository Receipts (GDRs) and Foreign Currency Convertible Bonds (FCCBs). The primary and secondary segments of the capital market expanded rapidly, with greater institutionalization and wider participation of individual investors accompanying this growth. However, many problems, including lack of confidence in stock investments, institutional overlaps, and other governance issues, remain as obstacles to the improvement of Indian capital market efficiency.

MARK-TO-MARKET

Under the current clearing and settlement system, if an investor buys and subsequently sells the same number of shares of stock during a settlement period, or sells and subsequently buys, it is not necessary to take or deliver the shares. The difference between the selling and buying prices can be paid or received. In other words, the squaring-off of the trading position during the same settlement period results in non-delivery of the shares that the investor traded.

FIIs and domestic institutional investors are, however, not permitted to trade without delivery, since non-delivery transactions are limited only to individual investors. One of SEBI's primary concerns is the risk of settlement chaos that may be caused by an increasing number of non-delivery transactions as the stock market becomes excessively speculative. Accordingly, SEBI has introduced a daily mark-to-market margin and intraday trading limit. The daily mark-to-market margin is a margin on a broker's daily position. The intraday trading limit is the limit to a broker's intraday trading volume. Every broker is subject to these requirements.

FOREIGN INSTITUTIONAL INVESTORS

FIIs have been allowed to invest in the Indian securities market since September 1992 when the Guidelines for Foreign Institutional Investment were issued by the Government. The SEBI (Foreign Institutional Investors) Regulations were enforced in November 1995, largely based on these Guidelines. The regulations require FIIs to register with SEBI and to obtain approval from the Reserve Bank of India (RBI) under the Foreign Exchange Regulation Act to buy and sell securities, open foreign currency and rupee bank accounts, and to remit and repatriate funds. Once SEBI registration has been obtained, an FII does not require any further permission to buy or sell securities or to transfer funds in and out of the country, subject to payment of applicable tax. Foreign investors, whether registered as FIIs or not, may also invest in Indian securities outside the FII process. Such investment requires case-by-case approval from the Foreign Investment Promotion Board (FIPB) in the Ministry of Industry and RBI, or only from RBI depending on the size of investment and the industry in which the investment is to be made. Investment in Indian securities is also possible through the purchase of GDRs.

Foreign currency convertible bonds and foreign currency bonds issued by Indians that are listed, traded, and settled overseas are mainly denominated in dollars. Foreign financial service institutions have also been allowed to set-up joint ventures in stock-broking, asset management companies, merchant banking, and other financial services firms along with Indian partners. Foreign portfolio investments in Indian companies are limited to individual foreign ownership at 10 percent of the total issued capital of any one company and to aggregate foreign ownership at 30 percent of the total issued capital of any one company.

REGULATION OF INTERMEDIARIES

Participants in the Indian capital market are required to register with SEBI to carry out their businesses. These include: stockbrokers, sub-brokers, share transfer agents, bankers to an issue, trustees of a trust deed, registrars to an issue, merchant bankers, underwriters, portfolio managers, investment advisers, and other such intermediaries who may be associated with the securities market in any manner:

Turnover in the Indian stock exchanges is high, implying that they are dominated by speculative investments, which is not unusual in emerging markets. However, trading volumes in the Indian capital market are fairly large compared to those in other emerging markets. While price levels have been depressed, the total turnover on BSE and NSE has been increasing. Account settlement period of stock exchanges that earlier had a 14-day trading cycle has been shortened to now just three days. In the case of BSE, the clearing house is operated by Bank of India Shareholding Ltd., which is jointly owned by BSE and the Bank of India.

Recent Capital Market Developments

While funds raised through public issues have fallen more than 94% in the first eight months of 2008-09 financial year, money raised through rights issues has climbed up marginally, About 18 rights issues during April-November 2008-09 raised Rs. 10,627 crore, slightly higher than in the year-ago period. Funds raised by the corporates through private placement of debt issues have kept pace with that in the 2007-period. Funds raised in the eight-month period is Rs. 86,604 crore, trailing last year's by a mere 2%. The falling-behind trend, here, has been arrested since October. The last two months in the review period registered a rise of 52% each in terms of amounts raised both on the BSE and NSE against last year.

While net resource mobilisation by mutual funds for the April-November period is negative at Rs. 30,530 crore as against last year's positive Rs. 1,35,124 crore, the figure for November is a positive Rs. 13,789 crore. However, net investment by mutual funds, which stands at Rs. 23,135 crore in April-November period, was more than halved in last two months of the period as funds liquidated Rs. 28,621 crore, mainly in debt. Even as foreign institutional investors (FIIs) liquidated Rs. 35,730 crore in the current financial year till November, there was a net inflow of foreign funds of Rs. 1,616 crore in November. In the review period, FIIs liquidated Rs. 43,304 crore in equity, whereas invested Rs. 7,574 crore in debt. And, mutual funds, in the period, invested Rs. 15,610 crore in debt, double of its investment of Rs. 7,526 crore in equities.

Corporation and Demutualization of Stock Exchanges : Out of the 23 erstwhile stock exchanges, 18 have since been corporatized and demutualised in 2007-08. One stock exchange. The RBI Act has been amended to empower RBI to develop and regulate market for Repos in corporate bonds. The limit of FII Investment in corporate debt has been increased from US$ 0.5 billion to US$ 1.5 billion. The trade reporting platform for corporate bonds has been operationalised since 1st January, 2007. The trading platforms for corporate bonds at the major exchanges has been operationalised from July 1, 2007.

The Securities Contracts Regulation Act, 1956 has been amended to include securitization instruments under the definition of "securities" and provide for disclosure based regulation for issue of the securitized instruments and the procedure thereof. This has been done keeping in view that there is considerable potential in the securities market for the certificates or instruments under securitization transactions. The development of the securitised debt market is critical for meeting the humungous requirements of the infrastructure sector, particularly housing sector, in the country. Replication of the securities markets framework for these instruments would facilitate trading on stock exchanges and in turn help development of the market in terms of depth and liquidity.

PAN as the Sole Identification Number : PAN has been made the sole identification number for all transactions in securities market. This is an investor friendly measure as he does not have to maintain different identification numbers for different kinds of transactions/different segments in financial markets. Further, identification through PAN would help the authorities in enforcement action.

Equity Finance for the Small and Medium Enterprises (SMEs): SMEs in India have traditionally relied on debt financing from banks and non-bank financial institutions. In order to develop the equity market for SMEs, SEBI has decided to create a separate exchange for the SMEs. There should be a single exchange for the SME sector for around 2-3 years to enable successful development of the market for SMEs.

IPO Grading: SEBI has made it compulsory for companies coming out with IPOs of equity shares to get their IPOs graded by at least one credit rating agency registered with SEBI from May 1, 2007. This measure is intended to provide the investor with an informed and objective opinion expressed by a professional rating agency after analyzing factors like business and financial prospects, management quality and corporate governance practices, etc.

Permitting Indian Mutual Funds to Invest in Overseas Securities: SEBI has fixed the aggregate ceiling for overseas investments at US $ 5 billion. Within the overall limit of US $ 5 billion, mutual funds can make overseas investments subject to a maximum of US $300 million per mutual fund. Further different regulations that allow individuals and Indian mutual funds to invest in overseas securities by permitting individuals to invest through Indian mutual funds has been converged.

New Derivative Products: Mini-derivative contract on Index (Sensex and Nifty) having a minimum contract size of Rs. 1 lakh have been introduced. It has been found that globally overall market liquidity and participation generally increases with introduction of mini-contracts. Since January 11, 2008 SEBI has also allowed trading on options contracts on indices and stocks with a longer life/tenure of upto five years. Since January 15, 2008 SEBI has permitted introduction of volatility index on futures and options contracts. An openly available and quoted measure of market volatility in the form of an index will help market participants. SEBI has issued a circular to permit short selling by institutional investors and securities lending and borrowing to support settlement of short sales.

Investment Options for Navaratna and Miniratna Public Sector Enterprises: The Navaratna and Miniratna Public Sector Enterprises have been allowed to invest in public sector mutual funds subject to the condition that they would not invest more than 30% of the available surplus funds in equity mutual funds and the Boards of PSEs would decide the guidelines, procedures and management control systems for such investment in consultation with their administrative Ministries.

Investor Protection and Education Fund (IPEF): SEBI has set-up the Investor Protection and Education Fund (IPEF) with the purpose of investor education and related activities. SEBI has contributed a sum of Rs. 10 crore toward the initial corpus of the IPEF from the SEBI General Fund. In addition, following amounts will also be credited to the IPEF namely: (i) Grants and donations given to IPEF by the Central Government, State Governments or any institution approved by SEBI for the purpose of the IPEF; (ii) Interest or other income received out of the investments made from the IPEF; and (iii) Such other amount that SEBI may specify in the interests of the investors.

External Commercial Borrowings: ECBs are permitted by the Government as an additional source of funds to Indian Corporate for expansion of their existing capacity as well as for fresh investment to augment the resources available domestically. A prospective borrower can access ECB under two routes, namely, the automatic route and the approval route.

The Government in consultation with Reserve Bank of India periodically reviews ECB policy in order to enable Indian corporates to have greater access to international capital market while keeping prudent debt management objective in view. ECB of more than USD 20 million both under automatic and approval route would be permitted only for foreign currency expenditure for permissible end-uses of ECB. ECB up to US$ 20 under the automatic route will also be permitted for foreign currency requirement. However, if company desires to bring the money into India for rupee cost requirement, they may do so with prior approval of RBI.

India's Sovereign Rating: Presently India is rated by five international credit rating agencies, namely, Standard and Poor's (S and P), Moody's Investor Services, FITCH, the Japanese Credit Rating Agency (JCRA) and the Rating and Investment Information Inc., Tokyo (R and I). Moody's foreign currency rating for India is Baa 3 (investment grade) with a stable outlook while Fitch's current rating is BBB– with a stable outlook. Standard and Poor's (S and P) have also upgraded India's rating to investment grade (BBB–) with stable outlook. Japan Credit Rating Agency (JCRA) has revised its ratings of Foreign Currency Long-term Senior Debts : as well as Domestic Currency Long-term Senior Debts from "BBB" to "BBB+" (Triple 'B' Plus) with rating outlook from Positive to Stable.

SECURITIES CONTRACT (REGULATION) ACT, 1956

The main purpose of passing of The Securities Contracts (Regulation) Act, 1956 was to prevent undesirable transactions in securities by regulating the business of dealing therein, and by providing for certain other matters connected therewith. The Act extends to the whole of India and came into force on 28th February, 1957. The Act defines various terms in relation to securities and provides the detailed procedure for the stock exchanges to get recognition from SEBI, procedure for listing of securities of companies and operations of the brokers in relation to purchase and sale of securities on behalf of investors.

This Act shall not apply to the Government, the Reserve Bank of India, any local authority or any corporation set-up by a special law or any person who has effected any transaction with or through the agency of any such authority as is referred to in this clause; and on any convertible bond or share warrant or any option or right in relation thereto, in so far as it entitles the person in whose favour any of the foregoing has been issued to obtain at his option from the company or other body corporate, issuing the same or from any of its shareholders' or duly appointed agents, shares of the company or other body corporate, whether by conversion of the bond or warrant or otherwise, on the basis of the price agreed upon when the same was issued.

If the Central Government is satisfied that in the interest of trade and commerce or the economic development of the country, it is necessary or expedient so to do, it by notification in the Official Gazette, specify any class of contracts as contracts which this Act or any provision contained therein shall not apply, and also the conditions, limitations or restrictions, if any, subject to which it shall not so apply.

The *'Securities' has been defined to* include:

- Shares, scrips, stocks, bonds, debentures, debenture stock or other marketable securities of a like nature or of any incorporated company body corporate.
- Derivative.
- Units or any other instrument issued by any

collective investment scheme to the Investors in such schemes.

- Government securities.
- Such other instruments as may be declared by the Central Government to be securities.
- Rights or interests in securities.

Stock Exchange means any body of individuals, whether incorporated or not, constituted for the purpose of assisting, regulating or controlling the business of buying, selling or dealing in securities. Recognized Stock Exchange means a stock exchange which is for the time being recognized by the Central Government. No person shall, except with the permission of the Central Government, organize or assist in organizing or be a member of any stock exchange (other than a recognized stock exchange) for the purpose of assisting in, entering into or performing any contracts in securities. No person shall, except with the permission of the Central Government, organize or assist in organizing or be a member of any stock exchange (other than a recognized stock exchange) for the purpose of assisting in, entering into or performing any contracts in securities. It will be effective in any State or area.

RECOGNITION OF STOCK EXCHANGES

1. Any stock exchange, which is desirous of being recognized for the purposes of this Act, may make an application in the prescribed manner to the Central Government.
2. An application has to be accompanied by a copy of the bye-laws of the stock exchange for the regulation and control of contracts and also a copy of the rules relating in general to the constitution of the stock exchange regarding:
   (i) Governing body of such stock exchange, its constitution and powers of management and the manner in which its business is to be transacted.
   (ii) Powers and duties of the office bearers of the stock exchange.
   (iii) Admission into the stock exchange of various

classes of members, the qualifications for membership, and the exclusion, suspension, expulsion and re-admission of members there from or there-into.

(iv) Procedure for the registration of partnerships as members of the stock exchange in cases where the rules provide for such membership; and the nomination and appointment of authorized representatives and clerks.

3. After making such inquiry as may be necessary the Central Government by obtaining such further information, if it is satisfied that the rules and bye-laws of a stock exchange applying for registration are in conformity with such conditions as may be prescribed with a view to ensure fair dealing and to protect investors and that the stock exchange is willing to comply with any other conditions (including conditions as to the number of members) which the Central Government, after consultation with the governing body of the stock exchange and having regard to the area served by the stock exchange and its standing and the nature of the securities dealt with by it, may impose for the purpose of carrying out the objects of this Act; and that it would be in the interest of the trade and also in the public interest to grant recognition to the stock exchange it may grant recognition to the stock exchange subject to the certain conditions.

4. The conditions which the Central Government may prescribe for the grant of recognition to the stock exchanges may relate to:

(i) Qualifications for membership of stock exchanges;

(ii) The manner in which contracts shall be entered into and enforced as between members;

(iii) Representation of the Central Government on each of the stock exchanges by such number of persons not exceeding three as the Central Government may nominate in this behalf;

(iv) Maintenance of accounts of members and their audit by chartered accountants whenever such audit is required by the Central Government.

5. Grant of recognition to a stock exchange shall be published in the Gazette of India and also in the Official Gazette of the State in which the principal office of the stock exchange is situated and such recognition shall have effect as from the date of its publication in the Gazette of India. Application for the grant of recognition will not normally be refused except and if refused the reasons for such refusal will be communicated to the stock exchange in writing. Rules of a recognized stock exchange relating to any of the matters approved should not be amended except with the approval of the Central Government.
6. The Central Government may in the interest of the trade or in the public interest withdraw recognition granted to the stock exchange by serving a notice on the governing body of the stock exchange by stating the reasons. However, such withdrawal will not affect the validity of any contract entered into or made before the date of the notification, and the Central Government may, after consultation with the stock exchange, make such provision as it deems fit in the notification of withdrawal or in any subsequent notification similarly published for the due performance of any contracts outstanding on that date.

POWERS OF CENTRAL GOVERNMENT

- Recognized stock exchanges have to furnish to the Securities and Exchange Board of India periodical returns relating to its affairs.
- A Recognized stock exchange and its members have to maintain and preserve for such periods not exceeding five years' books of account and other documents as the Central Government, after consultation with the stock exchange concerned, may prescribe in the interest of the trade or in the public

interest, and such books of account, and other documents shall be subject to inspection at all reasonable times by the Securities and Exchange Board of India.

- The Securities and Exchange Board of India, if it is satisfied that it is in the interest of the trade or in the public interest may by an order in writing upon a recognized stock exchange or any of its member to furnish in writing such information or explanation relating to the affairs of the stock exchange or of the member in relation to the stock exchange.
- SEBI may appoint one or more persons to make an inquiry in the prescribed manner in relation to the affairs of the governing body of a stock exchange or the affairs of any of the members of the stock exchange in relation to the stock exchange and submit a report of the result of such inquiry to SEBI within the time specified in the order or, in the case of an inquiry in relation to the affairs of any of the members of a stock exchange, direct the governing body to make the inquiry and submit its report to SEBI.
- In case an inquiry in relation to the affairs of a recognized stock exchange or the affairs of any of its members in relation to the stock exchange has been undertaken on:
  - Every director, manager, secretary or other officer of such stock exchange.
  - Every member of such stock exchange.
  - If the member of the stock exchange is a firm, every partner, manager, secretary or other officer of the firm.
  - Every other person or body of persons who has had dealings in the course of business with any of the persons mentioned above whether directly or indirectly; shall be bound to produce before the authority making the inquiry all books of account, and other documents in his custody or power relating to or having a bearing

on the subject-matter of such inquiry and also to furnish the authorities within the specified time any such statement or information relating thereto as may be required of him.

- A recognized stock exchange has to furnish the Central Government, a copy of the annual report which should contain such particulars as may be required of it.

POWERS OF RECOGNIZED STOCK EXCHANGES

A recognized stock exchange may make rules or amend any rules made by it to provide for all or any of the following matters:

1. Restriction of voting rights to members in respect of any matter placed before the stock exchange at any meeting.
2. Regulation of voting rights in respect of any matter placed before the stock exchange at any meeting so that each member may be entitled to have one vote only, irrespective of his share of the paid-up equity capital of the stock exchange.
3. Restriction on the right of a member to appoint another person as his proxy to attend and vote at a meeting of the stock exchange.
4. Any incidental, consequential and supplementary matters as may be necessary to give effect to any of the matters specified above.
5. Rules of a recognized stock exchange made or amended shall have effect only when they have been approved by the Central Government and published by that Government in the Official Gazette and, in approving it the Central Government may make such modifications therein as it thinks fit, and no such publication, the rules as approved by the Central Government shall be deemed to have been validly made, notwithstanding to anything contained in the Companies Act, 1956.

BYE-LAWS

Any recognized stock exchange may, subject to the previous approval of the SEBI may make bye-laws for the regulation and control of contracts. The bye-laws may provide for the following aspects:

1. Opening and closing of markets and the regulation of the hours of trade.
2. A clearing house for the periodical settlement of contracts and differences there under, the delivery of and payment for securities, the passing on of delivery orders and the regulation and maintenance of such clearing house.
3. Submission to SEBI by the clearing house any of the following particulars as it may require regarding: (i) the total number of each category of security carried over from one settlement period to another; (ii) the total number of each category of security, contracts in respect of which have been squared up during the course of each settlement period; (iii) the total number of each category of security actually delivered at each clearing.
4. Publication by the clearing house of all or any of the particulars submitted to SEBI.
5. Regulation or prohibition of blank transfers.
6. Number and classes of contracts in respect of which settlements shall be made or differences paid through the clearing house.
7. Regulation or prohibition of 'budlas' or carry-over facilities.
8. Fixing, altering or postponing of days for settlements.
9. Determination and declaration of market rates, including the opening, closing, highest and lowest rates for securities.
10. The terms, conditions and incidents of contracts, including the prescription of margin requirements, if any, and conditions relating thereto, and the forms of contracts in writing.

11. Regulation of the entering into, making, performance, rescission and termination, of contracts, including contracts between members or between a member and his constituent or between a member and a person who is not a member, and the consequences of default or insolvency on the part of a seller or buyer or intermediary, the consequences of a breach or omission by a seller or buyer, and the responsibility of members who are not parties to such contracts.
12. Regulation of 'taravani' business including the placing of limitations thereon.
13. Listing of securities on the stock exchange, the inclusion of any security for the purpose of dealings and the suspension or withdrawal of any such securities, and the suspension or prohibition of trading in any specified securities.
14. Method and procedure for the settlement of claims or disputes, including settlement by arbitration.
15. Levy and recovery of fees, fines and penalties from members.
16. Regulation of the course of business between parties to contracts in any capacity.
17. Fixing of a scale of brokerage and other charges.
18. Making, comparing, settling and closing of bargains.
19. The emergencies in trade which may arise, whether as a result of pool or syndicated operations or cornering or otherwise, and the exercise of powers in such emergencies, including the power to fix maximum and minimum prices for securities.
20. Regulation of dealings by members for their own account.
21. Separation of the functions of jobbers and brokers.
22. Limiting the volume of trade done by any individual member in exceptional circumstances.
23. The obligation of members to supply such information or explanation and to produce such documents relating to the business as the governing body may require.

24. A stock exchange may establish additional trading floor with the prior approval of the Securities and Exchange Board of India in accordance with the terms and conditions stipulated by the said Board. It means a trading ring or trading facility offered by a recognized stock exchange outside its area of operation to enable the investors to buy and sell securities through such trading floor under the regulatory framework of that stock exchange.
25. The bye-laws may specify that, contravention of it will make a member concerned liable to one or more of the following punishments, namely, fine or expulsion from membership, suspension from membership for a specified period, or any other penalty of a like nature not involving the payment of money.

Bye-laws made under this section shall be subject to such conditions in regard to previous publication, as may be prescribed, and, when approved by SEBI and published in the Gazette of India and also in the Official Gazette of the State in which the principal office of the recognized stock exchange is situate shall have effect as from the date of its publication in the Gazette of India. However, if SEBI is satisfied in any case that in the interest of the trade or in the public interest any bye-law should be made immediately, it may, by order in writing specifying the reasons therefore, dispense with the condition of previous publication.

AMENDMENT OF THE RULES OF STOCK EXCHANGE BY SEBI

- The Securities and Exchange Board of India may, either on a request in writing received by it in this behalf from the governing body of a recognized stock exchange or on its own motion, after consultation with the governing body of the stock exchange that it is necessary or expedient so to do and after recording its reasons for so doing, make bye-laws for such a stock exchange.

- Any bye-laws have been made or amended the bye-laws so made has to be published in the Gazette of India and also in the Official Gazette of the State in which the principal office of the recognized stock exchange is situate, and on the publication thereof in the Gazette of India, the bye-laws so made or amended shall have effect as if they had been made or amended by the recognized stock exchange concerned.
- In case the governing body of a recognized stock exchange objects to any bye-laws made or amended by SEBI on it own motion, it may, within two months of the publication thereof in the Gazette of India, apply to SEBI for revision, and it may, after giving an opportunity to the governing body of the stock exchange to be heard in the matter, revise the bye-laws so made or amended and where any bye-laws so made or amended are revised as a result of any action taken, the bye-laws so revised shall be published and shall become effective.
- The making or the amendment or revision of any bye-laws shall in all cases be subject to the condition of publication in the Gazette.
- If SEBI is satisfied that in the interest of the trade or in the public interest any bye-laws should be made, amended or revised immediately, it may, by order in writing specifying the reasons therefore carryout the amendment without previous publication.

By Central Government

After consultation with the governing bodies of stock exchanges generally or with the governing body of any stock exchange in particular, the Central Government is of opinion that it is necessary or expedient so to do, it may, by order in writing together with a statement of the reasons therefore, direct recognized stock exchanges generally or any recognized stock exchange in particular, as the case may be, to make any rules or to amend any rules already made within a period of two months from the date of the order.

If any recognized stock exchange fails or neglects to comply with any order made within the period specified therein, the Central Government may make the rules for, or amend the rules made by, the recognized stock exchange, either in the form proposed in the order or with such modifications thereof as may be agreed to between the stock exchange and the Central Government.

Rules so made or amended shall be published in the Gazette of India and also in the Official Gazette or Gazettes of the State or States in which the principal office or offices of the recognized stock exchange or exchanges is or are situated and on the publication it will have effect as if they had been made or amended by the recognized stock exchange. or stock exchanges itself.

GENERAL POWERS OF CENTRAL GOVERNMENT

Supersede Governing Body of Stock Exchanges : The Central Government is of opinion that the governing body of any recognized stock exchange should be superseded, it may serve on the governing body a written notice that it is considering the suppression of the governing body for the reasons specified in the notice and after giving an opportunity to the governing body it may, by notification in the Official Gazette, declare the governing body of such stock exchange to be superseded, and may appoint any person or persons to exercise and perform all the powers and duties of the governing body, and, when more persons than one are appointed, it may appoint one of such persons to be the chairman and another to be the vice-chairman thereof. The following consequences shall ensue, if Central Government supersedes the powers of the stock exchanges:

- Members of the governing body which has been superseded shall, as from the date of the notification of super session, cease to hold office as such members.
- The person or persons appointed may exercise and perform all the powers and duties of the governing body which has been superseded.

- All such property of the recognized stock exchange as the person or persons appointed may, by order in writing, specify in this behalf as being necessary for the purpose of enabling him or them to carry on the business of the stock exchange, shall vest in such person or persons.
- The person or persons appointed will hold office for such period as may be specified in the notification published by the Central Government may from time to time.
- The Central Government may at any time before the determination of the period of office of any person or persons appointed under this section call upon the recognized stock exchange to re-constitute the governing body in accordance with its rules and on such re-constitution all the property of the recognized stock exchange which has vested in, or was in the possession of, the person or persons appointed shall re-vest or vest, as the case may be, in the governing body so re-constituted.
- Until a governing body is so re-constituted, the person or persons appointed will continue to exercise and perform their powers and duties.

Suspend Business of Stock Exchanges: If there is an emergency, the Central Government may, by notification in the Official Gazette, for reasons to be set out therein, direct a recognized stock exchange to suspend its business for such period not exceeding seven days and subject to such conditions as may be specified in the notification. The Central Government, in the interest of the trade or the public interest requires that the period should be extended, may by notification extend the time.

PROHIBITION OF CERTAIN ACTIVITIES

- *Contracts void if entered in contravention of any bye-laws:* Any contract entered into in any State or area in contravention of any of the bye-laws specified in that behalf shall be void as respects the rights of any member of the recognized stock exchange who has entered into such contract in, and also on the rights of any other person who has knowingly participated in the transaction entailing such contravention. However, nothing shall be construed to affect the right of any person other than a member of the recognized stock exchange to enforce any such contract or to recover any sum under or in respect of such contract if such person had no knowledge that the transaction was in contravention of any of the bye-laws.

- *Members may not Act as Principals in Certain Circumstances:* No member of a recognized stock exchange shall in respect of any securities enter into any contract as a principal with any person other than a member of a recognized stock exchange, unless he has secured the consent or authority of such person and discloses in the note, memorandum or agreement of sale or purchase that he is acting as a principal, provided that where the member has secured the consent or authority of such person otherwise than in writing he shall secure written confirmation by such person or such consent or authority within three days from the date of the contract. No such written consent or authority of such person shall be necessary for closing out any outstanding contract entered into by such person in accordance with the bye-laws, if the member discloses in the note, memorandum or agreement of sale or purchase in respect of such closing out that he is acting as a principal.
- *Prevent Undesirable Speculation:* If the Central Government is of opinion that it is necessary to prevent undesirable speculation in specified securities in any State or area, it may, by notification in the Official Gazette, declare that no person in the State or area specified in the notification shall, save with the permission of the Central Government, enter into any contract for the sale or purchase of any

security specified in the notification except to the extent and in the manner, if any, specified therein.

- *Licensing of Dealers in Securities in Certain Areas:* No person shall carry on whether on his own behalf or on behalf of any other person, the business of dealing in securities in any State or area to which certain provisions of SCR Act has not been declared to apply and to which the Central Government declared would apply. The notification shall not be issued with respect to any State or area unless the Central Government is satisfied, having regard to the manner in which securities are being dealt with in such State or area, that it is desirable or expedient in the interest of the trade or in the public interest that such dealings should be regulated by a system of licensing. The restrictions imposed in relation to dealings in securities shall not apply to the doing of anything by or on behalf of a member of any recognized stock exchange.

PENALTIES

The following contraventions will attract penalty under the Act. On conviction such offenders will be punishable with imprisonment for a term which may extend to one year, or with fine, or with both:

- Without reasonable cause fails to comply with any requisition made under the Act.
- Enters into any contract in contravention of any of the provisions of the Act.
- Owns or keeps a place other than that of a recognized stock exchange which is used for the purpose of entering into or performing any contracts in contravention of any of the provisions of this Act and knowingly permits such place to be used for such purposes
- Manages, controls, or assists in keeping any place other than that of a recognized stock exchange which is used for the purpose of entering into or performing

any contracts in contravention of any of the provisions of this Act or at which contracts are recorded or adjusted or rights or liabilities arising out of contracts are adjusted, regulated or enforced in any manner whatsoever.

- Not being a member of a recognized stock exchange or his agent authorized as such under the rules or bye-laws of such stock exchange or not being a dealer in securities licensed wilfully represents to or induces any person to believe that contracts can be entered into or performed under this Act through him.
- Not being a member of a recognized stock exchange or his agent authorized as such under the rules or bye-laws of such stock exchange or not being a dealer in securities licensed canvasses, advertises or touts in any manner either for himself or on behalf of any other persons for any business connected with contracts in contravention of any of the provisions of this Act.
- Joins, gathers or assists in gathering at any place other than the place of business specified in the bye-laws of a recognized stock exchange any person or persons for making bids or offers or for entering into or performing any contracts in contravention of any of the provisions of this Act.
- Any person who enters into any contract in contravention of the provisions contained in section 15 or who fails to comply with the provisions of section 21 or with the orders of or section 22 shall, on conviction, be punishable with fine which may extend to one thousand rupees.
- *Offences by Companies:* Where an offence has been committed by a company, every person who, at the time when the offence was committed, was in charge of, and was responsible to, the company for the conduct of the business of the company, as well as the company, shall be deemed to be guilty of the offence, and shall be liable to be proceeded against and punished accordingly. However, it shall not render any such person liable to any punishment

provided in this Act, if he proves that the offence was committed without his knowledge or that he exercised all due diligence to prevent the commission of such offence.

Where an offence under this Act has been committed by a company and it is proved that the offence has been committed with the consent or connivance of, or is attributable to any gross negligence on the part of any director, manager, secretary or other officer of the company, such director, manager, secretary or other officer of the company, shall also be deemed to be guilty of that offence and shall be liable to be proceeded against and punished. A "company" means any body corporate and includes a firm or other association of individuals, and a "director", in relation to a firm, means a partner in the firm. Offences under this Act will be a cognizable offence within the meaning of that Criminal Procedure Code. No court inferior to that of a presidency magistrate or a magistrate of the first class shall take cognizance of or try any offence punishable under this Act.

The Central Government may make rules for the purpose of carrying out the objects of this Act for the following aspects:

(i) Manner in which applications may be made for grant of license of stock exchanges and the particulars which they should contain and the levy of a fee in respect of the applications.

(ii) Manner in which any inquiry for the purpose of recognizing any stock exchange may be made, the conditions which may be imposed for the grant of such recognition, including conditions as to the admission of members if the stock exchange concerned is to be the only recognized stock exchange in the area; and the form in which such recognition shall be granted.

(iii) The particulars which should be contained in the periodical returns and annual reports to be furnished to the Central Government.

(iv) Documents which should be maintained and preserved under section 6 and the periods for which they should be preserved.

(v) Manner in which any inquiry by the governing body of a stock exchange shall be made.

(vi) How the bye-laws to be made or amended under this Act shall before being so made or amended is published for criticism.

(vii) The procedures for making applications by dealers in securities regarding:
- Getting of licences.
- Fee payable and the period of such licences.
- Conditions subject to which licences may be granted.
- Conditions relating to the forms which may be used in making contracts.
- Documents to be maintained by licensed dealers and the furnishing of periodical information to such authority.
- Revocation of licences for breach of conditions.

(viii) Matter to be complied by public companies for the purpose of getting their securities listed on any stock exchange.

(ix) The form in which a reference shall be made and the particulars which such reference shall contain, and the evidence and the fees that should accompany such reference.

(x) Any other matter which may be prescribed.

(xi) Every rule made under this section shall, as soon as may be, after its publication in the Official Gazette, be laid before each House of Parliament, while it is in session, for a total period of thirty days which may be comprised in one session or in two to more successive sessions, and if, before the expiry of the session immediately following the session or the successive session aforesaid, both Houses agree in making any modification in the rule or both Houses agree that the rule should not be made, the rule shall thereafter have effect only in such modified form or be of no effect, as the case may be so, however, that any such modification or annulment shall be without prejudice to the validity of anything previously done under that rule.

(xii) *Protection of Action Taken in Good Faith:* No suit, prosecution or other legal proceeding whatsoever shall lie in any court against the governing body or any member, office bearer or servant of any recognized stock exchange or against any person or persons appointed for anything which is in good faith done or intended to be done in pursuance of this Act or of any rules or bye-laws made thereunder.

(xiii) *Power to Delegate:* The Central Government may, by order direct that the powers exercisable by it in relation to any matter and subject to the conditions, if any as may be specified in the order, be exercisable also by SEBI.

EXCLUSION OF SPOT DELIVERY CONTRACTS

If the Central Government is of opinion that in the interest of the trade or in the public interest it is expedient to regulate and control the business of dealing in spot delivery contracts also in any State or area may declare that the provisions shall also apply to such State or area in respect of spot delivery contracts generally or in respect of spot delivery contracts for the sale or purchase of such securities as may be specified in the notification, and may also specify the manner in which, and the extent to which the provisions apply.

REMEDY AGAINST REFUSAL OF STOCK EXCHANGES TO LIST SECURITIES

Where a recognized stock exchange refuses to list the securities of any public company, the company shall be entitled to be furnished with reasons for such refusal, and may within fifteen days from the date on which the reasons for such refusal are furnished to it, or where the stock exchange has omitted or failed to dispose of, within the reasonable time, the application for permission for the shares or debentures to be dealt with on the stock exchange, may apply to the Central Government for a remedy.

The Central Government may after giving the stock exchange an opportunity of being heard, vary or set aside the decision of the stock exchange or where the stock exchange has omitted or failed to dispose of the application within the specified time, grant or refuse the permission, and where the Central Government sets aside the decision of the recognized stock exchange or grants the permission, the stock exchange shall act in conformity with the orders of the Central Government.

TITLE TO DIVIDENDS

It shall be lawful for the holder of any security whose name appears on the books of the company issuing the said security to receive and retain any dividend declared by the company in respect thereof for any year, notwithstanding that the said security has already been transferred by him for consideration, unless the transferee who claims the dividend from the transferor has lodged the security and all other documents relating to the transfer which may be required by the company with the company for being registered in his name within fifteen days of the date on which the dividend became due.

The period specified in this section shall be extended :

(i) In case of death of the transferee, by the actual period taken by his legal representative to establish his claim to the dividend;

(ii) In case of loss of the transfer deed by theft or any other cause beyond the control of the transferee, by the actual period taken for the replacement thereof; and

(iii) In case of delay in the lodging of any security and other documents relating to the transfer due to causes connected with the post, by the actual period of the delay.

(iv) It shall not affect—(a) the right of a company to pay any dividend which has become due to any person whose name is for the time being registered in the books of the company as the holder of the security in respect of which the dividend has become due; or (b) the right of the transferee of any security to enforce against the transferor or any other person his rights, if any, in relation to the transfer in any case where the company has refused to register the transfer of the security in the name of the transferee.

7

Role of SEBI in Capital Market

SEBI ACT, 1992

The Board is a body corporate having perpetual succession and a common seal, with power subject to the provisions of this Act, to acquire, hold and dispose of property, both movable and immovable, and to contract, and shall, by the said name, sue or be sued. The head office of the Board shall be at Bombay and it may establish offices at other places in India.

Management of the Board

1. The Board shall consist of the following members, namely:
   - One Chairman.
   - Two members from amongst the officials of the Central Government dealing with Finance and administration of the Companies Act, 1956.
   - One member from amongst the officials of the Reserve Bank.

- Five other members of whom at least three shall be the whole-time members.

2. The general superintendence, direction and management of the affairs of the Board shall vest in a Board of members, which may exercise all powers and do all acts and things which may be exercised or done by the Board.
3. The Chairman shall also have powers of general superintendence and direction of the affairs of the Board and may also exercise all powers and do all acts and things which may be exercised or done by the Board.
4. The Central Government will appoint Chairman and the other members such that they are persons of ability, integrity and standing who have shown capacity in dealing with problems relating to securities market or have special knowledge or experience of law, finance, economics, accountancy, administration or in any other discipline which, in the opinion of the Central Government, shall be useful to the Board.

Functions of the Board

It shall be duty of the Board to protect the interests of the investors in securities and to promote and development of, and to regulate the securities market by such measures as it thinks fit. The measures referred to therein may provide for:

- Regulating the business in stock exchanges and any other securities markets.
- Registering and regulating the working of stock brokers, sub-brokers, share transfer agents, bankers to an issue, trustees of trust deeds, registrars to an issue, merchant bankers, underwriters, portfolio managers, investment advisers and such other intermediaries who may be associated with securities markets in any manner.
- Registering and regulating the working of the depositories, participants, custodians of securities, foreign institutional investors, credit rating agencies

and such other intermediaries as the Board may, by notification, specify in this behalf.

- Registering and regulating the working of venture capital funds and collective investment schemes including mutual funds.
- Promoting and regulating self-regulatory organizations.
- Prohibiting fraudulent and unfair trade practices relating to securities markets.
- Promoting investors' education and training of intermediaries of securities markets.
- Prohibiting insider trading in securities.
- Regulating substantial acquisition of shares and take-over of companies.
- Calling for information from, undertaking inspection, conducting inquiries and audits of the stock exchanges, mutual funds and other persons associated with the securities market and intermediaries and self-regulatory organizations in the securities market;
- Calling for information and record from any bank or any other authority or board or corporation established or constituted by or under any Central, State or Provincial Act in respect of any transaction in securities which is under investigation or inquiry by the Board.
- Performing such functions and exercising such powers under the provisions of Securities Contracts (Regulation) Act, 1956, as may be delegated to it by the Central Government.
- Levying fees or other charges for carrying out the purpose of this section.
- Conducting research for the above purposes.
- Calling from or furnishing to any such agencies, as may be specified by the Board, such information as may be considered necessary by it for the efficient discharge of its functions.
- Performing such other functions as may be prescribed.

- ❖ Take measures to undertake inspection of any book, or register, or other document or record of any listed public company or a public company which intends to get its securities listed on any recognized stock exchange where the Board has reasonable grounds to believe that such company has been indulging in insider trading or fraudulent and unfair trade practices relating to securities market.

Powers of SEBI

The Board shall have the same powers as are vested in a civil court under the Code of Civil Procedure, 1908 while trying a suit, in respect of the following matters, namely:

- The discovery and production of books of account and other documents, at such place and such time as may be specified by the Board.
- Summoning and enforcing the attendance of persons and examining them on oath.
- Inspection of any books, registers and other documents of any person at any place.
- Inspection of any book, or register, or other document or record of the company.
- Issuing commissions for the examination of witnesses or documents.
- The Board may, by an order, for reasons to be recorded in writing, in the interests of investors or securities market, take any of the following measures, either pending investigation or inquiry or on completion of such investigation or inquiry, namely:
  - ❖ Suspend the trading of any security in a recognized stock exchange;
  - ❖ Restrain persons from accessing the securities market and prohibit any person associated with securities market to buy, sell or deal in securities;
  - ❖ Suspend any office-bearer of any stock exchange or self-regulatory organization from holding such position;

  - Impound and retain the proceeds or securities in respect of any transaction which is under investigation;
  - Attach, after passing of an order on an application made for approval, by the Judicial Magistrate of the first class having jurisdiction, for a period not exceeding one month, one or more bank account or accounts of any intermediary or any person associated with the securities market in any manner involved in violation of any of the provisions of this Act, or the rules or the regulations made thereunder.
  - Only the bank account or accounts or any transaction entered therein, so far as it relates to the proceeds actually involved in violation of any of the provisions of this Act, or the rules or the regulations made thereunder shall be allowed to be attached.
- Direct any intermediary or any person associated with the securities market in any manner not to dispose of or alienate an asset forming part of any transaction which is under investigation.
- The Board may take any of the measures in respect of any listed public company or a public company which intends to get its securities listed on any recognized stock exchange where the Board has reasonable grounds to believe that such company has been indulging in insider trading or fraudulent and unfair trade practices relating to securities market.
- Either before or after passing such orders, give an opportunity of hearing to such intermediaries or persons concerned.
- Board can regulate or prohibit issue of prospectus, offer document or advertisement soliciting money for issue of securities for the protection of investors.
- The matters relating to issue of capital, transfer of securities and other matters incidental thereto.
- The manner in which such matters shall be disclosed by the companies.

- By general or special orders prohibit any company from issuing prospectus, any offer document, or advertisement soliciting money from the public for the issue of securities.
- Specify the conditions subject to which the prospectus, such offer document or advertisement, if not prohibited, may be issued.
- The Board may specify the requirements for listing and transfer of securities and other matters incidental thereto.
- *Power to Issue Directions*: After making or causing to be made an enquiry, the Board is satisfied that it is necessary, in the interest of investors, or orderly development of securities market; or to prevent the affairs of any intermediary or other persons referred to in section 12 being conducted in a manner detrimental to the interests of investors or securities market; or to secure the proper management of any such intermediary or person, it may issue such directions, to any person or class of associated with the securities market; or to any company in respect of any matter as may be appropriate in the interests of investors in securities and the securities market.
- *Power to Adjudicate:* The Board shall appoint any of its officer not below the rank of a Division Chief to be an adjudicating officer for holding an inquiry in the prescribed manner after giving any person concerned a reasonable opportunity of being heard for the purpose of imposing any penalty. While holding an inquiry the adjudicating officer shall have power to summon and enforce the attendance of any person acquainted with the facts and circumstances of the case to give evidence or to produce any document which in the opinion of the adjudicating officer, may be useful for or relevant to the subject matter of the inquiry and if, on such inquiry, he is satisfied that the person has failed to comply with the provisions of Act, he may impose such penalty as he thinks fit.

Registration of Intermediaries

- No stock-broker, sub-broker, share transfer agent, banker to an issue, trustee of trust deed, registrar to an issue, merchant banker, underwriter, portfolio manager, investment adviser and such other intermediary who may be associated with securities market shall buy, sell or deal in securities except under, and in accordance with, the conditions of a certificate of registration obtained from the Board in accordance with the regulations made under this Act.
- No depository, participant, custodian of securities, foreign institutional investor, credit rating agency or any other intermediary associated with the securities market as the Board may by notification in this behalf specify, shall buy or sell or deal in securities except under and in accordance with the conditions of a certificate of registration obtained from the Board in accordance with the regulations made under this Act.
- No person shall sponsor or cause to be sponsored or carry on or cause to be carried on any venture capital funds or collective investment schemes including mutual funds, unless he obtains a certificate of registration from the Board in accordance with the regulations.

The following activities or initiatives are taken by SEBI against to prohibit manipulative practices and no person can use these deceptive practices:

- No person shall directly or indirectly—use or employ, in connection with the issue, purchase or sale of any securities listed or proposed to be listed on a recognized stock exchange, any manipulative or deceptive device or contrivance in contravention of the provisions of this Act or the rules or the regulations made thereunder.
- Employ any device, scheme or artifice to defraud in connection with issue or dealing in securities which

are listed or proposed to be listed on a recognized stock exchange.

- Engage in any act, practice, course of business which operates or would operate as fraud or deceit upon any person, in connection with the issue, dealing in securities which are listed or proposed to be listed on a recognized stock exchange, in contravention of the provisions of this Act or the rules or the regulations made there-under.
- Engage in insider trading.
- Deal in securities while in possession of material or non-public information or communicate such material or non-public information to any other person, in a manner which is in contravention of the provisions of this Act or the rules or the regulations made there-under.
- Acquire control of any company or securities more than the percentage of equity share capital of a company whose securities are listed or proposed to be listed on a recognized stock exchange in contravention of the regulations made under this Act.

PENALTY IMPOSABLE UNDER SEBI ACT

1. *Penalty for Failure to Furnish Information etc.:* If any person, who is required under this Act or any rules or regulations made there under, to furnish any document, return or report to the Board, fails to furnish the same, he shall be liable to a penalty of one lakh rupees for each day during which such failure continues or one crore rupees, whichever is less or fails to file any return or furnish any information, books or other documents within the time specified therefore in the regulations, fails to file return or furnish the same within the time specified therefore in the regulations, he shall be liable to a penalty of one lakh rupees for each day during which such failure continues or one crore rupees, whichever is less or fails to maintain books of accounts or records, fails to maintain the same, he shall be liable

to a penalty of one lakh rupees for each day during which such failure continues or one crore rupees, whichever is less.

2. *Penalty for Failure by any Person to Enter into an Agreement with Clients:* If any person, who is registered as an intermediary and is required under this Act or any rules or regulations made there-under, to enter into an agreement with his client, fails to enter into such agreement, he shall be liable to a penalty of one lakh rupees for each day during which such failure continues or one crore rupees, whichever is less.
3. *Penalty for Failure to Redress Investors' Grievances:* If any listed company or any person who is registered as an intermediary, after having been called upon by the Board in writing, to redress the grievances of investors, fails to redress such grievances within the time specified by the Board, such company or intermediary shall be liable to a penalty of one lakh rupees for each day during which such failure continues or one crore rupees, whichever is less.
4. *Penalty for Certain Defaults in Case of Mutual Funds:*
   (a) If any person, who is required under this Act or any rules or regulations made there under to obtain a certificate of registration from the Board for sponsoring or carrying on any collective investment scheme, including mutual funds, sponsors or carries on any collective investment scheme, including mutual funds, without obtaining such certificate of registration, he shall be liable to a penalty of one lakh rupees for each day during which he sponsors or carries on any such collective investment scheme including mutual funds, or one crore rupees, whichever is less.
   (b) If any person, who is registered with the Board as a collective investment scheme, including mutual funds, for sponsoring or carrying on any investment scheme, fails to comply with the terms and conditions of certificate of

registration, he shall be liable to a penalty of one lakh rupees for each day during which such failure continues or one crore rupees, whichever is less.

(c) If any person, who is registered with the Board as a collective investment scheme including mutual funds, fails to make an application for listing of its schemes as provided for in the regulations governing such listing, he shall be liable to a penalty of one lakh rupees for each day during which such failure continues or one crore rupees, whichever is less.

(d) If any person, who is registered as a collective investment scheme, including mutual funds, fails to despatch unit certificates of any scheme in the manner provided in the regulation governing such despatch, he shall be liable to a penalty of one lakh rupees for each day during which such failure continues or one crore rupees, whichever is less.

(e) If any person, who is registered as a collective investment scheme, including mutual funds, fails to refund the application moneys paid by the investors within the period specified in the regulations, he shall be liable to pay a penalty of one lakh rupees for each day during which such failure continues or one crore rupees, whichever is less.

(f) If any person, who is registered as a collective investment scheme, including mutual funds, fails to invest money collected by such collective investment schemes in the manner or within the period specified in the regulations, he shall be liable to a penalty of one lakh rupees for each day during which such failure continues or one crore rupees, whichever is less.

5. *Penalty for failure to observe rules and regulations by an asset management company 15E*: Where any asset management company of a mutual fund registered under this Act fails to comply with any of the

regulations providing for restrictions on the activities of the asset management companies, such asset management company shall be liable to [a penalty of one lakh rupees for each day during which such failure continues or one crore rupees, whichever is less.

6. *Penalty for fFailure in Case of Stock Brokers:* If any person, who is registered as a stock broker under this Act—
   - Fails to issue contract notes in the form and manner specified by the stock exchange of which such broker is a member, he shall be liable to a penalty not exceeding five times the amount for which the contract note was required to be issued by that broker;
   - Fails to deliver any security or fails to make payment of the amount due to the investor in the manner or within the period specified in the regulations, he shall be liable to [a penalty of one lakh rupees for each day during which such failure continues or one crore rupees], whichever is less;
   - Charges an amount of brokerage which is in excess of the brokerage specified in the regulations, he shall be liable to [a penalty of one lakh rupees] or five times the amount of brokerage charged in excess of the specified brokerage, whichever is higher.
7. *Penalty for Insider Trading:* If any insider who—
   - Either on his own behalf or on behalf of any other person, deals in securities of a body corporate listed on any stock exchange on the basis of any unpublished price sensitive information; or
   - Communicates any unpublished price sensitive information to any person, with or without his request for such information except as required in the ordinary course of business or under any law; or
   - Counsels, or procures for any other person to deal in any securities of any body corporate on

the basis of unpublished price sensitive information, shall be liable to a penalty [twenty-five crore rupees] or three times the amount of profits made out of insider trading, whichever is higher.

8. *Penalty for Non-disclosure of Acquisition of Shares and Takeovers:* If any person, who is required under this Act or any rules or regulations made there-under, fails to—(i) disclose the aggregate of his shareholding in the body corporate before he acquires any shares of that body corporate; or make a public announcement to acquire shares at a minimum price, he shall be liable to a penalty [twenty-five crore rupees] or three times the amount of profits made out of such failure, whichever is higher or make a public offer by sending letter of offer to the shareholders of the concerned company; or make payment of consideration to the shareholders who sold their shares pursuant to letter of offer.
9. *Penalty for Fraudulent and Unfair Trade Practices:* If any person indulges in fraudulent and unfair trade practices relating to securities, he shall be liable to a penalty of twenty-five crore rupees or three times the amount of profits made out of such practices, whichever is higher.
10. *Penalty for Contraventions where no Separate Penalty has been Provided*: Whoever fails to comply with any provision of this Act, the rules or the regulations made or directions issued by the Board there-under for which no separate penalty has been provided, shall be liable to a penalty which may extend to one crore rupees.

SECURITIES APPELLATE TRIBUNAL

A Securities Appellate Tribunal shall consist of a Presiding Officer and two other Members, to be appointed, by notification, by the Central Government:

Powers of the Securities Appellate Tribunal

The Securities Appellate Tribunal shall not be bound by the procedure laid down by the Code of Civil Procedure, 1908, but shall be guided by the principles of natural justice and, subject to the other provisions of this Act and of any rules, the Securities Appellate Tribunal shall have powers to regulate their own procedure including the places at which they shall have their sittings.

The Securities Appellate Tribunal shall have, for the purposes of discharging their functions under this Act, the same powers as are vested in a civil court under the Code of Civil Procedure, 1908, while trying a suit, in respect of the following matters, namely: (a) summoning and enforcing the attendance of any person and examining him on oath; (b) requiring the discovery and production of documents; (c) receiving evidence on affidavits; (d) issuing commissions for the examination of witnesses or documents; (e) reviewing its decision; (f) dismissing an application for default or deciding it ex-parte; (g) setting aside any order of dismissal of any application for default or any order passed by it ex-parte; and (h) any other matter which may be prescribed.

Every proceeding before the Securities Appellate Tribunal shall be deemed to be a judicial proceeding within the meaning of sections 193 and 228, and for the purposes of section 196, of the Indian Penal Code and the Securities Appellate Tribunal shall be deemed to be a civil court for all the purposes of section 195 and Chapter XXVI of the Code of Criminal Procedure, 1973.

Power of Central Government to Issue Directions

The Board, in exercise of its powers or the performance of its functions under this Act or the Depositories Act, 1996 , be bound by such directions on questions of policy as the Central Government may give in writing to it from time to time. Provided that the Board shall, as far as practicable, be given an opportunity to express its views before any direction is given under this sub-section. The decision of the Central Government whether a question is one of policy or not shall be final.

Power of Central Government to Supersede the Board

In the following circumstances the Central Government may supersede the powers of the Board :

- On account of grave emergency, the Board is unable to discharge the functions and duties imposed on it by or under the provisions of this Act.
- That the Board has persistently made default in complying with any direction issued by the Central Government under this Act or in the discharge of the functions and duties imposed on it by or under the provisions of this Act and as a result of such default the financial position of the Board or the administration of the Board has deteriorated.
- That circumstances exist which render it necessary in the public interest so to do, the Central Government may, by notification, supersede the Board for such period, not exceeding six months, as may be specified in the notification.
- When notification is made all the members shall, as from the date of suppression, vacate their offices and all the powers functions and duties which may, by or under the provisions of this Act, be exercised or discharged by or on behalf of the Board, shall until the Board is reconstituted be exercised and discharged by such person or persons as the Central Government may direct; and all property owned or controlled by the Board shall, until the Board is reconstituted vest in the Central Government.
- On the expiration of the period of suppression specified in the notification, the Central Government may reconstitute the Board by fresh appointment and in such case any person or persons who vacated their offices and shall not be deemed disqualified for appointment. However, the Central Government may, at any time, before the expiration of the period of suppression, take action.
- The Central Government shall cause a notification issued, a full report of any action taken and the

circumstances leading to such action to be laid before each House of Parliament at the earliest.

REGULATIONS ON PORTFOLIO MANAGERS

An application by a portfolio manager for grant of the certificate shall be made to SEBI in the prescribed form-A. Incomplete applications shall be rejected after the applicant is given an opportunity to remove within the time specified such objections on the application as may be indicated by SEBI. Before disposing the application, SEBI may require the applicant to furnish further information or clarification and the applicant or its principal officer who is mainly responsible for the activities as a portfolio manager, shall appear before the SEBI to make a personal representation, if required.

Contract with Clients and Disclosures

The portfolio manager shall before taking up an assignment of management of funds or portfolio of securities in writing on behalf of a client, enter into an agreement in writing with such client clearly defining the interse relationship, and setting out their mutual rights, liabilities and obligations relating to management of funds or portfolio of securities. The agreement between the portfolio manager and the client shall, *inter alia*, contain:

- The investment objectives and the services to be provided;
- Areas of investment and restrictions, if any, imposed by the client with regard to the investment in a particular company or industry;
- Type of instruments and proportion of exposure;
- Tenure of portfolio investments;
- Terms for early withdrawal of funds or securities by the clients;
- Attendant risks involved in the management of the portfolio;
- Period of the contract and provision of early termination, if any;

- Amount to be invested subject to the restrictions provided under these regulations;
- Procedure of settling client's account including form of repayment on maturity or early termination of contract;
- Fees payable to the portfolio manager;
- The quantum and manner of fees payable by the client for each activity for which service is rendered by the portfolio manager directly or indirectly, where such service is out-sourced;
- Custody of securities;
- In case of a discretionary portfolio manager a condition that the liability of a client shall not exceed his investment with the portfolio manager;
- The terms of accounts and audit and furnishing of the reports to the clients as per the provisions of these regulations; and
- Other terms of portfolio investment subject to these regulations.

The portfolio manager shall provide to the client, the Disclosure Document, along with a certificate, at least two days prior to entering into an agreement with the client. The Disclosure Document shall *inter alia* contain the following:

- The quantum and manner of payment of fees payable by the client for each activity for which service is rendered by the portfolio manager directly or indirectly (where such service is out sourced);
- Portfolio risks;
- Complete disclosures in respect of transactions with related parties as per the accounting standards specified by the Institute of Chartered Accountants of India in this regard;
- The performance of the portfolio manager;
- Provided that the performance of a discretionary portfolio manager shall be calculated using weighted average method taking each individual category of investments for the immediately preceding three

years and in such cases performance indicators shall also be disclosed;

- The audited financial statements of the portfolio manager for the immediately preceding three years.
- The contents of the Disclosure Document shall be certified by an independent chartered accountant; and
- The portfolio manager shall file with the Board, a copy of the Disclosure Document before it is circulated or issued to any person and every six months thereafter or whenever any material change is effected therein whichever is earlier, along with the certificate in Form C as specified in Schedule I.

The portfolio manager shall charge an agreed fee from the clients for rendering portfolio management services without guaranteeing or assuring, either directly or indirectly, any return and the fee so charged may be a fixed fee or a return based fee or a combination of both. The portfolio manager may, subject to the disclosure in terms of the Disclosure Document and specific permission from the client, charge such fees from the client for each activity for which service is rendered by the portfolio manager directly or indirectly where such service is out sourced.

Investment of Clients' Moneys and Management of Clients' Portfolio of Securities

- The money or securities accepted by the portfolio manager shall not be invested or managed by the portfolio manager except in terms of the agreement between the portfolio manager and the client. Any renewal of portfolio fund on maturity of the initial period shall be deemed as a fresh placement.
- The funds or securities can be withdrawn or taken back by the client before the maturity of the contract under the following circumstances, namely—
- Voluntary or compulsory termination of portfolio management services by the portfolio manager or the client.

- Suspension or cancellation of the certificate of registration of the portfolio manager by the Board.
- Bankruptcy or liquidation of the portfolio manager.
- The portfolio manager shall invest funds of his clients in money market instruments [or derivatives] or as specified in the contract.
- Provided that leveraging of portfolio shall not be permitted in respect of investment in derivatives and also that the portfolio manager shall not deploy the clients' funds in bill discounting, badla financing or for the purpose of lending or placement with corporate or non-corporate bodies.
- The portfolio manager shall not while dealing with clients' funds indulges in speculative a transaction that is, he shall not enter into any transaction for purchase or sale of any security which is periodically or ultimately settled otherwise than by actual delivery or transfer of security except the transactions in derivatives.
- The portfolio manager shall, ordinarily purchase or sell securities separately for each client. However, in the event of aggregation of purchases or sales for economy of scale, interse allocation shall be done on a prorata basis and at weighted average price of the day's transactions. The portfolio manager shall not keep any open position in respect of allocation of sales or purchases effected in a day.
- Any transaction of purchase or sale including that between the portfolio manager's own accounts and client's accounts or between two clients' accounts shall be at the prevailing market price.
- The portfolio manager shall segregate each client's funds and portfolio of securities and keep them separately from his own funds and securities and be responsible for safekeeping of clients' funds and securities.
- The portfolio manager may hold the securities belonging to the portfolio account in own name on behalf of clients only if the contract so provides and in such an event the records of the portfolio manager

and report to the client should clearly indicate that the securities are held by on behalf of the portfolio account.

- The portfolio manager may, subject to authorisation by the client in writing, participate in securities lending.
- That the portfolio manager may manage funds raised or collected or brought from outside India in accordance with the Securities and Exchange Board of India (Foreign Institutional Investors) Regulations, 1995.

Contents of Agreement between the Portfolio Manager and his Clients

The following shall be mentioned in the agreement:

1. Appointment of Portfolio Manager
2. *Scope of Services*: Scope of services to be provided by the Portfolio Manager subject to the activities permitted under SEBI (Portfolio Managers) Regulations, 1993, viz, advisory, investment management, custody of securities, keeping track of corporate benefits associated with the securities. The Portfolio Manager shall act in a fiduciary capacity and as a trustee and agent of the clients' account.
3. *Functions, Obligations, Duties and Responsibilities:* Functions, obligations, duties and responsibilities as discretionary and non discretionary to be given separately) with specific provisions regarding instructions for non discretionary portfolio manager, inter alia : (i) terms in compliance with the Act, SEBI (Portfolio Managers)Regulations, 1993, rules, regulations, guidelines made under the Act and any other laws/rules/regulations/guidelines etc.; (ii) providing reports to clients; (iii) maintenance of client wise transaction and related books of accounts; (iv) provisions regarding audit of accounts as required under the SEBI (Portfolio Managers) Regulations, 1993; (v) settlement of accounts and procedure therefore including the provisions for

payment on maturity or early termination of the contract;

4. *Investment Objectives and Guidelines*: (i) Types of securities in which investment would be made specifying restrictions, if any. (ii) Particulars regarding amount, period of management, repayment or withdrawal. (iii) Taxation aspects such as Tax Deducted at Source etc., if any. (iv) Condition that the portfolio manager shall not lend the securities of the client unless authorized by him in writing.
5. *Risk Factors*: A detailed statement of risks associated with each type of investment including the standard risks associated with each type of investment and the risk factors specific to the scheme as well as those attendants to specific investment policies and objectives of the scheme.
6. *Period of Agreement*: Minimum period, if any, and provision for renewal, if any, to be mentioned.
7. *Conditions*: Conditions under which agreement may be altered, terminated and implications thereof, such as settlement of amounts invested, repayment obligations, etc. (i) Voluntary/mandatory termination by the Portfolio Manager, (ii) Voluntary/mandatory termination by the client, and (iii) Suspension by the Board or other regulatory authority.
8. *Maintenance of Accounts:* Maintenance of accounts separately in the name of the client as are necessary to account for the assets and any additions, income, receipts and disbursements in connection therewith, as provided under SEBI (Portfolio Managers) Regulations, 1993.
9. *Change in the Quantum of Funds to be Managed:* The conditions under which the client may withdraw cash or securities from the portfolio account or bring in additional cash to be managed as per the terms and conditions that apply. The portfolio manager shall not change any terms of the agreement without prior consent of the client.

10. *Access to Information:* Provisions enabling client to get the books of accounts of the portfolio manager relating to his transactions audited by a chartered accountant appointed by him and permitting the client an access to relevant and material documents of portfolio manager, provisions listing the documents for inspection along with timings for such inspection, furnishing of reports to the client subject to furnishing at least once in six months and the reports to be made available on the web site of the portfolio manager with restricted access to each client and other rights of clients, etc. The provision that the statements/documents/report furnished by the portfolio manager to the client present a true and fair picture of the actual transactions.
11. *Terms of Fees*: The quantum and manner of payment of fees and charges for each activity for which services are rendered by the portfolio manager directly or indirectly where such service is outsourced, such as investment management, advisory, transfer, registration and transaction costs with specific references to brokerage costs, custody charges, cost related to furnishing regular communication, account statement, miscellaneous expenses (individual expenses in excess of 5% to be indicated separately), etc. The provision that the portfolio manager shall take prior permission from the client in this respect.
12. *Billing:* Periodicity of billing, whether payment to be made in advance, manner of payment of fees, whether setting-off against the account, etc., type of documents evidencing receipt of payment of fees.
13. *Liability of Portfolio Manager:* Liability of Portfolio Manager in connection with recommendations made, to cover errors of judgment, negligence, wilful misfeasance in connection with discharge of duties, acts of other intermediaries, brokers, custodians, etc.
14. *Liability of Client:* Restricting the liability of the client to the extent of his investment.

15. *Death or Disability:* providing for continuation/termination of the agreement in event of client's death/disability. Succession, nomination, representation, etc. to be incorporated.
16. *Assignment:* Conditions for assignment of the agreement by client.
17. *Governing Law:* The law/jurisdiction of country/state which governs the agreement to be stated.
18. *Settlement of Grievances:* Provisions to cover protection of act done in good faith, risks and losses, redressal of grievances, dispute resolution mechanism, reference for arbitration and the situations under which such rights may arise, may be made.

Code of Conduct of Portfolio Manager

1. A Portfolio Manager shall, in the conduct of his business, observe high standards of integrity and fairness in all his dealings with his clients and other Portfolio Managers.
2. The money received by a portfolio manager from a client for an investment purpose should be deployed by the portfolio manager as soon as possible for that purpose and money due and payable to a client should be paid forthwith.
3. A Portfolio Manager shall render at all times high standards of service, exercise due diligence, ensure proper care and exercise independent professional judgment. The portfolio manager shall either avoid any conflict of interest in his investment or disinvestment decision, or where any conflict of interest arises; ensure fair treatment to all his customers. He shall disclose to the clients, possible sources of conflict of duties and interests, while providing unbiased services. A portfolio manager shall not place his interest above those of his clients.
4. A Portfolio Manager shall not make any statement or become privy to any act, practice or unfair competition, which is likely to be harmful to the interests of other Portfolio Managers or is likely to

place such other Portfolio Managers in a disadvantageous position in relation to the Portfolio Manager himself, while competing for or executing any assignment.

5. A Portfolio Manager shall not make any exaggerated statement, whether oral or written, to the client either about the qualification or the capability to render certain services or his achievements in regard to services rendered to other clients.
6. At the time of entering into a contract, the portfolio manager shall obtain in writing from the client, his interest in various corporate bodies which enables him to obtain unpublished price-sensitive information of the body corporate.
7. A Portfolio Manager shall not disclose to any clients, or press any confidential information about his client, which has come to his knowledge.
8. The portfolio manager shall where necessary and in the interest of the client take adequate steps for registration of the transfer of the clients' securities and for claiming and receiving dividends, interest payments and other rights accruing to the client. He shall also take necessary action for conversion of securities and subscription/renunciation of/or rights in accordance with the clients' instruction.
9. A Portfolio Manager shall endeavour to:
   - Ensure that the investors are provided with true and adequate information without making any misguiding or exaggerated claims and are made aware of attendant risks before any investment decision is taken by them.
   - Render the best possible advice to the client having regard to the client's needs and the environment, and his own professional skills.
   - Ensure that all professional dealings are effected in a prompt, efficient and cost effective manner.
10. A Portfolio Manager shall not be a party to:
    - Creation of false market in securities.
    - Price rigging or manipulation of securities.

- Passing of price sensitive information to brokers, members of the stock exchanges and any other intermediaries in the capital market or take any other action which is prejudicial to the interest of the investors.

11. No Portfolio manager or any of its directors, partners or manager shall either on their respective accounts or through their associates or family members, relatives enter into any transaction in securities of companies on the basis of unpublished price sensitive information obtained by them during the course of any professional assignment.
12. A Portfolio Manager or any his employees shall not render, directly or indirectly any investment advice about any security in the publicly accessible media, whether real-time or non-real-time, unless a disclosure of his long or short position in the said security has been made, while rendering such advice.
13. In case an employee of the Portfolio Manager is rendering such advice, he shall also disclose the interest of his dependent family members and the employer including their long or short position in the said security, while rendering such advice.
14. The portfolio manager shall abide by the Act, and the Rules, Regulations made there-under and the Guidelines/Schemes issued by the Board.
15. The portfolio manager shall comply with the model code of conduct specified in the SEBI (Prohibition of Insider Trading) Regulations, 1992.
16. The portfolio manager shall not use his status as any other registered intermediary to unduly influence the investment decision of the clients while rendering portfolio management services.

General Responsibilities of a Portfolio Manager

- The discretionary portfolio manager shall individually and independently manage the funds of each client in accordance with the needs of the client in a manner which does not par take character of a

Mutual Fund, whereas the non-discretionary portfolio manager shall manage the funds in accordance with the directions of the client. The portfolio manager shall not accept from the client, funds or securities worth less than five lacks rupees.

- The portfolio manager shall act in a fiduciary capacity with regard to the client's funds.
- The portfolio manager shall keep the funds of all clients in a separate account to be maintained by it in a Scheduled Commercial Bank.
- The portfolio manager shall transact in securities within the limitation placed by the client himself with regard to dealing in securities under the provisions of the Reserve Bank of India Act, 1934 (2 of 1934).
- The portfolio manager shall not derive any direct or indirect benefit out of the client's funds or securities.
- The portfolio manager shall not borrow funds or securities on behalf of the client.
- The portfolio manager shall not lend securities held on behalf of clients to a third person except as provided under these regulations.
- The portfolio manager shall ensure proper and timely handling of complaints from his clients and take appropriate action immediately.

UNDERWRITERS REGULATION

No person shall act as underwriter unless he holds a certificate granted by the Board under the regulations, Provided that such person, who was engaged as underwriter prior to the coming into force of the Act, may continue to carry on activity as underwriter if he has made an application for such registration till the disposal of such application. Every stock broker or merchant banker holding a valid certificate of registration shall be entitled to act as an underwriter without obtaining a separate certificate for underwriting activities.

Conditions for Grant or Renewal of Certificate to Underwriter: The certificate of registration or its renewal, as the case may be, shall be valid for a period of three years from the date of its issue to the underwriter. The Board may grant or renew a certificate to an underwriter subject to the following conditions namely:

- In case of any change in the status and constitution, the underwriter shall obtain prior permission of the Board to continue to act as underwriter;
- The underwriter shall enter into a valid agreement with the body corporate on whose behalf he is acting as underwriter and the said agreement amongst other things may define the allocation of duties and responsibilities between him and such body corporate;
- He shall pay the amount of fees of registration in the manner provided in the regulations;
- He shall abide by the rules and regulations made under the Act in respect of the activities carried on by him as an underwriter; and
- The certificate of registration or its renewal, as the case may be, shall be valid for a period of three years from the date of its issue to the underwriter.

Application for Grant of Certificate

An application by an underwriter for grant of a certificate shall be made to the Board in form A. The Board may require the applicant to furnish further information or clarification regarding matters relevant to underwriting to consider the application for grant of a certificate. If the Board, on receipt of further information, is of the opinion that the information so furnished is not sufficient to decide on the application and seeking further information through correspondence is likely to delay the matter, it may require the applicant or its principal officer to appear before the Board in order to give an opportunity to the applicant to give further clarifications on the application.

Application to Conform to the Requirements

Any application, which is not complete in all respects and does not conform to the instructions specified in the form, shall be rejected. Before rejecting any such application, the applicant shall be given an opportunity to remove within one month, such objections as may be indicated by the Board. The Board may also on sufficient reasons being shown extend the time by another one month in order to enable the applicant to comply with the requirements of the Board.

Consideration of Application

The Board shall take into account for considering the grant of a certificate, all matters which are relevant to or relating to underwriting and in particular the following, namely, whether the applicant—has the necessary infrastructure like adequate office space, equipments, and manpower to effectively discharge his activities:

- Has any past experience in underwriting or has in his employment minimum two persons who had the experience in underwriting or any person, directly or indirectly connected with the applicant has not been granted registration by the Board under the Act. For the purposes of this clause the Board shall take into account whether a previous application for a certificate of any person directly or indirectly connected with the applicant has been rejected by the Board or any disciplinary action has been taken against such person under the Act or any of the Rules or any of the Regulations made under the Act.
- Fulfils the capital adequacy requirements.
- Any of its director, partner or principal officer is or has at any time been convicted for any offence involving moral turpitude or has been found guilty of any economic offence.
- The applicant is a fit and proper person.

Capital Adequacy Requirement

- The capital adequacy requirement shall not be less than the net worth of rupees twenty lakhs.
- Every stock broker, who acts as an underwriter shall fulfil the capital adequacy requirements specified by the stock exchange of which he is a member;

- Every merchant banker, who acts as an underwriter shall fulfill the capital adequacy requirements the Securities and Exchange Board of India (Merchant Banker) Regulations, 1992. For the purposes of this regulation, "net worth" means in the case of an applicant being a proprietary concern or a firm or an association of persons or any body of individuals, the value of capital contributed to such business by the applicant and the free reserves of any kind belonging to the business of the applicant; and in the case of a body corporate, the value of the paid-up capital and the free reserves as disclosed in the books of accounts of the applicant at the time of making the application.

Procedure for Registration and Renewal

The Board on being satisfied that the applicant is eligible, shall send an intimation within one month of such satisfaction of the applicant mentioning that he has been found eligible for the grant of certificate and grant a certificate in form B subject to payment of fees. An underwriter may, if he so desires, make an application in form A for renewal of certificate before three months of the expiry of the period of certificate. The application for renewal of certificate shall be dealt with in the same manner as if it were an application for grant of a certificate.

Procedure where Registration is not Granted

Where an application for grant of a certificate or of renewal does not fulfil the requirements, the Board may reject the application, after giving an opportunity of being heard. The decision shall be communicated by the Board within thirty days of such decision stating therein the grounds on which the application has been rejected. Any applicant may, being aggrieved by the decision of the Board, apply within a period of thirty days from the date of receipt of such intimation, to the Board for reconsideration of its decision. On receipt of the application made, the Board shall reconsider its decision and communicate its findings thereon as soon as possible in writing to the applicant.

Any underwriter whose application for grant or renewal of a certificate has been refused by the Board shall on and from the date of the receipt of the communication, cease to act as an underwriter. If the Board is satisfied that it is in the interest of the investors, it may permit the underwriter to undertake the underwriting commitments already entered into by him during the validity period of the certificate.

Payment of Fees and the Consequences of Failure to Pay Fees

Every applicant eligible for grant or renewal of a certificate shall pay fees in such manner and within time. A stock broker or a merchant banker who, has been granted a certificate and pays fees under the Securities and Exchange Board of India (Stock Brokers and Sub-Brokers) Regulations, 1992 or Securities and Exchange Board of India (Merchant Bankers) Regulations, 1992, shall not be required to pay fees again. Where an underwriter fails to pay the fees as, the Board may suspend the certificate, whereupon the underwriter shall forthwith cease to act as an underwriter.

GENERAL OBLIGATIONS AND RESPONSIBILITIES

Agreement with Clients: Every underwriter shall enter into an agreement, with each body corporate on whose behalf he is acting as underwriter and the said agreement shall, amongst other things, provide for the following, namely :

- The period for which the agreement shall be in force;
- The amount of underwriting obligations;
- The period, within which the underwriter has to subscribe to the issue after being intimated by or on behalf of such body corporate;
- The amount of commission or brokerage payable to the underwriter; and
- Details of arrangements, if any, made by the underwriter for fulfilling the underwriting obligations.

General Responsibilities of an Underwriter

1. The underwriter shall not derive any direct or indirect benefit from underwriting the issue other than the commission or brokerage payable under an agreement for underwriting.
2. The total underwriting obligations under all the agreements referred to in clause (b) of rule 4 shall not exceed twenty times the net worth referred to in regulation 7.
3. Every underwriter, in the event of being called upon to subscribe for securities of a body corporate pursuant to an agreement referred to in clause (b) of rule 4 shall subscribe to such securities within 45 days of the receipt of such intimation from such body corporate.

To maintain proper books of accounts and records, etc.

- Subject to the provisions of any other law, every underwriter shall keep and maintain the following books of accounts and documents, namely :
- In relation to underwriter being a body corporate—a copy of the balance sheet and profit and loss account as specified in sections 211 and 212 of the Companies Act, 1956 or a copy of the auditor's report referred to in section 227 of the Companies Act.
- In relation to an underwriter not being a body corporate—records in respect of all sums of money received and expended by them and the matters in respect of which the receipt and expenditure take place; and their assets and liabilities.
- Every underwriter shall, after the close of each financial year as soon as possible but not later than six months from the close of the said period furnish to the Board if so required copies of the balance sheet, profit and loss account, statement of capital adequacy requirement and such other documents as may be required by the Board.

- Every underwriter shall also maintain the following records with respect to—details of all agreements.
- Total amount of securities of each body corporate subscribed.
- Statement of capital adequacy requirements.
- Other records as may be specified by the Board for underwriting.
- Every underwriter shall intimate to the Board the place where the books of accounts, records and documents are maintained.
- Every underwriter shall preserve the books of accounts and other records and documents mentioned under this chapter for a minimum period of five years.

Appointment of Compliance Officer

Every underwriter shall appoint a compliance officer who shall be responsible for monitoring the compliance of the Act, rules and regulations, notifications, guidelines, instructions, etc. issued by the Board or the Central Government and for redressal of investors' grievances. The compliance officer shall immediately and independently report to the Board any non-compliance observed by him.

Power to Call for Information

The Board may at any time call for any information from an underwriter with respect to any matter relating to underwriting business. Where any information is called for it shall be the duty of the underwriter to furnish such information.

INSPECTION AND DISCIPLINARY PROCEEDINGS

Board's right to inspect : Where it appears to the Board so to do, it may appoint one or more persons as inspecting authority to undertake the inspection of the books of accounts, other records and documents of the underwriter for any of the following purposes:

- To ensure that the books of accounts and other

records and documents are being maintained in the manner required;

- That the provisions of the Act, rules and regulations are being complied with;
- To investigate into the complaints received from investors, other underwriters or any other person on any matter having a bearing on the activities of the underwriter; and
- To investigate *suo-moto* in the interest of securities business or investors' interest into the affairs of the underwriter.

Procedure for Inspection

- Before undertaking an inspection, the Board shall give a reasonable notice to the underwriter, for that purpose.
- Where the Board is satisfied that in the interest of the investors or in the public interest no such notice should be given, it may by an order in writing direct that the inspection of the affairs of the underwriter be taken up without such notice.
- On being empowered by the Board, the inspecting authority shall undertake the inspection and the underwriter against whom an inspection is being carried out shall be bound to discharge his obligations.

Obligations of Underwriter on Inspection by the Board

- It shall be the duty of every director, proprietor, partner, officer and employee of the underwriter who is being inspected to produce to the inspecting authority such books, accounts and other documents in his custody or control and furnish him with the statements and information relating to an underwriter within such time as the inspecting authority may require.
- The underwriter shall allow the inspecting authority to have a reasonable access to the premises occupied

by such underwriter or by any other person, on his behalf and also extend reasonable facility for examining any books, records, documents and computer data in the possession of the underwriter or any such other person on their behalf and also provide copies of documents or other material which in the opinion of the inspecting authority are relevant for the purposes of the inspection.

- The inspecting authority shall in the course of inspection, be entitled to examine or record statements of any principal officer, director, partner, proprietor and employee.
- It shall be the duty of every director, proprietor, partner, officer or employee of the underwriter to give to the inspecting authority all assistance in connection with the inspection which the underwriter may reasonably be expected to give.
- The inspecting authority shall, as soon as may be possible, submit an inspection report to the Board. The Board shall after consideration of the inspection report communicate the findings to the underwriter to give him an opportunity of being heard before any action is taken by the Board on the findings of the inspecting authority.
- On receipt of the explanation, if any, from the underwriter the Board may call upon the underwriter to take such measures as the Board may deem fit in the interest of the securities market and for due compliance with the provisions of the Act, rules and regulations.

Appointment of Auditor

The Board may appoint a qualified auditor to investigate into the books of account of the affairs of the underwriter. Provided that the auditor so appointed shall have the same powers of the inspecting authority and the obligation of the underwriter and his employees shall be applicable to the investigation under this regulation. The expression "qualified auditor" shall have the same meaning as given to it in section 226 of the Companies Act, 1956.

Liability for Action in case of Default

An underwriter or a stock broker or a merchant banker entitled to carry on business of underwriting without obtaining a separate certificate who:

- Fails to comply with any conditions subject to which certificate has been granted.
- Contravenes any of the provisions of the Act, rules or regulations; shall be liable to penalties.
- The penalties may be either suspension of registration after enquiry for a specified period or cancellation of registration.

Suspension, Cancellation of Certificate

A penalty of suspension of certificate granted to an underwriter or a certificate of registration granted to a stock broker or a merchant banker entitled to carry on business of underwriting without obtaining a certificate, may be imposed where an underwriter or such stock broker or merchant banker:

1. Violates the provisions of the Act, rules or regulations.
2. Does not follow the code of conduct.
3. Fails to furnish any information relating to his business as underwriter as required by the Board.
4. Furnishes wrong or false information.
5. Does not submit periodical returns as required by the Board.
6. Does not co-operate in any enquiry conducted by the Board.
7. Indulges in manipulating or price rigging or cornering activities.
8. Is guilty of misconduct or improper or un-business like or unprofessional conduct.
9. Fails to maintain the capital adequacy.
10. Fails to pay the fees.
11. Violates the conditions of registration.
12. Fails to fulfil his underwriting obligations.
13. The Board for reasons to be recorded in writing, may in case of repeated defaults of the type mentioned

above impose a penalty of cancellation of certificate on the underwriter or cancellation of certificate of registration granted on a stock broker or a merchant banker.

14. A penalty of cancellation of certificate granted to an underwriter or a certificate of registration granted to a stock broker or a merchant banker entitled to carry on the business of underwriting under rule 3, may be imposed where they.
15. Indulge in deliberate manipulation or price rigging or cornering activities affecting the securities market and the investors' interest.
16. Are guilty of fraud, or is convicted of a criminal offence.
17. Violate any provision of Securities and Exchange Board of India.
18. Violate the provisions of the Act, rules and regulations;
19. Fails to fulfil more than once their underwriting obligations.
20. No order of penalty of suspension or cancellation shall be imposed except after holding an inquiry in accordance with the procedure.

Manner of Holding Enquiry before Suspension or Cancellation

1. For the purpose of holding an enquiry, the Board may appoint an enquiry officer.
2. The enquiry officer shall issue to the underwriter a notice at the registered office or the principal place of business of the underwriter.
3. The underwriter may, within thirty days from the date of receipt of such notice, furnish to the enquiry officer a reply together with copies of documentary or other evidence relied on by him or sought by the Board from the underwriter.
4. The enquiry officer shall, give a reasonable opportunity of hearing to the underwriter to enable him to make submissions in support of his reply.

5. Before the enquiry officer, the underwriter may either appear in person or through any person duly authorized by the underwriter.
6. No lawyer or advocate shall be permitted to represent the underwriter at the enquiry.
7. Where a lawyer or an advocate has been appointed by the Board as a presenting officer, it shall be lawful for the underwriter to present its case through a lawyer or advocate.
8. If it is considered necessary, the enquiry officer may ask the Board to appoint a presenting officer to present its case.
9. The enquiry officer shall, after taking into account all relevant facts and submissions made by the underwriter, submit a report to the Board and recommend the penalty to be awarded as also the justification of the penalty proposed.

Show-cause Notice and Order

1. On receipt of the report from the enquiry officer, the Board shall consider the same issue a show-cause notice as to why the penalty as it considers appropriate should not be imposed.
2. The underwriter shall within thirty days of the date of the receipt of the show-cause notice send a reply to the Board.
3. The Board after considering the reply to the show-cause notice, if received, shall as soon as possible but not later than thirty days from the receipt of the reply, if any, pass such order as it deems fit.
4. Every order passed shall be self-contained and give reasons for the conclusions stated therein including justification of the penalty imposed by that order.
5. The Board shall send a copy of the order to the underwriter.

Effect of Suspension and Cancellation of Certificate Granted to Underwriter

On and from the date of the suspension of the certificate

or certificate of registration granted to a stock broker or a merchant banker, the underwriter shall cease to act as an underwriter during the period of suspension. The Board may in the interest of the investors and securities market, permit the underwriter to complete his underwriting obligations specified in the agreement. On and from the date of cancellation of certificate or certificate of registration granted to a stock broker or a merchant banker, the underwriter shall with immediate effect cease to act as an underwriter. The order of the Board passed shall be published in at least two daily newspapers by the Board.

CODE OF CONDUCT FOR UNDERWRITERS

1. Every underwriter shall maintain high standards of integrity, dignity and fairness in all his dealings with his clients and other Underwriters in the conduct of his business.
2. An underwriter shall ensure that he and his personnel will act in an ethical manner in all his dealings with a body corporate making an issue of securities.
3. Every underwriter shall, at all times, render high standards of service, exercise due diligence, ensure proper care and exercise independent professional judgment.
4. Every underwriter shall disclose to the Issuer Company his possible source or potential areas of conflict of duties and interest while providing underwriting services.
5. Underwriter shall not indulge in any unfair competition, which is likely to be harmful to the interest of other underwriters carrying on the business of underwriting or likely to place such other underwriters in a disadvantageous position in relation to the underwriter while competing for, or carrying out any assignment.
6. No underwriter shall make any statement, either oral or written, which would misrepresent—the services that the underwriter is capable of performing for the,

or has rendered to other Issuer Company; his underwriting commitment.

7. No underwriter shall divulge to other Issuer, Press or any party any confidential information about his Issuer Company, which has come to his knowledge and deal in securities of any Issuer Company without making disclosure to the Board as required under the regulations and also to the Board of Directors of the Issuer Company.
8. No underwriter shall wilfully make untrue statement or suppress any material fact in any documents, reports, papers or information furnished to the Board.
9. An underwriter or any of his employees shall not render, directly or indirectly any investment advice about any security in the publicly accessible media, whether real-time or non-real-time, unless a disclosure of his interest including his long or short position in the said security has been made, while rendering such advice.
10. In case, an employee of the underwriter is rendering such advice, he shall also disclose the interest of his dependent family members and the employer including their long or short position in the said security, while rendering such advice

SEBI RULES ON REGISTRARS TO AN ISSUE AND SHARE TRANSFER AGENTS

Conditions for Grant or Renewal of Certificate

The Board may grant or renew a certificate to a registrar to an issue or a share transfer agent subject to the following conditions, namely :

- In case of any change in the status and constitution, it or he shall obtain prior permission of the Board to continue to act as registrar to an issue or share transfer agent;
- The registrar to an issue or share transfer agent, shall enter into a valid agreement with the body corporate

or the person or group of persons for or on whose behalf he is buying or selling or dealing in securities as a registrar to an issue or as a transfer agent and the said agreement amongst other things may define the allocation of duties and responsibilities between him and such body corporate or persons or group of persons, as the case may be;

- He pays the amount of fees for registration in the manner provided in the regulations;
- He maintains capital adequacy requirements specified in the regulations at all times during the period of the certificate or renewal thereof; and
- He shall take adequate steps for redressal of grievances of the investors within one month of the date of the receipt of the complaints and he shall keep the Board informed about the number, nature and other particulars of the complaints received and the manner in which such complaints have been redressed.

STOCK-BROKERS AND SUB-BROKERS REGULATIONS

(a) Application for Registration of Stock Broker

An application by a stock-broker for grant of a certificate shall be made through the stock exchange or stock exchange of which he is admitted as a member. The stock exchange shall forward the application form to the Board as early as possible, but not later than thirty days from the date of its receipt. The Board may require the applicant to furnish such further information or clarifications, regarding the dealings in securities and matters connected thereto to consider the application for grant of a certificate.

The Board shall take into account for considering the grant of a certificate all matters relating to buying, selling, or dealing in securities and in particular the following, namely, whether the stock broker is eligible to be admitted as a member of a stock exchange; has the necessary infrastructure like adequate office space, equipments and manpower to effectively discharge his activities; has any past experience in the business of buying, selling or dealing in securities; is subjected to disciplinary proceedings under the rules, regulations and bye-laws of a stock exchange with respect to his business as a stock-broker involving either himself or any of his partners, directors or employees.

The Board on being satisfied that the stock-broker is eligible shall grant a certificate in Form D to the stock-broker and send an intimation to that effect to the stock exchange or stock exchanges as the case may be. The stock-broker holding a certificate shall at all times abide by the Code of Conduct.

(b) Procedure where Registration is not Granted

A stock-broker, whose application for grant of a certificate has been refused by the Board, shall not, on and from the date of the receipt of the communication, buy, sell, or deal in securities as a stock-broker.

Where an application for grant of a certificate, does not fulfill the requirements, the Board may reject the application after giving a reasonable opportunity of being heard. The refusal to grant the registration certificate shall be communicated by the Board within thirty days of such refusal to the concerned stock exchange and to the applicant stating therein the grounds on which the application has been rejected. An applicant may, being aggrieved by the decision of the Board may apply within a period of thirty days from the date of receipt of such intimation, to the Board for reconsideration of its decision. The Board shall reconsider an application made and communicate its decision as soon as possible in writing to the applicant and to the concerned stock-exchange.

(c) Application for Registration of Sub-broker

An application by a sub- broker for the grant of a certificate shall be made. The application for registration shall be accompanied by a recommendation letter from a stock-broker of a recognized stock exchange with whom he is to be affiliated along with two references including one from his banker. The application form shall be submitted to the stock exchange of which the stock-broker with whom he is to be affiliated is a member. The stock exchange on receipt of an application shall verify the information contained therein and shall also certify that the applicant is eligible for registration as per criteria. The eligibility criteria for registration as a sub-broker shall be as follows, namely:

In the case of an individual:

- The applicant is not less than 21 years of age.
- The applicant has not been convicted of any offence involving fraud or dishonesty.
- The applicant has at least passed 12th standard equivalent examination from an institution recognized by the Government.
- The applicant is a fit and proper person.
- The Board may relax the educational qualifications on merits having regard to the applicant's experience.

In the case of partnership firm or a body corporate it has the necessary infrastructure like adequate office space, equipment and manpower to effectively discharge his activities and shall be a person recognized by the Stock Exchange as a sub-broker affiliated to a member broker of a stock exchange. The Board on being satisfied that the sub-broker is eligible, shall grant a certificate in Form E to the sub-broker and send an intimation to that effect to the stock exchange or stock exchanges as the case may be. The Board may grant a certificate of registration to the appellant subject to the terms and conditions as stated in rule.

(d) Application for Registration of Trading Member or Clearing Member

An application for grant of certificate of registration by a trading member of a derivatives exchange or derivatives segment of a stock exchange shall be made in Form AA of Schedule I, through the concerned derivatives exchange or derivative segment of a stock exchange of which he is a member. An application for grant of certificate of registration by a clearing member or self-clearing member of the clearing corporation or clearing house of a derivatives exchange or derivatives segment of a stock exchange, shall be made in Form AA of Schedule I, through the concerned clearing corporation or clearing house of which he is a member. The derivatives exchange or segment or clearing house or corporation as the case may be shall forward the application to the Board as early as possible but not later than thirty days from the date of its receipt.

CODE OF CONDUCT FOR STOCK BROKERS

Integrity: A stock-broker, shall maintain high standards of integrity, promptitude and fairness in the conduct of all his business.

Exercise of Due Skill and Care: A stock-broker, shall act with due skill, care and diligence in the conduct of all his business.

Manipulation: A stock-broker shall not indulge in manipulative, fraudulent or deceptive transactions or schemes or spread rumours with a view to distorting market equilibrium or making personal gains.

Malpractices: A stock-broker shall not create false market either singly or in concert with others or indulge in any act detrimental to the investor's interest or which leads to interference with the fair and smooth functioning of the market. A stock-broker shall not involve himself in excessive speculative business in the market beyond reasonable levels not commensurate with his financial soundness.

Compliance with Statutory Requirements: A stock-broker shall abide by all the provisions of the Act and the rules, regulations issued by the Government, the Board and the stock exchange from time to time as may be applicable to him.

DUTY TO THE INVESTOR

Execution of Orders: A stock-broker, in his dealings with the clients and the general investing public, shall faithfully execute the orders for buying and selling of securities at the best available market price and not refuse to deal with a Small Investor merely on the ground of the volume of business involved. A stock-broker shall promptly inform his client about the execution or non-execution of an order, and make prompt payment in respect of securities sold and arrange for prompt delivery of securities purchased by clients.

Issue of Contract Note: A stock-broker shall issue without delay to his client or client of sub-broker a contract note for all transactions in the form specified by the stock exchange.

Breach of Trust: A stock-broker shall not disclose or discuss with any other person or make improper use of the details of personal investments and other information of a confidential nature of the client which he comes to know in his business relationship.

Business and Commission: A stock-broker shall not encourage sales or purchases of securities with the sole object of generating brokerage or commission. A stock-broker shall not furnish false or misleading quotations or give any other false or misleading advice or information to the clients with a view of inducing him to do business in particular securities and enabling himself to earn brokerage or commission thereby.

Business of Defaulting Clients: A stock-broker shall not deal or transact business knowingly, directly or indirectly or execute an order for a client who has failed to carry out his commitments in relation to securities with another stock-broker.

Fairness to Clients: A stock-broker, when dealing with a client, shall disclose whether he is acting as a principal or as an agent and shall ensure at the same time that no conflict of interest arises between him and the client. In the event of a conflict of interest, he shall inform the client accordingly and shall not seek to gain a direct or indirect personal advantage from the situation and shall not consider clients' interest inferior to his own.

Investment Advice: A stock-broker shall not make a recommendation to any client who might be expected to rely thereon to acquire, dispose of, retain any securities unless he has reasonable grounds for believing that the recommendation is suitable for such a client upon the basis of the facts, if disclosed by such a client as to his own security holdings, financial situation and objectives of such investment. The stock-broker should seek such information from clients, wherever he feels it is appropriate to do so.

Investment Advice in publicly accessible media: A stock broker or any of his employees shall not render, directly or indirectly, any investment advice about any security in the publicly accessible media, whether real—time or non real-time, unless a disclosure of his interest including the interest of his dependent family members and the employer including their long or short position in the said security has been made, while rendering such advice. In case, an employee of the stock broker is rendering such advice, he shall also disclose the interest of his dependent family members and the employer including their long or short position in the said security, while rendering such advice.

Competence of Stock Broker: A stock-broker should have adequately trained staff and arrangements to render fair, prompt and competent services to his clients.

STOCK-BROKERS *VIS-A-VIS* OTHER STOCK-BROKERS

Conduct of Dealings: A stock-broker shall co-operate with the other contracting party in comparing unmatched transactions. A stock-broker shall not knowingly and willfully deliver documents which constitute bad delivery and shall co-operate with other contracting party for prompt replacement of documents which are declared as bad delivery.

Protection of Clients Interests: A stock-broker shall extend fullest co-operation to other stock-brokers in protecting the interests of his clients regarding their rights to dividends, bonus shares, right shares and any other right related to such securities.

Transactions with Stock-Brokers: A stock-broker shall carry out his transactions with other stock-brokers and shall comply with his obligations in completing the settlement of transactions with them.

Advertisement and Publicity: A stock-broker shall not advertise his business publicly unless permitted by the stock exchange.

Inducement of Clients: A stock-broker shall not resort to unfair means of inducing clients from other stock-brokers.

False or Misleading Returns: A stock-broker shall not neglect or fail or refuse to submit the required returns and not make any false or misleading statement on any returns required to be submitted to the Board and the stock exchange.

SEBI RULES ON BANKERS TO AN ISSUE

Conditions for Grant or Renewal of Certificate

The Board may grant or renew a certificate to a banker to an issue subject to the following conditions, namely:

- He shall enter into a legally binding agreement with the body corporate for or on whose behalf he is acting as banker to an issue stating therein the duties and responsibilities between himself and the body corporate for the issue for which he is acting as a banker to an issue;
- He shall pay the amount of fees for registration in the manner provided in the regulations;
- He shall take adequate steps for redressal of grievances of the investors within one month of the date of the receipt of the complaints and he shall keep the Board informed about the number, nature and other particulars of the complaints received and the manner in which such complaints have been redressed;
- The certificate granted shall be valid for a period of three years from the date of the grant of the same; and
- The Board may grant the renewal of the certificate to a banker to an issue.

SEBI RULES ON DEBENTURE TRUSTEES

No person shall act as debenture trustee unless he holds a certificate granted by the Board under the regulations, provided that such person who was engaged as debenture trustee prior to the coming into force of the Act, may continue to act as debenture trustee if he has made an application for such registration till the disposal of such application.

Conditions of Grant or Renewal of Certificate

The certificate or its renewal, as the case may be, shall be valid for a period of three years from the date of its issue to the debenture trustee. The Board may grant or renew a certificate to an debenture trustee subject to the following conditions, namely:

- In case of any change in the status and constitution the debenture trustee shall obtain prior Permission of the Board to continue to act as debenture trustee;
- He pays the amount of fees of registration or renewal as the case may be in the manner provided in the regulations;
- He shall abide by the rules and regulations; and
- He shall take adequate steps for redressal of grievances of the investors within one month of the date of the receipt of the complaints and he shall keep the Board informed about the number, nature and other particulars of the complaints received and the manner in which such complaints have been redressed.

8

Merchant Banking

Amsterdam was the international finance capital for a long time. Hence, Amsterdam merchants became the first masters of the various financial techniques and developments which, in the course of time, became identified with the emergent profession of Merchant Bankers. The term 'Merchant Banking' came from the early years of banking when only merchants required the facilities of finance. The term has been retained because; it reflects the nature of those banks which provide financial services to the business community.

INDIAN HISTORY OF MERCHANT BANKING

Merchant Banking in India is of recent origin. It had its beginning in India in 1967, when Grindlays Bank established a division followed by City Bank in 1970 (now it has ceased to provide merchant banking services) and the State Bank of India in 1972. Later on ICICI set-up their merchant banking division followed by a few other banks likes Syndicate Bank, Bank of India, Bank of Baroda, Charted Bank, Mercantile Bank, etc. The merchant banks, as they have developed in our country could be broadly classified into three categories. The first category consists of the division of commercial banks, the second category comprises of National and State level financial corporations. The third category includes leading broker firms who have extended their activities into merchant banking.

After setting up of SEBI, the term 'Merchant Banker' was officially defined. Accordingly, "A Merchant Banker means any person who is engaged in the business of Issue Management either by making arrangements regarding selling, buying or subscribing to Securities as Manager, Consultant, Adviser of rendering Corporate Advisory Service in relation to such Issue Management". This is stated in the SEBI (Merchant Bankers) Rules, 1922.

Commercial Banking and Investment Banking are often confused, with Merchant Banking. In many ways, there may be similarities in their functions. However, in certain ways, Merchant Banking is distinctly different from commercial Banking and Investment Banking. The primary function of a commercial bank is to receive deposits from customers and lend the same to others. But the functions of a merchant banker are different. Commercial banks can undertake some of the merchant banking activities like Issue management, etc. The Merchant Banker mainly deals the issue management, post issue services, corporate advisory services, etc.

Investment Banker does more services than the merchant banker which include issue of securities, undertaking merger and acquisitions for clients, global custody services to local fund managers, trading and market making, and so on. Merchant banking is purely fee-based service whereas; investment banker service is both fee and fund-based service. The Merchant Banker advises corporation and firms relating to opening of issues, receiving loans and the like, which the management consultants also do. The management consultant (have a wide area operations like production, Marketing, Personnel Relations, to finance, etc. But they lack statutory recognition to undertake capital market related activities which has enabled the merchant banker to cater to the heeds the Corporate Sector. A merchant bank may be considered as an institution which centers its operations on all or most of the following activities.

- Corporate financial advice, on such diverse matters as new share and bond issues, capital reconstructions, mergers and acquisitions;
- The takings of deposits and currency, money market operations including foreign exchange dealings;
- Medium-term lending and syndication of loans;
- Acceptance credits and all forms of export finance;
- The holding and dealing in quoted and unquoted investments; and
- Fund management on behalf of clients, most typically pension funds, unit trust, investment trusts and wealthy individuals.

The Merchant Banking provide a number of specialized services like lending money on short or medium-terms or advising companies on the best method of raising long-term loans. Merchant Banking may also run something akin to a "Marriage Bureau"—matching companies wishing to expand by amalgamation or help fight against a takeover bid. They provide fund management services and advices on the best methods of using these funds profitably. They also run their own unit trusts and also manage pension funds for their clients. Authorization for a Merchant Banker. If any person or body is interested in the business of merchant banking either to start it as a new business or to add it to its existing business, would need Authorization from SEBI. This will grant a certificate of registration as a merchant banker. SEBI will look into the following aspects before granting certificate to this effect:

- *Professional Competence:* Whether the person or the body requiring authorization has the necessary professional know-how and the competence to successfully run the business smoothly.
- *Capital:* Whether they have adequate capital and ready financial resources.
- *Track Record:* The person or firm should possess a clear record and their performance in the past is considered. The amount of experience they have,

their general reputation and fairness in all their transactions are also scrutinized.

- *Infrastructure:* The quality of their personnel and the basic foundation and infrastructure are also considered by SEBI.
- *Net Worth:* The most important factor is the net worth of a prospective merchant banker. SEBI lays down that all MB must be worth at least Rupees one crore. However, this rule has now been amended for the benefit of Merchant Bankers and now a varying net worth level has been introduced based on the category that an applicant opts for.

ELIGIBILITY FOR GRANT OF MERCHANT BANKER CERTIFICATION

1. The applicant shall be a body corporate other than a non-banking financial company.
2. Only a bank or a public financial institution can be granted a certificate of registration as merchant banker.
3. The applicant has the necessary infrastructure like adequate office space, equipments and manpower to effectively discharge his activities.
4. The applicant has in his employment a minimum of two persons who have the experience to conduct the business of the merchant banker.
5. A person directly or indirectly connected with the applicant has not been granted registration by SEBI.
6. The applicant fulfils the capital adequacy requirement.
7. The applicant, his partner, director or principal officer is not involved in any litigation connected with the securities market which has an adverse bearing on the business of the applicant.
8. The applicant, his director, partner or principal officer has not at any time been convicted for any offence involving moral turpitude or has been found guilty of any offence.

9. The applicant has the professional qualification from an institution recognized by the Government in finance, law or business management.
10. The applicant is a fit and proper person; grant of certificate to the applicant is in the interest of investors.

FUNCTIONS OF A MERCHANT BANKER

1. *Issue Management:* This consists *inter alia,* the preparation of prospectus and other information relating to the issue of shares, bonds, debentures, etc. Tie-up of financiers and determining the financial structure are also taken up by the Merchant bankers. The following are the services rendered by merchant bankers in issue related matters:
   - Advising the company on planning and timing of the issue.
   - Obtaining the consent of the SEBI including their approval for reservation of shares for non-residents (on repatriation basis) employees and business associates.
   - Drafting and finalizing the letter of offer and getting the same approved by the stock exchanges wherever the shares are listed in case of right issues.
   - Computation of amount of debentures that can be raised as per the prevailing government guidelines.
   - Making necessary arrangements for underwriting the issue by financial institutions, banks and/or brokers.
   - Selection and appointment of a principal broker, brokers and bankers to the issue.
   - Selection and appointment of an issue house and fixing their remuneration.
   - Selection and appointment of advertising consultants/agencies for organizing the necessary publicity campaign including press

and brokers/investors' conferences at important centers.

- Preparing the draft prospectus, where necessary, 'having it approved by solicitors.
- Obtaining the clearance of financial institutions, bankers, other underwriters and stock exchanges for the draft prospectus.
- Arranging for designing and printing of draft prospectus as well as despatch of the final prospectus.
- Filing a copy of the prospectus along with the other necessary documents required.
- Making an application to stock exchanges to have the shares listed and comply with all the listing requirements.
- Obtaining permission from the Reserve Bank of India for offering shares/debentures to non-residents and for opening Foreign Currency Collection Accounts at overseas branches.
- Advising the strategy of marketing the issue amongst non-residents.
- Arranging investors' conferences and publicity campaigns abroad.
- Arranging for collection of application moneys at overseas branches.

2. *Post-issue Services:* This includes the issuing of refund orders for rejected applications or over-subscribed issues and also partial payment towards the shares such as the call money, etc.
3. *Portfolio Management Services*: Portfolio management include, advising the right mix of securities for maximum returns with minimum risk and undertaking to sell/buy securities on authorization.
4. *Corporate Advisor Services:* It advises corporations and firms relating to opening of issues receiving loans.
5. *Project Appraisal and Project Counseling:* This includes helping those people who have finance but who do not have the competence or the technical know-how required for running a successful business. The Merchant banker brings such people together and

guides them to invest their money in the right kind of business suitable to them as well as quite profitable. Assist corporate houses for incorporation and obtain letter of intent/industrial license. And license for imports and exports for import of capital goods. Assists appointing outside technical consultancy organizations, if considered necessary, for preparation of a detailed project report, market survey report, feasibility study, etc. scrutinize the project from all angles. Undertaking of obtaining consents of the government agencies such as Ministry of Industry, SEBI, Reserve Bank of India, and other agencies from whom permission need to be obtained as per law.

6. *Loan Syndication:* Sometimes the merchant banker might be approached for loans by its clients. In such cases, it surveys the market and acquires loans from rich organizations and also sometimes from foreign organizations to be invested in the country. Thus, it also helps its clients and at the same time increases the foreign currency reserve of the country. Various services offered by merchant bankers under this banner includes:
   - Assist promoters to raise finance from financial institutions and banks for modernization and expansion.
   - Arrange consortium meetings.
   - Prepare necessary documents.
   - Execution of necessary documents, registration of charges, etc.
   - Arrange Syndication of foreign currency loans or guarantees whenever required.
7. *Bought out Deals:* Some portion of equity to be offered to the investing public is taken up in the first instance by the merchant banker. Later these shares are placed with the public at a price which will fetch reasonable and adequate return.
8. *Venture Finance*: At the initial period of venture, merchant banker provide long-term start up funds for high risk and hi-tech ventures promoted by new

entrepreneurs, who suffer from capital deficiencies but have a high profit potential. Funding an emerging high risk, hi-tech project based purely on research and development activities can be termed as venture financing. It is a long-term financial arrangement and oriented towards capital gains. It is a source of financing for hi-tech industries that uses a new technology. It supports the early stages of a company's life.

9. *Off-shore Banking:* Merchant Bankers are now allowed to get loans from other countries and invest it in safe and profitable ventures. Here, the MB receives loans from a foreign country which can be invested in the home country but the same cannot be done vice-versa.
10. *Management of Fixed Deposits*: The merchant bankers are the intermediaries in fulfilling the financial needs of the corporate houses. In the matters of raising money through fixed deposits the following services are offered by them:
    - Ascertaining the amount that a company can be raised by way of deposits.
    - Advising the company on terms and conditions for acceptance of fixed deposits and the rate of interest to be paid thereon keeping in view the prevailing market conditions.
    - Assisting the company in fulfilling the conditions for raising deposits.
    - Drafting and filing a copy of an advertisement.
    - Arranging for issue of advertisement in newspapers.
    - Drafting of application form and arranging printing thereof.
    - Arranging for collection of deposits at various branches of the bank and presenting periodical statements on the collection of deposits to the company.
    - Arranging through the company for payment of interest warrants.

From 1st July1998, SEBI has advised that merchant bankers shall undertake only those activities which relate to securities market. These activities are:

- Managing of public issue of securities.
- Underwriting connected with the aforesaid public issue management business.
- Managing/Advising on international offerings of debt/equity, i.e. GDR, ADR, bonds and other instruments
- Private placement of securities.
- Primary or satellite dealership of government securities.
- Corporate advisory services related to securities market including takeovers, acquisition and disinvestment.
- Stock broking.
- Advisory services for projects.
- Syndication of rupee term loans.
- International financial advisory services.

Merchant bankers permitted to carry on activities of primary dealers. SEBI has permitted merchant bankers who are registered with RBI as NBFC for primary and satellite dealership of Government securities.

Following are the primary market intermediaries approved by SEBI:

- Merchant Bankers/Lead Managers.
- Portfolio Managers
- Registrars and Transfer Agents.
- Bankers to issue.
- Debenture Trustees.
- Underwriters.

With the assistance of these intermediaries, a company reaches its prospective investors and work as a team to complete the issue. After the abolition of the Capital Issues (Control) Act, SEBI has introduced a free pricing system in which the issuer and the merchant bankers are entrusted with the task of pricing the issue in a reasonable manner. SEBI has issued guidelines in respect of each intermediary to ensure proper services to be rendered by them to the investors and the capital market.

The activities of the merchant bankers in the Indian capital market are regulated by SEBI (Merchant Bankers) Rules, 1992 and SEBI (Merchant Bankers) Regulations. Merchant Banker according to the regulation means 'any person engaged in the business of issue management by making arrangements regarding selling, buying or subscribing to securities or acting as manager/consultant/advisor or rendering corporate advisory services in relation to such issue management'. No person shall carry on any activity as a merchant banker unless it holds a certificate of registration granted by SEBI under the relevant regulations. This certificate to a merchant banker may be renewed subject to the following conditions:

- The merchant banker in case of any change in its status or constitution shall obtain prior permission of SEBI to carry on its activities as a merchant banker.
- He shall pay the amount of fees for registration for renewal.
- He shall take adequate steps for redressal of grievances of the investors within one month of the date of receipt of the complaint and keep the board informed about the number, nature and other particulars of the complaints received.
- He shall abide by the rules and regulations made under the Act in respect of the activities carried on by the merchant banker.

OBLIGATIONS OF MERCHANT BANKERS

1. **Specific responsibilities must be taken up by each divisional or lead manager. A statement of *inter-se* allocation of responsibilities in the prescribed format, jointly signed by all lead managers has to be submitted to SEBI.**
2. **A certificate of due-diligence certifying the contents of the Prospectus/Letter of offer and the**

reasonableness of the views expressed therein also has to be submitted to SEBI.
3. The above-mentioned documents together with a copy of the draft prospectus has to be submitted to SEBI at least 15 days before filing it with the registrar of companies.
4. Each Lead Manager has to accept a minimum underwriting obligation of 5% of the total underwriting or Rs. 25 lakhs whichever is lower.
5. The Lead Managers have to ensure that the issue-related publicity and all advertising material is in conformity with the contents of the prospectus. The information given or views expressed in conferences also cannot be materially different from the contents of the prospectus.

CODE OF CONDUCT OF MERCHANT BANKER

- A merchant banker in the conduct of his business shall observe high standards of integrity and fairness in all his dealings with his clients and other merchant.
- A merchant banker shall render at all times high standards of service, exercise diligence, ensure proper care and exercise independent professional judgment.
- It shall wherever necessary, disclose to the clients, possible sources of conflict of duties and interests.
- A merchant banker shall not make any statement or become privy to any act, practice or unfair competition, which is likely to be harmful to the interests of other merchant bankers or is likely to place such other merchant bankers in a disadvantageous position in relation to the merchant banker, while competing for or executing any assignment.
- A merchant banker shall not make any exaggerated statement, whether oral or written, to the client either about the qualification or the capability to render certain services or his achievements in regard to services rendered to other clients.

- A merchant banker shall always endeavour to render the best possible advice to the clients having regard to the client's needs and the environments and his own professional skill; and
- It has to ensure that all professional dealings are effected in a prompt, efficient and cost effective manner.
- A merchant banker shall not divulge to other clients, press or any other party any confidential information about his client, which has come to his knowledge; and deal in securities of any client company without making disclosure to the Board as required under the regulations and also to the Board of Directors of the client company.
- A merchant banker has to ensure that the investors are provided with true and adequate information without making any misguiding or exaggerated claims and are made aware of attendant risks before any investment decision is taken by them and copies of prospectus, memorandum and related literature are made available to the investors.
- It should see that adequate steps are taken for fair allotment of securities and refund of application money without delay and grievance from investors are adequately dealt with.
- The merchant bankers should not generally and particularly in respect of issue of any securities be a party to creation of false market or price rigging or manipulation or passing of price sensitive information to brokers, members of the stock exchanges and other players in the capital market or take any other action which is unethical or unfair to the investors.
- A merchant banker shall abide by the provisions of the Act, rules and regulations and which may be applicable and relevant to the activities carried on by the merchant banker.

SEBI GUIDELINES ON LEAD MERCHANT BANKER

All public issues should be managed by at least one merchant banker functioning as the lead merchant banker. In the case of issue of rights shares to the existing members with or without the right of renunciation, the amount of the issue of the body corporate does not exceed Rs. 50 lakhs, the need not be a lead merchant banker. Every lead merchant banker shall, before taking up the assignment relating to an issue, enter into an agreement with the issuing company setting out their mutual rights, liabilities and obligations relating to such issue and in particular to disclosures, allotment and refund.

RESPONSIBILITIES OF LEAD MANAGERS

1. No lead manager shall agree to manage or be associated with any issue unless his responsibilities relating to the issue mainly those of disclosures, allotment and refund are clearly defined, allocated and determined.
2. A statement specifying such responsibilities is furnished to SEBI at least 1 month before the opening of the issue for subscription.
3. **Where there are more than 1 lead merchant banker to the issue, the responsibility of each such lead merchant banker shall clearly be demarcated and the statement specifying such responsibilities shall be furnished to SEBI at least 1 month before the opening of the issue for subscription.**
4. **No lead merchant banker shall agree to manage the issue made by anybody corporate if such body corporate is an associate of the lead merchant banker.**
5. ***Underwriting Obligation*: In respect of every issue to be managed, the lead merchant banker holding a certificate under Category I shall accept a minimum underwriting obligation of 5% of the total underwriting commitment or Rs. 25 lakhs whichever is less but if the lead merchant banker is unable to accept the minimum underwriting obligation, that lead merchant banker shall make arrangement for**

having the issue underwritten to that extent by a merchant banker associated with the issue and shall keep SEBI informed of such arrangement.

6. *Due Diligence by Merchant Banker*: The lead merchant banker, to be responsible for verification of the contents of a prospectus or the letter of offer in respect of an issue and reasonableness of the views expressed therein, to submit to SEBI at least 2 weeks prior to the opening of the issue for subscription, a due diligence certificate in the prescribed form, confirming that the draft prospectus/letter of offer forwarded to SEBI is in conformity with the documents, materials and papers relevant to the issue, that all the legal requirements connected with the said issue have been duly complied with and that the disclosures made in draft prospectus/letter of offer are true, fair and adequate to enable the investors to make a well informed decision as to the investments in the proposed issue.
7. Merchant Banker shall also examine various documents including those relating to litigation like commercial disputes, patent disputes, disputes with collaborators etc. and also discuss with the company its directors and other officers and other agencies on matters including objects of the issue, projected profitability, price justification, etc. before giving the due diligence certificate.
8. A merchant banker shall also include in the due diligence certificate, important documents including documents in support of the track record and experience of the promoters and their professional competence, listing agreement of the company for existing securities traded on the stock exchanges, consent letters from company's auditors, bankers to issue, bankers to the company, lead managers, brokers, proposed trustees, etc., auditor's certificate regarding tax benefits available to the company, shareholders and debenture holders, reports from Government agencies/expert agencies/consultants/ company regarding market demand and supply for

the product, industry scenario, standing of the foreign collaborators, etc., certification of revaluation of Company's assets given by' government valuer, certificate of compliance with FEMA/MRTP/RBI regulations in relation to prospectus/NRI allotments/ foreign collaboration terms obtained from Company's Solicitors. In other words, the merchant bankers have to apply their mind to every important aspect of the company's past performance and future prospects in order to protect the interest of the capital market to the investors.

9. The merchant banker shall ensure that every draft offer document submitted to SEBI shall be accompanied by undertakings and certificates from CEO of the Company Secretary/Promoters/Lead Manager to assure that all necessary arrangements have been made to ensure compliance of the various laws falling within their responsibility and to offer due protection to the investors.
10. These matters include investors' complaints, refunds, issue of certificates for the securities, and promoters' contribution, underwriting arrangements, etc.
11. The lead managers among other things should issue clear instructions/advice to the investors and the bankers and ensure compliance in regard to the utilization of the stock invest scheme, buy back arrangement for purchase of non-convertible partion of partly convertible debentures (PCD), creation of trust for disposal of odd lots, etc.
12. The Merchant Bankers should see that the listed company appoints a compliance officer to directly liaise with SEBI in regard to implementation/ compliance of the various laws, rules and regulations and directives and for settlement of investors' complaints.
13. The name of the compliance officer should be intimated to SEBI and also mentioned in the offer document relating to the capital issue with details, telephone number, fax number and address of the said compliance officer.

14. The lead manager shall ensure that the disclaimer clause and the risk factors are printed prominently in the offer document/prospectus while highlighting issue highlights, capital structure, etc.
15. The lead manager should also see that the various intermediaries associated by the issue are registered with SEBI and that they are competent and capable to discharge their responsibilities.
16. They should also ensure that the bankers to the issue are appointed in all the mandatory collection centers all over the country.
17. The issue material meant for the public should be despatched well in advance to the stock exchanges, brokers, and underwriters to avoid compliance of non-availability of application forms.
18. In the case of rights issue the lead manager should see to it that the letters of offer are despatched to all the existing shareholders at least one week before the date of opening of the issue.
19. Regarding underwriting, the lead manager should observe all the conditions prescribed by SEBI and that in the case of a devolvement on underwriters, the underwriters should give a letter of acceptance for the amount of devolvement within 60 days from the date of closure of the issue and pay the amount within 90 days. Any dispute in this regard shall be brought to the notice of SEBI by the lead manager.
20. Wrong and misleading advertisements should be prevented by the lead manager, ensuring compliance with SEBI guidelines on the subject.

POST-ISSUE OBLIGATIONS

1. The lead manager shall among other things confirm to SEBI within 7 days from the date of closure of the issue as to whether the issue is subscribed to the extent of 90%.
2. It shall submit the 45 days compliance report to SEBI before the close the next working day without fail, maintaining close co-ordination with the Registrars to

the issue and bankers to the issue to monitor all the aspects of assignment.

3. Irrespective of the level of subscription, the post-issue lead merchant banker shall ensure the submission of the post-issue monitoring reports as per formats specified schedule XVI of the SEBI Guidelines.
4. The due date for submitting post-issue monitoring report in case of public issues by listed and unlisted companies is the 3rd day from the date of allocation in the book built portion or one day prior to the opening of the fixed price portion whichever is earlier.
5. The lead manager responsible for the issue shall furnish SEBI the following documents 2 weeks prior to the date of filing the draft prospectus/letter of office with the Regional Stock Exchange or ROC—Particulars of the issue, Draft prospectus or the draft letter of offer and any literature to be circulated to the investors including to the existing shareholders and other documents which are relevant.

CANCELLATION OR SUSPENSION OF REGISTRATION

- Suspension of registration of a merchant banker may be imposed where.
- Violates the provisions of the Act, rules and regulations.
- Fails to furnish any information relating to his activity as merchant banker as required by SEBI or furnishes wrong or false information or does not submit periodical returns as required by SEBI or does not cooperate in any enquiry conducted by SEBI.
- Fails to resolve the complaints of the investors or fails to give a satisfactory reply to SEBI in this behalf.
- Indulges in manipulating or price rigging or cornering activities the merchant banker is guilty of misconduct or improper or unprofessional conduct which is not in accordance the Code of Conduct.
- Fails to maintain the prescribed capital adequacy requirements.

- Fails to pay the fees.
- Violates the conditions of registration.

PROCEDURE FOR INSPECTION

SEBI is empowered with the power of inspection following is the procedure for inspection of the merchant bankers' offices and records by SEBI:

- Appoint one or more persons as inspecting authority to undertake inspection of books of accounts, records etc. of the merchant banker, to ensure that such books and records are maintained in the prescribed manner; to investigate into complaints from investors, other merchant bankers or other persons, on any matter having a bearing on the activities of the merchant banker and to investigate *suo-motu* in the interest of the securities business or investors interest m the working of the merchant banker.
- To undertake such inspection with or without notice and the obligations of the merchant bankers in relation to such inspection.

9

Borrowings and Deposits

POWERS OF INVESTMENT

A company can invest its funds by purchase of shares in other companies or by making loans to other companies. But there are restrictions in respect of the overall limit of such investments or loans, both in case of companies under the same management and those not under the same management, as well as provides for the statutory procedure to be adopted before making such investments and loans.

Investments in Other Bodies Corporate

A company, whether by itself or together with its subsidiaries, shall not be entitled to acquire, by way of subscription, purchase or otherwise (whether by itself or by any individual or association of individuals in trust for it or for its benefit or on its account) the shares of any other body corporate except to the extent, and except in accordance with the restrictions and conditions.

Restrictions and Conditions

The restrictions and conditions imposed on inter-corporate investments under Sec. 372 are as follows:

- The Board of directors of the investing company shall be entitled to invest in any shares of any other body corporate up to sixty per cent of the subscribed equity share capital or the aggregate of the paid-up equity and preference share capital of such other body corporate, whichever is less. Where the investments are made by a company together with its one or more subsidiary companies, the percentage specified in this sub-rule shall be computed with reference to the aggregate of the investments made by the company and its subsidiaries.
- The above, mentioned particulars must be entered in the register within seven days of making the investment or, in the case of investments made before the commencement of 1960 Amendment Act, within six months from such commencement, or within such further time as the Central Government may grant in this behalf.
- The register must be kept at the registered office of the investing company. It must remain open to inspection by any member and the members shall have the right to take extracts there from to the same extent and in the same manner as the register of members on payment of the same fees.
- If default is made in complying, the company, and every officer of the company who is in default, shall be punishable with fine of up to Rs. 500 and also with a tine of Rs. 50 per day after the first day for a continuing default.
- Every investing company must annex, with each Balance sheet prepared by it, a statement showing the names of the Companies in the shares of which investments have been made. The names of the companies in the same group must be indicated separately showing the nature and extent of investment made in each company. Particulars regarding all investments, whether existing or not, made subsequent to the date of the last balance sheet should be included in the statement. However, in the case of an investment company, only the investments

existing on the date of the balance sheet are to be shown.

- The restrictions and conditions imposed on investments by a company will not apply to: (a) any banking or insurance company; (b) a private company, unless it is a subsidiary of a public company; (c) any company established with the object of financing private industrial enterprises in India, by way of loans or advances or subscribing to their capital. In any case where the Central Government had made or agreed to make to the company a special advance for the purpose or has guaranteed or agreed to guarantee the borrowings of the company from a foreign institution; (d) investments by a holding company in its subsidiary, and (e) to investments by a managing agent or secretaries and treasurers in a company managed by him/them.

Procedure for Investment under Sec. 372

The following procedure has to be adopted by a company when making investment:

- A resolution has to be adopted in the meeting of the Board of directors sanctioning the investment in shares of other companies. The notice of the resolution to be moved at the Board meeting for this purpose must be given to every director as required u/s 286 of the Act. The resolution must have to be passed with the consent of all the directors present and entitled to vote.
- Where investment is proposed to be made in excess of the limits prescribed, the company must take steps to convene a general meeting to adopt a resolution sanctioning the proposal, in addition to a Board resolution. The investing company must also obtain the previous approval of the Central Government. The previous approval of the Central Government has been made compulsory by the Companies (Amendment) Act, 1988.

- For obtaining the approval of the Central Government, an application will have to be made in Form No. 34B of the Companies (Central Government's) General Rules and Forms, 1956, along with the prescribed fees and accompanied by the f0110wing documents: (a) a copy of the Board's resolution approving the investment; (b) a copy of the Board's resolution passed in the general meeting; (c) copies of memorandum and articles of association of the investing company as well as the investee company; (d) copies of the balance sheets of both the companies for the last three years; and (e) copy of the prospectus, if any, issued by the other company.
- On receipt of approval from the Central Government, make necessary Investment.
- Where necessary, steps should also be taken to obtain approval of the Reserve Bank of India under the FERA, 1973.
- Within seven days of making the investment, the particulars of must be entered in the Register of Investments.
- A statement has to be prepared and annexed to each Balance Sheet showing the names of the companies in the shares of which investments have been made.
- The Stock Exchange where the company is listed, must be sent three copies of the notice and a copy of the proceedings of the General body meeting.

Loans to Companies under 'Same Management'

- No company shall make any loan, or give any guarantee, or provide any security in connection with loans made by any other person to, or to any other person by, any body corporate unless it is authorized by a special resolution of the lending company.
- No special resolution shall be necessary in the case of loans made to other bodies corporate not under the some management as the lending company, where the aggregate of such loans do not exceed thirty per cent of the aggregate of the subscribed capital of the

lending company and its free reserves. The aggregate of the loans made by the lending company to all other bodies corporate shall not except with the prior approval of the Central Government exceed (a) sixty per cent of the aggregate of the subscribed capital of the lending company and its free reserves, where all such other bodies corporate are not under the same management as the lending company; and (b) sixty per cent of the aggregate of the subscribed capital of the lending company and its free reserves, where all such other bodies corporate are under the same management as the lending company.

- If a special resolution has been passed by the lending company authorizing the making of loans up to the limit of sixty per cent then no further special resolution or resolutions shall be deemed to be necessary for the making of any loan or loans within such limit. If a special resolution has been passed by the lending company authorizing the Board to give any guarantee or provide any security up to a limit specified in the resolution, then no further special resolution(s) shall be deemed to be necessary for giving any guarantee or providing any security within such limit.
- Where the lending company (a) makes any loan to or (b) gives any guarantee or provides any security, in connection with a loan made by any other person to or to any other person by a firm in which a partner is a body corporate under the same management as the lending company : (i) the loan shall be deemed to have been made to, or (ii) the guarantee or the security shall be deemed to have been given or provided in connection with the loan made by such other person to or to such other person by, a body corporate under the same management.
- Two bodies corporate (companies) will be deemed to be under the same management: (i) if the managing director or manager of one body corporate is the managing director or manager of the other body corporate; or (ii) if a majority of directors of one body

corporate constitute, or constituted at any time within 6 months immediately preceding, a majority of directors of the other body corporate; or (iii) if one-third or more of the total voting power, with respect to any matter relating to each of the two bodies corporate, is expected or controlled by the same individual or body corporate; or (iv) if the holding company of one body corporate is under the same management as the other body corporate; or (v) if one or more directors of one body corporate while holding, by themselves or together with their relatives, the majority of shares in that body corporate also hold, by themselves or together with their relatives, the majority of shares m the other body corporate.

Register of Investment

Every investing company must keep a register of all investments made by it in shares of other company or companies, whether in the same group or not. The following particulars in respect of each investment must be shown in the register:

- The name of the company in which investment has been made.
- The date on which the investment has been made.
- Where the other company is in the same group, the date on which the company came into the same group.
- The names of all companies in the same group as the investing company.

PUBLIC DEPOSITS

The practice of mobilizing public deposits as a source of short-term working capital has been increasingly adopted by non-banking companies during the last two decades because of its various advantages. Companies are able to obtain cheaper credit through the elimination of financial intermediaries. Timely and easy credit is available for short-term needs as non-banking companies can attract investors by offering higher rates of interest than banking companies. As a result deposits with non-banking companies, rose sharply during the 'sixties and early 'seventies. This also inevitably gave rise to many abuses affecting the monetary and credit system of the country, as well as the interest of the investors. In many cases, companies accepted deposits far beyond their capacities at very high rates of interest. There was a proliferation of companies depending mainly on public deposits. Ultimately, many of these companies failed to repay the deposits on the due dates and some of them even went into liquidation. To enable the Reserve Bank of India to control and regulate acceptance of deposits by non-banking companies and to protect the interest of the investors, the Reserve Bank of India Act, 1934 was amended in 1963. Later, the Reserve Bank of India promulgated the Non-Banking, Non-Financial Companies (Reserve Bank) Directions, 1966 and the Miscellaneous Non-Banking Companies (Reserve Bank) Directions, 1973.

Regulation of Public Deposits

In order to prevent the misuse of this practice and to regulate acceptance of deposits by public companies other than banking companies the following were provided:

1. The Central Government may, in consultation with the Reserve Bank of India, prescribe limits up to which deposits may be invited or accepted by a company either from the public or from its members. It may also prescribe the manner in which and the conditions subject to which such deposits' may be invited or accepted.
2. No company shall invite or allow any other person to invite or cause any invitation to be made in this behalf, except in accordance with the rules to be framed by the Government and without issuing an advertisement in the prescribed form and manner, which shall include therein a statement showing the financial position of the company.
3. Every deposit accepted by a company before the commencement of the Amendment Act of 1974, in

accordance with the directions made by the Reserve Bank of India, shall be repaid in accordance with the terms and conditions of such deposit, unless it renewed.

4. A Company shall not default in the repayment of any deposit or part there of and any interest on such deposit.
5. Every deposit accepted by a company shall be repaid in accordance with the terms and conditions of such deposit unless renewed in accordance the terms and conditions of such deposit unless renewed.
6. Where any deposit is accepted by a company in contravention of the rules made by the Central Government, such deposit must be repaid by the company within thirty days from the date of acceptance or such further time as the Central Government may allow.
7. Where a company omits or fails to repay a deposit in accordance with the provisions or within the prescribed time, the company shall be punishable with fine which shall not be less than twice the amount of the deposit not repaid out of this fine, if realized, an amount equal to the amount of the deposit not repaid shall be paid by the Court to the person entitled to the repayment and on such payment the liability of the company to the extent of the amount paid by the Court shall stand discharged. In addition, every officer of the company who is in default for such non-payment shall be punishable with imprisonment of up to five years and also with fine.
8. Where a company accepts or invites, or allows or causes any other person to accept or invite, any deposit in excess of the limit prescribed under in contravention of the manner or condition prescribed, the company shall be punishable where such contravention relates to acceptance of any deposit, with fine which shall not be less than the amount of the deposit, and where such contravention relates to

invitation for deposit, with fine which may extend to one lakh rupees but shall not be less than five thousand rupees.

9. Every officer of the company who is in default shall be punishable with imprisonment of up to five years and also with fine.
10. The Central Government may also if it considers necessary for avoid legal hardship or for any other just or sufficient reason, by order issued prospectively or retrospectively, grant extension of time to any company or class of companies either generally or for any specified period, subject to such conditions as may be specified in the order.
11. Where a company has failed to repay any deposit or part thereof in accordance with the terms and conditions of such deposit, the Company Law Board may, if it is satisfied either on its own or on the application of the depositor that it is necessary in order to safeguard the interests of the company or the depositors or in public interest to do so, direct the company by order to make repayment of such deposit or part thereof forthwith or within such time and subject to such conditions as may be specified in the order. However, before making such order the CLB may give a reasonable opportunity to the company or any other interested persons to be heard.
12. Whoever fails to comply with the order of the Company Law Board hall be punishable with imprisonment which may extend to three years and also with fine extending to not less than Rs. 50 for each day during which such non-compliance continues.
13. A depositor whose matured deposits have not been repaid by the company can make an application to Company Law Board. The application has to be made in the prescribed form, i.e., Form No. 4. Following are required to be accompanied along with the application the copy of deposit receipt, copy of the correspondence exchanged, demand draft evidencing payment of application fee of Rs. 50.

Deposits not Considered as Deposits

- Deposit made for advance booking for purchase of car, scooter etc. is not a deposit u/s 58A.
- Deposits accepted by a sick industrial company in respect of which BIFR has, by specific order, suspended the operation of any contracts.
- Deposits accepted by financial companies which receive deposits under any specified scheme by way of subscription/contribution.
- Deposits accepted by relief undertakings notified as such under the various State Laws.

Application of Deposit Rules: These rules are applicable to all types of non-banking and non-financial companies, including guarantee companies and companies having share capital but set-up not for profit. However, it does not apply to a banking company and such other companies as may be specified by the Central Government.

Exemptions

The following companies are exempted:

- A banking company.
- Companies specified by the Central Government after consultation with the RBI.
- Except the provisions relating to advertisement, such financial companies as may be specified by the Central Government consultation with the RBI.

Financial Companies exempted. The Central Government has by a notification specified, after consultation with the Reserve Bank of India, all classes of financial companies exempt. For this purpose, a "financial company" means a non-banking company which is a "financial institution" within the meaning of clause (c) of Section 45I of the Reserve Bank of India Act, 1934.

Powers of Central Government to Grant Extension of Time/ Exemption

The Central Government may grant extension of time or

grant partial or total exemption to a company or class of companies to avoid hardship or for any other just and reasonable cause. The order granting the extension of time must be issued after consultation with the Reserve Bank of India. While granting the extension of time or exemption, the Central Government may impose such conditions as it may think fit and proper. The extension of time or exemption may be granted generally, or for any specified period. The power to grant extension of time or exemption has been delegated by the Central Government to the Company Law Board. A company seeking extension of time or exemption has to make an application to the Company Law Board in the prescribed form along with the prescribed documents.

Penalties for Contravention

Penalties for omission or failure to repay deposits are imposed. The penalty for the company is fine extending to twice the amount of the deposits not repaid. For the officers of the company in default, the penalty is imprisonment of up to 5 years and also fine. Penalty is impossable for accepting or inviting deposits in excess of the limits prescribed or in contravention of the manner or condition prescribed. The penalties for the company are: (a) fine of not less than an amount equal to the deposit, where such contravention relates to acceptance of deposit; (b) fine which may extend to rupees one lakh but not less than Rs. 5000, where the contravention relates to invitation for deposits. For the officers of the company in default, the penalties are imprisonment of up to 5 years and also fine.

COMPANIES (ACCEPTANCE OF DEPOSITS) RULES, 1975

Definition of Deposits: "Any deposit of money with, and includes any amount borrowed by, a company but shall not include such categories of amount as may be prescribed in consultation with the Reserve Bank of India."

'Deposit' has been defined as any deposit of money with, or any money borrowed by, a company but excluding the following types of deposits, loans and advances:

- Any loan received from, or guaranteed by, the Central Government or a State Government, or receipts from a local authority, a foreign government or any other foreign citizen, authority or person.
- Any loan from a banking company or from the State Bank of India or any of its subsidiaries or any other banking Institution.
- Any loan from any specified financial institution or from any other financial company owned by the Central or State Government or from any other financial company or public financial institution notified by the Central Government.
- Any amount received from any other company.
- Any amount received from an employee of the company as security deposit.
- Any amount received as security or advance from any purchasing or selling agent or other agents in the course of or for the purpose of the business of the company or any advance received from customers for supply of any goods or properties or for rendering of any service.
- Any amount received as subscription to any shares, stock, bonds or debentures pending their allotment, or calls received in advance on shares in accordance with the Articles so long as such amount is not repayable to members.
- Any amount received in trust or any amount in transit.
- Any amount received from a director of the company or from its shareholders by a private company or by a private company which is deemed to be a public company, provided such director or shareholder gives a written declaration, at the time of giving the money, that the amount is not being given out of funds acquired by him by borrowing or accepting deposits from others.
- Any amount raised by the issue of bonds or the issue of debentures secured by the mortgage of any immovable property or with an option to convert them into shares in the company, provided the

amount of such bonds or debentures does not exceed the market value of such immovable property.

- Any amount brought in by the promoters of a company by way of unsecured loan in pursuance of stipulations of financial institutions, subject to the fulfilment of the following conditions:
  1. The loans are brought in by the promoters in pursuance of the stipulation imposed by the financial institutions in fulfilment of the obligation of the promoters to contribute such finance.
  2. The loans are provided by the promoters themselves and/or by their relatives, and not from their friends and business associates.
  3. The exemption under this clause shall be available only till the loans of financial institutions are repaid and not thereafter.

Free Reserves

Free reserves include the balance of share premium account, capital and debenture redemption reserve and any other reserves shown or published in the balance sheet and created out of profits of the company, but does not include any reserve created for repayment of liability or for depreciation in assets or for bad debts, or created by revaluation of assets.

While calculating the aggregate of paid-up share capital and free reserves, the amount of accumulated loss, the balance of deferred revenue expenditure and other intangible assets are to be excluded. However, the amount of surplus of profit and loss account appearing in the balance sheet of the company forms a part of the free reserves; and the subsidy received under the Central Government Outright Grant and Subsidies Scheme, 1971 is "free reserves" for the purpose of the Companies (Acceptance of Deposits) Rules, 1975, provided the following conditions are fulfilled:

- The subsidy is received in cash.
- The subsidy is utilized for the purpose for which it is received.

- The period of five years from the commencement of production has already elapsed and the subsidy has not become recoverable under the conditions of the grant.

Changes in paid-up Capital: In calculating the aggregate of paid-up share capital and free reserves for the purpose of reckoning the limit for acceptance of deposits, any change in the paid-up share capital occurring after the close of the financial year of the company is to be disregarded.

Acceptance of Deposits—Restrictions and Limits

The following restrictions and limits on the acceptance of deposits by a company are made:

- No company shall accept any deposit which is repayable on demand or on notice or repayable after a period; and
- No company shall renew any deposit accepted by it, except where such deposit is repayable after the expiry of six months but not later than thirty-six months from the date of acceptance of renewal of such deposits.

However, for the purpose of meeting any of its short-term requirements for funds, a company may accept or renew such deposits for repayment earlier than six months from the date of deposit or renewal, provided such deposits do not exceed 10 per cent of the aggregate of paid-up share capital and free reserves of the company and are repayable not earlier than three months from the date of such deposit of renewal.

- No company shall invite or accept or renew any deposits in any form on a rate of interest exceeding 15 per cent per annum.
- No company can pay brokerage to any broker for collecting deposits at a rate exceeding: (a) 1 per cent of deposits up to one year; (b) 1.5 per cent for deposits of more than one year but up to two years; and (c) 2 per cent for deposits exceeding two years.

The brokerage can be paid on deposits collected by or through such broker, and such payment shall be on one-time basis.

No company, other than a Government company, shall accept (i) any deposit against an unsecured debenture or any deposit from a shareholder (not being a deposit accepted by a private company from its shareholders) or any deposit guaranteed by any person who, at the time of giving such guarantee, is a director of the company, if the amount of any deposit together with the amount of such deposits of all or any of the kinds, outstanding on the date of acceptance or renewal of such deposit exceeds ten per cent of the aggregate of the paid-up share capital and free reserves of the company; (ii) any other deposit, if the amount of such deposit together with the amount of such other deposit, other than any of the deposits referred above outstanding on the date of acceptance or renewal, exceeds twenty-five percent of the paid-up share capital and free reserves of the company.

Maintenance of Liquid Assets

Every company is required to deposit or invest, before 30th April every year, a sum which is not less than 15 per cent of its deposits maturing during the year ending on 31st March next. The deposit or investment must be in anyone or more of the following: (a) in a current or deposit account in a scheduled bank; (b) In unencumbered securities of the Central Government or any State government; (c) in unencumbered securities. The purpose was to provide a limited safeguard to the depositors and to enable the companies to meet their obligations for repayment of the deposits. The securities include (a) promissory notes, debentures, stock and other securities of any State Government or of the Central Government; (b) securities on which both the principal and interest have been fully and unconditionally guaranteed by any State Government or the Central Government; (c) stock or debentures or shares of corporations, the interest whereon has been guaranteed by the Central Government; (d) debentures or other securities for money issued under the authority of any Central or State Act or on behalf of any municipal body, port trust or city improvement trust; and (e) units issued by the Unit Trust of India.

The amount so deposited or invested must not be utilized for any purpose other than for repayment of deposits maturing during the year, However, the amount remaining deposited or invested shall not at any time fall below 15 per cent of amount of the deposits maturing, until 31st March of that year.

Advertisement and Statement in lieu of Advertisement: Every company intending to invite public deposits must issue an advertisement in a leading English newspaper and a vernacular newspaper circulating in the State in which its registered office is situated, the advertisement in the vernacular newspaper must be in the language of that newspaper and not in English. Such advertisement must be issued under the authority of the Board of Directors and must contain the terms and conditions under which the deposit will be accepted, the date of approval of the advertisement by the Board and other particulars required.

Each advertisement must be issued on the authority and in the name of the Board of directors of the company and it must state the date on which the text of the advertisement was approved by the Board of directors.

An advertisement inviting deposits is a prospectus and all the provisions of the Companies Act applicable to the prospectus are also applicable to the advertisement inviting deposits. Before issuing the advertisement a copy of the same, signed by a majority of the directors at the time of its approval or their agents, must be delivered to the Registrar for registration. An advertisement issued under this rule will remain valid for six months from the last date of the financial year in which it is issued or until the date on which the balance sheet is laid before the general meeting, whichever is earlier. A fresh advertisement must be made in each financial year for the acceptance of deposits during that year.

Where a company intends to accept deposits without inviting deposits from the public, it must deliver to the Registrar a Statement in lieu of Advertisement before accepting the deposit. The statement must contain all the particulars required to be included in the advertisement and other provisions relating to advertisement are also applicable to a Statement in lieu of Advertisement.

Contents of Advertisement

1. The name of the company.
2. The date of incorporation of the company.
3. The business carried on by the company and its subsidiaries with details of branches or units, if any.
4. Brief particulars of the management of the company.
5. Names, addresses and occupations of the directors.
6. Profits of the company before and after making provision for tax, for the three financial years immediately preceding the date of advertisement.
7. Dividends declared by the company in respect of the said years.
8. Summarized financial position of the company as in the two audited balance sheets immediately preceding the date of advertisement.
9. The amount which the company will raise by way of deposits under these rules and the aggregate of deposits actually held on the last day of the immediately preceding financial year.
10. A statement to the effect that on the day of the advertisement, the company has no overdue deposits other than unclaimed deposits, or a statement showing the amount of such overdue deposits, as the case may be.
11. A declaration to the effect that the company has complied with the provisions of these rules and that compliance with these rules does not imply that repayment of deposits is guaranteed by the Central Government; that the deposits accepted by the company (other than secured deposits, if any, accepted under the provisions of these rules, the aggregate amount of which may be indicated) are unsecured and ranking *pari passu* with other unsecured liabilities.

Receipts to Depositors and Register of Deposits

Every company accepting deposits must issue a receipt in the prescribed form to each depositor or his agent, signed by an officer of the company authorized in that behalf. The deposit receipt shall be signed by an officer of the company duly authorized in this behalf and shall state the date of deposit, name and address of the depositor, the amount of deposit, the rate of interest payable and the date when the deposit is repayable. The company shall not reserve to itself the right to alter the terms and conditions of the deposit, to the prejudice of the depositor, after the deposit is accepted. Every such company must maintain a Register or Registers where particulars of the deposit from each depositor must be entered. The Register or Registers must be preserved for a period of not less than 8 years from the financial year in which the last entry is made.

The following particulars are required to be entered in the register or registers of deposits separately for each deposit: (a) name and address of the depositor; (b) date and amount of deposit; (c) duration of the deposit and the date when the deposit will be repayable; (d) rate of interest; (e) date or dates on which payment of interest will be made; and (f) any other particulars relating to deposit.

Repayment of Deposits

Where a deposit is repaid after six months of its receipt but before the expiry of the period for which the deposit was accepted the rate of interest payable by the company must be reduced by 1 per cent from the rate which the company would have paid had the deposit been accepted for the period which it had run. However, this rule will not apply to the repayment of any deposit before the expiry of the period for which it was accepted, if such repayment is made solely for the purpose of complying with the provisions of the Non-Banking Non-Financial Companies (Reserve Bank Directions) 1966. The above rules will also not apply if the deposits are converted into secured debentures, with the consent of the depositors in accordance with the guidelines issued by the Government of India from time to time regarding the issue of 'rights debentures'.

Application Form for Deposits

A company can accept or renew deposits only if an application is made by the intending depositor for acceptance or renewal of such deposit in the form to be supplied by the company. While making the application, the intending depositor must declare that the amount is not being deposited out of funds acquired by him by borrowing or accepting deposits from any other person. The form of application to be supplied by the company must be accompanied by a statement by the company giving the same particulars as are required to be given in the Advertisement for deposits or in the Statement in lieu of Advertisement.

Filing of Return

Every company to which these rules apply is required to file with the Registrar, on or before 30th June of each year, .a return in the prescribed form duly certified by the auditor of the company and giving the required information as on 31st March of that year. A copy of the return must also be furnished to the Reserve Bank of India. The form of return as prescribed in Rule 10 has been revised w.e.f. 19.4.85.

Procedure for Acceptance of Deposits

- The Board of Directors have the powers to borrow money by accepting public deposits, unless the Articles provide that this power must be exercised duly with the sanction of the shareholders in a general meeting: Usually, the decision to accept public deposits is taken by a resolution passed in the Board meeting. The terms and conditions under which such deposits will be invited and accepted are also decided by the Board. The total amount of deposits that can be accepted is limited to 35% of the paid-up share capital and free reserves of the company. Out of this 35%, ten per cent can be in the form of deposits against unsecured debentures or deposit from shareholders (not being a deposit accepted by a private company from its shareholders) or deposit guarantee by directors of the company.

The other 25% can be any other deposit. From 1.4.1980, in case the total of other deposits which have already been accepted by the company exceeds 25% of paid-up capital and free reserves, no fresh deposits or renewal could be made.

- After the Board decides to invite and accept deposits from the public, a draft of the Advertisement to be issued is prepared. If the company decides to accept deposits without issuing invitation for the same, a draft of Statement in lieu of Advertisement must be prepared.
- A meeting of the Board of Directors is then held to approve the Advertisement or Statement in lieu of Advertisement. No company can accept or renew deposits unless an application is made by the intending depositor. The application must be made in the form to be supplied by the company. It must be accompanied by a statement containing all the particulars required to be given in the Advertisement. The draft of the Application form and the accompanying statement must also be placed before the Board meeting for approval along with the Advertisement.
- After the Advertisement has been approved by the Board, arrangement is made for its publication in a leading English newspaper and a vernacular newspaper circulating in the State in which the registered office of the company is situated.. Before the date of its issue, a copy of the Advertisement signed by a majority of the directors is filed with the Registrar for registration. If the company decides not to issue advertisement inviting deposits, a Statement in lieu of Advertisement is filed with the Registrar before the deposit is accepted.
- The advertisement is valid until the expiry of 6 months from the date of closure of the financial year in which it is issued or delivered or until the date on which the balance sheet is laid before the company in General Meeting or where the AGM for any year has not been held, the latest day on which that meeting

should have been held as per the provisions of the Companies Act, whichever is earlier.

- The advertisement inviting public deposits, besides giving the particulars required under the Rules, also indicates the minimum amount below which the applications will not be entertained, the rates of interest, mode of interest payment, the place from where application forms will be issued and the manner of making the deposits. Usually application forms are issued from the registered office of the company and intending depositors are required to submit the applications at the registered office along with the amount of deposit payable by cheque or bank draft. Arrangement may also be made for accepting application forms and deposits through the company's banker.
- On receipt of the application and amount of the deposit from an applicant, the application is scrutinized and, if found in order, arrangement is made to issue a receipt to the depositor or his agent. The Deposit Receipt must be signed by an officer of the company authorized in this behalf. The particular of the deposit received from each depositor is then entered in a Register of Deposits.
- The aggregate of investments made by the Board in all other bodies corporate shall not except with the previous approval of the central Government exceed (i) sixty per cent of the aggregate of the subscribed capital and free reserves of the investing company; and (ii) sixty per cent of the aggregate of the subscribed capital and free reserves of the investing company, where such other bodies corporate are in the same group.
- While computing the percentages, the aggregate of investments made by the investing company in other company or companies up to that time shall be taken into account.
- Sec. 372 prohibit the company that has defaulted in the repayment, if any deposit or part there of or any

interest, from making any investment till the default is made good.

- The investing company can make investments in shares of other companies in excess of the percentages only if the investment is sanctioned by a resolution in general meeting and it is previously approved by the Central Government.
- The percentages will not apply in case of investment in rights shares offered to the investing company. However, if the investing company at any time intends to invest in shares other than rights shares, then the investment in rights share will be included in computing the aggregate investment of the investing company.
- A company cannot make any investment in share, unless it is sanctioned by a resolution passed in the Board meeting with consent of all directors present and entitled to vote. Further, the notice of the resolution to be moved at the meeting must be given to every director as required to every director for the time being in India, and at the usual address in India of every other director.
- A company will be deemed to be in the same group as the investing company:
  (a) if the company is the managing agent of the investing company, and
  (b) if the company and the investing company are deemed to be under the 'same management'.

10

Pricing of Securities

A listed company whose equity shares are listed on a stock exchange, may freely price its equity shares and any security convertible into equity at a later date, offered through a public or rights issue. An unlisted company eligible to make a public issue and desirous of getting its securities listed on a recognized stock exchange pursuant to a public issue, may freely price its shares or any securities convertible at a later date into equity shares.

NORMS FOR ISSUE OF SECURITIES

Infrastructure Company: An eligible infrastructure company shall be free to price its equity shares subject to the compliance with the disclosure norms as specified by SEBI from time to time.

Initial Public Issue by Banks: The banks (whether public sector or private sector) may freely price their issue of equity shares or any securities convertible at a later date into equity share subject to approval by the Reserve Bank of India.

Differential Pricing: Any unlisted company or a listed company making a public issue of equity shares or securities convertible at a later date into equity shares, may issue such, securities to applicants in the firm allotment category at a price different from the price at which the net offer to the public is made, provided that the price at which the security is being offered to the applicants in firm allotment category is higher than the price at which securities are offered to public. The net offer to the public means the offer made to the Indian public and does not include firm allotments or reservations or promoters' contributions.

A listed company making a composite issue of capital may issue securities at differential prices in its public and rights issue. In the public issue which is a part of a composite issue differential pricing is also permissible. Justification for the price difference shall be given in the offer document.

Price Band : Issuer company can mention a price band of 20% (cap in the price band should not be more than 20% of the floor price) in the offer documents filed with the Board and actual price can be determined at a later date before filing of the offer document With ROCs. If the Board of Directors has been authorized to determine the offer price within a specified price band such price shall be determined by a Resolution to be passed by the Board of Directors: The Lead Merchant Bankers shall ensure that in case of the listed companies, a 48 hours notice of the meeting of the Board of Directors for passing resolution for determination of price is given to the Regional Stock Exchange. The final offer document shall contain only one price and one set of financial projections, if applicable.

Payment of Discounts/Commissions: No payment direct or indirect in the nature of a discount, commission, allowance or otherwise shall be made either by the issuer company or the promoters in public issue, to the persons who have received firm allotment in such public issue.

Denomination of Shares: Freedom to determine the denomination of shares for public/rights is and to change the standard denomination. An eligible company shall be free to make public or rights issue of equity shares in any denomination determined by it in accordance with sub-section (4) of sec. 13 of the Companies' Act, 1956. The companies which have already issued shares in the denomination of Rs. 10 or Rs. 100 may change the standard denomination of the shares by splitting/consolidating the existing shares. The companies proposing to issue shares in any denomination or changing standard denomination shall comply with following:

- The shares shall not be issued in the denomination of decimal of a rupee
- The denomination of the existing shares shall not be altered to a denomination of decimal of a rupee.
- At any given time there shall be only one denomination for the shares of the company.
- The companies seeking to change the standard denomination may do so by amending the Memorandum and Articles of Association, if required.
- The company shall adhere to the disclosure and accounting norms specified by SEBI from time to time.

BASIS FOR ISSUE PRICE

Following information shall be disclosed for all issues irrespective of the issue price:

- Earnings per share. EPS pre-issue for the last three years (as adjusted for changes in capital).
- PIE pre-issue and comparison thereof with industry PIE where available (giving the source from which industry PIE has been taken).
- Average return on net worth in the last three years.
- Minimum return on increased net worth required to maintain pre-issue EPS.
- Net Asset Value per share based on last balance sheet.
- Net Asset Value per share after issue and comparison thereof with the issue price.

The above is subjected to conditions that the projected earnings shall not be used as a justification for the issue price in the offer document. And the accounting ratios disclosed in the prospectus in support of basis of the issue price shall be calculated after giving effect to the consequent increase in capital on account of compulsory conversions outstanding, as well as on the assumption that the options outstanding, if any, to subscribe for additional capital will be exercised.

The issuer company and the lead merchant banker shall provide the accounting ratios to justify the basis of issue price. Provided that, the lead merchant banker shall not proceed with the issue in case the accounting ratios mentioned above, do not justify the issue price. In case of book built issues, the offer document shall state that the final price has been determined on the basis of the demand from the investors.

Pricing of Issues of DFIs (Development Financial Institutions)

DFIs may freely price their issues subject to the following conditions:

- ❖ The DFIs have 3 years' track record of consistent profitability with profits shown in their respective audited profit and accounts after providing for interest, tax and depreciation in 3 out of immediately preceding 5 years with profit during the last 2 years prior to the issue.
- ❖ Where interest charged on debts outstanding for more than three years has been taken into Profit and Loss Account, the same shall be excluded for reckoning net profit.
- ❖ DFI determines the issue price in consultation with the lead manager.
- ❖ The issue price shall be authorized by a resolution passed at a duly convened meeting of the shareholders/company's Board.
- ❖ The offer document shall contain justification for the premium disclosing the following:
  1. Mode of calculation of the parameters including selection of any particular capitalization rate and reasons therefor.
  2. Whether revaluation reserves have been taken into account for determining book value; if so, the date of revaluation and whether such

revaluation was done by an approved valuer and certified by the auditors.

3. Revaluation reserves shall be excluded if such revaluation has been done within 3 years from the close of previous financial year.
4. Past performance with reference to the earnings per share and book value for the past 5 years.
5. Projected earnings per share/book value for the next 3 years as per DFI's own assessment.
6. Stock market data covering average high and low price of the share for the last 2 years and monthly high and low for the last 6 months, wherever applicable.
7. All other factors which have been taken into account by the issuer for determining the premium.

Pricing of the Issue when Issue of Shares on a Preferential Basis is Made

The issue of shares on a preferential basis can be made at a price not less than the higher of the following:

- The average of the weekly high and low of the closing prices of the related shares quoted on the stock exchange during the six months preceding the relevant date.
- The average of the weekly high and low of the closing prices of the related shares quoted on a stock exchange during the two weeks preceding the relevant date. "Relevant date" for the purpose of this clause means the date thirty days prior to the date on which the meeting of general body of shareholders is held, in terms of Section 81 (1A) of the Companies Act, 1956 to consider the proposed issue.
- "Stock exchange" for the purpose of this clause means any of the recognized stock exchanges in which the shares are listed and in which the highest trading volume in respect of the shares of the company has been recorded during the preceding six months prior to the relevant date.

Pricing of Shares Arising Out of Warrants: Where warrants are issued on a preferential basis, with an option to apply for and be allotted shares, the issuer company shall determine the price of the resultant shares. The relevant date for the above purpose may, at the option of the issuer be a date 30 days prior to the date on which the holder of the warrants becomes entitled to apply for the said shares. The resolution to be passed in terms of section 81(1A) shall clearly specify the relevant date on the basis of which price of the resultant shares shall be calculated. An amount equivalent to at least ten percent of the price fixed shall become payable for the warrants on the date of their allotment. The amount shall be adjusted against the price payable subsequently for acquiring the shares by exercising an option for the purpose. The amount shall be forfeited if the option to acquire shares is not exercised.

Pricing of Shares on Conversion

Where PCDs/FCDs/other convertible instruments are issued on a preferential basis, providing for the issuer to allot shares at a future date, the issuer shall determine the price at which the shares could be allotted in the same manner as specified for pricing of shares allotted in lieu of warrants. The explanatory statement to the notice for the general meeting in terms of section 173 of the Companies Act, 1956 shall contain:

- The objects of the issue through preferential offer.
- Intention of promoters/directors/key management persons to subscribe to the offer.
- Shareholding pattern before and after the offer.
- Proposed time within which the allotment shall be complete.
- The identity of the proposed allottees and the percentage of post-preferential issue capital that may be held by them.

Pricing Norms in for sale of equity share or any other security under OTCEI: Any offer for sale of equity share or any other security convertible at a later date into equity shares resulting out of a Bought out Deal (BOD) registered with OTCEI is exempted from the pricing norms specified in Clause 3.2 of

Chapter III of these guidelines subject to the following conditions:

1. The promoters after such issue shall retain at least 20% of the total issued capital with the lock-in of three years from the date of the allotment of securities in the proposed issue.
2. At least two market makers (one Compulsory and one additional market-maker) are appointed in accordance with the Market Making guidelines stipulated by the OTCEI.

11

New Issue Market

PRIMARY MARKET

The primary market plays an important role in the securities market by forming a link between the savings and investments. It is through this market that the borrower's viz., the Government and the corporates issue securities in which the investors deploy their savings. The primary market comprises, the public issues and the private placement market. A public issue consists of a company entering the market to raise funds from all types of investors; its debut is known as the initial public offer (IPO). In case of private placement, there are only a few select subscribers to the issue. The securities can be issued at a face value, or at a discount/premium; they may take a variety of forms such as equity, debt or some hybrid instrument.

Apart from raising funds in domestic markets, resources are mobilized in international markets through the issuance of American Depository Receipts (ADRs)/Global Depository Receipts (GDRs) and External Commercial Borrowing (ECB) route. In order to refine the primary market design and boost the waning investors' confidence, various measures have been taken by the Government, RBI and SEBI. Given the SEBI's commitment to protect the investors' interests and to increase the transparency and efficiency of the primary market, stringent disclosure and eligibility norms have been issued. Further, various operational procedures for the issuers have been simplified to facilitate smooth mobilization of resources. In this regard, SEBI has set-up various committees, which constantly review the guidelines.

The year 2003-04 witnessed an upsurge in the primary market activity induced by a buoyant secondary market, sharp economic recovery, and political stability. The resource mobilization by way of IPOs and new issues by listed companies leaped to Rs. 200,592 million in 2003-04 from Rs. 40,703 million in 2002-03. As compared with 52 total schemes in 2003-04, there were only 26 in the previous year. The share of public issues in the total resources mobilized rose from 89% in 2002-03 to 92% in 2003-04. The mobilization by rights issues also witnessed a manifold increase as compared to the previous year. The turnaround in the fortunes of the rights issues both by numbers and by amount has come about primarily because of the steady conditions in the secondary market and drying up of the ECB market. Companies offer shares on rights basis either to expand, diversify or simply to restructure their balance sheets.

CLASSIFICATION OF ISSUES

Primarily, issues can be classified as a Public, Rights or preferential issues (also known as private placements). While public and rights issues involve a detailed procedure, private placements or preferential issues are relatively simpler. The classification of issues is illustrated below: Public issues can be further classified into Initial Public offerings and further public offerings. In a public offering, the issuer makes an offer for new investors to enter its shareholding family. The issuer company makes detailed disclosures as per the SEBI guidelines in its offer document and offers it for subscription. The significant features are illustrated below:

1. *Initial Public Offering (IPO)* is when an unlisted company makes either a fresh issue of securities or an offer for sale of its existing securities or both for the first time to the public. This paves way for listing and trading of the issuer's securities.
2. *A follow on public offering (FPO)* is when an already listed company makes either a fresh issue of securities to the public or an offer for sale to the public, through an offer document. An offer for sale in such scenario is allowed only if it is made to satisfy listing or continuous listing obligations.
3. *Rights Issue (RI)* is when a listed company which proposes to issue fresh securities to its existing shareholders as on a record date. The rights are normally offered in a particular ratio to the number of securities held prior to the issue. This route is best suited for companies who would like to raise capital without diluting stake of its existing shareholders unless they do not intend to subscribe to their entitlements.
4. *A preferential issue* is an issue of shares or of convertible securities by listed companies to a select group of persons under Section 81 of the Companies Act, 1956 which is neither a rights issue nor a public issue. This is a faster way for a company to raise equity capital. The issuer company has to comply with the Companies Act and the requirements contained pertaining to preferential allotment in SEBI guidelines which *inter alia* include pricing, disclosures in notice etc.

ELIGIBILITY NORMS FOR MAKING ISSUES

SEBI has laid down eligibility norms for entities accessin the primary market through public issues. There is n eligibility norm for a listed company making a rights issue it is an offer made to the existing shareholders who a expected to know their company. The main entry norms companies making a public issue (IPO or FPO) are summari as here.

Entry Norm I (EN I): The company shall meet the following requirements:

- Net Tangible Assets of at least Rs. 3 crores for 3 full years.
- Distributable profits in atleast three years.
- Net worth of at least Rs. 1 crore in three years.
- If change in name, atleast 50% revenue for preceding 1 year should be from the new activity.
- The issue size does not exceed 5 times the pre-issue net worth.

To provide sufficient flexibility and also to ensure that nuine companies do not suffer on account of rigidity of the rameters, SEBI has provided two other alternative routes to npany not satisfying any of the above conditions, for ssing the primary market, as under:

Norm II (EN II)

Issue shall be through book building route, with at least 50% to be mandatory allotted to the Qualified Institutional Buyers (QIBs).

The minimum post-issue face value capital shall be Rs. 10 crore or there shall be a compulsory market-making for at least 2 years.

m III (EN III)

e "project" is appraised and participated to the ent of 15% by FIIs/Scheduled Commercial Banks hich at least 10% comes from the appraiser(s).

minimum post-issue face value capital shall be crore or there shall be a compulsory market-g for at least 2 years.

lition to satisfying the aforesaid eligibility the company shall also satisfy the criteria of at least 1000 prospective allotees in its

Exempted from the Aforesaid Eligibility Norms: SEBI (DIP—Disclosures and Investors Protection) guidelines have provided certain exemptions from the eligibility norms. The following are eligible for exemption from entry norms.

- Private sector banks.
- Public sector banks.
- An infrastructure company whose project has been appraised by a Project financing institution or a bank which was earlier a PFI and not less than 5% of the project cost is financed by any of these institutions.
- Rights issue by a listed company.

SEBI'S ROLE IN AN ISSUE

Any company making a public issue or a listed company making a rights issue of value of more than Rs. 50 lakhs is required to file a draft offer document with SEBI for its observations. The company can proceed further on the issue only after getting observations from SEBI. The validity period of SEBI's observation letter is three months only ie. the company has to open its issue within three months period. SEBI does not recommend any issue nor does take any responsibility either for the financial soundness of any scheme or the project for which the issue is proposed to be made or for the correctness of the statements made or opinions expressed in the offer document.

1. *SEBI Approval :* It is to be distinctly understood that submission of offer document to SEBI should not in any way be deemed or construed that the same has been cleared or approved by SEBI. The Lead manager certifies that the disclosures made in the offer document are generally adequate and are in conformity with SEBI guidelines for disclosures and investor protection in force for the time being. This requirement is to facilitate investors to take an informed decision for making investment in the proposed issue. The investors should make an

informed decision purely by themselves based on the contents disclosed in the offer documents. SEBI does not associate itself with any issue/issuer and should in no way be construed as a guarantee for the funds that the investor proposes to invest through the issue. However, the investors are generally advised to study all the material facts pertaining to the issue including the risk factors before considering any investment. They are strongly warned against any 'tips' or news through unofficial means.

2. *DIP Guidelines:* The primary issuances are governed by SEBI in terms of (Disclosures and Investor protection) guidelines. SEBI framed its DIP guidelines in 1992. Many amendments have been carried out in the same in line with the market dynamics and requirements. In 2000, SEBI issued *"Securities and Exchange Board of India (Disclosure and Investor Protection) Guidelines, 2000" which is compilation of all circulars organized in chapter forms. These guidelines are last amended in 2005. These guidelines and amendments thereon are* issued by SEBI under section 11 of the Securities and Exchange Board of India Act, 1992. SEBI (Disclosure and investor protection) guidelines 2002 are in short called DIP guidelines. It provides a comprehensive framework for issuances the companies.

3. *Compliance with DIP:* The Merchant Banker are the specialized intermediaries who are required to do due diligence and ensure that all the requirements of DIP are complied with while submitting the draft offer document to SEBI. Any non-compliance on their part, attract penal action from SEBI, in terms of SEBI (Merchant Bankers) Regulations. The draft offer document filed by Merchant Banker is also placed on the website for public comments. Officials of SEBI at various levels examine the compliance with DIP guidelines and ensure that all necessary material information is disclosed in the draft offer documents.

CENTRAL LISTING AUTHORITY (CLA)

The Central Listing Authority's (CLA) functions have been detailed under Regulation 8 of SEBI (Central Listing Authority) Regulations, 2003 (CLA Regulations) issued on August 21, 2003 and amended up to October 14, 2003. In brief, it covers processing applications for letter precedent to listing from applicants; to make recommendations to the Board on issues pertaining to the protection of the interest of the investors in securities and development and regulation of the securities market, including the listing agreements, listing conditions and disclosures to be made in offer documents; and; to undertake any other functions as may be delegated to it by the Board from time to time. SEBI as the regulator of the securities market examines all the policy matters pertaining to issues and will continue to do so even during the existence of the CLA.

ISSUE DOCUMENTS

(a) *"Offer document"* means *Prospectus* in case of a public issue or offer for sale and *Letter of Offer* in case of a rights issue which is filed with Registrar of Companies (ROC) and Stock Exchanges. An offer document covers all the relevant information to help an investor to make his/her investment decision.

(b) *"Draft Offer Document"* means the offer document in draft stage. The draft offer documents are filed with SEBI, atleast 21 days prior to the filing of the Offer Document with ROC/SEs. SEBI may specifies changes, if any, in the draft Offer Document and the issuer or the Lead Merchant banker shall carry out such changes in the draft offer document before filing the Offer Document with ROC/SEs. The Draft Offer document is available on the SEBI website for public comments for a period of 21 days from the filing of the Draft Offer Document with SEBI.

(c) *"Red Herring Prospectus"* is a prospectus which does not have details of, either price .or number of shares being offered or the amount of issue. This means that in case price is not disclosed, the number of shares and the upper and lower price bands are disclosed. On the other hand, an issuer can state the issue size and the number of shares are determined later. An RHP for and FPO can be filed with the RoC without the price band and the issuer, in such a case will notify the floor price or a price band by way of an advertisement one day prior to the opening of the issue. In the case of book-built issues, it is a process of price discovery and the price cannot be determined until the bidding process is completed. Hence, such details are not shown in the Red Herring prospectus filed with ROC in terms of the provisions of the Companies Act. Only on completion of the bidding process, the details of the final price are included in the offer document. The offer document filed thereafter with ROC is called a prospectus.

(d) *"Abridged Prospectus"* means the memorandum as prescribed in Form 2A under sub-section (3) of section 56 of the Companies Act, 1956. It contains all the salient features of a prospectus. It accompanies the application form of public issues.

PRICE OF AN ISSUE

Indian primary market ushered in an era of free pricing in 1992. Following this, the guidelines have provided that the issuer in consultation with Merchant Banker shall decide the price. There is no price formula stipulated by SEBI. SEBI does not play any role in price fixation. The company and merchant banker are however required to give full disclosures of the parameters which they had considered while deciding the issue price. There are two types of issues one where company and Lead Manager fix a price (called fixed price) and other, where the company and Lead Manger stipulate a floor price or a price band and leave it to market forces to determine the final price (price discovery through book building process).

Fixed Price Offers

An issuer company is allowed to freely price the issue. The basis of issue price is disclosed in the offer document where the issuer discloses in detail about the qualitative and quantitative factors justifying the issue price. The Issuer company can mention a price band of 20% (cap in the price band should not be more than 20% of the floor price) in the Draft offer documents filed with SEBI and actual price can be determined at a later date before filing of the final offer document with SEBI/ROCs.

SEBI's Disclosure and Investor Protection guidelines for new issues are:

- An unlisted company may make an initial public offering (IPO) of equity shares or any other security, which may be converted into or exchanged with equity shares at a later date. Provided, it has a track record of profitability, and meets the conditions of net worth, net tangible assets, etc. as specified in the guidelines.
- An unlisted company not complying with any of the above conditions may still make an IPO, if it meets the conditions:
  - (a) (i) The issue is made through the book-building process, with at least 50% of the issue size being allotted to the Qualified Institutional Buyers (QIBs). Failing which the full subscription money have to be refunded, OR
  - (a) (ii) The "project" has at least 15% participation by Financial Institutions/Scheduled Commercial Banks, of which at least 10% comes from the appraiser(s). In addition, at least 10% of the issue size is to be allotted to QIBs, otherwise, the full subscription monies is to be refunded, AND
  - (b) (i) The minimum post-issue face value capital of the company has to be Rs. 10 crore, OR
  - (b) (ii) There should be a compulsory market-making for at least 2 years from the date of listing of the shares subject to certain conditions as specified in the guidelines.
- A listed company is eligible to make a public offer of equity shares or any other security which is

convertible into equity shares. But, the aggregate issue size of the proposed issue along with all the previous issues made during the same financial year should not exceed 5 times its pre-issue net worth as per the audited balance sheet of the last financial year. If the name of the company has been changed in the last one year, then the revenue accounted for by the activity suggested by the new name should not be less than 50% of its total revenue in the preceding one full-year period.

- No company can make a public or rights issue of debt instruments (whether convertible or not), unless the following conditions are satisfied: Credit rating of not less than investment grade is obtained from not less than two SEBI registered credit rating agencies and the company should not be in the list of willful defaulters of RBI. They should not have defaulted payment of interest or repayment of principal, if any, for a period of more than 6 months.
- An issuer company should not allot non-convertible debt instrument pursuant to a public issue, if the proposed allottees are less than fifty. In such a case, the company should forthwith refund the entire subscription amount received; a delay beyond 8 days attracts a penal charge of 15% per annum.
- Prior to an IPO, the shares held by the persons other than the promoters, which are locked in may be transferred to any other person holding shares. This should be subjected to continuation of lock-in in the hands of transferees for the remaining period and compliance with the SEBI (Substantial Acquisition of Shares and Takeovers) Regulations, 1997.
- Shares held by promoter(s), which are locked-in, may be transferred to and amongst promoter/promoter group or to a new promoter or persons in control of the company. Provided the lock-in of shares in the hands of transferees for the remaining period remains. They should also comply with the SEBI (Substantial Acquisition of Shares and Takeovers) Regulations, 1997.

- As in case of equity shares, the transfer of the locked in preference shares/instruments is subject to the same norms and comply with SEBI (Substantial Acquisition of Shares and Takeovers) Regulations, 1997.
- The lock-in period in respect of the shares issued on preferential basis pursuant to a scheme approved under Corporate Debt Restructuring framework should commence from the date of allotment. The lock-in period should continue for a period of one year. In case of partly paid up shares the lock-in period should commence from the date of allotment and continue for a period of one year from the date when shares become fully paid up.
- Unless the entire shareholding is held in dematerialized form, no listed company is permitted to make preferential issue of equity shares, warrants, Partly Convertible Debentures (PCDs), Fully Convertible Debentures (FCDs) or any other financial instruments convertible into or exchanged with equity shares at a later date.
- In case of the shares, warrants, PCDs, FCDs or any other financial instruments convertible into equity shares, which are issued on preferential basis, the entire pre-preferential allotment shareholding should be under lock-in. The lock-in period shall start from the relevant date up to a period of six months from the date of preferential allotment. In addition, the shareholders, who have sold their shares during the six months period prior to the relevant date, would not be eligible for allotment of shares on preferential basis.
- Following the withdrawal of the concept of a regional stock exchange, companies have to choose one stock exchanges as a designated stock exchange for the purpose of finalization of the basis of allotment.

NEW ISSUE *VIS-À-VIS* BOOK-BUILDING

Book-building is a process undertaken by which a demand

for the securities proposed to be issued by a body of corporate is elicited and built up and the price for such securities is assessed for the determination of the quantum of such securities to be issued by means of a notice, circular, advertisement, document. Book Building is basically a capital issuance process used in Initial Public Offer (IPO) which aids price and demand discovery. It is a process used for marketing a public offer of equity shares of a company. It is a mechanism where, during the period for which the book for the IPO is open, bids are collected from investors at various prices, which are above or equal to the floor price. The process aims at tapping both wholesale and retail investors. The offer/issue price is then determined after the bid closing date based on certain evaluation criteria.

BOOK BUILDING AND NORMAL PUBLIC ISSUE

Fixed Price Process

- Price at which the securities are offered/allotted is known in advance to the investor.
- Demand for the securities offered is known only after the closure of the issue.
- Payment if made at the time of subscription wherein refund is given after allocation.

Book Building Process

- Price at which securities will be offered/allotted is not known in advance to the investor. Only an indicative price range is known.
- Demand for the securities offered can be known everyday as the book is built.
- Payment is made only after allocation.

Types of Book-Building Process

Book building is a price discovery mechanism. Based on the bids received at various prices from the investors, demand is assessed and then the price of the securities is discovered. The issuer proposing to issue capital through book building has *two options*, viz., 75% book building route and 100% book building route. In case of issue of securities through the first route, 75% of the net offer is made through book building process and 25% at the price determined by book building. In this case not more than 50% should be available for allocation to QIBs and not less than 25% to non-QIBs. The balance 25% should be made to the public at the price determined through book building. In case a company makes a issue of 100% of the net offer to public through 100% book building process, then not less than 25% should be available for allocation to retail individual investors, not less than 25% to non-institutional investors and not more than 50% for QIBs. Allotment to retail individual investors and non-institutional investors are made on the basis of the proportionate allotment system within 15 days of the closure of the issue; failing of which attracts a penal charge of 15% which is paid to the investors. In case of under subscription in any category, the unsubscribed portions can be allocated to the bidders in other categories.

Besides, book building also requires that: issuer should provide indicative floor price and no ceiling price, bids to remain open for at least 5 days, only electronic bidding is permitted, bids are submitted through syndicate members, investors can bid at any price, retail investors have option to bid at cut-off price, bidding demand is displayed at the end of every day, the lead manager analyses the demand generated and determines the issue price in consultation with the issuer, etc.

Book Building through On-line IPO System: Book building is basically a process used in IPO for efficient price discovery. During the period when the offer is open, bids are collected from investors at various prices, which are above or equal to the floor price. The offer price is determined after the bid closing date. In its endeavor to continuously improve the Indian securities market, NSE has offered an infrastructure for conducting online IPOs through book building. It helps to discover prices as well as demand for the security to be issued through a process of bidding. The advantages are:

(a) The investor parts with money only after the allotment,

(b) It eliminates refunds except in case of direct applications, and

(c) It reduces the time taken to process the issue. The securities get listed within 15 days from the closure of the issue. Though the guidelines for book building were issued in 1995, it is being also used for IPOs only from 1999. Till June 2004, 36 issuers have used this route for making IPO issues. Several issues have hit the market after that.

Total public issue (i.e., net offer to the public): 75% of the public issue can be offered to institutional investors who had participated in the bidding process.

Fixed price method: 25% of the public issue can be offered to the public through prospectus and shall be reserved for allocation to individual investors who had not participated in the bidding process of book-building. It defined the term as "an international practice that refers to collecting orders from investment bankers and large investors based on an indicative price range. In capital markets, with sufficient width and depth, such a pre-issue exercise often allows the issue to get a better idea of the demand and the final offer price of an intended public offer."

BOOK BUILDING PROCESS IN INDIA

Offer to Public through Book-Building Process: The process specifies that an issuer company may make an issue of securities to the public through prospectus in the following manner:

- 100 per cent of the net offer to the public through book building process, or
- 75 per cent of the net offer to the public through book building process and 25 per cent of the net offer to the public at a price determined through book building process.

SEBI has redefined the retail individual investor as one who applies or bids for securities of or for a value not exceeding Rs. 1 lakh. It has reduced the non-institutional category, popularly known as high net worth individuals (HNI), allocation from 25 per cent to 15 per cent. Institutional investors include foreign financial institutions (FII) banks, mutual funds and Indian financial institutions like LIC or IDBI.

The principal parties/intermediaries involved in a book building process are:

- The issuer company,
- The Book Running Lead Manager (BRLM) who is a Category I Merchant Banker registered with SEBI, and
- *The Syndicate*: Members who are intermediaries registered with SEBI and who are permitted to carryon activities as underwriters. Syndicate Members are appointed by Book Running Lead Manager.

Pre Book-building Activities

1. Nominate Book Runner.
2. Form Syndicate of Brokers, Arrangers, Underwriters, Financial Institutions, etc.
3. Submit Draft Offer Document to SEBI without mentioning Coupon Rate or Price.
4. Circulate offer Document among the Syndicate Members.
5. Ask for Bids on Price.
6. Aggregate and forward all offers to Book Runner.
7. Run the Book to maintain a record of Subscribers and their Orders.
8. Consult with Issuer and determine the issue Price as Weighted Average of the Offers Received.
9. Firm up Underwriting Commitments.
10. Allot Securities among Syndicate Members.
11. Securities Issued and Listed.
12. Trading Commences on Exchanges.

The steps for book building process are :

1. Preparation of draft prospectus,
2. Formation of Syndicate,
3. Record of orders,
4. Consolidation,
5. Closure of order book,
6. Determination of price,
7. Agreement with syndicate members,
8. Payment in advance,
9. Filling of prospectus,
10. Two Separate accounts are opened by the issuer company for collection of application money,
11. Collection of application for securities,
12. Allotment of placement and public portions,
13. The placement portion may be used to adjust under subscription,
14. Rate of allotment, and
15. Maintenance of records.

Book Building Guidelines

1. The issuer company should enter into an agreement with one or more stock exchange(s), which have the requisite system to offer on-line securities. The agreement should specify the rights, duties, responsibilities and obligations of the company and the stock exchange(s). The agreement should also provide for a dispute resolution mechanism between them.
2. The freedom is given to the issuer company to list the securities on any other exchange and not necessarily on the exchange through which the company has offered the securities.
3. The book runner(s)/syndicate members should appoint SEBI registered brokers to accept bids, applications and placing orders with the company. The appointed brokers should be financially capable of honouring their commitments arising out of defaults of their clients/investors, if any.

4. The company should pay the broker/s a commission/fee for the services rendered.
5. The brokers are not allowed to levy a service fee on his clients/investors for his services.
6. If the offer is through 100% book building process, then the following rules apply: (a) not less than 25% of the net offer should be made to retail individual investors; (b) not less than 25% of the net offer to non-institutional investors, i.e. other than retail individual investors and QIBs; and (c) not more than 50% of the net offer for QIBs.
7. If 75% of the net offer is through book building process and 25% at the price determined through book building, then (a) in the book built portion, not less than 25% and not more than 50% of the net offer should be available for allocation to non QIBs; (b) the balance 25%, offered at a price determined through book building, should be available only to retail individual investors. They will be either those who have not participated or have not received any allocation, in the book built portion. It is mandatory that 50% of the issue size is allotted to the QIBs.
8. *Pricing of Issues*: For an IPO by an unlisted company, if the issue price is Rs. 500 or more, the issuer company has the discretion to fix the face value below Rs. 10 per share subject to a lower limit of not less than Re. 1 per share. In case the issue price is below Rs. 500 per share, the face value ought to be Rs. 10 per share. The face value of shares should be disclosed in the advertisements and offer documents.
9. *Post Issue Obligations:* The allotment of shares should be on a proportionate basis within the specified categories, rounded-off to the nearest integer. This will be subject to a minimum allotment being equal to the minimum application size as fixed and disclosed in the offer document.
10. *Green Shoe Option*: An issuer company making a public offer of equity shares can avail of the Green Shoe Option (GSO) for stabilizing post listing of its shares, subject to certain provisions in the guidelines

such as: A company desirous of availing the option should seek authorization in the general meeting for allotment of the additional shares to the 'stabilizing agent' (SA) at the end of the stabilization period. The company should appoint one of the merchant bankers or book runners, as the SA. They will be responsible for the price stabilization process, if required. Prior to filing of offer document with SEBI, the SA should enter into an agreement with the issuer company clearly stating all the terms and conditions relating to this option including fees charged/ expenses to be incurred. The SA should also enter into an agreement with the promoter(s) or pre-issue shareholders who will lend their shares. The agreement should specify the maximum number of shares that may be borrowed from the promoters or the shareholders which should not be in excess of 15% of the total issue size. The allocation of these shares should be on pro-rata basis to all the applicants. The stabilization mechanism should be available for not more than 30 days from the date when trading is permitted on the exchange(s). The promoters and pre-issue shareholders, of both unlisted and listed company, holding more than 5% shares should lend the shares for the purpose of GSO.

11. *Contents of Offer Document*: The draft offer document and the final offer document should be approved by the Board of Directors and signed by all the Directors (including the managing director), Chief Executive Officer and Chief Financial Officer. They should also certify that all the disclosures made in the offer document are true and correct.
12. *Disclose pertinent information:* Some of the pertinent information have to be disclosed irrespective of the issue prices viz., Earnings per share, EPS pre-issue for the last three years, P/E pre-issue, average return on net worth in the last 3 years, minimum return on increased net worth required to maintain pre-issue EPS, NAV per share based on last balance sheet, NAV

per share after issue and comparison thereof with the issue price, comparison of all the accounting ratios of the issuer company. However, the projected earnings should not be used as a justification for the issue price in the offer document. Further, the accounting ratios disclosed in the offer documents in support of the issue price should be calculated after giving effect to the consequent increase in capital on account of compulsory conversions outstanding as well as on the assumption that the options outstanding, if any, to subscribe for additional capital will be exercised.

13. *Guidelines for Issue of Advertisements:* Every time the issue is advertised on television screen, the risk factors should not be scrolled on the screen, but the advertisement should advise the viewers to refer to the red herring prospectus or other offer document for details.
14. *Miscellaneous:* The Board should provide exemptions regarding any particular provision(s) of these guidelines viz., (i) on an application made by any listed company or intermediary connected with the issue, (ii) of a technical violation or a possible violation, or (iii) on being satisfied that the violation was caused or may be caused due to factors beyond the control of the applicant.
15. The minimum application value should be within the range of Rs. 5,000 to Rs. 7,000 and in multiples thereof.
16. In a public issue by a listed company, the reservations can be made for the shareholders, who hold shares worth up to Rs. 50,000 on the record date, for allotment on proportionate basis as in case of allotment in public category.

POINTS TO BE KEPT IN MIND BY INVESTORS ENTERING PRIMARY MARKET/BOOK BUILDING ROUTE

1. *Price band:* The red herring prospectus may contain either the floor price for the securities or a price band within which the investors can bid, the spread

between the floor and the cap of the price band shall not be more than 20%. In other words, it means that the cap should not be more than 120% of the floor price. The price band can have a revision and such a revision in the price band shall be widely disseminated by informing the stock exchanges, by issuing press release and also indicating the change on the relevant website and the terminals of the syndicate members. In case the price band is revised, the bidding period shall be extended for a further period of three days, subject to the total bidding period not exceeding thirteen days.

2. *Decision on the price band:* It may be understood that the regulatory mechanism does not playa role in setting the price for issues. It is up to the company to decide on the price or the price band, in consultation with Merchant Bankers. The basis of issue price is disclosed in the offer document. The issuer is required to disclose in detail about the qualitative and 'quantitative factors' justifying the issue price.
3. *Firm allotment:* A company making an issue to public can reserve some shares on "allotment on firm basis" for some categories as specified in DIP guidelines. Allotment on firm basis indicates that allotment to the investor is on firm basis. DIP guidelines provide for maximum percent of shares which can be reserved on firm basis. The shares to be allotted on "firm allotment category" can be issued at a price different from the price at which the net offer to the public is made provided that the price at which the security is being offered to the applicants in firm allotment category is higher than the price at which securities are offered to public.
4. *Reservation on competitive basis:* Reservation on Competitive Basis is when allotment of shares is made in proportion to the shares applied for by the concerned reserved categories. Reservation on competitive basis can be made in a public issue to the Employees of the company, Shareholders of the promoting companies in the case of a new company

and shareholders of group companies in the case of an existing company, Indian Mutual Funds, Foreign Institutional Investors (including non-resident Indians and overseas corporate bodies), Indian and Multilateral development Institutions and Scheduled Banks.

5. *Preference on allotment:* The allotment to the Qualified Institutional Buyers (QIBs) is on a discretionary basis. The discretion is left to the Merchant Bankers who first disclose the parameters of judgment in the Red Herring Prospectus. There are no objective conditions stipulated as per the DIP Guidelines. The Merchant Bankers are free to set their criteria and mention the same in the Red Herring Prospectus.
6. *Eligibility for reservation:* In a book built issue allocation to Retail Individual Investors (RIIs), Non-Institutional Investors (NIIs) and Qualified Institutional Buyers (QIBs) is in the ratio of 35 : 15 : 50 respectively. In case the book built issues are made pursuant to the requirement of mandatory allocation of 60% to QIBs in terms of Rule 19(2)(b) of SCRR, the respective figures are 30% for RIIs and 10% for NIIs. This is a transitory provision pending harmonization of the QIB allocation in terms of the aforesaid Rule with that specified in the guidelines.
7. *Retail Investor:* 'Retail individual investor' means an investor who applies or bids for securities of or for a value of not more than Rs. 1,00,000
8. *Retail investor in a book-built issue:* He can bid in a book-built issue for a value not more than Rs. 1,00,000. Any bid made in excess of this will be considered in the HNI category.
9. *"Online bidding":* A company proposing to issue capital to public through the on-line system of the stock exchange for offer of securities can do so if it complies with the requirements. The appointment of various intermediaries by the issuer includes a prerequisite that such members/registrars have the required facilities to accommodate such an online

issue process. An investor may place his bids through the online terminals offered by some of the brokers.

10. *How to get a form for applying/bidding for the shares:* The form for applying/bidding of shares is available with all syndicate members, collection centers, the brokers to the issue and the bankers to the issue.
11. *Relying of the documents:* The document is prepared by an independent specialized agency called Merchant Banker, which is registered with SEBI. They are required to do through due diligence while preparing an offer document. The draft offer document submitted to SEBI is put on website for public comments. In case, you have any information about the issuer or its directors or any other aspect of the issue, which in your view is not factually reflected, you may send your complaint to Lead Manager to the issue or to SEBI, Division of Issues and Listing.
12. *Demat Account:* As per the requirement, all the public issues of size in excess of Rs. 10 crore, are to made compulsorily in the demat more. Thus, if an investor chooses to apply for an issue that is being made in a compulsory demat mode, he has to have a demat account and has the responsibility to put the correct DP ID and Client ID details in the bid/application forms.
13. *Things to do and not to do:* The investors are generally advised to study all the material facts pertaining to the issue including the risk factors before considering any investment. They are strongly warned against any 'tips' or relying on news obtained through unofficial means.
14. *Open of issues:* Subscription list for public issues shall be kept open for at least 3 working days and not more than 10 working days. In case of Book built issues, the minimum and maximum period for which bidding will be open is 3-7 working days extendable by 3 days in case of a revision in the price band. The public issue made by an infrastructure company, may be kept open for a maximum period of 21 working

days. As per clause 8.8.2., Rights issues shall be kept open for at least 30 days and not more than 60 days.

15. *Revise a bid:* The investor can change or revise the quantity or price in the bid using the form for changing/revising the bid that is available along with the application form. However, the entire process of changing of revising the bids shall be completed within the date of closure of the issue.
16. *Proof for bid:* The syndicate member returns the counterfoil with the signature, date and stamp of the syndicate member. The investor can retain this as a sufficient proof that the bids have been taken into account.
17. *Allotted of shares:* In case of fixed price issues, the investor is intimated about the CAN/Refund order within 30 days of the closure of the issue. In case of book built issues, the basis of allotment is finalized by the Book Running lead Managers within 2 weeks from the date of closure of the issue. The registrar then ensures that the demat credit or refund as applicable is completed within 15 days of the closure of the issue. The listing on the stock exchanges is done within 7 days from the finalization of the issue.
18. *Reliable sources to get information about response to issues:* In the case of book-built issues, the exchanges (BSE/NSE) display the data regarding the bids obtained (on a consolidated basis between both these exchanges). The data regarding the bids is also available category-wise. After the price has been determined on the basis of bidding, the statutory public advertisement containing, interalia, the price as well as a table showing the number of securities and the amount payable by an investor, based on the price determined, is issued.
19. *Timeframe on refund or allotment:* The investor is entitled to receive a Confirmatory Allotment Note (CAN) in case he has been allotted shares within 15 days from the date of closure of a book Built issue. The registrar has to ensure that the demat credit or

refund as applicable is completed within 15 days of the closure of the book built issue.

20. *Listing:* The listing on the stock exchanges is done within 7 days from the finalization of the issue. Ideally, it would be around 3 weeks after the closure of the book built issue. In case of fixed price issue, it would be around 37 days after closure of the issue.
21. *Place of getting draft offer document:* SEBI issues press releases every week regarding the draft offer documents received and observations issued during the period. The draft offer documents are put up on the website under *Reports/Documents* section. The final offer documents that are filed with SEBI/ROC are also put up for information under the same section. Copies of the draft offer documents in hard copy form may be obtained from the office of SEBI, Mittal Court, 'A' wing, Ground Floor, 224, Nariman Point, Mumbai-400021 on a payment of Rs. 100 or from SES, LMs, etc. The soft copies can be downloaded from the SEBI website under *Reports/ Documents* section. Some LMs also make it available on their web sites for download. The final offer documents that are filed with SEBI/ROC can also be downloaded from the same section of the website.

THE ROLE OF INTERMEDIARIES IN SECURITIES

Intermediary: Merchant Bankers to the issue or Book Running Lead Managers (BRLM), syndicate members, Registrars to the issue, Bankers to the issue, Auditors of the company, Underwriters to the issue, Solicitors, etc. are the intermediaries to an issue. The issuer discloses the addresses, telephone/fax numbers and email addresses of these intermediaries. In addition to this, the issuer also discloses the details of the compliance officer appointed by the company for the purpose of the issue.

Eligibility: A Merchant banker possessing a valid SEBI registration in accordance with the SEBI (Merchant Bankers) Regulations, 1992 is eligible to act as a Book Running lead Manager to an issue.

Role of a Lead Managers: In the pre-issue process, the lead Manager (LM) takes up the due diligence of company's operations, management, business plans, legal etc. Other activities of the LM include drafting and design of Offer documents, Prospectus, statutory advertisements and memorandum containing salient features of the Prospectus. The BRLMs shall ensure compliance with stipulated requirements and completion of prescribe formalities with the Stock Exchanges, RoC and SEBI including finalization 0 Prospectus and RoC filing. Appointment of other intermediaries viz. Registrar(s), Printers, Advertising Agency and Bankers to the Offer is also included in the pre-issue processes. The LM also draws up the various marketing strategies for the issue.

The post-issue activities including management of escrow accounts coordinate non-institutional allocation, intimation of allocation and dispatch of refunds to bidders etc are performed by the LM. The post Offer activities for the Offer will involve essential follow-up steps, which include the finalization of trading and dealing of instruments and dispatch of certificate: and demat of delivery of shares, with the various agencies connected with the work such as the Registrar(s) to the Offer and. Bankers to the Offer are the bank handling refund business. The merchant banker shall be responsible for ensuring that these agencies fulfil their functions and enable it to discharge this responsibility through suitable agreements with the Company.

Role of a Registrar: The Registrar finalizes the list of eligible allotees after deleting the invalid applications and ensures that the corporate action for crediting of shares to the demat accounts of the applicants is done and the dispatch of refund orders to those applicable are sent. The Lead manager coordinates with the Registrar to ensure follow-up so that that the flow of applications from collecting bank branches, processing of the applications and other matters till the basis of allotment is finalized, dispatch security certificates and refund orders completed and securities listed.

Role of Bankers to the Issue: Bankers to the issue, as the name suggests, carries out all the activities of ensuring that the funds are collected and transferred to the Escrow accounts. The Lead Merchant Banker shall ensure that Bankers to the Issue are appointed in all the mandatory collection centers as specified in DIF Guidelines. The Lead Manager also ensures follow-up with bankers to the issue to get quick estimates of collection and advising the issuer about closure of the issue, based on the correct figures.

Due diligence: The Lead Managers state that they have examined various documents including those relating to litigation like commercial disputes, patent disputes, disputes with collaborators, etc. and other materials in connection with the finalization of the offer document pertaining to the said issue; and on the basis of such examination and the discussions with the Company, its Directors and other officers, other agencies, independent verification of the statements concerning the objects of the issue, projected profitability, price justification, etc., they state that they have ensured that they are in compliance with SEBI, the Government and any other competent authority in this behalf.

CONTENTS OF OFFER DOCUMENT

1. *Cover Page:* The Cover Page of the offer document covers full contact details of the issuer company, lead managers and registrars, the nature, number, price and amount of installments offered and issue size, and the particulars regarding listing. Other details such as Credit Rating, risks in relation to the first issue, etc. are disclosed if applicable.
2. *Risk Factors:* The issuer's management gives its view on the Internal and external risks faced by the company. The company also makes a note on the forward looking statements. This information is disclosed in the initial pages of the document and it is also clearly disclosed in the abridged prospectus. It is generally advised that the investors should go through all the risk factors of the company before making an investment decision.
3. *Introduction:* The introduction covers a summary of the industry and business of the issuer company, the offering details in brief, summary of consolidated financial, operating and other data. General

Information about the company, the merchant bankers and their responsibilities, the details of brokers/syndicate members to the Issue, credit rating (in case of debt issue), debenture trustees (in case of debt issue), monitoring agency, book building process in brief and details of underwriting Agreements are given here. Important details of capital structure, objects of the offering, funds requirement, funding plan, schedule of implementation, funds deployed, sources of financing of funds already deployed, sources of financing for the balance fund requirement, interim use of funds, basic terms of issue, basis for issue price, tax benefits are covered.

4. *About issuer:* This presents a review of on the details of the business of the company, business strategy, competitive strengths, insurance, industry-regulation (if applicable), history and corporate structure, main objects, subsidiary details, management and board of directors, compensation, corporate governance, related party transactions, exchange rates, currency of presentation, dividend policy and management's discussion and analysis of financial condition and results of operations are given.
5. *Financial Statements:* Financial statement, changes in accounting policies in the last three years and differences between the accounting policies and the Indian Accounting Policies (if the Company has presented its Financial Statements also as per either US GAAP/IAS are presented.
6. *Legal and other information:* Outstanding litigations and material developments, litigations involving the company and its subsidiaries, promoters and group companies are disclosed. Also material developments since the last balance sheet date, government approvals/licensing arrangements, investment approvals (FIPB/RBI, etc.), all government and other approvals, technical approvals, indebtedness, etc. are disclosed.

7. *Other regulatory and statutory disclosures:* Under this head, the information includes authority for the Issue, prohibition by SEBI, eligibility of the company to enter the capital market, disclaimer clause, disclaimer in respect of jurisdiction, distribution of information to investors, disclaimer clause of the stock exchanges, listing, impersonation, minimum subscription, letters of allotment or refund orders, consents, expert opinion, changes in the auditors in the last 3 years, expenses of the issue, fees payable to the lead managers, fees payable to the issue management team, fees payable to the registrars, underwriting commission, brokerage and selling commission, previous rights and public issues, previous issues for cash, issues otherwise than for cash, outstanding debentures or bonds, outstanding preference shares, commission and brokerage on previous issues, capitalization of reserves or profits, option to subscribe in the issue, purchase of property, revaluation of assets, classes of shares, stock market data for equity, shares of the company, promise *vis-a-vis* performance in the past issues and mechanism for redressal of investor grievances.
8. *Offering information:* Under this head, the information includes Terms of the Issue, ranking of equity shares, mode of payment of dividend, face value and issue price, rights of the equity shareholder, market lot, nomination facility to investor, issue procedure, book building procedure if applicable, bid form, who can bid, maximum and minimum bid size, bidding process, bidding bids at different price levels, escrow mechanism, terms of payment and payment into the escrow collection account, electronic registration of bids, build up of the book and revision of bids, price discovery and allocation, signing of underwriting agreement and filing of prospectus' with SEBI/ROC, announcement of statutory advertisement, issuance of confirmation of allocation note ("can") and allotment in the issue, designated date, general instructions, instructions for completing the bid form,

payment instructions, submission of bid form, other instructions, disposal of application and application moneys, interest on refund of excess bid amount, basis of allotment or allocation, method of proportionate allotment, dispatch of refund orders, communications, undertaking by the company, utilization of issue proceeds, restrictions on foreign ownership of Indian securities, etc.

9. *Other Information:* This covers description of equity shares and terms of the Articles of Association, material contracts and documents for inspection, declaration, definitions and abbreviations, etc.

NEW TERMS AND CONCEPTS IN SECURITIES ISSUE

1. *Green-shoe Option:* A Green Shoe option means an option of allocating shares in excess of the shares included in the public issue and operating a post-listing price stabilizing mechanism for a period not exceeding 30 days, which is granted to a company to be exercised through a Stabilizing Agent. This is an arrangement wherein the issue would be over allotted to the extent of a maximum of 15% of the issue size. From an investor's perspective, an issue with green shoe option provides more probability of getting shares and also that post listing price may show relatively more stability as compared to market.
2. *E-IPO:* A company proposing to issue capital to public through the on-line system of the stock exchange for offer of securities can do so if it complies with the requirements under Chapter 11A of DIP Guidelines. The appointment of various intermediaries by the issuer includes a prerequisite that such members/registrars have the required facilities to accommodate such an online issue process.
3. *Safety Net:* Any safety net scheme or buy-back arrangements of the shares proposed in any public issue shall be finalized by, an issuer company with

the lead merchant banker in advance and disclosed in the prospectus. Such buy back or safety net arrangements shall be made available only to all original resident individual allottee is limited up to a maximum of 1000 shares per allottee and the offer is kept open for a period of 6 months from the last date of dispatch of securities. The details regarding Safety Net are covered under Clause 8.18 of DIP Guidelines.

4. *Syndicate Member:* The Book Runner(s) may appoint those intermediaries who are registered with the Board and who are permitted to carryon activity as an 'Underwriter' as syndicate members. The syndicate members are mainly appointed to collect entire bid forms in a book-built issue.
5. *Open book/closed book:* Presently, in issues made through book building, Issuers and merchant bankers are required to ensure online display of the demand and bids during the bidding period. This is the Open book system of book building. Here, the investor can be guided by the movements of the bids during the period in which the bid is kept open. Under closed book building, the book is not made public and the bidders will have to take a call on the price at which they intend to make a bid without having any information on the bids submitted by other bidders.
6. *Hard underwriting:* Hard underwriting is when an underwriter agrees to buy his commitment at its earliest stage. The underwriter guarantees a fixed amount to the issuer from the issue. Thus, in case the shares are not subscribed by investors, the issue is devolved on underwriters and they have to bring in the amount by subscribing to the shares. The underwriter bears a risk which is much higher in soft underwriting.
7. *Soft underwriting:* Soft underwriting is when an underwriter agrees to buy the shares at later stages as soon as the pricing process is complete. He then, immediately places those shares with institutional players. The risk faced by the underwriter as such is reduced to a small window of time. Also, the soft

underwriter has the option to invoke a *'force Majeure'* (acts of God) clause in case there are certain factors beyond the control that can affect the underwriter's ability to place the shares with the buyers.

8. *Cut-off Price:* In Book building issue, the issuer is required to indicate either the price band or a floor price in the red herring prospectus. The actual discovered issue price can be any price in the price band or any price above the floor price. This issue price is called "Cut-off price". This is decided by the issuer and Lead Manager after considering the book and investors' appetite for the stock. SEBI (DIP) guidelines permit only retail individual investors to have an option of applying at cut-off price.
9. *Differential pricing:* Pricing of an issue where one category is offered shares at a price different from the other category is called differential pricing. In DIP Guidelines differential pricing is allowed only if the securities to applicants) in the firm allotment category is at a price higher than the price at which the net offer to the public is made. The net offer to the public means the offer made to the Indian public and does not include firm allotments or reservations or promoters' contributions.
10. *Basis of Allocation/Basis of Allotment:* After the closure of the issue, the bids received are aggregated under different categories i.e., firm allotment, Qualified Institutional Buyers (QIBs), Non-Institutional Buyers (NIBs), Retail, etc. The over subscription ratios are then calculated for each of the categories as against the shares reserved for each of the categories in the offer document. Within each of these categories, the bids are then segregated into different buckets based on the number of shares applied for. The oversubscription ratio is then applied to the number of shares applied for and the number of shares to be allotted for applicants in each of the buckets is determined. Then, the number of successful allottees is determined. This process is followed in case of proportionate allotment. In case of allotment for

QIBs, it is subject to the discretion of the post-issue lead manager.

11. *Qualified Institutional Buyer (QIBs):* Qualified Institutional Buyers are those institutional investors who are generally perceived to possess expertise and the financial muscle to evaluate and invest in the capital markets. These entitles are not required to be registered with SEBI as QIBs. Any entity falling under the categories specified above are considered as QIBs for the purpose of participating in primary issuance process. A 'Qualified Institutional Buyer' shall mean:
    - Public financial institution as defined in section 4A of the Companies Act, 1956.
    - Scheduled commercial banks.
    - Mutual funds.
    - Foreign institutional investor registered with SEBI.
    - Multilateral and bilateral development financial institutions.
    - Venture capital funds registered with SEBI.
    - Foreign Venture capital investors registered with SEBI.
    - State Industrial Development Corporations.
    - Insurance Companies registered with the Insurance Regulatory and Development Authority (IRDA).
    - Provident Funds with minimum corpus of Rs. 25 crores.
    - Pension Funds with minimum corpus of Rs. 25 crores.

12

Derivatives Market

SNAP SHOTS ON DERIVATIVES

- In November 1996 L.C. Gupta Committee was set-up and in 1998 the recommendations of L.C. Gupta Committee was accepted by the Government.
- Subsequently in February 1999, Securities Contract (Amendment) Act was passed and definition of derivatives was inserted in SCRA.
- In June 2000, the actual trading in Index Futures started on Bombay Stock Exchange (BSE) and National Stock Exchange (NSE).

Derivatives include options and futures. Certain options are short-term in nature and are issued by investors. These options may be long-term in nature and are issued by companies in the process of financing their activities. The trading in derivatives are things of US origin and in US the Organized exchanges began trading in options on equities in 1973 and on debt from 1982.

In India the term 'derivatives' initially, had its reference to the bank transaction when banks created deposits out of primary deposits. The primary deposit is received by banks and the same is lent on book credit. The bank does not give cash to the borrower but provides him with a cheque book and allows him to draw for payment. When these cheques presented in the bank, they create deposits and they were referred to as the derivatives. In a similar fashion, the stocks are traded in exchanges either as spot-delivery against payment or on forward market-delivery on future payment. This may or may not happen, but the purpose is to prevent any fall in price of stocks which is an insurance of the risk of volatility in prices. The derivatives market consists of forward contract, futures contract, options trading and swaps market.

Contract Size

The Standing Committee on Finance, a Parliamentary Committee, at the time of recommending amendment to Securities Contract (Regulation) Act, 1956 had recommended that the minimum contract size of derivative contracts traded in the Indian Markets should be pegged not below Rs. 2 Lakhs. Based on this recommendation SEBI has specified that the value of a derivative contract should not be less than Rs. 2 Lakh at the time of introducing the contract in the market.

Lot Size of a Contract

Lot size refers to number of underlying securities in one contract. Additionally, for stock specific derivative contracts SEBI has specified that the lot size of the underlying individual security should be in multiples of 100 and fractions, if any, should be rounded-off to the next higher multiple of 100. This requirement of SEBI coupled with the requirement of minimum contract size forms the basis of arriving at the lot size of a contract.

FUTURES CONTRACT

Futures contract means a legally binding agreement to buy or sell the underlying security on a future date. Future contracts are the organized/standardized contracts in terms of quantity, quality (in case of commodities), delivery time and place for settlement on any date in future. The contract expires on a pre-specified date which is called the expiry date of the contract. On expiry, futures can be settled by delivery of the underlying assets or cash. Cash settlement entails paying/ receiving the difference between the prices at which the contract was entered and the price of the underlying asset at the time of expiry of the contract.

A futures contract is an agreement to buy a particular product at a particular price on a particular future date. Apparently, it looks similar to a forward contract. However, in futures contract the defects of the forward contracts are removed. A futures contract is an instrument which has particular product as an underlying asset. The buyer of the futures agrees to buy the underlying asset on the specified date. Similarly, the seller of the futures agrees to sell the underlying asset on the specified date. Further, in futures transactions there is no one to one transaction. All the transactions are routed through exchange and the exchange acts as a counter party to all the contracts, i.e. if one of the parties fails to perform the other party would not suffer.

The exchange regulates the futures transactions, i.e. it sets the standards of quality for the underlying asset, the quantity of the underlying asset (i.e. 100 kg, 500 kg etc.) which would represent one futures contract, market lots for the futures contracts (i.e., futures contracts can be traded only in multiple of 100, etc.), the maturity date of the contract (i.e., the date of which the seller of the futures is required to give delivery of the underlying asset), margin requirements, etc. The futures can be bought and sold in the secondary market like any other financial instrument (shares, debentures, etc.) and market price of the futures is determined on the basis of the underlying asset.

The buyer of the futures contract may either take actual delivery of the underlying asset or may square-off the contract before the maturity date. Further, since the value of the futures contract is based on the value of the underlying asset the market price of the futures would be close to that of the underlying asset as the maturity date (i.e., the date on which the contract is to be honoured and delivery is to be given) approaches and on the maturity date both the prices would match. As a result of these futures contracts are widely used as a hedge instrument and most of the times are squared off by entering into a reverse transaction before the maturity date.

The Indian Contract Act, 1872 governs the contracts in India, and is very interesting to examine whether the contracts in futures and options are valid in terms of the provisions of the law governing contracts, Section 30 of the Indian Contract states that agreement by way of wager are void. The Contract Act does not define what is wager however over a period of time it has emerged that the following features make a transaction a wager:

(1) Uncertain event,
(2) Mutual chances of gain or loss,
(3) Neither part has control over the event, and
(4) No other interest in the event.

The fourth condition above indicates that the parties do not have any other interest in the agreement except the wager. For example, in an insurance contract the person taking insurance has interest in the property insured and accordingly such contract can not be said to be a wager. If the characteristics of futures and option contracts are analyzed it can be observed that such contracts are speculative in nature and satisfy the above test. Accordingly, futures and option contracts are void in terms of section 30 of the Indian Contract Act, 1872. Further, section 20 of the Securities Contracts (Regulation) Act, 1956 (SCRA) specifically prohibited options in securities. The government has taken following steps to ensue that the contracts in futures and options are not void in terms of the law. Section 20 of SCRA was deleted w.e.f. January 25, 1995 by the Securities Laws (Amendment) Act, 1995. Section 18A was inserted in SCRA by Securities Law (Amendment) Act, 1999. In terms of this section notwithstanding anything contained in any other law for the time being in force, contracts in derivative shall be legal and valid if such contracts are: (a) traded on a recognized stock exchange, and (b) settled on the clearing house of the recognized stock exchange. Thus, notwithstanding the provisions of section 30 of the Contract Act, 1872 contracts in futures and options would be legal and valid if the requirements of section 18A are satisfied.

Utility of futures market: Futures are widely used as a hedge instrument and improve quality of the market. Worldwide futures form integral part of the capital markets and add depth to the market. Further, badals are withdrawn from the Indian market and futures are introduced as a sophisticated product.

FORWARD CONTRACTS

Forward contracts are similar to futures contracts in that they are agreements to buy or sell an asset at a certain time in the future for a certain price. However, unlike futures contracts, they are not traded on an exchange. They are private agreements between two financial institutions or between a financial institution and one of its corporate clients.

One of the parties to a forward contract assumes a long position and agrees to buy the asset at a certain specified date for a certain price. The other party assumes a short position and agrees to sell the asset on the same date for the same price. Forward contracts do not have to conform to the standards of a particular exchange. The delivery date in the contract can be any date mutually convenient to the two parties. Usually, in forward contracts, a single delivery date is specified, whereas in futures contracts, there is a range of possible delivery dates. Forward contracts are not marked to market daily like futures contracts. The two parties contract to settle up on the specified delivery date. Whereas most futures contracts are closed out prior to delivery, most forward contracts do lead to delivery of the physical asset or to final settlement in cash.

Forwards *vs.* Futures

Forwards	*Futures*
Private contract between two parties	Traded on an exchange
Not standardized	Standardized contract
Usually one specified delivery date	Range of delivery dates
Settled at end of contract	Settled daily
Delivery or final cash settlement usually takes place	Contract usually closed out prior to maturity

Delivery Price: The specified price in a forward contract will be referred to as the delivery price. At the time the contract is entered into this is chosen so that the value of the contract to both parties is zero. This means that it costs nothing to take a long or a short position.

Forward Price: The forward price for a forward contract is similar in general concept to the futures price for a futures contract. A contract's current forward price is the delivery price that would apply if the contract were negotiated today. More formally, we can say that the forward price for a certain contract is defined as the delivery price which would make that contract have zero value. The forward price and the delivery price are by definition equal at the time the contract is entered into. However, as time passes, the forward price is liable to change while the delivery price, of course, remains the same. The two are not therefore equal, except by chance, at any time after the start of the contract. Generally, the forward price at any given time varies with the maturity of the contract being considered. For example, the forward price for a contract to buy or sell in three months will typically be different from that for a contract to buy or sell in six months.

Forward Contracts on Foreign Exchange

Forward contracts on foreign exchange are very popular. Large banks have a "forward desk" within their foreign exchange trading room. This is devoted to the trading of forward contracts. Forward foreign exchange rates are frequently quoted alongside spot rates.

Foreign Exchange Quotes

Futures prices are always quoted as the number of Indian Rupee per unit of the foreign currency or as the number of Indian Rupee per unit of the foreign currency, forward prices are always quoted in the same way as spot prices. This means that for the British pound, the forward quotes show the number of U.S. dollars per unit of the foreign currency and are directly comparable with futures quotes. For most other countries, forward quotes show the number of units of the foreign currency per U.S. dollar. Thus, in the forward market, a futures price of 0.6050 dollars per Swiss franc would be expressed as 1.6529 francs per dollar. This is because 1.6529 = 1/0.6050.

Forward-Rate Agreements

Forward contracts are frequently arranged on domestic interest-rate-bearing instruments as well as on foreign currencies. For example, two companies might agree that a 7 percent per annum rate of interest will apply to a one-year deposit in six months time. If the actual rate proves to be different from 7 percent per annum, one company pays and the other receives the present value of the difference between two sets of interest cash flows. This is known as a forward-rate agreement (FRA).

Disadvantages of forward contracts: The forward contract offers solution to both the parties, i.e. the buyer and the seller. However, forward contracts suffer from certain defects as follows:

- *Default risk*: In case the farmer fails to deliver wheat or the buyer fails to pay the price then the other party has no option but to go under the normal provisions of the law for the remedy which could be a long drawn procedure and their normal business would be disturbed.
- *One to One agreements:* Forward contracts are one to one agreements and there is no third party (agency) involved who would regulate and guarantee the transaction.
- *Quality of product:* In absence of standardization of the quality of the product it could lead to dispute between the buyer and the seller.

Margin Requirements

Margins are special features of the futures contract. The futures contracts are guaranteed by the exchange and it takes the counter-party risk. In fact, the margin requirements (i.e., mark to market system) works in such a manner that the contracts are settled every day and the maximum possible loss which may arise on default by either party is always recovered from the parties in the form of margins. The following example indicates how mark to market system works:

Data:

Contract size	1 futures = 1,000 kg. of Paddy
Futures price	10000
Margin	2000
Type	Sell

Day	*Futures Price*	*Daily Gain*	*Cumulative Gain*	*Margin A/c Balance*	*Margin Call*	*Margin Balance*
1	10000	—	—	2000	—	—
2	10100	(100)	(100)	1900	100	2000
3	10200	(100)	(200)	1900	100	2000
4	10150	50	(150)	2050	(50)	2000

In the above table column 2 represents the price of the futures contract in the market, column 3 represents daily gain (loss) due to change of the price of the futures, column 4 indicates the cumulative gain (loss), column 5 indicates change in the margin a/c due to change in price of the futures, column 6 indicates the margin call made to restore the margin a/c balance at 2000, column 7 indicates the margin a/c balance after the margin call.

The seller has sold one futures contract of above description for Rs. 10,000 i.e. the seller has agreed to deliver 1,000 kg. of paddy on the maturity date for Rs. 10,000. As per the requirements of the exchange he is required to maintain margin of Rs. 2000 with the, exchange. On day two the futures price moves to Rs. 10,100. This means that the seller has made a loss of Rs. 100. As mentioned above conventionally, majority of the futures contracts are settled without actual delivery.

Hence, the underlying assumption in the mark to market system is that the contract is entered into for hedging purpose and would ultimately be settled by entering into a reverse contract. Thus, if the contract is to be squared-off on day two then the seller would have to buy futures at Rs. 10,100 whereas he has sold it for Rs. 10,000. Thus, the difference of Rs. 100

represents his loss. Considering this loss of Rs. 100 the balance in his margin account goes down to Rs. 1900 and the exchange would ask (margin call) for Rs. 100 to restore his balance at Rs. 100. On day three also the market price of the futures goes up and the seller makes further loss of Rs. 100 and has to pay further call of Rs. 100. His cumulative loss on day three is Rs. 200. On day four the futures goes down to Rs. 10,150 and this fall in price indicates gain of Rs. 50 for the seller. The margin account balance goes up to Rs. 2050 and the seller will be paid the excess balance in the margin account, i.e. Rs. 50.

TYPES OF FUTURES

Index Futures: Since, futures contracts were introduced Index Futures were introduced for the first time in the Indian Capital markets. Index Futures are futures whose value is based on the value of Index, i.e. SENSEX in the case of BSE and NIFTY in the case of NSE. Index Futures were introduced for the first time in July 2000. The underlying asset in the case of Index Futures is Index itself. Index Futures work in the same manner as the commodity futures discussed above. However, since the underlying asset, i.e. Index cannot be delivered the settlement is always in the form of payment of differences in cash.

Specific Scrip Futures: Futures on specific scrip's (i.e., futures on shares of a particular company) were introduced in the market w.e.f. July 2001. The underlying asset in this case is the shares of a particular company. To begin with the settlement of specific scrip futures was cash settlement, i.e. by way of payment of difference. However, gradually it would become compulsory to settle contracts by way of actual delivery of underlying shares. Thus futures contracts in the Indian Capital markets can be broadly divided in three categories as follows:

- Index Futures.
- Specific Scrip Futures—settlement in cash.
- Specific Scrip Futures—settlement by actual delivery of underlying shares.

PLAYERS IN FUTURES MARKET

Issuer: It is interesting to note that the futures are issued by no one. Although it may be futures on shares of a company, the company does not issue such futures. The company only issues shares which are traded in the market. Futures are written by the participants in the market.

Participants: Participants in futures consist of all types of investors, i.e. individuals, financial institutions, mutual funds, foreign institutional investors, banks etc. Since, the amount required to be invested is comparatively low (i.e., only margins) it is possible even for the small investors to participate in the market.

WHETHER FUTURES TRANSACTIONS ARE SPECULATIVE?

A general view prevailing amongst the investors is that the futures transactions are speculative transactions and various reports appearing in the media also give an impression that futures transactions are speculative. The next requirement for classifying a transaction as speculative transaction is that the transaction for purchase or sale of delivery is settled otherwise than by actual delivery or transfer of the commodity or the scrip. In other words, the section requires that actual delivery of the commodity or shares contracted is to be given if the transaction is not to be treated as speculative transaction. However, the section does not require delivery of something which the parties have not agreed to deliver.

As mentioned above the futures can be broadly classified in three categories. In the case of Index Futures and Specific Scrip Futures (cash settlement) on the maturity day the transaction is settled by paying the difference in the prices and no actual delivery of underlying asset takes place. Whereas in the third type of futures, i.e. Specific Scrip Futures (actual delivery) the settlement is possible by actual delivery of the underlying shares.

Settlement of Contracts: The section uses the words "settlement of contract". However, the words "settled" or "settlement" in connection with contracts has not been defined in the Indian Contract Act, 1872 or in the Sale of Goods Act, 1930.

Index Futures and Specific Scrip Futures (Cash Settlement)

In the case of Index Futures the underlying asset is the value of the index. Strictly speaking the underlying is not an asset but only a numerical expression. As far as delivery is concerned if one closely examines the nature of the product, i.e. Index Futures and the way it functions it can be said that the product is originally designed in such a .manner that no actual delivery of the underlying asset is possible. When one enters into an agreement to buy shares of a particular company then in that case actual delivery is possible. When one buys futures on a particular commodity then actual delivery is possible. However, in the case of Index Futures its value is based on value of index which is not any commodity but just a numerical expression and a numerical expression cannot be delivered.

The product is such that every transaction is divided into two limbs and these two limbs of the contract are inseparable from each other. When one enters into the first limb of the contract—say buys Index Futures he automatically enters into the second leg also i.e., contract to sell Index Futures on the maturity date and get the price differential. The life of the product is only three months and the second limb of the transaction becomes effective automatically. Hence, buying Index Futures cannot be compared with buying shares of any company which could be held till the company is liquidated.

Even if it is assumed that the futures are commodity, it cannot be said that transactions in Index Futures or Specific Scrip Futures (cash settlement) are settled otherwise than by actual delivery of the shares as the parties never contract for the actual delivery of the shares in such contracts. Thus, such contracts cannot be said to be speculative transactions.

Specific Scrip Futures (Physical Settlement)

In the case of Specific Scrip Futures (physical settlement) it is possible to actually deliver the underlying shares. However, if the product is designed in such a manner that the only way in which contract can be settled is by payment of cash and actual delivery of underlying shares is not possible. In both the above cases it is not possible to perform the contract by actual delivery of underlying assets. More importantly when the parties enter into the agreement, the agreement is not at all for delivery of actual shares but it is for cash settlement. Thus, as observed above, section 43(5) requires the parties to deliver the commodity which was the subject matter of the contract. In the case of Index Futures and Specific Scrip Futures (cash settled) the parties have never agreed to deliver the actual shares.

Deemed Speculation Business

Explanation to section 73 of SCR Act makes any transaction of purchase or sale of shares undertaken by a company (other than certain types of companies) a speculative transaction. It should be noted that this Explanation creates a deeming fiction and even though the transaction is settled by actual delivery of the shares as required by section 43(5) it would still be treated as a speculative business. However, it should be noted that the Explanation uses the word "share" and no other security. Futures cannot be treated as shares and the Explanation cannot be applied to transactions in Futures.

Specific Scrip Futures (physical settlement): If such contracts are squared off before the maturity date then it would amount to settlement of contract otherwise than by actual delivery of the commodity. Thus such contract would amount to a speculative transaction (however with the assumption that futures are commodity).

OPTIONS

Option contract is a type of derivatives contract which gives the buyer/holder of the contract the right (but not the obligation) to buy/sell the underlying asset at a predetermined price within or at end of a specified period. The buyer/holder of the option, purchases the right from the seller/writer for a consideration which is called the premium. The seller/writer of an option is obligated to settle the option as per the terms of the contract when the buyer/holder exercises his right. The underlying asset could include securities, an index of prices of securities, etc.

Option is a right but not an obligation to do something. The Options can be divided in two parts, i.e. Call Option and Put Option. A Call Option is a right but not an obligation to buy the underlying asset at a predetermined price. A Put Option is a right but not an obligation to sell the underlying asset at a predetermined price. The person who buys the Option is called the buyer of the Option. The person who sells the Option, i.e. the person who has agreed to perform or who takes up the obligation is called the seller of the Option. Alternatively such person is also called writer of the Option. The underlying asset could be anything such as wheat, oil, currency, shares, etc. Let us take the example which was taken for the purpose of explaining Futures.

If farmer who grows wheat, then the cultivation, etc. starts—for instance in May 2006 and his crop is ready by August 2006. In May 2006, he can predict with certainty that total he would be able to produce 1,000 kg of wheat in August 2006. His total estimated cost of production is Rs. 5,000. However, he is not certain about what would be the demand for wheat in August 2006 and what would be the price prevailing in the market at that time.

The farmer is happy with profit of Rs. 2,000 and is willing to sell his production of 1,000 kg of wheat for Rs. 7,000. To lock in this profit of Rs. 2,000 he would buy a put option wherein he will have the option of selling 1,000 kg of wheat for Rs. 7,000 on August 1, 2006 to the buyer. If on August 1, 2006 if he is in a position to sell what produced by him in the market for a price more than Rs. 7,000 then he will not exercise his option (i.e. will not sell wheat to the buyer for Rs. 7,000). Instead he will go to the market and would sell his production at the prevailing market price. However, he would not get back the premium which he has paid to the writer of the Option. On August 1, 2006, if the prevailing market price is less than Rs. 7,000 then he would sell his production to the buyer who has written the Option. Thus, it can be observed that the farmer is in a position to lock his minimum required profit and at the same time also enjoys the liberty to sell the same goods to some third party if there is possibility of earning more profit. For enjoying this freedom obviously he has to pay price, i.e. Premium to the writer of the Option.

If compared with forward or futures contracts, Options look much more improved product. As examined earlier the maximum price that the farmer would have obtained is Rs. 7,000 had he written futures on wheat. Whereas in the case of Options, there is no upper limit for the price which he can fetch for his product and his maximum loss is the premium which he has paid. The buyer of the Option enjoys potential gains which has no limit. However, he pays a fixed price (premium) for it. The seller/writer of the Option bears unlimited loss. Whereas he gains a fixed assured return, i.e. premium.

American Option and European Options

Under the Securities Contracts (Regulations) Act, 1956, options on securities has been defined as "option in securities" means a contract for the purchase or sale of a right to buy or sell, or a right to buy and sell, securities in future, and includes a teji, a mandi, a teji mandi, a galli, a put, a call or a put and call in securities. An Option to buy is called Call option and option to sell is called Put option. The price at which the option is to be exercised is called Strike price or Exercise price. Depending on the date of delivery the Options can be divided into two categories, i.e., American Option and European Option. Further, if an option that is exercisable on or before the expiry date is called American option. In American Option the buyer has the right to exercise his option at any time during the period of contract. For example, if one buys an Option on April 1, which matures on June 30 then in case of American Option the buyer can ask for delivery of goods at any time between April 1 and June 30. The one that is exercisable only on expiry date, is called European option. In European Option the buyer has the right to exercise his option only on a specified day, i.e. at the end of the contract. In the above example, in case of European Option the buyer can ask for delivery only on June 30 and on no other day.

Therefore, in the case of American options the buyer has the right to exercise the option at anytime on or before the expiry date. This request for exercise is submitted to the

Exchange, which randomly assigns the exercise request to the sellers of the options, who are obligated to settle the terms of the contract within a specified time frame. As in the case of futures contracts, option contracts can also be settled by delivery of the underlying asset or cash. However, unlike futures cash settlement in option contract entails paying/receiving the difference between the strike price/exercise price and the price of the underlying asset either at the time of expiry of the contract or at the time of exercise/assignment of the option contract.

Types of Options

Currently, two types of Options are traded on the courses, viz. Index Options and Specific Scrip Options. Index Options are of European type and Specific Scrip Options are American Options. Their operations are explained hereunder.

Index Futures and Index Option Contracts

Futures contract based on an index i.e., the underlying asset is the index, are known as Index Futures Contracts, For example, futures contract on Nifty Index and BSE-30 Index. These contracts derive their value from the value of the underlying index. Similarly, the options contracts, which are based on some index, are known as Index options contract. However, unlike Index Futures, the buyer of Index Option Contracts has only the right but not the obligation to buy/sell the underlying index on expiry. Index Option Contracts are generally European Style options, i.e. they can be exercised/assigned only on the expiry date.

An index in turn derives its value from the prices of securities that constitute the index and is created to represent the sentiments of the market as a whole or of a particular sector of the economy (Sectoral Index). By its very nature, index cannot be delivered on maturity of the Index futures or Index option contracts therefore, these contracts are essentially cash settled on expiry.

Index Options: In the case of Index Option the underlying asset is value of Index, i.e. Sensex or SandP CNX Nifty. However, as the Index cannot be delivered the settlement is done by paying the difference in cash. For example, let Mr. X buy a call option on Nifty from Mr. Y at strike price of Rs. 1,300. Premium payable by X say Rs. 10. If on the agreed date if value of Nifty is more than Rs. 1,300 (say 1400), then X would exercise his option and Y would pay him Rs. 100 (i.e., 1,400-1,300). However, if the Nifty is at Rs. 1,200 then X would not exercise the option.

Specific Scrip Option: Specific Scrip Options started trading on NSE from July 2, 2001. For example, X may enter into an Option contract with Y whereby Y agrees to sell 100 shares of SVS Ltd. @ Rs. 50 per share after three months if X decides to buy such shares. Thus, X has the option to buy or not to buy shares after three months on the basis of prevailing market price. For enjoying the potential gain X would pay price to Y which would be Y's consideration for bearing the potential price risk. Let us assume this premium to be Rs. 4 per share. In the above example, the actual settlement is done by giving actual-delivery of shares of SVS Ltd. However, the contracts introduced on NSE and BSE the settlement is done by paying the price differential as against delivery of actual shares. Gradually the contracts may be required to be settled only by giving actual delivery.

Thus Options can be divided in three categories as follows:

- Index Options.
- Specific Scrip Options (cash settlement).
- Specific Scrip Options (physical settlement).

PLAYERS IN OPTIONS

Issuer: It is interesting to note that the options are issued by no one. Although it may be options on shares of a company, the company does not issue such options. The company only issues shares which are traded in the market. Options are written by the participants in the market.

Participants: Participants in options consists of all types of investors such as individuals, financial institutions, mutual funds, FIIs, banks, etc. Since the amount required to be invested is comparatively low, it is possible even for the small investors to participate in the market.

Utility of options market: It is widely used to hedge instruments and improves quality of market. Worldwide options form integral part of the capital markets and add depth to the market. Further, badlas are withdrawn from the Indian capital market and options are introduced as a sophisticated product.

HEDGING

Like futures contracts, forward contracts can be used for hedging. Suppose a Indian company knows that it is due to pay Rs. 10,00,000 in 90 days and the 90 days forward rate is 1.8381. It can choose at no cost to enter into a long forward contract to buy Rs. 10,00,000 in 90 days for Rs. 18,38,100. In this way, it hedges its foreign exchange risk by locking in the exchange rate that will apply to the sterling it requires. Similarly, an Indian company that knows it is due to receive Rs. 10,00,000 in 90 days can at no cost enter into a short forward contract to sell Rs. 10,00,000 in 90 days for Rs. 18,38,100. In this way, it hedges its foreign exchange risk by locking in the price that will apply to the sterling it receives.

Speculation

Forward contracts can be used for speculation as well as hedging. An investor who thinks that sterling will increase in value relative to the Indian rupees can speculate by taking a long position in a forward contract on sterling. Similarly, an investor who feels that sterling will fall in value can speculate by taking a short position in a forward contract on sterling.

Many of the participants in futures markets are hedgers. Their aim is to use futures markets to reduce a particular risk that they face. This risk might relate to the price of oil, a foreign exchange rate, the level of the stock market, or some other variable. A perfect hedge is one that completely eliminates the risk. In practice, perfect hedges are rare. To quote one trader: "The only perfect hedge is in a Japanese garden". A study of hedging using futures contracts is, therefore, for the most part a study of the ways in which hedges can be constructed so that they perform as close to perfectly as possible.

When an individual or company chooses to use futures markets to hedge a risk, the objective is usually to take a position that neutralizes the risk as far as possible. Consider a company that knows it will gain Rs. 10,000 for each Paisa increase in the price of a commodity over the next three months and lose Rs. 10,000 for each paisa decrease in its price during this period. To hedge, the company's treasurer should take a short futures position that is designed to offset this risk. The futures position should lead to a loss of Rs. 10,000 for each paisa increase in the price of the commodity over the three months and a gain of Rs. 10,000 for each paisa decrease in its price during the period. If the price of the commodity goes down, the gain on the futures position offsets the loss on the rest of the company's business. If the price of the commodity goes up, the loss on the futures position is offset by the gain on the rest of the company's business.

Short Hedges

A short hedge is a hedge, such as the one just described, that involves a short position in futures contracts. A short hedge is appropriate when the hedger already owns an asset and expects to sell it at some time in the future. For example, it could be used by a farmer who owns some hogs (small animal) and knows that they will be ready for sale at the local market in two months. A short hedge can also be used when a hedger does not own an asset right now, but knows that the asset will be owned at some time in the future.

Consider for example, an Indian exporter who knows that he or she will receive German marks in three months. The exporter will realize a gain if the mark increases in value relative to the Indian Rupees and a loss if the mark decreases in value relative to the Indian rupee. A short future position leads to a loss if the mark increases in value and again if it decreases in value. It has the effect of offsetting the exporter's risk.

Interest-rate Future

An interest-rate futures contract is a futures contract on an asset whose price is dependent solely on the level of interest rates. Hedging a company's exposure to interest rates is more complicated than hedging its exposure to, say, the price of copper. This is because a whole term structure is necessary to provide a full description of .the level of interest rates, whereas the price of copper can be described by a single number. A company, when wishing to hedge its interest rate exposure, must decide not only the maturity of the hedge it requires but also the maturity of the interest rate to which it is exposed. It must then find a way of using available interest rate futures contracts so that an appropriate hedge is obtained.

Spot and Forward Interest Rates

The n-year spot interest rate or n-year zero-coupon rate is the interest rate on an investment that is made for a period of time starting today and lasting for n-years. Thus, the three-year spot rate is the rate of interest on an investment lasting three years; the five year spot rate is the rate of interest on an investment lasting five years and so on. The investment considered should be a 'pure' for the number of years of investment with no intermediate payments. This means that all the interest and the principal are repaid to the investor at the end of last year.

SWAPS

Swaps are private agreements between two companies to exchange cash flows in the future according to a prearranged formula. They can be regarded as portfolio of forward contracts. The study of swaps is, therefore, a natural extension of the study of forward and futures contracts. In US the first swap contracts were negotiated in 1981. Since then, the market has grown very rapidly. Hundreds of billions of dollars of contracts are currently negotiated each year.

MECHANICS OF INTEREST-RATE SWAPS

The most common type of swap is a "plain vanilla" interest-rate swap. In this, one party, B, agrees to pay to the other party, A, cash flows equal to interest at a predetermined fixed rate on a notional principal for a number of years. At the same time, party A agrees to pay party B cash flows equal to interest at a floating rate on the same notional principal for the same period of time. The currencies of the two sets of interest cash flows are the same. The life of the swap can range from two years to over 15 years.

Why should A and B enter into such an agreement? The reason most commonly put forward concerns comparative advantages. Some companies appear to have a comparative advantage in fixed-rate markets while other companies appear to have a comparative advantage in floating-rate markets. When obtaining a new loan, it makes sense for a company to go to the market where it has a comparative advantage. However, this may lead to a company borrowing fixed when it wants floating or borrowing floating when it wants fixed. This is where a swap comes in. A swap has the effect of transforming a fixed rate loan into a floating-rate loan or vice versa.

London Inter-bank Offer Rate

The floating rate in many interest-rate swap agreements is the London Inter-bank Offer Rate (LIBOR). LIBOR is the rate of interest offered by banks on deposits from other banks in Eurocurrency markets. One-month LIBOR is the rate offered on one-month deposits, three-month LIBOR is the rate offered on three-month deposits, and so on. LIBOR rates are determined by trading between banks and change continuously as economic conditions change. Just as prime is often the reference rate of interest for floating-rate loans in the domestic financial market, LIBOR is frequently a reference rate of interest for loans in international financial markets. To understand how it is used, consider a loan where the rate of interest is specified as six-month LIBOR + 0.5 percent per annum. The life of the loan is divided into six-month time periods. For each period, the rate of interest is set 0.5 percent per annum above the six-month LIBOR rate at the beginning of the period. Interest is paid at the end of the period.

13

Leasing

Lease is defined as a contract between a lessor and a lessee for the hire of a specific asset for a specified period payment of specified rentals. As such, it is a right to use equipment or capital goods on payment of periodical amount. There are parties to a lease, namely, the lessor and the lessee. A person who is the owner of the equipment permitting the use of the same by the other party on payment of a periodical amount is called the Lessor and the other person who acquires the right to use equipment for which he pays periodically is called the Lessee.

The subject of the lease is the asset, article or property leased. Property over the asset vests with the lessor and is never intended to pass to the lessee. This feature distinguishes it from hire purchase where the title is transferred to the person using the asset after the payment of all the instalments. Since the ownership of the asset vests with the lessor in a lease, it is he who can show the asset in his Balance Sheet and claim depreciation and other allowances in respect thereof. This is not so in a hire purchase agreement where the user of the asset is entitled to claim depreciation and other allowances in respect of the asset in use.

ORIGIN AND GROWTH OF LEASING IN INDIA

The concept of leasing in India was mainly restricted to real estate leasing agreements. The pioneer of leasing industry in India is the First Leasing Company of India Limited set-up in Madras in 1973. Even though, there were suggestions to the Citibank in Bombay as early as the sixties to go in for equipment leasing it was not taken up on the ground that the concept was too sophisticated for India. In 1973, a management qualified professional from the Citibank. Farouk Irani was invited by a corporate group to set-up the First Leasing Company of India Limited in 1973.

By the early 1980s, a number of financial institutions and commercial banks started leasing. In 1983, the public financial institution, ICICI joined the fray. During the year 1984, the Banking Regulation Act, 1949 was amended enabling commercial banks to promote their subsidiaries to engage in leasing activities. Thereafter, the industry grew at a faster pace. From 1982 to 1985 there was an eight-fold increase in the gross value of the leased assets. Leasing as an alternative to long-term financing has come more as a result of constraints imposed by the commercial and development banks during the eighties. Lease financing was a welcome development as it widened the capital market. Indian industries found leasing as a circumventing tool around high taxation rates and the off-balance sheet aspects of leasing was an added factor.

After 1988, the mushroom growth of leasing companies began to decline. Lack of resources, knowledge on cost of funds and the rate war have caused mainly of the newly formed companies to diversify out of the industry. The number of active lessors declined and only a few, consisting of financial banks and private corporative lessors with efficient professionals have stood up the decadence. The First Leasing Company of India Ltd., 20th Century Leasing Limited, leasing divisions of ICICI and Sundaram Finance and a handful of lesser known lessors have not only survived, but have shown consistently strong financial results for more than a decade. The initial boom and the subsequent downslide which are inherent to every innovative activity, the Indian leasing industry showed consistency later. The high profitability has led the commercial banks the initial resistance to the concept in India delayed any further I to convince the RBI to permit them to directly undertake leasing.

The First Leasing Company of India promoted by the Chidambaram group in 1973 in Madras was the first of its kind in India. This was followed by the Twentieth Century Leasing Company in 1980 at Mumbai. Four other finance companies, namely, Shelly Investment and Finance, Motor and General Finance, Jayabharati Credit and Finance and Sundaram Finance joined the stream in 1982. Equipment leasing was first introduced by the ICICI, which now provides leasing for computerization, exports, expansion, etc. Leasing Companies may be independent ones, like the Twentieth Century Leasing or subsidiaries of manufacturing companies, like Tata Industries Ltd., or even as public sector financial institutions such as the ICICI, IFCI, etc.

Lease financing being helpful for the small and medium-sized units that may face short-term which face financial problems. It has gained importance with the increasing number of entrepreneurs starting business on a small scale. Leasing is accepted as an alternative source of finance. The new industrial policy and other economic measures of the Government, withdrawal of investment allowance, etc. have made leasing as a financing option. It plays an important role in the financing of machinery, plant and equipment. Thus, a lot of optimism has been brought about in the leasing industry due to liberalization.

The expansion of financial services at a very fast pace has left its impact on the financial services Scenario in the Country. The organized player in the financial services sector were too few to cope with demands placed on it from the economy and as a result the present position shows the effect of unplanned growth. With the growth of the financial services sector, there has also been a spurt in number of market intermediaries such as sub-brokers and so on.

Government has taken several steps to reorganize and restructure of the financial services industry due to the presence of large number of intermediaries. Several committees in the past such as Narasimhan Committee on reforms in the financial sector, the Pherwani Committee on reorganization of stock exchanges, the Bhave Committee on mutual funds, etc. have made a reasonable attempt in streamlining the system of governance of intermediaries. Apart from this, the watchdog body of the SEBI has now been given legislative teeth.

Lease Rentals

The lessor receives in return for the vesting of the property rights with the lessee, compensation in the following forms:

- Collects charges borne by him in respect of repairs, insurance, maintenance charges incurred on the property leased-out, etc.
- Claim of depreciation on the property for tax and profit calculation purposes.
- Interest on the lessor's investment made in the property leased.
- Servicing charges.

TYPES OF LEASES

Financial Lease

Under this form of lease, the asset is provided to the lessee for a long period that sometimes granted for the entire life of the asset. The lessor assumes the role of a financier and hence services of repairs, maintenance, etc. are not provided by him. The legal tile is retained by the lessor so that he can exercise the option to terminate the lease agreement in case the lessee does not carry out the lease as per the contract of lease. He recoups the principal and interest incurred by him through lease rentals collected during the payback period.

The lessee may reserve the right to purchase the leased asset on the expiry of the lease period on payment of an agreed price or may only have a share in the sale proceeds of the assets or may renew the lease agreement at a lower rent. A finance lease also called a capital lease is a loan in disguise. According to T.M. Clark, "It is a contract involving payment over an obligatory period of specified sums sufficient in total to amortize the capital outlay of the lessor and give some profit".

The lessor thus is typically a financial institution and does not render specialized service in connection with the asset.

Operating Lease

It is where the asset is not wholly amortized during the non-cancelable period, if any, of the lease and where the lessor does not rely for his profit on the rentals in the non-cancelable period. The lessor bears the all expenses. The lessee uses the asset for a specified time. The lessor bears the risk of obsolescence and incidental risks. Either party to the lease may terminate the lease after giving due notice of the same, since the asset may be leased out to other willing lessees.

Specialized services are provided by the lessor who has specialized knowledge in handling and operating the asset. This type of a lease is usually preferred when the long-term suitability of the asset is uncertain, where the asset is needed to solve a temporary problem and the asset is subject to rapid obsolescence.

Sale and Lease Back Leasing

In order to raise funds, a company may sell an asset which belongs to it to the lessor with whom the ownership vests from then on. Subsequently, the lessor leases the same asset to the same company that sold the asset and which presently who uses it. The asset thus remains with the lessee with the change in title to the lessor thus enabling the company to procure needed finance.

Sales Aid Lease

The lessor under this arrangement agrees with the manufacturer to market his product through his leasing operations, in return for which the manufacturer agrees to pay him a commission.

Specialized Service Lease

Under this agreement, the lessor provides specialized personal services in addition to providing its use.

Small Ticket and Big Ticket Leases

Leases of assets of smaller value are generally referred to

as small ticket leases and that of assets of larger value are referred to as big ticket leases.

Cross Border Lease

Leasing across national frontiers is referred to as cross border leasing. This still remains underdeveloped.

Merits of Leasing

1. Flexibility is a distinct merit of leasing. The leasing company modifies the arrangements to suit the lessees' requirements.
2. It is an alternative to obtain loan and other facilities from financial institutions.
3. Full financing for the cost of equipment may be made available by a leasing company whereas banks and other financial institutions may not provide for the same.
4. Less documentation is involved in a lease agreement when compared to term loans from banks or other financial institutions.
5. The lessor bears the risk of obsolescence in the case of an operating lease.
6. The debt equity or current ratio of the lessee remains unaffected by a lease. The reason is that the use of the asset by the lessee does not affect the borrowing capacity of the lessee in any way, since the payment can be made from income of the operating period and may not call for credit.
7. The 'Sale and Lease Back' arrangement enables the lessee to borrow in case of any crisis.
8. In case debt financing is not possible then a borrower may opt leasing.
9. The lessee can bring tax benefits depending upon his tax status.

Demerits

1. Leasing does not prove very useful in the setting up

of new projects as the rentals become payable soon after acquisition of the assets.

2. The lessor generally leases out assets, which are purchased by him with the help of bank credit. In the event of a default made by the lessor in making the payment to the bank, the banks sometimes, to the disadvantage of the lessee would seize the asset.
3. The cost of interest in lease financing is very high.
4. The asset reverts back to the owner on the termination of the lease period and the lessee loses his claim on the residual value.

ACCOUNTING FOR LEASE

Worldwide there is a strong dissenting group opposing the introduction of accounting standards to leasing. In India too, adopting the Accounting Standards has met with severe resistance and they were for sometime stayed by an order of the Madras High Court. It is contended by such persons that such a standard will impair the growth of the leasing industry and the national economy.

The USA can be said to be the first country to have promulgated accounting procedures for leasing. In 1949 the Committee on Accounting Procedures of the American Institute of Accountants issued a statement called Disclosure of Long-term Leases in Financial Statements of Lessees. Among other things, the statement requires, in case of long-term leases where rental and other obligations are material, disclosures in the financial statements or its notes about the amount of annual rentals to be paid with some indication of the periods for which they are payable and any other important obligation assumed or guarantee made in connection therewith.

Since deficiencies were noted regarding the model of capitalizing of the lease and treating the outstanding liability in profit and loss account, they were subsequently sought to be remedied by the opinion of the Accounting Principles Boards (APB). In 1964, Opinion No. 5 was issued for 'Reporting of leases in financial statements of lessees'. In 1967, Opinion No. 7 was issued for 'Accounting for leases in financial statements of lessors Later, Opinions No. 27 and 31 were issued respectively for 'Accounting for lease transactions by manufacturer or dealer lessors and for 'Disclosure of lease commitments by lessees'.

The International Accounting Standards Committee had published the International Accounting Standard (IAS) No.17 on Accounting for leases which came into effect since 1st January, 1984. In India, the Research Committee of the Institute of Chartered Accountants of India (ICAI) published an Exposure Draft of Guidance Note on Accounting for leases in 1986. But due to controversies between the ICAI and the Association of leasing companies, its operation has been stayed.

Accounting for lease is the subject matter of many controversies. While the problem of lease accounting is looked at mainly from the lessee's view point in the western countries, in India it is viewed mainly as the lessor accounting. Essentially, accounting involves spreading of cash inflows and outflows over a certain period of time and the basic principle is to match the revenues and expenses over that period. In case of a lease, it is necessary for income recognition for the lessor and for asset disclosure for the lessee and therefore, a special method of accounting is desired for leases.

The need for a special method is due to the reason that a financial lease will be mentioned as a lease in the record, whereas the intention of the parties will be to exchange a loan for a commitment to pay. The position of the lessor would be not that of an asset owner, but akin to a lender and the position of lessee would be like an asset owner instead of an asset hirer. Hence, in the case of a lease, its legal form varies from its substance and financial reality which creates the difficulty as the legal form and financial reality in other normal transactions are mutually reinforcing.

ACCOUNTING STANDARD ON LEASE

The IAS-17 defines a financial lease as "a lease that transfers substantially all the risks and rewards incident to ownership of an asset. Title may or may not eventually be transferred". Leases other than finance leases are operating leases.

The classification of leases is based on the extent to which risks and rewards incidental to ownership of a leased asset lie with the lessor or the lessee. Risks include the possibilities of losses from idle capacity or technological obsolescence and of variations in return due to changing economic conditions. Rewards may be represented by the expectation of profitable operation over the asset's economic life and of gain from appreciation in value or realization of a residual value.

According to the standard, whether a lease is a finance lease or not depends on the substance of the transaction rather than on the form of the contract. A finance lease is normally non-cancelable and secures for the lessor the recovery of his capital outlay and there return for the funds invested. It also provides examples of situations where a lease would normally be classified as a finance lease, they are:

- Lease transfers ownership of the asset to the lessee by the end of the lease term.
- The lessee has the option to purchase the asset at a price which is expected to be sufficiently lower than the fair value at the date the option becomes exercisable that at the inception of the lease, it is reasonably certain that the option will be exercised.
- The lease term is for the major part of the useful life of the asset and the title may or may not eventually be transferred.
- The present value at the inception of the lease of the minimum lease payments is greater than or equal to substantially all of the fair value of the leased asset net of grants and tax credits to the lessor at that time. Title mayor may not eventually be transferred.

Accounting Treatment by the Lessee

- A finance lease should be reflected in the balance sheet of the lessee. The asset and a liability must be recorded at a fair value of the leased property net of grants and tax credits receivable by the lessor at the present value of the minimum lease payments. While calculating the present value, the interest rate implicit in the lease will be the discount factor. If it is not practicable to determine the interest rate, the lessee's incremental borrowing rate should be used.

- Rentals should be apportioned between the finance charge and the reduction of the outstanding liability.
- The finance charge should be allocated to periods during the lease term so as to produce a constant periodic rate of interest on the remaining balance of the liability for each period.
- The leased asset should be, depreciated, similar to depreciable asset which are owned. If there is no reasonable certainty that the lessee will obtain ownership by the end of the lease term the asset should be fully depreciated over the lease term or its useful life, whichever is shorter.
- In case of operating leases, the charge to income should be the rental expenses for the accounting period, recognized on a systematic basis that is representative of the time pattern of the user's benefit.
- The lessee should disclose assets taken under a finance lease by way of a note to the accounts disclosing interalia the future obligations of the lessee as per agreement.
- Lease rentals should be accounted not on accrual basis over the lease term in order to arrive at an appropriate charge in this respect in the profit and loss account with a separate disclosure thereof. The excess of lease rentals paid over the amount accrued in respect thereof should be treated as prepaid lease rental and *vice versa*.

Accounting Treatment by the Lessor

- The balance sheet should not show the leased asset as a fixed asset. The investment should be shown as a receivable, at an amount equal to the net investment in the lease.
- The rental income should be treated on a pattern reflecting a constant periodic rate of return on either

the lessor's net investment outstanding or the net cash investment outstanding in respect of the lease.

- Manufacturer or dealer, lessors should include selling profit or loss in income in accordance with the policy normally followed for outright sales. If artificially low rates of interest are quoted, selling profit should be restricted to that which would apply if a commercial rate of interest were charged. Initial direct costs should be charged to income at the inception of the lease.
- In case of operating leases, the assets should be recorded as property, plant and equipment in the balance sheet and the rental income should be recognized on a straight line basis over the lease term. The depreciation of the leased asset should be on a basis consistent with the lessor's normal depreciation policy for similar assets.
- In case of sale and leaseback transactions resulting in a finance lease, any excess of side proceeds over the carrying amount should not be immediately recognized in income in the financial statements of the seller-lessee. In case of excess, it should be deferred and amortized over the lease term.
- Assets should be disclosed as "assets given on lease" under the head 'Fixed Asset' in the balance sheet.
- The finance income for the period should be calculated by applying the interest rate implicit in the lease to the net investment in the lease during the relevant period.
- Initial direct costs, such as commissions and legal fees incurred while negotiating and arranging the lease should normally be expensed in the year in which they are incurred. Income on account of lease like the management fees should be recognized in the year in which they accrue.
- Accounting policies should be disclosed.
- Lease rentals in a finance lease should be shown separately under 'Gross Income' in the profit or loss account of the relevant period and a matching charge is to be made against the lease rental representing

recovery of the net investment fair value of the leased asset over the lease term.

Disclosures on Lease

In Case of Lessee

- The amount of asset that is the subject of finance leases at each balance sheet date. Liabilities related to them should be shown separately from other liabilities, differentiating between the current and long term portions.
- The commitments for minimum lease payments, mentioning the amounts and periods in which the payments will become due.
- Significant financing restrictions, renewal or purchase options, contingent rentals and other contingencies arising from leases.

In Case of Lessor

- The gross investment in finance leases at each balance sheet date, and the related unearned finance income and unguaranteed residual values of leased assets.
- The basis used for allocating income so as to produce a constant periodic rate of return indicating whether the return relates to the net investment outstanding or the net cash investment outstanding in the lease.

FIXATION OF LEASE RENTALS AND LEASE EVALUATION

The consideration for a lease transaction is the lease rentals. The consideration may be towards the interest on the investment in the asset or the depreciation of the asset or towards servicing or packaging charges or towards the charges for cost of repairs, insurance, maintenance or operation where the lessor bears such costs. The last mentioned charges on costs will be absent in the case of net leases as it is net of those charges.

Lease rentals are generally mentioned in terms of a sum of rupees per thousand rupees of the cost of the leased equipment based upon a flat rate concept or compounding period. In the flat rate concept, the fact that the lessor's capital investment is reduced during the lease period is ignored. The flat rate is roughly twice the true rate less one.

In computing rentals, generally four steps are involved (there may be variations to these steps):

1. The basic cost of the equipment is to be determined for the lessor.
2. To this the lessor's mark up or profit projection is added.
3. The amortization payment factor is worked out.
4. The capitalized cost is multiplied by the service finance factor

The lease rentals may be fixed or variable. If the amount of rental payments are changeable neither by the lessor nor by the lessee, as is the case in small and medium ticket leases, the lease rentals are said to be fixed. In big ticket leases, changes in exchange rates, interest rates, tax rates, monetary controls and depreciation allowances require variations at different stages in lease rentals. The rates of return by the rentals depend upon the cost of capital and cost of operations of a lessor. Hence provisions for future tax liability also have to be incorporated to meet out the financing and operational costs and to provide minimum desired return on the owned asset.

While drafting lease documents, the amount of rentals and the periodicity of their payments are usually mentioned in a schedule appended to the agreement and the lessees may also be required to give instructions to their bankers for regular payment as and when they fall due in order to avoid delayed payment of rentals.

LEASE EVALUATION

A number of factors are considered in evaluating the

available leasing alternatives. There are no general merits or demerits for leasing and everything depends upon the circumstances relevant to the requirements of the lessor or lessee. Normally, the evaluation of a lease is influenced by qualitative factors or quantitative analysis.

Qualitative factors: There are many principal qualitative factors influencing the preference for leasing and also against it. Leasing frees the cash flow and enables the utilization of working capital for a more productive use. Another significant factor of leasing is its flexibility to adapt the terms of the contract to the needs of the borrower lessee. As a means of acquiring, capital assets, leasing usually costs less than other alternative methods. Lease finance is off the balance sheet finance and increases the borrowing capacity of the lessee. Lease rentals provide tax benefits. Leasing companies usually do not impose restrictive covenants which are inevitable in case of loans from financial institutions or banks.

There are some disadvantageous factors also. Since the asset reverts back to the lessor at the determination of lease, there is the loss of residual value to the lessee. Contrary to this will be an advantage to the lessor. Leasing may incur double sales tax, that is, at the time when the asset is purchased and when it is leased out. It is basically another form of debt financing and may lead to failure of proper appreciation of the lease commitments as it does not appear as a liability in the balance sheet.

Quantitative Analysis

Quantitatively in any decision on a financial lease evaluation the choice of the cheapest alternative and its advantage over others is involved. The costs either as lease rentals in leasing or as interest in borrowing or as earnings lost in direct purchases have to be computed as after tax costs, so that the tax benefits are also taken into account. As money has time value, present values also are important factors. Therefore, a comparison of present value of after tax cash flows in leasing with that of other alternatives is also considered essential. In zero-tax situations leasing will be costlier than borrowing or buying. If the taxation is very high, leasing will be cheaper to the lessee than an outright purchase as there will be a passing on of tax benefits to the lessee from the lessor.

Another factor which influences lease evaluation is the residual value. Also called as salvage value it means the value of the asset left over at the end of its economic life. Where the lessee is allowed to enjoy the benefits of the residual value even after the end of the lease period, there will be no difference regarding the value between leasing and direct purchasing. If the leased asset has an economic life beyond the period of lease and the lessor is taking it back after the end of the lease, the lessee will be deprived of the benefit which he would be enjoying in case of direct purchasing. In such cases it will be quantified as an outflow.

Methods of Lease Evaluation

In financial management the problem of lease evaluation constitutes a difficult financial decision-making. Several models have been suggested to answer this problem. The first of such analytical tools for evaluation of leases was proposed by Richard F. Vancil. Subsequent to Vancil's models many more were proposed. Basically it was proposed to find out whether leasing is a financing decision or an investment decision and the role of discounting rates. The investment decision concerns the acquisition and disposal of assets and the modes of investments and disinvestments.

The financing decision is related to the sources of funds for the investments, ranging from funds available internally through retained earnings to funds available externally through capital markets. Since leasing is considered to be an alternative to borrowing and buying, investment decisions which cannot be made with borrowed finance can be made in lease financing. Hence, a lease decision is considered to be a blend of investment and financing decisions. By treating leasing as a finance decision, two types of models were evolved based upon present value and internal rates of return. Models have also been developed by treating leasing as an investment decision and as a mix of investment and financing decisions.

NPV Model

Under NPV model, the net present value of cash flows

under leasing option and the net present value of cash flows under a buying or borrowing option are found out. There must be a positive figure to accept an individual project itself and among the options, the one with the greater positive figure of net present value is preferable for investment.

Vancil's Model

Unlike investment decisions where financing is separated from investment decisions, in leasing these two decisions are made simultaneously. Hence, at the time of evaluating lease, separation of investment decision from the financing decision necessitated and it has resulted in the development of several models. One such model was developed by Vancil in involving Basic Interest Rate. In this method a basic rate, which would be the minimum rate at which the company expects to borrow from the market by issuing the attractive Securities is established. After ascertaining this, the payments are discounted at the basic rate. Then the equivalent depreciation of the lease payments is calculated. The lease payments consist of interest payments and amortization of the asset value. From this lease payment, an imputed interest on the outstanding amount at the BIR is deducted and the remainder will be the equivalent depreciation. On this equivalent depreciation, tax savings are calculated and deducted from the lease payments. It gives the net cash flows.

These net cash flows are discounted at the discounting rate of the company. The sum of these present values of tax benefits is deducted from the already discounted value of lease payments and it will give the cost of lease. Bower, Herringer and Williamson emphasize that a lease plan should be adopted only if it results in increasing the market value of the lessee company's stock in accordance with the objective of the firm to maximize the wealth of stockholders.

Internal Rate of Return Model: This method has been suggested as an alternative to the above mentioned NPV methods. It is based upon the internal rate of return. The IRR is the implicit interest rate built into the lease payments.

Internal Rate of Return: IRR is the rate which the company will discount lease rentals and the residual value to the cost of the asset. The cash flows are reduced at a later time by the effect of the rate of discount. If the rate of discount is higher, the NPV will be reduced. To increase the positive NPV, lower discount rate can be used. When such is the case, there will be a discount rate which will give IRR and NPV exactly equal to zero. This rate which gives the NPV exactly at zero is called the internal rate of return or implicit rate of return. It means that if the cost of capital is equal to IRR, there will be no profit or loss from the project and that the IRR is the actual return being obtained from the project. Once the rate of return is known, by comparing IRR with the cost it can be decided whether to accept or reject the proposal.

If the IRR is greater than the cost of the capital, the project will be acceptable and if it is lesser, be project is liable to the rejected. If both are equal we will have the option to accept or reject. Even though there are some drawbacks in the IRR method it is considered to be theoretically sound and it has been advised to those who accept that leasing is purely a method of financing. By some, the present value methods are considered to be unsuitable for evaluation of leases, which according to them is a financing device, as those methods are considered to be suitable for investment decisions alone.

Johnson and Lewellen Model

Leasing is also considered to be a purely investment decision. This view was subscribed by W.R. Johnson and W.G. Lewellen. They opted to treat leasing as an investment opportunity on the ground that the attractiveness of a capital investment opportunity should be appraised without reference to the specific form of financing employed in its execution and without including explicit finance charges such as dividend and interest payments as part of the cash flows whose present values influence project worth.

While making capital investment decision, they contended that leasing should be approached as an investment opportunity in order to avoid the problem of considering alternative financing strategies. According to them the decision to acquire an asset should not be affected by whether the funds needed for it come by leasing or borrowing. Similar to a purchase lease is also a means of acquiring a service and so will be a capital project, since the aim of any capital project is to acquire the services for economic benefit. They claimed that to analyze a lease the purchase price of an asset is not relevant since lease project possesses separate set of cash flow and so should be analyzed on that basis.

Johnson and Lewellen adopted two discounting rates instead of the simple discounting rate used in the above mentioned NPV model which represented the after tax overall cost of capital. One of the two adopted by Johnson and Lewellen is to discount the cash inflows associated will have the asset which is the firms overall after-tax cost of capital. The other is to discount payments on account of the lease contract which is the company's after-tax debt rate.

14

Hire Purchase

Hire purchase is a mode of financing the price of goods to be sold out at future date. In hire purchase, subject to payment of all installments i.e., hire charges, the goods let on hire will become the property of the user (hirer). Hire purchaser is free to return the goods without being required to pay any further installments falling due after the return.

There are two methods of operation. In the first case, the hire purchase company purchases the equipment from the supplier and let it on hire to the hirer, who makes the down payment and balance with interest in equal installments. In the second method hirer deposits fixed amounts with finance company who provides the entire finance. There is no down-payment, instead, the entire amount is repayable with interest in equal instalments over a period. The deposit with interest will be returned to the hirer after payment of the final instalment.

According to Park W.D. "true hire purchase is a bailment by the owner of a movable article by an agreement which also gives an option to the hirer to return or purchase the goods at some stage. It is the hybrid of a simple hiring and sale and that it contains 'an element of sale' is recognized in several decisions. In a credit sale the property passes at the beginning; the object of hire purchase is to prevent the purchaser passing a good title in the goods to a third party, so that the -vendor can always recover them".

According to Fox-Smith, hire purchase is "the system where a person hires an article, pays rent for it and only becomes the legal owner when all the payments are completed Should default be made in the payment of the hire rent, that is the installment, the goods can be retaken by the owner, who may be a retailer manufacturer or finance house, Payments already made are then forfeited subject to the conditions set out in the hire purchase agreement, Although physical possession passes to the hirer, the legal ownership of the goods comprised in the agreement does not vest in the hirer until he has completed his obligation. That is, to pay the total hire rent and the option to purchase".

HIRE PURCHASE ACT, 1972

The Hire Purchase Act was enacted in 1972 to regulate the rights and obligations of the owner and hirer under hire purchase transactions, however, the Act enforcement was delayed due to certain lacunae found. Subsequently, the Reserve Bank of India also has issued regulatory directions for leases and hire purchases. Section 2(c) of the Hire Purchase Act, 1972 defines hire-purchasing agreement. "Hire purchasing agreement means an agreement under which goods are let on hire and under which the hirer has an option to purchase them in accordance with the terms of the agreement and includes an agreement under which:

- Possession of goods is delivered by the owner thereof to a person on condition that such person pays the agreed amount in period instalments.
- The property in the goods is to pass to such person on the payment of the last of such instalments and
- Such person has a right to terminate the agreement at any time before the property so passes.

ORIGIN AND GROWTH

The origin of the concept of hire purchase can be traced to the period of industrial revolution in United Kingdom. During the early nineteenth century, after a few stray incidents of hire purchasing, Singer Sewing Machine Company in the U.K. introduced an installment credit scheme, letting out machines to its customers under a hiring agreement with an option to purchase. The concept slowly extended to other types of consumer goods which were beyond the means of persons who wanted to acquire it and who could not afford to pay the cost in one lump sum. It was developed by wagon companies which financed the purchase of wagons by collieries. A characteristic of these early hire purchase transactions is that all the finances were made by manufacturers or dealers themselves. Only subsequently, the concept was adopted by independent financial houses which began to finance for a wide variety of consumer articles, automobiles and industrial machineries.

During the earlier stages, the manufacturers and dealers had to oblige the finance companies by selling them the goods at a discount. As the hire-purchase business began to flourish, the competition among the financing companies increased the dealer's bargaining power which eventually led to the situation where the financing companies were forced to pay commission to the manufacturers and dealers if business is to be obtained.

In France, the practice began with the affluent people who retired to holiday resorts during the summer. The French Lords used to hire bungalows in Paris during the summer season. There the furniture makers equipped those bungalows with necessary furniture with the offer that they could be purchased if they liked them. This sort of inducing a consumer, first by offering it on hire and later to acquire ownership became the basis for hire purchase system. With U.K. as a pioneer in the field of hire purchase, the concept spread to the U.S.A., Canada, Australia and India.

In India, hire purchasing as an organized service had its birth in the automobile sector where the auto supply companies provided finance for the purchase of automobiles. The period after the World War I witnessed rapid development in road transport and it led to a phenomenal growth 'in hire purchase business. A large number of private financiers started to offer hire purchase service for automobiles and consumer durable and the industry attained noticeable development subsequent to the World War II. During the 1960's the State Agro Industries Corporation entered into the field of hire purchase finance.

The Industrial Development Bank of India (IDBI) indirectly participated in financing hire purchase business by rediscounting usance bills/promissory notes which arose out of sales of indigenous machinery on hire purchase-basis. Manufacturers of cotton and sugar mill machinery, machine tools, electrical machinery, oil solvent extraction plants and agro-industries resorted to IDBI facility. Such a discounting scheme is run by the Industrial Credit and Investment Corporation of India (ICICI) too.

The Law Commission in its Twentieth report on Indian Sale of Goods Act had suggested for legislating a separate statute to regulate hire purchase contracts. The Law Commission observed that a separate Act on the lines of the English Hire Purchase Acts and other similar laws should be enacted in India to regulate the hire purchase transactions. This report led the way to the enactment of Hire Purchase Act in 1972 in the line of the English Act. Government of India intended to enforce the Act twice but cancelled the notifications issued in this behalf on both the occasions and the Act is yet to come into force. At present the hire purchases are mainly subject to the Contract Act.

Many Government committees formed to study the working of non banking companies have emphasized the need for encouraging this line of financial activity. The Study Group on Road Transport Financing under the Chairmanship of R.G. Saraya in 1968, the Study Group on Non-banking Finance Intermediaries under the Chairmanship of B.K. Dutt in 1971 and the James S. Raj committee constituted by the Reserve Bank of India were all of the said view. The report of the James Raj committee observed that hire purchase institutions are 'para bankers' and that their activities should be further regulated on the lines of the Banking Regulation Act.

The report of the Banking Laws Committee headed by P.V. Rajamannar, acknowledged the important role played by hire purchase companies in the country. The committee's report on personal Property Security Law in 1977, recommended certain reforms. The report covered security devices being employed for obtaining security interest in personal property, like hypothecation, pledge, mortgage and hire purchase.

Prior to 1977 there were no restrictions on the acceptance of deposits by the Non-Banking Financing Companies (NBFC) and mobilization of resources was taking place on different lines. Subsequent to the James Raj Committee, it was decided by the RBI that the hire purchase and leasing companies should accept deposits up to ten times the eligible network and that these deposits should not be for periods less than six months and more than 36 months. The deposits accepted prior to 1977 payable on demand or for long periods should be repaid on maturity and renewals should be accepted on the new basis. In case of deposit for more than three years, the maximum permissible rate of interest payable is only 15 percent.

Subsequent to the independence there was a shift in the traffic of hire purchase business from rail sector to the road sector after the implementation of five year plans. The demand for finance to acquire transport vehicles gained momentum. This resulted in the entry of more number of hire purchase companies.

POLICY MEASURES ON HIRE PURCHASE

Funds are very essential for the efficient performance and sustained growth of hire purchase companies. The major sources of funding are through mobilization of deposits from the public and borrowings from banks. The Reserve bank of India regulates the mobilization of funds through public deposits. Before 1977, there were no restrictions on the acceptance of deposits by the NBFC's. Only after the report of the James Raj committee, the RBI had decided that the hire purchase and leasing companies should accept deposits up to ten times the eligible net worth and that these deposits should not be for periods less than six months and more than 36 months.

After the report of the Tandon Committee it was felt that specific norms should be laid down for the sanctioning of cash credit limits to NBFC's also. This question was examined by the G.S.Dahitre Committee which made its recommendations in 1988. The hire purchase and leasing companies can secure credit from banks up o three times their eligible net worth. It was also considered desirable that NBFC's should be encouraged to reduce dependence on banks and centrally owned institutions and others for loans.

In 1990, the RBI allowed banks to enter the business of hire purchase business imposing certain conditions such as:

- The banks should not enter into the hire purchase business directly.
- Those banks which have set-up subsidiaries for various finance service activities may enter hire purchase through such subsidiary or by setting up a new subsidiary, subject to getting prior approval from the RBI for undertaking the hire purchase business.
- Banks may invest in shares of other hire purchase companies subject to the limits set by the Banking Regulation Act, 1949, with the approval of the RBI, but cannot act as promoters of such companies.
- The existing bank subsidiaries intending to enter hire purchase business and the new subsidiaries being set-up for the said purpose should not finance the other companies engaged in hire purchase business.
- The aggregate investment by a bank in the shares of its subsidiaries undertaking hire purchase and leasing business and in the shares of other companies carrying on such business should not exceed ten, percent of the paid up capital and reserves of the bank.
- The RBI may require necessary information from time to time from the banks carrying on hire purchase business through its subsidiaries.

While most of the restrictive guidelines are considered to be justified for the healthy growth of the industry and for the safety of the depositors some of the guidelines are considered to be retrogressive requiring review the hire purchase companies when imposed with the conditions minimum and maximum periods for accepting deposits, banks and industrial companies are not burdened with such restrictions. The RBI had stated that no interest should be paid for the expired period of the deposit. In case the depositor wants to withdraw the amount for genuine reasons before maturity. In such cases, the depositor will be put to great hardships and financial losses which will not make them favourable to the hire purchase companies which, having utilized the funds of the depositor are bound by the restrictions imposed by the RBI. Hence the guidelines and other regulatory measures have to be reviewed according to the changes restructuring the economy of the country.

Hire Purchase and Transport Industry

There has been a shift in the traffic from the rail sector to the road sector after the implementation of the five year plans. There has been a tremendous increase in the demand for financing the purchase of transport vehicles. This has been due to the fact that road transport is preferable for transporting goods from point to point rather than depending upon the rail transport which often requires further transportation. Hence movement of goods by road has been found to be economical and faster than by rail transport. It has resulted in increased production of vehicles necessitating the requirement of more funds for the acquisition of vehicles by operators. So there was a spurt in the number of hire purchase companies in the organized sector as well as the individual and partnership firms.

Banks play an important role in financing transport business. However, HP companies in the private sector have grown because of their fast, efficient and personalized services and because of the flexibility and ease with which the transaction can be put through. To finalize proposal, commercial banks will require longer time because of the formalities involved and the paper work because of their accountability. But a hire purchase company evaluates the willingness and repaying capacity of the hirer with ease and speed and at the same time ensures quick and proper documentation. Further, the hire purchase companies usually support the small operators in the acquisition of new vehicles. They also grant finance on used vehicles already being owned by operators, for working capital requirements like repairing, etc. The role of commercial banks is also very important in hire purchase sector due to the large number of vehicles being put on the every year.

In the transport industry, a type of sale and hire back transaction is, being utilized by the operators as a mode of finance. Throughout our nation, financing money on the security of old vehicles is in vogue. Industrial establishments raise money for their working capital requirements upon their existing assets. But a truck operator can avail a similar facility and it need not be necessarily for his working capital requirements such as for purchase of batteries or for maintenance, repair, etc.

Depending upon the credit-worthiness and past record of the owner of the vehicle, an advance equivalent up to sixty percent of the market value of the vehicle is given. Under this system, the existing owner will be selling a vehicle already owned by him to the hire purchase financier but the vehicle continues to remain under the control and custody of the hirer and only its legal ownership and title are changed in favour of the financier. Thus, there is a transfer of ownership of the vehicle from the hirer to the hire purchase financier and on termination of the agreement there will be transfer of, ownership for a second time from the hire purchase financier to the hirer.

In the hire purchase of a motor vehicle, the hirer is permitted to build a body on the chassis at his own expense. The vehicle thus built would be deemed to be a normal part of the motor vehicle and it will be the sale and absolute property of the owners. The additions would not make the hirer a co-owner i.e., construction of a body on a motor vehicle would not by itself give part ownership or proportionate right to the extent of the value improved by the hirer.

Another factor is that with the restructuring of the economy of the country, there is an increase in the setting up of new industries. Local entrepreneurs face stiff competition from

NRIs, FIIs and multinationals who can pool money with ease for outright purchases of assets and equipments, while inter-corporate funds have become very costly for the Indian entrepreneurs. All these will result in a steep increase in demand for funds and at this critical juncture if enough encouragement is not given to the hire purchase sector it will retard the growth of Indian industrialists. Especially the road transport sector, which is expected to grow as a core sector, has to be favoured since it will be very difficult for the government of India to find the large resources that would be required to expand the Indian railway network to the rural areas where seventy percent of the Indian population lives.

Hire Purchase Agreement

An agreement of hire purchase is a simple contract in writing. Since the agreement relates to transaction in movable assets registration is not required. The contract of hire purchase is an agreement enforceable under law, made between the owner of goods and the hirer, whereby the owner lets out the goods on hire for a specified period of time with a provision for payment of rentals at regular intervals and provided with an option to the hirer to purchase the goods at the expiry of the stipulated time.

The essential features of a valid hire purchase contract are:

- A proposal from the hirer to acquire the goods and acceptance of the proposal by the owner on mutually agreed upon terms to be reduced in writing in the form of an agreement after consent between the parties.
- An express intention to create a legal relationship by the delivery of goods on bailment to the hirer with the option to purchase after a specified period of time.
- The owner and hirer should have the capacity, as mentioned under the contract act, to enter into the contract.
- The contract should not oppose public policy.
- The hire purchase agreement is supported by consideration in the form of rentals payable by the

hirer to the owner at regular intervals for the right to use the goods.

- The agreement must confer the power of termination undercircumstances that will be prescribed under the agreement.

HIRE PURCHASE V. LEASING

Hire Purchase

- Ownership of asset is transferred to user on payment of the last instalment.
- Asset is capitalized in the books of user
- Depreciation on the asset is claimed by user.
- Value of capital asset is low as compared to lease transactions
- Hire purchase finance is subject to margin requirements.
- Seller claims tax benefits in respect of interest payable on acquiring asset.

Leasing

- Ownership is never transferred to user.
- Leased asset is capitalized in the books of Lessor/ Leasing Company/Owner.
- Depreciation is claimed by the lessor or leasing co-owners.
- Value of assets is very high in leasing, (aircrafts, ships, etc.).
- In Lease, 100% financing is available.
- Lessee claims benefit of tax on rentals paid by him.

TYPES OF HIRE PURCHASE

Consumer Instalment Credit

Consumer instalment credit is finance offered to consumers for acquiring consumer durables. Instalment credit may be in the form of a personal loan credit sale, rental or conditional sale in the form of hire purchase. The consumer acquires goods by utilizing the funds being advanced under the hire purchase agreement. Retail hire purchase may be in different forms depending upon the mode of collection. It may be in the form of direct collection, agency collection or block discounting.

Industrial and Commercial Credit

In industrial and commercial fields finance may be provided through loans, credit sales, leasing, factoring or hire purchase. The financing house desirous of financing a commercial concern for the purchase of equipments, itself purchases the equipment from the manufacturer or dealer through hire purchase and lets it on hire purchase to the said commercial concern instead of lending money,

Some of the important recommendations of Rajmannar committee involving hire purchase financiers and banks which extend instalment credit are: (The recommendations of this committee were also taken into consideration while the Hire Purchase (Amendment) Bill, 1989 was introduced in the parliament).

- Making the registration of the security a compulsory one as a form of public notification in order to protect the hirer's interest.
- Hire purchase endorsement in the registration certificate in respect of the security to continue with each vehicle to safeguard financier's interest.
- In the event of default, the right to take possession of the security without recourse to court, if necessary with the help of court.
- After the adjustment of all the dues of the hirer the surplus has to be returned to him.
- To finally discard the concept of instalment sale.
- High priority ranking over the security.

FINANCIAL ASPECTS OF HIRE PURCHASE

Certain aspects of finance are required to be considered before deciding to go in for a hire purchase. They relate to the hire purchase price, evaluation of the hire purchase offer, choosing between a hire purchase and a lease and the structuring of the hire purchase plan.

A. Hire Purchase Price

The hire purchase charges or the add-on rate, and the interest factors are of importance to a consumer who goes for a hire purchase.

1. Add-on Rate

In most of the borrowings the interest being charged is expressed as a percentage to be paid all the outstanding balance of the loan at any given point of time. Whereas, in hire purchase transactions, the financing charges are usually not stated as a fraction of the outstanding balance, but are stated as a percent of the original cash price of the equipment. This is referred to as add-on rate interest. The agreement may also quote the total quantum of interest instead of specifying a rate. Consumers who are not well-versed with financial intrigues tend to make the mistake of identifying the add-on rate as the true rate of interest.

On the contrary the add-on rate is not the true rate of interest because the add-on rate is specified as a percentage of the original cash price of the asset, while actually the outstanding balance will steadily decrease with each periodic payment. Hence, the true rate of interest will be much more than the add-on rate of interest. Sometimes, another rate referred to as the Discount rate of interest is mentioned. It is a flat rate applied to a loan figure from which the discount is deducted at the beginning. Hence, it is also misleading since the amount being financed actually is less than the amount on which the rate is mentioned. Since the consumers who are ignorant and illiterate may be deceived and misguided by these financial ruses, steps have been taken worldwide through legislations requiring proper disclosure.

2. True Rate of Interest

The true rate of interest may be calculated from the add-on rate of payment schedule. The true rate of interest is calculated by applying the present value factors and finding the internal rate of interest. The rate which equates the stream of installments to the cash price of the goods will be the true rate of interest. For calculating add-on rate, finance charge and the monthly payment corresponding to various rates of interest, different tables are used. Capital recovery factor tables are also being used. By locating the factor before the relevant number of years in the tables, true rate of interest is found out. Applying the tables and by locating the factors the true rate of interest can be calculated mathematically.

B. Evaluation of the Hire Purchase Offer

Generally hire purchase plans are evaluated by applying the same principles involved in evaluation of leases. In a loan and a hire purchase scheme, the one which has lesser financing costs has to be preferred because a hire purchase scheme need not necessarily be an effective alternative to a loan scheme as the treatment under income tax is same to both transactions. However, financial techniques of evaluation are not necessary for comparing the finance costs of hire purchase and a loan as the cost of the hire purchase can be evaluated with the ready reckoning tables available for the purpose.

C. Choosing Between Hire Purchase and a Lease

It may be necessary for a consumer who is acquiring an equipment to decide whether to adopt a hire purchase scheme or a lease scheme for various reasons. The tax treatments for hire purchase are opposite to those of a lease. In hire purchase, the hirer is entitled to the benefits arising out of depreciation and other deductions. But in a lease, the lessor is entitled to claim these benefits. The hirer under a hire purchase is given the benefit of only the finance charge part of the instalments, whereas in a lease the lessee gets full deductions of the lease rentals.

Quantitative and non-quantitative factors are also involved in choosing between hire purchase and a lease. A major non-quantitative reason for not favouring a lease is that it is unsuitable in case of low capitalized enterprises when: the requirement is to show a strong asset position in the balance sheet. But the advantages of off-Balance sheet financing tend to favour leasing. Quantitatively speaking, the relative position of leasing and hire purchase will depend upon the effective tax rate and the rate of depreciation admissible on the equipment, provided the financing costs of both are equal. Broadly speaking, a high tax company will be benefited by taking low depreciation items on lease instead of hire purchase and a low tax company would be benefited by taking high depreciation items on lease rather than on hire purchase.

D. Structuring the Hire Purchase

The most important part of the financial activities in a hire purchase is its structuring. While structuring a hire purchase plan, the important decisions involved are :

- Amount to be financed
- Initial payment required
- Period of hire purchase
- Periodicity of payments
- Number of instalments
- Rental computation.

ACCOUNTING FOR HIRE PURCHASE

Basically, hire purchase transaction involves the letting out of an asset on hire and receiving the total amount of hire from the hirer in equally proportioned monthly instalments. These instalments are arrived at by dividing the total agreement value with the number of months for which the hiring contract is entered into. Sometimes, the monthly instalments are: made flexible by front loaded payments or rear end loaded instalments. When the owner receives large amounts in the first few months it is called front loaded payments and when the hire moneys are higher at the later stages of the instalments they; are referred to as rear end loaded instalments. These flexibilities are known as ballooning effect in lease contracts and similar practices are adopted in hire purchase contracts too.

In hire purchase and leases, the principal and the opportunity cost. Viz., the finance charges are received every month and the profit is realized throughout the period of contract. So it is a matter of arriving at the internal rate of return. Hence, it is obvious that a transaction of hire purchase is similar to that of a lease in many respects. Hence, fundamentally, leasing and hire purchase are to be accounted in the same way as recognized by several accounting standards. Yet, in many countries, including India, the accounting for leasing and hire purchase are differentiated.

The Guidance Note on Accounting for Leasing Transactions issued by the Institute of Chartered Accountants of India, are expressly exclude from being applied to hire purchase contracts in contrast to the International Accounting Standard No. 17, where hire purchase contracts have been included in leasing contracts.

According to IAS No. 17, no different accounting standard is prescribed for leases and hire purchase. Hence, as per the standard, the hire purchase transaction also should be accounted for according to its substance, as a secured loan. The sum of digits or Rule of 78 method and the actuarial method are considered as methods distributing the finance charges in conformity with the IAS. In India, the even spread method of apportioning the finance charges equally is prevalent but it is not considered to be in accordance with the international standards.

HP Accounting Methods

Even Spread Method

It is also referred to as the straight line method or the add-on rate method. Under this method, the income is spread over the term of the contract in equal proportion. The total finance charges are spread evenly over entire period of contract, by dividing the said finance charges with the number of months of the contract. The amount arrived at is the income for each month of the contract and the balance is regarded as principal recovery. Obviously, the method is very simplistic and primitive and it is not considered to be in conformity with financial principles as it fails to take note of the decline in the outstanding balance.

Sum of Digits Method

It is also known as Rule of 78 methods, the name was derived from the sum of the 12 months in a year, viz., the numbers 1 to 12 are added, amounting to 78. Unlike the even spread method, this method is intended for a proper distribution of the finance charges so that it declines with each repayment. So, a large income is apportioned in the initial few months and it declines gradually in the later part of the contractual period. However, this method also is considered to be crude one, since it fails to exactly identify the interest.

The Actuarial Method

In this method, the internal rate of return (IRR) is found out and then it is applied on the outstanding principal at the time of receiving each instalment.

Lease *v.* Hire Purchase—Accounting Differences

Certain features distinguish hire purchase accounting from lease accounting. The major distinguishing features are:

- In a lease, the asset is treated as the fixed asset of the lessor. Whereas, the asset is shown in the balance sheet of the hirer in case of hire purchase even though the legal title remains with the hire vendor who shows the assets being hired as stock-in-trade or as receivables.
- In lease, the entire receipts from the lessee are taken to the lessor's profit and loss account. But in case of hire purchase, a receipt from the hirer is separated into principal and interest and only the interest is taken to the profit and loss account of the hire vendor.
- Since the leased assets are shown in the lessor's balance sheet, it is he who depreciates such asset. The lessor's income tends to decline with the decline of the investment outstanding in the lease. But, in hire purchases, the general practice is to allocate finance charges to the hire purchase period equally.
- In a sale type hire purchase, the activity of selling is combined with the activity of financing. So, the selling profit should be recognized when the goods

are let out on hire purchase and the finance income should be spread over the entire period of hire purchase. Hence, the normal selling profit is to be separated from the profit on account of financing. Such differences do not exist in lease.

15

Factoring

Factoring is defined as an outright purchase of credit approved accounts receivable with the factor assuming bad debt losses. 'Biswe' defines factoring as 'Credit Factoring' is a continuing legal relationship between a financial institution (the 'Factor') selling goods providing services to trade customer ('Factor') and a business concern (The 'Client') selling goods or providing services to trade customers ('the customers') whereby the factor purchases the clients book debts either with or without recourse to the client, and in relation thereto controls the credit extended to customers and administers the sales ledger.

Factoring is one where, an asset based method of financing as well as a specialized service being the purchase of book debts of a company by the factor, thus releasing the capital tied up in accounts receivables and providing financial accommodation to the company. The book debts are assigned to the factor that undertakes the liability to collect them when due for which he charges an amount as discount or rebate deducted from the bills. Thus, the factor is an intermediary between the supplier and customers who performs financing and debt collection services. Factoring a form service extended on a large scale in USA, UK, many European countries, Central/South American countries, South East and Far Eastern parts of Asia.

In an economy where competition is tough, it is natural for the weaker units, small scale and medium scale sectors to be left behind. This has been the matter of concern for bankers, creditors, government and society in general. Delay in payments of sales bills leads to inadequate tie-up of working capital which results in industrial sickness. Despite several measures taken by banks like inventory related finance against pledge of goods like loans and cash credits and receivables related finance i.e., discounting bills of exchange, supply bills finance or overdraft against book debts, the problems continued. In this context the policy makers thought of helping the small and medium scale sectors to recover their dues from buyers of its goods more quickly by establishing "Factoring Services" as an alternative.

The term 'factor' has its origin in the Latin word 'Facere. meaning' to make or to get things done. During the 15th and 16th centuries, Factors were appointed by manufacturers in England, France and Spain to arrange for the sale and distribution of their goods and to collect the proceeds thereof. Factors never received title, but were responsible for the safe keeping of the goods as well as the proceeds of sale. During the 19th and 20th centuries, the manufacturers retained their distribution function, but transferred the financing, credit and collection functions to the Factor. A 'Factor' is an agent who finances the seller through the purchase of accounts receivables. Though this form was prevalent earlier through traveling merchants, it became significant during 16th century in UK, France and Spain.

IMPORTANCE OF FACTORING

The industrialization of country and increase in the production and sales of companies, during recent times in India has led to the feeling of timely collection of receivables and management of the same. In a buyer's market, delay in collection of debts results in problems of working capital as a result of which the small suppliers with a limited finance 'raising capacity' ultimately suffer. Delay or Non-realization of dues had been the main reason for the sickness in the small-scale sector.

Traditionally, collection of book debts was not undertaken by banks, though they provide collection services in respect of bills purchased/discounted by them. The client must reimburse the dishonored bills and the latter thus enjoys no protection against default by the buyers. In addition to the working capital problems forced by the seller, no interest is realized for the period for which the payments are delayed beyond the estimated time. Manufacturers refrain from insisting on the payment of overdue interest due to severe competition in the market, which ultimately results in the decrease in profits and deficits in working capital. Hence, there is a need for an efficient system of receivable management and collection machinery which will enable the manufacturers to concentrate on other important matters.

Characteristic Features of Factoring Services

- It aims at replacing high cost market credit.
- It is a financial service product.
- Factor takes care of the collection of sales bills of clients.
- Its rate of interest is comparable to that of banks.
- It offers a continuous relationship between factor and his client.
- It also includes a package of services like, collection and follow up of each in voice, credit insurance, MIS support, etc.
- Very minimal service charges.
- It is classified as other current liability.
- These services are available to all sectors, *viz.*, manufacturing, Trading and services.
- It substitutes sundry creditors.
- Factoring is different from bill discounting.

Factoring in India

The varied services provided by the factors could benefit the large number of suppliers in India. The need for factoring in India arises due to the limitations of the banking industry in the provision of finance, Credit protection or Collection Services. Moreover, an efficient system of receivables management for the manufacturers is the need of the hour. Numerous sellers in India, more so from the SSI sector are in need of advice on various aspects of credit-extension, recovery of dues, receivables management, etc., which could be provided only by those who posses specialized knowledge of the same, This is more feasible by the factors unlike banks because the factors have a better knowledge of the affairs of the seller.

The Reserve Bank of India has already accepted the recommendation of Kalyana Sundaram Committee and initiated on working out the details. The factoring services in the initial stages are to be introduced only for domestic trade and commerce. Four of five Zonal organizations are set-up as subsidiaries of State Bank of India and other nationalized banks. The Nationalized Banks for this purpose have already been short listed and State Bank had already floated its subsidiary to look after factoring service in the West Zone. Canara Bank has also floated a subsidiary in the Southern Region. Private sector is being presently kept out of the factoring services. Reserve Bank has also approached Central Government for exempting factors from stamp duty.

Though factoring is not by itself a complete answer for delays and defaults in payment, their professional approach in matters of credit is expected to improve the culture of payments. Factors such as estimation of potential demand for factoring services, prices of such services, infrastructural facilities needed for providing them, type of organizations which may provide them, linkages between banks and factors, etc., must be considered while taking a view on the introduction of factoring services in India.

On the initiation of the RBI four of five zonal organizations are set-up as subsidiaries of the SBI and other nationalized banks factoring has been introduced only for domestic trade and the private sector has been kept out so far. Much more has to be done in this sphere. There is a good prospect for factoring in India.

Functions of Factors

The factor purchases the book debts of the client. As such he performs certain basic services as well as auxiliary services.

Basic Services

- Provision of finance.
- Absorption of the Risk of bad debts.
- Collection of debts.
- Administration of the client's sales ledger.

Modern factoring which involves a continuing arrangement under which a financing institution assumes the credit and collection function its client, purchases its receivables as they arise either with or without recourse to him for credit losses, maintains the sales ledger, attends to other book keeping relating to such accounts receivables and performs other services. Provision of finance is normally the basic service which brings factoring into existence. The risk of bad debts may not be absorbed by him as he may discount the bills subject to a term of resource, i.e., reverting back to the client where the customer fails to pay the bills. Likewise the collection and accounting function may also be left to the client. The aforesaid services may be provided separately by different agencies. The unique feature about factor is that he provides all those services in one package.

SERVICES RENDERED BY FACTORS

1. *Financing of Receivables*: This is the key feature of factoring. The factor purchases the book debts of a supplier client at a price in whose favour the debts are assigned. It could be with recourse in which case the factor renders collection services and the supplier is obliged to refund the amount in the event of failure to pay by the customer, or it may be without recourse where the factor is obvious obliged to pay the client on the due date of invoice. While the banks only finance the receivables, the factor purchases the

same as a result of which the suppliers balance sheet discloses an improve current ratio.

2. *Maintenance of Sales Ledger:* The factor undertakes to maintain sales ledger of the client for a service charge. The client forwards a copy of an invoice sent by him to his customer. The client need not maintain individual sales ledgers for his customers as the factor undertakes to do it. The factors due to large-scale operations computerize the same which contribute to expeditious book keeping. The factor reports to the client about the current status of receivables from customers and other reports of importance at regular intervals as agreed upon.
3. *Collection of Accounts Receivables:* The factor undertakes to do the collection and thus relieves the client. This reduces the time, effort and money spent there on. Besides the client is in a position to concentrate on improving purchases, production, marketing and other managerial aspects of the business. A systematic follow-up is made possible (by the use of computers by the factors) as a result of which the client makes a timely demand on the debtors to pay the amount. The debtors who dislike going down in the esteem of the factor respond promptly to the reminders sent to them.
4. *Credit Control and Credit Protection:* Factoring enables better credit control as the factor with the help of extensive information provides quality services in this area. The credit rating and records of payments of customers are intimated to the client. Thus, the factor advises the client as to whom credit should be extended, if so how much, etc., which is possible, since the factor serves many clients with the same customers who become familiar in due course of time. This enables the clients to handle a great volume of business than would have been otherwise possible.
5. *Advisory Services:* The specialized experience in matters of finance and credit enables the factor to advise the clients' developments in their industries.

The factors also employ those with extensive manufacturing experience to advice on work load analysis and other technical aspects of a client's business. Moreover, the factor, develop close relationship within an industry due to the scope of operations and this helps them to give advice regarding matters of importance.

How does Factoring Work?

1. The customer places an order with the seller—the client.
2. The factor and the seller enter into a factoring agreement about the various terms of factoring.
3. Sale contract is entered into with the buyer and the goods are delivered. The invoice with the notice to pay the factor is sent along with.
4. The copy of invoice covering the above sale is to the factor, who maintains the sales ledger.
5. The factor prepays up to 80% of the invoice value.
6. Monthly statements are sent by the factor to the buyer. If there are any unpaid invoices follow-up action is initiated.
7. The buyer settles the invoices on expiry of credit period allowed.
8. The balance 20% less the Cost of Factoring is paid by the Factor to the Client.

Banks Facilitate Factors

Financial services can be obtained by the suppliers from the banks and factoring organizations. Thus, a proper linkage between the two assumes importance, Banks and factors must furnish information to each other about those parties who approach more than one agency. The debt may be assigned to the factors by the suppliers and the factor may borrow from the banks. The supplier may as an alternative borrow from the banks and avail of all other services from a factor. Linkages between banks and factor are to the advantage of the factors and suppliers who would avail-off the services. Both the agencies would be able to bring about timely action and thus prevent the sellers and buyers' units from becoming sick.

The pricing of various services rendered by the factors depends upon the creditworthiness of the customers, his track record, turnover, etc. But, the cost of funds and other costs to be borne by the factors influence the pricing. The price of financial services is suggested to be around 16% p.a. and for other services on the aggregate not to exceed 2.5% to 3% of the serviced debts.

The establishment of SBI Factors and Commercial Services (P) Ltd., is a boon to Indian Industries. It was set-up by State Bank of India in collaboration with Small Industries Development Bank India, Union Bank of India and State Bank of Saurashtra on 26th February, 1991 to serve the Indian industries and commercial concerns. Since the establishment of SBI Factor and Commercial Services (P) Ltd., the sellers of the industrial products, particularly the manufacturers have improved their cash flows through repayment facilities, leading to increased sales, continuity of suppliers and reduction in the cost of maintenance.

Types of Factoring

- *Maturity Factoring:* Under this method, the factor may agree to pay an amount t9 the client for the bills purchased by him either immediately or on maturity. The latter refers to a date agreed upon on which the factor pays the client.
- *Non-Recourse Factoring:* Also termed 'old-line factoring', it is an arrangement whereby the factor has no recourse to the client when the bill remains unpaid by the customer. Thus, the risk of bad debt is absorbed by the factor.
- *Recourse Factoring*: The credit risk remains with the client though the debt is assigned to the factor, i.e., the factor can have recourse to the client in the event of non-payment by the customer.
- *Full Factoring:* It is just opposite of recourse factoring. The factor offers comprehensive services to the client.

- *Supplier Guarantee Factoring*: This is also referred to as drop shipment factoring. This happens when the client is a mediator between supplier and customer. When the client is a distributor, the factor guarantees the supplier against the invoices raised by the supplier upon the client and goods may be delivered to the customers. The client thereafter raises bills.
- *Advance Factoring:* Where the payment is made by the factor immediately it is called Advance Factoring. Under this type of factoring, the factor provides financial accommodation apart from non-financial services rendered by him.
- *Confidential and Undisclosed Factoring:* The arrangement between the factor and the client are left un-notified to the customers and the client collects the bills from the customers without intimating them of the factoring arrangements.
- *Agency factoring:* The facilities of finance and protection against bad debts are provided by the factor whereas; the sales ledger administration and collection of debts are carried out by the client.
- *Bank Participation Factoring*: The bank takes a floating charge on the Client's equity, i.e., the amount payable by the factor to the client in respect of his receivables. On this basis, the bank lends to the client and enables him to have double financing.
- *Bull factoring*: It is a modified form of invoice discounting. Here notification of assignment of debts is given to the customers. However, the client is subject to full recourse and he carries out his own administration and collection.

Merits of Factoring

1. *Increase in the Turnover of Stocks:* Turnover of stock into cash is speeded up and this results in larger turnover on the same investment.
2. *Improved Credit Standing:* It improves the credit rating of an industrial unit.
3. *Reduces Risk:* The present risk in bills financing like

finance against accommodation bills can be reduced to minimum.

4. *Offers specialized Service:* Since the factor collects the debts on behalf of the client, specialized service is obtained at a minimum cost. The clients also get advice in matters relating to marketing, finance and production. The factor with its own specialised expertise is in a position to provide information regarding product design/mix prices, market conditions and economic prospects to its clients. Thus, the services concerning the commercial viability (marketing, demand and supply aspects) of a project are provided by the factor.
5. *Obviates Collection Department:* The client need not undertake any responsibility of collecting the dues from the buyers of the goods. Thus, the industrial units, especially in the tiny and small sector need not have any administrative set-up for the credit realisation.
6. Prompt payment and reduction of debt.
7. Improves current ratio.

Demerits of Factoring

1. It is not suitable for companies with speculative business.
2. It is not suitable for companies which have in-efficient management.
3. It is not suitable for companies which have high bad debt past experience.
4. It is not suitable for companies manufacturing and selling highly specialized items, because the factor may not have sufficient expertise to assess the credit risk,
5. It is not suitable for companies selling large number of small products to various types of people or companies having large number of debtors for small amounts.
6. *It associates high risk:* Factoring is a high risk prone area and it may result in over dependence on

factoring, mismanagement, over trading or even dishonesty on behalf of the clients.

7. *Existence of Teething Problems:* In a developing economy like India, the Institution of factoring in its infant state may have its teething problems, arising from lack of professionalism competence, developed expertise, non-acceptance of change, etc.
8. *Unsuitability:* All companies may not be suitable for entering into factoring contracts. Some of the limiting factors may be: It is uneconomical for small companies with a lesser turnover. Factoring may not suit the needs of certain business concerns. Due to the following reasons:
   - Concerns which accept only cash sales.
   - For firms that undertake job works.
   - Organizations, where payments are made in instalments.

BILLS DISCOUNTING *v.* FACTORING

Bills Discounting

- Under bills discounting it is always offered with recourse to the clients.
- In bills discounting the notice of assignment is not given to the debtors.
- It is purely a financial accommodation.
- It is an advance against bills.
- It cannot be an "Off balance sheet financially".
- Charges recovered upfront and this increases total effective cost.
- In bills discounting entire amount of the bill is to be drawn on the rate of discount.
- Under bills discounting penalty is charged if payment is not paid on due date.
- In bills discounting the grace period is allowed to the maximum of 3 days.
- The procedures to be followed in bills discounting is difficult.

- It is individual transaction-oriented and the amount of finance extended is usually a lesser amount.

Factoring

- Factoring may be both with recourse and without recourse to the client
- Under factoring notice of assignment is given by pre-printed invoices.
- It provides a package of service including finance, collection of invoices, credit protection, sales ledge administration, etc. That is, factoring is financial and service agreement.
- It is a purchase of debt of assignment "Off balance sheet financially" is possible under factoring.
- In factoring there is no upfront recovery of charges.
- In factoring amount can be drawn and when recovered charge is levied only on actual drawings.
- Under factoring no penal interest charged till the expiry of grace period.
- Under factoring the grace period allowed to the maximum of 75 days.
- Under certain circumstances it can be extended up to 150 days.
- The procedure to be followed in factoring is very easy.
- It is whole turn over oriented and the amount of finance is bulk.

INTERNATIONAL FACTORING

International factoring is an efficient alternative to more traditional trade tools and helps the exporters to take advantage of the new markets abroad. Although their products are sold in the open market abroad, they are covered for credit risk as the collection is made through export factoring.

TYPES ON INTERNATIONAL FACTORING

Two Factor System: This is the most common system of

international factoring and involves four parties i.e., Exporter, Importer, Export Factor in exporter's country and Import Factor in Importer's country. The functions of the export Factor are:

- Assessment of the financial strength of the exporter.
- Prepayment to the exporter.
- Follow-up with the Import Factor.
- Sharing of commission with the import Factor.

The functions of the Import Factor are:

- Maintaining the books of the exporter in respect of sales to the debtors in his country.
- Collection of debts from the importer and remitting the proceeds to the exporter's factor providing credit protection in case of financial inability on the part of any of the debtors.

Single/Direct Factoring System: In this system, a special agreement is signed between two Factoring companies for single Factoring. Whereas in Two Factor System, credit is provided by import Factor and pre-payment, book keeping and collection responsibilities remain with export Factor. For this system to be effective there should be strong co-ordination and co-operation between two Factoring companies. Pricing is lower when compared to Two Factor System.

Direct Export Factoring: Here only one Factoring company is involved, i.e., export Factor, which provides all services including finance to the exporter.

Direct Import Factoring: Under this system, the seller chooses to work directly with Factor of the importing country. The Factoring agreement is executed between the exporter and the import Factor. The import Factor is responsible for sales ledger administration, collection of debts and providing bad debt protection upto the agreed level of risk cover. .

Back to Back Factoring: It is a very specialized form of International Factoring, used when suppliers are selling large volumes to a few debtors for which it is difficult to cover the credit risk in International Factoring. In this case, International Factor can sign a domestic Factoring agreement with the debtor whereby it will be getting the receivables as security for the credit risk taken in favour of Export Factor.

EXPORT FACTORING

In case of international factoring, four parties are involved:

- Seller (exporter)
- Buyer (importer)
- Export factor (in the exporting country)
- Import factor (in the importing country).

The following procedure is normally adopted:

An exporter contacts the export factor in connection with his export of products. The export factor appoints an import factor in the importing country. The exporter submits a list of buyers in the importing country.

- The import factor evaluates the creditworthiness of the buyer and reports back to the exporter indicating the credit limits of the buyers.
- Once the credit limit is approved, the exporter enters into an export factoring agreement with the export factor.
- All export receivables are assigned to the export factor which in turn assigns them in favour of the import factor.
- The exporter ships the merchandise to the approved importer. All invoices bear the notification that all moneys due in the invoices have been assigned and must be paid to the appointed import factor.
- A copy of such notification is sent to the import factor who will handle the collection. The import factor is responsible for all invoices and also for all aspects of the factoring operations.

- Once the authorized sales take place, the import factor is responsible for remitting the funds collected in the fastest possible way.
- If the importer fails to pay the amount due on the invoice on the due date, the import factor arranges to make the collection in accordance with the local practice. In case of any dispute, between the exported, and importer; the import factor also resolves the issue.
- The import factor settles the account with the export factor as soon as it receives payment from the buyer. It should be noted that the import factor is responsible for all invoices factored up to the approved limit.
- In case the approved buyer fails to payer delays the payment, the import factor pays the receivables to the export factor at least about 100 days after the due date.

Advantages of Export Factoring

- *Protection against Bad Debts*: Since the export factor undertakes the responsibility of collection, it will bear the credit risk in case of failure to effect payment by the importer.
- *Guarantee for Receipt of Money with the Specified Period*: Upon maturity the exporter will receive the full value of the invoices as the payment period is guaranteed.
- *Prompt Collection:* Exporter can entrust the responsibility of collection with the import factor in the respective buyer's countries. Since the import factors have flexible form of financing
- *Healthier Customer Portfolios*: The import factor evaluates the creditworthiness of the buyer. Since export of goods is done only after this, the exporters can expect a healthy relationship with such buyers.
- *Advantage of Using International Factors*: Being specialists in the field of international business, the export factor advises the exporters as to how they may have to proceed in the export trade with the

help of the import factor and buyers with good reputation are identified. The sellers are able to take advantage of the situation and export quality products without any hesitation. The buyers in the importing country can also expect quality products and prompt delivery if they make use of import factors.

- *Provision of multi-sales ledger*: Since the export factor provides a multi-currency sales ledgering system, the local exporter is able to understand the sales without any difficulty. This system makes the local exporter to concentrate on production, planning and marketing without any botheration of collection of funds.
- *Hedges against Fluctuation in Foreign Exchange:* The value of the currency is fluctuating from time to time. The export factor can make the necessary arrangements for appropriate forward exchange covers to protect exporters against such fluctuations.

16

Consumer Finance and Credit Cards

When a financial intermediary finances the purchase of consumer durables, it is called consumer finance. A consumer may obtain finance for the purchase of vehicles, refrigerator, washing machines, television and other durable items for the household. A consumer with a limited income may not be in a position to buy high cost durables; however, he may be in the long-run able to pay for the goods. In such a situation, he needs the helping hand from the financiers in the organized or organized sector to finance him for purchase of durables. In this chapter only organized form of consumer finance is discussed.

CHANGING CONSUMER ATTITUDES IN INDIA

- The key to the success of the Indian consumer finance market can be attributed to the following factors, such as, fast changing consumer habits, borrowing money to buy the products he wants and not content with buying what he can afford.

- ❖ Consumer finance today is a win-win system in which everyone stands to gain. For the Indian consumer, it is an opportunity to upgrade his standard of living right now instead of waiting for years for his savings to accumulate. For manufacturers, it stimulates demand and lowers inventory. For middlemen, it's a sales boosting device. For players of consumer finance, it's a means of profit generation.
- ❖ The buy-now-pay-later culture is a system of consumer behavior in India. This led to the system of evolving, through various forms of consumer lending, consumer credit, consumer loans, friendly and family borrowings, daily payment schemes and so on.
- ❖ The basic underpinning of consumer financing is the consumers present spending habits tend to be geared by the expectations of future income.
- ❖ Along with buying a home, consumers prefer consumer finance to buy home appliances and vehicles, opting for finance based on the rate of interest, administrative fee, processing fee, commitment charges, pre-payment penalty, types of facilities' standard and kind of services mix and sundry terms and conditions.
- ❖ These are the members of a growing breed of normally conservative middle-class Indians who are shedding their inhibitions about opting for loans despite the high interest rates.

GROWTH OF CONSUMER FINANCING

1. Consumer Durables Banks have entered almost all the segments in retail finance. They are gaining share from NBFCs. Private Banks have started offering loans for low-ticket items like consumer durables and two-wheelers, besides personal loans.
2. *Reduction in Interest Rates*: Falling interest rates, coupled substantially reduced the EMIs affordable to more people.

3. *Housing Loans*: Housing loans have been the product of choice for nationalized banks because of their attractive profitability, low risk and the ease of processing loans.
4. *Expanding Target Market*: Loans becoming more affordable and the target market has become expanded. This effect is particularly because the incomes of middle and upper-middle class households have increased considerably and hence it is the target market for retail loans.
5. *Increasing Risk of Disintermediation in Corporate Lending*: Retail finance has become the preferred business of banks on account of its higher spreads. It is due to the fact of the increasing risk of disintermediation in corporate lending. The abnormal growth in retail finance has made it the primary driver of banks financing.
6. The retail finance boom has a direct impact on the fortunes of the consumer durables market, including two-wheelers and passenger cars. This correlation is already clear from the surge in demand in recent times. Availability of cheaper loans for two-wheelers and cars has made these sales of these industries to grow at an even faster rate. The car finance market has reached a new level of maturity, so much so that the car-maker, the automobile dealer and the financier now work together to provide better features and funding options for the buyer. Depending on the manufacturer, tenure of the loan and credit history of the car buyer, interest rates, on a reducing balance basis.
7. *Key Issues and Success Factors:* For the consumer finance companies to flourish there is a need to develop a credit information system, which will ease the process, making it faster and easier to determine the creditworthiness of customers. The following measures will speed up consumer finance:
   - Ability to offer simple, convenient and innovative consumer finance products, a wide

distribution network and choice of repayment tenure, documentation and loan offer.

- As a result of the large number of players, market pressures, increased competition, increased awareness and wider offerings, consumer-financing activities need to become customer-oriented and user-friendly.
- Rating of consumer credit worthiness: One of the perceived problems relating to consumer finance is the absence of credit bureaus to rate the creditworthiness of consumers.

8. *Innovative Solutions:* The banks are lending against collateral and have concentrated on small potential borrowers to achieve disbursal targets.
9. *Consumer Durables in Rural India:* Penetration of consumer durables would be deeper in rural India, if banks were ready to finance them. Banks have shown reluctance in this sector and restrict themselves to tractors and diesel pumps. Transportation has helped people in rural India to have access to consumer durables through consumer finance. While the consumer durables market is facing a slowdown due to saturation in the urban market, rural consumers are ready to put their money on the counter if consumer finance is made available and basic infrastructure requirements such as electricity and voltage are ironed out. Currently, rural consumers purchase their durables from the nearest towns, leading to increased expenses due to transportation.
10. *Consumer Preferences:* Indian consumers identify ease and speed of the loan application and approval process, as well as flexibility of evaluation procedures, as the key drivers of financing satisfaction. Consumer Financing Satisfaction Performance is measured by four factors: Application process, Approval and documentation, Finance advising and Loan value. Customers who obtained their loans from a nationalized bank are relatively more satisfied than those choosing a non-banking finance company (NBFC) or a foreign bank. Low

interest rates and the reputation of the finance company are among the key reasons for customers who opted either for an NBFC or a foreign bank.

FEATURES OF CONSUMER FINANCE

1. *Parties and Structure of the Transaction:* A consumer finance transaction can either be bipartite or tripartite. A bipartite transaction involves the dealer-*cum*-financier and the borrower or customer while in tripartite transaction, the dealer and financier are two separate parties transactions can be either structured in the form of hire purchase, conditional sale or credit sale, but a majority of the tripartite consumer finance transactions are of the hire purchase type.
2. *Payment for the transaction:* Consumer finance schemes are divided into two categories: Down Payment Schemes and Deposit Linked Schemes. The down payment varies from according to the value of goods and financing is available for up to 80% or as the case may be. In a deposit linked scheme, the down payment varies between 15% and 25% of the total value of the asset. The financier pays the full amount to the seller. Deposits are of cumulative nature and carry a prescribed interest rate. Zero Deposit schemes are also available, under which the Equated Monthly Instalment (EMI) is higher than the EMI under 15%-25% deposit schemes.
3. *Rate of Interest and Repayment Period:* The borrower can choose a repayment period ranging from 12-60 months. Finance companies notify the customer indicating the amount of equated monthly instalments that need to be paid through post-dated cheques.
4. *Security:* The credit provided is secured through first charge on the asset concerned. The borrower is prohibited from disposing, pledging or hypothecating the asset during the credit period.
5. *Eligibility Criteria for Borrowers:* Individuals, partnership firms and private and public limited

companies are eligible to borrow. Different companies follow different criteria for financing. A sample hire purchase may include the following conditions:

Individual Borrowers

- The net take-home monthly salary should be about three times the Equated Monthly Instalment likely to be calculated on the loan financed.
- Having a minimum of level of annual income.
- A minimum of one or two years of employment with the current employer.
- At least five years of service left, for retirement or till the repayment of the current scheme.
- Should not have often changed the employment.

Corporate Borrowers

- Consistency in profits for two or three years.
- The Net Profit plus Depreciation must be at least three times the annual instalment.
- A minimum net worth as expected by the financier.
- Set-up and functioning at least for a minimum period of four years.

CREDIT CARDS

A credit card is a monetary instrument that enables the cardholder to obtain goods and services without actual payment at the time of purchase. It is also popularly known as plastic money. The value of purchases made by the cardholder using the card is recovered at the end of a specified period, usually a month, called the billing cycle. It can be said that a credit card is basically a "Pay Later" card that is provided to a customer.

Benefits of Credit Cards

- Credit can be availed for a period of 30-50 days.

- A cardholder need not have the required amount in his account to the extent of the transaction made.
- The card carries a predetermined limit up to which the holder can spend.
- At the end of each billing cycle, the cardholder has to pay a minimum sum of the bill normally 5-10% and the rest can be paid in instalments over the next few months/years.
- On outstanding balance, a nominal rate of 1.5 to 3% per month is charged as interest.
- Regular use of the credit card by the user earns him additional points that provide the cardholder with discounts on purchases.

How do Credit Cards Work?

Every transaction made on a credit card involves three parties:

- Card Issuer
- Cardholder
- Trader

A credit card holder, subsequent to making a purchase or availing a service at a designated trader, presents his credit card instead of paying cash. The trader checks the number of the card against the Hot List provided to him by the Card Issuer, to ascertain the authenticity of the cardholder. The signature of the cardholder on the voucher provided by the trader should tally with the signature on the credit card. The trader then presents the sales vouchers to the bank, which reimburses it, after charging commission. At the end of each billing cycle, the value of the transaction is included in the statement mailed to the cardholder.

Business Associates: The card issuer sometimes enters into a contract with organizations that also issue cards on behalf of the issuer to the clients. The organizations that issue cards are known as Business Associates or Member Affiliates. Cards issued by Member Affiliates are similar to credit cards except for the name and logo of the Member Affiliate besides the name and logo of the issuer. This type of arrangement enlarges the scope and operations of the credit card issuer.

Clearing Houses: The card issuer generally affiliates itself with the clearing house usually, MasterCard International or Visa Card International act as on behalf of the issuer. This enables the cardholder of one affiliate to use his card at the Merchant Establishment of another affiliate.

DEBIT CARD

Debit card is the opposite of a credit card. While in credit card without having any balance in the account a holder is enabled to overdraw his account. A credit card holder need not be an account holder of the bank (savings or current account). Whereas, a debit card holder should be an account holder and he is allowed to debit his account whenever he goes for purchase. Banks now-a-days offer card as ATM cum Debit cards.

An account holder is issued with the Debit card. The retailer swipes the card over an electronic terminal at his outlet, you enter the personal identification number on a PIN pad and the money is immediately debited at the bank. Citibank and a few domestic banks like Times Bank offer this. Debit cards have been witnessing a slow and steady growth. It has made a delayed entry into India during 1998. The growth is phenomenal today. The issuance and usage of debit cards has been steadily increasing over the last two years. But the awareness about the benefits and technology used is very low. Creating awareness among the customers will mark the future of debit cards in India.

Benefits of Debit Cards

1. The card is issued free.
2. One can plan budget within the savings instead of going for credit.
3. He can access his own money 24 hours a day.
4. He saves fee and other service changes on cash withdrawals.

5. He can carry one card to use both at ATMs and at merchant locations.
6. Free personal accident insurance cover for cardholders
7. Insurance to holders of the card from the time of by the bank.
8. Free cash withdrawal facility at the bank ATMs.
9. Discounts will be arranged at selected merchant establishments for using debit card to settle the bill.
10. Cardholder can access his accounts in one branch through a card in the ATMs.

Working of Debit Cards

The technology involved in making the debit cards is sophisticated and almost all the issuing banks use the same kind of technology. Some of the features of the technology involved include:

- Technology is more or less similar to credit cards.
- Debit cards can be used only at Point of Sale terminals and at ATMs where the data is read from the magnetic stripe positioned on the back of the card.
- There will not be any individual card limit. Whatever the balance maintained by cardholder, is accessible for usage.
- Debit cards are Personal Identification Number (PIN) based; some other cards are both PIN and signature based.

Security Features Cards

To safeguard the interests of the customer the bank ensures the following:

- The card and the Personal identification Number PIN are sent separately.
- The bank has a department that closely monitors all high-risk transactions on debit cards. Special reports on spend patterns are generated on a daily basis to mitigate potential loss on account of misuse of cards.

- The card has an inactive status it cannot be used for transactions at ATMs or at POS. The cardholder needs to activate his card by carrying out a transaction at the ATM using his PIN number.
- Debit cards use magnetic stripe-based technology. Debit cards can only be used for online transactions whereas Credit cards can also be used for offline transactions. Debit card transactions are subject to daily limits on the card and subject to the available balance in the customer's account whereas Credit Cards transactions are subject to the credit limit of the customer.
- The magnetic stripe and signature have been used on plastic cards since the early 1970s but they no longer form the best form of security. Chip and PIN will make payments more secure and are expected to dramatically reduce fraud losses.
- There are two elements involved in making a plastic card transaction secure. The first is to ensure that the card is genuine and secondly that the person presenting the card is the true owner.
- The chip protects against counterfeit fraud and the PIN against lost and stolen cards and those intercepted in the post.
- Bank and brands like Visa and Master Card are investing significantly in migration from magnetic stripe technology to microchip technology. The microchip is embedded into debit or credit card and provides both highly secure memory and complex processing capabilities.
- The chip not only holds the same personal data as the magnetic stripe card holder name, card number, expiry date, but also adds a range of indications and counter mechanism reduce the opportunities for misuse of the card. Chip technology uses highly sophisticated processing to identify genuine cards and makes counterfeiting more complex and expensive.
- The PIN is a four-digit code assigned to or chosen by card holders to prove that they are the rightful

owners of the card when paying for goods and services. It will replace signature when the card is chip-enabled and when the retailer terminal is PIN-enabled.

TYPES OF CARDS

1. *VISA Card*: VISA card is a product of VISA, USA and along with MasterCard it is distributed by financial institutions around the world. A VISA card holder borrows money against a credit line and repays the money with interest if the balance is carried over from month to month in a revolving line of credit.
2. *Master Card:* MasterCard is a product of MasterCard International and along with VISA is distributed by financial institutions; around the world. Cardholders borrow money against a line of credit: and pay it back with interest if the balance is carried over from month to month
3. *Standard Card and Classic Card:* It is the usual form of card issued by most of the issuers. Classic card is the brand name for the standard card issued by VISA.
4. *Gold Card or Executive Card:* Gold card is a credit card that offers a higher line of credit than a basic card. Income eligibility is also higher. In addition, issuers provide extra incentives to cardholders.
5. *Platinum Card:* Platinum card is a credit card with a higher limit and additional perks than a gold card.
6. *Affinity Cards:* A card offered by two organizations, one by the financing institution, the other a non-financial group. Schools, non-profit groups, pro-wrestlers, popular singerr5 and airlines are among those featured on affinity cards. Usually use of the card entitles holders to special discounts or deals from the non-financial group.
7. *Titanium Card:* Titanium card is a card with an even higher limit than platinum card.
8. *Charge Card:* It falls between a debit and credit card. This is equal to a credit card but the holder need not be an accountholder. The cardholder has to pay in

full, when the bill arrives with the mail. No outstanding are allowed, no other words, no revolving credit facility either.

9. *Rebate Card:* This is a card that allows the customer to accumulate cash, merchandise or services based on card usage.
10. *Travel Card:* These cards works mostly as debit cards for the limited purpose of travel. Citibank Dollar Card, American Express, Bobcard Global and Hong Kong Bank Thomas Cook International Card are among the players in this section.
11. *Secured Card:* It is a credit card that a cardholder secures with a savings deposit to ensure payment of the outstanding balance if the cardholder defaults in payments.
12. *Co-branded Card:* This is an agreement between two service providers who want a trade off with the other strengths. Specific facilities are made to members through these tie-ups. So, Times Bank and Citibank have a co-branded card that allows concessional rates for add-on cards or telephone banking.
13. *Cash Card:* Cash cards, similar to pre-paid phone cards, contain a set amount of value, which can be read by a special cash card reader. Participating retailers will use the reader to debit the card in instalments until the value is gone. The cards are like cash. They have no built-in security, so if lost or stolen, they can be used by anyone.
14. *Laghu Udyami Credit Card (LUCC) Scheme:* Encouraged by the response given to Kisan Credit Card Scheme the Government launched a Laghu Udyami Credit Card Scheme (LUCC) in the Budget 2002-03. The Public Sector Banks would issue Credit Cards to small businessmen, retail traders, artisans, small entrepreneurs, professionals and other self-employed persons including those in the tiny sector. The scheme aims at providing simplified and borrower friendly credit facilities.
15. *Global Card:* Credit cards issued in India can only be used in India and Nepal. To overcome this drawback,

a new card called a "Global Card" has been introduced. The card can be used anywhere across the globe as well as in India. The card can also be used to make foreign payments through the net, to import books etc.

16. *Corporate Credit Cards*: Companies, both public and private sector, issue these cards. The companies also issue other add-on cards to directors, secretaries and other persons depending upon their requirements. The name of the company is embedded on the add-on cards issued to the cardholder. Generally, the main card has a dummy card, which is used for the purpose of billing all the charges of the add-on cards. All transactions made through add-on cardholders are billed to the main cards which are debited from the company's account.
17. *Smart Cards:* Smart cards mark the next natural step in the world of plastic cards. A smart card has an integrated step embedded into it, which enables it to perform different functions. It has the capacity to store up to 80 times more information than other magnetic stripe cards. Smart cards are now available with 16 Kilobytes of memory. When read by special terminals, the cards can perform a number of functions or access data stored in the chip. Smart cards carry the electronic proof of its holder's identity enabling its holder to make secure purchases anywhere on the globe, leading to a dramatic increase in electronic commerce. These cards can be used as cash cards or as credit cards with a preset credit limit, or used as ID cards with stored-in passwords. Smart cards allow companies to deliver more personalized products and service that suit the individual life style of the customers. Smart cards also allow the consumers to carry multiple currencies when traveling. One can make secure purchases over the internet anytime, anywhere and can pay for public transportation and public phone calls as well as make traditional credit and debit purchases.

CONSIDERATIONS FOR ISSUE OF CREDIT OR DEBIT CARD

1. *Place of Residence:* One of the important criteria for getting a card is that the applicant has to own a house. If an applicant stays in a rented house, the criteria would be that he should have stayed in the rented house fairly long period of time.
2. *Landline phone connection:* Another criterion is that the applicant must have a telephone connection. It is because that the customer can easily be tracked down in case of default.
3. *Organization working:* Card issuers look for good clients from reputed organizations.
4. *Profession:* Profession is yet another criterion for granting the service.
5. *Place of Work:* Card issuers will normally check the reputation of the company you work in, the number of years you have put up there and your designation.
6. *Age:* The applicant should have attained the legal age to hold card.
7. *Other factors:* Other than this broad set of factors, issuers will also like to check the number of dependents of the applicant, whether the person is servicing a loan and whether the applicant has another credit card. If a person possesses more than one credit card, one's credit history.

COSTS ASSOCIATED WITH CREDIT CARD

1. *Service charge:* While issuing cards normally banks do not charge any service charge. Usually, the first year the service charge is waived. Banks have started to issue life time free cards.
2. *Renewal:* The card has to be renewed every year for which the cardholder have to pay renewal Charges. Often, the card issuer or bank will slip in renewal fees and even an unsolicited upgrade of class of card.
3. *Interest-free period on every bill:* Interest is not charged for one month on every bill. In practice, part

payments in a month by a cardholder are adjusted in the next bill.

4. *Purchases on credit:* In some shops or retail outlets, card payments means an extra payment added to the bill by an establishment that does not want to encourage plastic money.
5. *Fuel on credit:* Every time a person fills the tank, the service charge that accompanies each transaction could be 2.5 per cent. Small charge adds up to the sum in the total. Likewise for gold purchases the service charge is charged by the seller.
6. *Billing period:* Every cardholder gets the bill in regular monthly cycles. If a person makes a purchase close to the billing date, he or she gets shorter pay time.
7. *Cash advance:* There are two sets of interest that are applied the moment the cash leaves the teller machine. First, there is a flat transaction fee. Second, there is a rate of interest that is applied on a daily basis. Thus in the bill one ends up with a dual interest and the cash advance payment is not included, usually, in the general bill.

POINTS TO CONSIDER WHILE APPLYING FOR CARD

There are numerous cards in the market; a person intending to get a card should look for the following before applying for card:

- *Residence:* In some of the towns still use of cards are not introduced. Hence, before applying a person should see where a person is about to spent most of the time/purchases.
- *Acceptability:* This determines how widely the card is accepted. It depends on the network and the affiliation. For instance, Visa and Master Cards are more widely accepted than Diners or American Express. Also, a global card scores higher on acceptability than a domestic one.
- *Consortium:* Some banks have consortium among

them and allow other bank cards to use in their ATMs.

- *Eligibility:* All cards have basic minimum income criterion for issuing cards.
- *Fees:* One of the most important factors, the fees includes admission fees, annual subscription and fees for add on cards. All these fees are billed in the first bill and are not charged upfront.
- *Credit Period:* Most cards have different credit periods ranging from 30 days to 50 days. That is the length of the billing cycle. This implies that the bill comes to you every 10th day which is the credit period. Also, credit covers finance charges. Most cards carry heavy credit charges ranging from 1.7% per month to 3% p.m.
- *Cash Advance.* Cardholders can take money out of the cards in ATMs, but obviously pay interest charges on that. You also have to pay cash withdrawal charges—generally 2.5% of the amount withdrawn. Interest is also charged on the amount withdrawn again around 2.5% p.m. Every card has a limit for the amount withdrawn. Some cards have an absolute limit like Rs.10,000 p.m. while most cards have a cash withdrawal limit as a percentage of total credit limit.
- *Insurance Cover.* Insurance cover on cards is available only in the case of an accident. The limits are higher for air accidents than for other types.
- *Other Charges:* Extra charges are payable for late payment. These are only in case a person does not pay the minimum required amount. Late payment charges range from 2.5% of outstanding to 3% p.m.

USES OF CREDIT CARDS

- Many problems associated with credit can be avoided through the use of credit cards. In many businesses, particularly in the retail and consumer service fields, credit arrangements for customers are available through the use of these cards. Under these plans, there is little or no commitment of the business's own capital, and the costs and risks of administration and collection are almost entirely the responsibility of the Credit Card Company or bank.

- Credit card service is available from one's regular commercial bank. Receipts from bank credit card purchases can be deposited daily and are immediately credited. The bank assumes all credit risks provided that one follows instructions for approval of credit card purchases. Typically, these instructions require that one checks the validity of the card against a master list of canceled cards and contact the credit service before accepting the customer's card for purchase above a certain limit.
- Credit card services are particularly vital for businesses with a large number of relatively small accounts. They eliminate the need for credit approval, invoice preparation, record maintenance, and collections. They also minimize one's commitment of capital and virtually eliminate the risk of uncollectible accounts. From a marketing standpoint, the availability of instant credit could often encourage a customer to buy immediately, rather than postpone the decision to a later date or bypass it completely.
- Credit cards are most often used for retail accounts. However, they have also been used successfully in selling to small commercial accounts. Businesses such as repair shops, supply firms, and stationery stores, which have a mixture of consumer and commercial accounts, often find it convenient and economical to extend credit card service to small commercial accounts. Benefits provided by credit cards are not limited to the credit facility alone.

Additional benefits offered to cardholders

1. *Personal Accident Insurance*: Credit card issuers have introduced a free insurance cover to the cardholder against loss of life due to accidents.
2. *Cash Withdrawal Facility*: A pre-determined credit and

cash limit is provided to the cardholder at Automated Teller Machine (ATM) facilities.

3. *Increase in Credit*: Cardholders with a good credit track record are provided with increased credit limit for a short period of time, whenever required.
4. *Add-on Cards*: The spouse, parents and children, over eighteen, of the cardholder, are provided with add-on cards on payment of a specified fee.
5. *Leveraged Investment Facility*: This facility enables the cardholders to subscribe to designated equity or debenture issues in the primary market and schemes floated by mutual funds.

FACTORS THAT CONTRIBUTED TO THE INCREASED USES OF CREDIT CARDS

1. The perception to own credit cards has changed and cards are being viewed as a convenient substitute to carrying cash and also availing credit for short periods.
2. India ranks at the bottom in terms of usage of credit cards when compared to China, Taiwan and Malaysia.
3. Usage of credit card picked up only last ten years.
4. Indians viewed the cards as a luxury and so, Indian banks were not willing to venture it.
5. Over the last ten years, things have changed drastically since the idea of owning a credit card has had its roots in the minds of millions of Indians.
6. Enlightened customer has started viewing the card as a convenient substitute to carrying cash.
7. The change in mindset is clear from the growth, both in terms of absolute numbers and growth rates.
8. The importance of having a pie in the credit cards segment was not lost on any bank, and most banks started their credit card operations. Currently, there are more than 20 banks offering credit cards, but the market share of the top five exceeds 75%.
9. Credit card is a low-margin but high-volume business.

10. The initial investments required by a bank are very high.
11. The income per card is low, thereby requiring large volumes in terms of cards issued and the transactions finance to make the operations profitable.
12. The bigger businesses and merchants are already acquired by the existing players, so for new banks, braking into this business and convincing a merchant is increasing because the banks are shifting towards lower end merchants.
13. Competition in acquiring business, new categories of merchants are coming up.
14. The foreign banks have a dominant share due to various reasons like having been in the field for decades, sound operational and financial strength, strong brand recognition, etc. They were catering to the upper segments and charged high annual fees.
15. According to Visa International, an average Indian cardholder uses his card 9.3 times. A number of card owners do not use their cards and almost 20-30% cards are inactive.
16. In India, two players dominate the credit cards industry—Visa and MasterCard and 15 out of 17 banks provide credit card services through Visa or MasterCard.
17. Banks adopted a strategy of reaching lower down the income strata by lowering down their eligibility norms, the credit limits are set at lower levels as compared to the foreign banks. As a result of this strategy, the credit cards base is widening day by day with the increase of base in B-grade cities.

17

Venture Capital

Venture capital is a significant term of financial innovation in the twentieth century. It is the source of long-term finance provided to small/medium sized business promoted by individuals or firms. These projects involve new technology or products while promoters lack finance. Venture capital implies investments of equity finance on projects. It is the capital committed as shareholdings for the formation and setting up of firms specializing in new ideas or new technologies with an element of risk for the owners, but with a potential for rapid growth. Venture capitalists expect to earn a return, nearly double their original investment in 2 to 3 years. They select the deals which offer good growth possibilities and confine to few big deals. They do not finance small deals as the yield is limited and the control over the financed enterprise is difficult to be monitored.

After a careful analysis a structured deal would be entered between the venture capitalist and the entrepreneur. The deal contains matters relating to the method of financing, total outlay of funds, nature of business, payment of royalty on the sales effected, payment of changes for value-added services, option for further financing, exit conditions, appointment of the board of directors, restriction on use, sale or transfer of technology, control on operations of the company, etc. method of valuation of shares in care of management buy-outs are also dealt with in the agreement signed by the venture capitalist and the entrepreneur.

ORIGIN OF VENTURE FINANCING

This concept originated in the United States late in 1948 and became familiar worldwide in the second half of the seventies. In U.K., the concept venture capital was adopted during the eighties of this century. Venture capital in India can be traced back from the seventies, when a special committee set up for the development of small and medium industries found that, the promoter's interest in the business constituted only a few lakhs collected from his own resources and that the bank financial institution's loan was in the form of 'loan for interest'. This committee recommended for a better equity base, from the contributions of both by the entrepreneur and the funding agency which would make the funds more secure. Thus emerged the Equity Capital Corporation, which extended finance in the form of equity to new entrepreneurs. In the venture capital history of India, it was given shape in the 1986-87 budget. The CCI (now stands replaced by SEBI) in Nov. 1988 issued venture capital guidelines, which insisted for institutionalization of venture funding. SEBI through its circular dt., 13.2.1996 issued further guidelines for registration and regulation of venture capital companies.

FORMS OF VENTURE FINANCING

1. Equity Financing

Venture capital companies (VCCs) finance the first generation entrepreneurs with hi-tech and innovative projects. Venture financing in India is available in the following ways; equity, conditional loans, income notes and participating loans/ debentures. Equity form of financing is provided by all VC funds, but private venture funds confine themselves largely to equity participation only. This type of finance is considered to be an effective control over the ownership of the enterprises.

The Companies Act was amended to offer more teeth to the venture funds, by permitting companies under sec. 370, to invest in other companies 60% of its subscribed capital without the approval of the Central Government. This enabled the VCCs to have a higher percentage of equity holdings in the enterprise. As VCCs join the entrepreneur as a co-promoter in projects and share the risk and rewards of the enterprise with the objective of long term capital appreciation, inter corporate investments permitted up to 60% of aggregate paid up equity reserves to Venture Capital Funds (VCFs) help them a lot.

2. Conditional Loan

A conditional loan is provided in the form of loan which is repayable as royalty after the moratorium period which is fixed based on the capacity of the project to generate sales. Normally, no interest is charged for the loan, but sometimes interest is substituted for royalty.

3. Income Notes

Income notes form of financing carries interest as well as the royalty. The rate of interest and royalty are fixed depending upon the estimated return on the project.

4. Participating Loan

Few of the private venture capital companies provide participating loan/debenture facilities, in which interest is charged for the loan at different slabs at different periods.

MOTIVATING FACTOR OF VCCs

The form of financing a project will depend upon the agreement between the VCCs and the entrepreneur/firm. The functions of the VCCs would be motivated by removal certain restrictions put under different legislations. The buy back shares enabled greater flow of funds to industries. Despite the above, allowing companies to buy back their shares enabled the new entrepreneurs to pay back the equity subscribed by the VCCs. At the same time, the VCCs had an exit to that venture and they could look for fresh deals.

Tax Exemption

The Indian venture capital association (IVCA) has succeeded in its efforts in getting tax exemption for the VCFs. For a long time, the association was raising its voice to the government to exempt venture funds from tax as that of mutual funds. Its cry has been noted, and the Government of India in the Union Budget 1996-97, fully exempted venture capital funds tax, but income is taxable in the hands of shareholders. The above tax dispensations are restricted to companies registered with SEBI.

PLAYERS IN VC MARKET

The major VCCs in the fray may be conveniently grouped under four categories; they are All India Financial institutions, State level financial institutions, Indian and foreign banks and Private institutions. Initially there were 4 National Level Institutions (IFCI, ICICI, IDBI, SIDBI), 2 State level institutions (GVFL, APIDC), 3 Commercial banks (SBI, Canara bank, Grindlays bank) operated in the field. Now several private VCCs (like Indus venture fund, 20th century finance company, credit capital venture fund, Shopper's Investment Ltd., and so forth) have floated their VCFs.

Features of Venture Capital Financing

Some of the features of venture capital financing are as under:

1. Venture capital is usually in the form of equity participation.
2. It may also take the form of convertible debt or long-term loan.
3. Investment is made only in high risk but high growth potential projects.
4. Venture capital is available only for commercialization of new ideas or new technologies and not for enterprises which are engaged in trading, broking, financial services, agency, liaison work or research and development.
5. Venture capitalist companies/firms joins with the

entrepreneur as a co-promoter, in projects and share the risks and rewards of the enterprise.

6. There is continuous involvement in business after making an investment by the investor.
7. Once the venture has reached the full potential the venture capitalist disinvests is holdings either to the promoters or in the market. The basic objective of investment is not profit but capital appreciation at the time of disinvestment.
8. Venture capital is not just injection of money but also an input needed to set-up the firm, design its marketing strategy and organize and manage it.
9. Investment is usually made in small and medium scale enterprises.

Conditions for Financing under Venture Capital

All new projects will not become eligible for venture capital financing unless they have the following attractions:

- A novel idea or new invention or improved technology.
- Capitability of commercial exploitation and application.
- Large sales potential for the product or services.
- Must have attained pre-production stage.

Financing of a new venture involves high risk. Investing companies always goes through the draft plan carefully and thoroughly to understand the prospects of the new business at assess the risk involved. This would enable the venture capitalist to eliminate the chances of wrong selection of projects. A careful study of the past performance of the entrepreneur, his expertise, competence in managing money men and matters will also help in deciding the acceptance or rejection of a project.

Stages in Venture Capital Financing

- *Financing/Seed Capital:* It is the initial stage of finance given to the entrepreneur to enable him to demonstrate the worth or usefulness of the new invention i.e., for pilot production of the product.

- *Research and Development financing:* At this stage financing enables the entrepreneur to develop the product with a view to commercialize it for practical application. At this stage the finance enjoys tax benefits.
- *Startup capital:* This is the take-off stage where the product is fully developed and is launched for commercial use. Market penetration of the technology is enhanced.
- *Harvesting the Investments:* This refers to the final stage of investment. The venture capital company after the intermediate investment, when satisfied with the yield prospects of the project, decides on final financing on the project. Hence, it is called harvesting. Strategies of harvesting are:
  (a) Outright sale of the company.
  (b) Initial Public Offerings (IPOs) to the public.
  (c) Management buy-outs.
  (d) Mergers/acquisitions or control transfer.
  (e) Liquidation of the company.

When advance level of the project is attained in its growth stage of technological life cycle, either exit or harvesting is done. It then reaches maturity when the profits are stagnated and slowly and gradually the technology becomes obsolete and the profits start declining. Among all exist strategies the most common and preferred avenue of reaping high profits is through Initial Public Offering. After assessing the viability of projects, the investors decide for what stage they should provide venture capital so that it leads to greater capital appreciation.

VENTURE CAPITAL FUNDS REGULATIONS, 1996

Registration of Venture Capital Funds

1. Eligibility Criteria

For the purpose of the grant of a certificate by the Board

the applicant shall have to fulfil in particular the following conditions, namely:

In case of a company or body corporate:

- Memorandum of association has as its main objective, the carrying on of the activity of a venture capital fund.
- It is prohibited by its memorandum and articles of association from making an invitation to the public to subscribe to its securities;
- Its director, trustees, or principal officer or employee is not involved in any litigation connected with the securities market which may have an adverse bearing on the business of the applicant;
- Its director, trustees, principal officer or employee has not at any time been convicted of any offence involving moral turpitude or any economic offence.
- It is a fit and proper person.
- It is set-up or established under the laws of the Central or State Legislature.

In case of a trust:

- The instrument of trust is in the form of a deed and has been duly registered under the provisions of the Indian Registration Act, 1908.
- The main object of the trust is to carry on the activity of a venture capital fund;
- The directors of its trustee company, if any, or any trustee is not involved in any litigation connected with the securities market which may have an adverse bearing on the business of the applicant;
- The directors of its trustee company, if any, or a trustee has not at any time, been convicted of any offence involving moral turpitude or of any economic offence;
- The applicant is a fit and proper person.

2. *Application for Grant of Certificate*

Any company or trust or a body corporate to carry on any activity as a venture capital fund on or after the commencement of these regulations shall make an application to the Board for grant of a certificate. An application for grant of certificate shall be made to the Board in Form A and shall be accompanied by a non-refundable application fee. The Board may in the interest of the investors issue directions with regard to the transfer of records, documents or securities or disposal of investments relating to its activities as a venture capital fund.

3. *Consideration of Application*

An application which is not complete in all respects shall be rejected by the Board, provided that, before rejecting any such application, the applicant shall be given an opportunity to remove, within thirty days of the date of receipt of communication, the objections indicated by the Board. Provided further that the Board may, on being satisfied that it is necessary to extend the period specified in the first provison, extend such period by such further time not exceeding ninety days.

4. *Procedure for Grant of Certificate*

If the Board is satisfied that the applicant is eligible for the grant of certificate, it shall send intimation to the applicant. On receipt of intimation, the applicant shall pay to the Board; the registration fee specified in Part A of the Second Schedule in the manner specified in Part B thereof. The Board shall on receipt of the registration fee grant a certificate of registration in Form B.

5. *Conditions of Certificate*

The certificate granted shall be *inter-alia,* subject to the following conditions, namely:

- The venture capital fund shall abide by regulations
- The venture capital fund shall not carry on any other activity other than that of a venture capital fund.
- The venture capital fund shall forthwith inform the Board in writing if any information or particulars

previously submitted to the Board are found to be false or misleading in any material particular or if there is any change in the information already submitted.

6. *Procedure where Certificate is not Granted*

- After considering an application, if the Board is of the opinion that a certificate should not be granted, it may reject the application after giving the applicant a reasonable opportunity of being heard.
- The decision of the Board to reject the application shall be communicated to the applicant within thirty days.

7. *Effect of Refusal to Grant Certificate*

- Any applicant whose application has been rejected under regulation 9 shall not carry on any activity as a venture capital fund.
- Any company or trust or a body corporate whose application for grant of certificate has been rejected by the Board shall, on and from the date of the receipt of the communication cease to carry on any activity as a venture capital fund.
- The Board may in the interest of the investors issue directions with regard to the transfer of records, documents or securities or disposal of investments relating to its activities as a venture capital fund. The Board may in order to protect the interests of the investors appoint any person to take charge of records, documents, securities and for this purpose also determine the terms and conditions of such an appointment.

INVESTMENT CONDITIONS AND RESTRICTIONS

1. Minimum Investment in a Venture Capital Fund

(a) A venture capital fund may raise monies from any

investor whether Indian, foreign or non-resident Indians by way of issue of units.

(b) No venture capital fund set-up as a company or any scheme of a venture capital fund set-up as a trust shall accept any investment from any investor which is less than five lakh rupees.

(c) This condition will not apply to employees or the principal officer or directors of the venture capital fund, or directors of the Trustee Company or trustees where the venture capital fund has been established as a trust or the employees of the fund manager or asset Management Company.

(d) Each scheme launched or fund set-up by a venture capital fund shall have firm commitment from the investors for contribution of an amount of at least Rupees five crores before the start of operations by the venture capital fund.

2. Investment Conditions and Restrictions

All investment made or to be made by a venture capital fund shall be subject to the following conditions, namely:

(a) Venture capital fund shall disclose the investment strategy at the time of application for registration.

(b) Venture capital fund shall not invest more than 25% corpus of the fund in one venture capital undertaking.

(c) Venture capital fund may invest in securities of foreign companies subject to such conditions or guidelines that may be stipulated or issued by the Reserve Bank of India and the Board from time to time

(d) It shall not invest in the associated companies.

(e) Venture capital fund shall disclose the duration of life cycle of the fund.

(f) Venture capital fund shall make investment in:

- At least 66.67% of the investible funds shall be invested in unlisted equity shares or equity linked instruments of venture capital undertaking.

- Not more than 33.33% of the investible funds may be invested by way of—
- Subscription to initial public offer of a venture capital undertaking whose shares are proposed to be listed.
- Debt or debt instrument of a venture capital undertaking in which the venture capital fund has already made an investment by way of equity.
- Preferential allotment of equity shares of a listed company subject to lock in period of one year.
- The equity shares or equity linked instruments of a financially weak company or a sick industrial company whose shares are listed. Financially weak company" means a company, which has at the end of the previous financial year accumulated losses, which has resulted in erosion of more than 50% but less than 100% of its net worth as at the beginning of the previous financial year.
- Special Purpose Vehicles which are created by a venture capital fund for the purpose of facilitating or promoting investment.

3. Restrictions on Investment by a Venture Capital Fund

All investments made or to be made by a venture capital fund shall be subject to the following restrictions:

1. The venture capital fund shall not invest in the equity shares of any company or institution providing financial services.
2. At least 80 percent of funds raised by a venture capital fund shall be invested in:
   - "The equity shares or equity related securities issued by a company whose securities are not listed on any recognized stock exchange. Provided that a venture capital fund may invest in equity shares or equity-related securities of a company whose securities are to be listed or are listed where the venture capital fund has made

these investments through private placements prior to the listing of the securities.

- The equity shares or equity related securities of a financially weak company or a sick industrial company, whose securities may or may not be listed on any recognized stock-exchange. No venture capital fund shall be entitled to get its units listed on any recognized stock exchange till the expiry of three years from the date of the issuance of units by the venture capital fund.
- Providing financial assistance in any other manner to companies in whose equity shares the venture capital fund has invested. Funds raised means, the actual monies raised from investors for subscribing to the securities of the venture capital fund and includes monies raised from the author of the trust in case the venture capital fund has been established as a trust but shall not include the paid up capital of the trustee company, if any".

GENERAL OBLIGATIONS AND RESPONSIBILITIES

1. *Prohibition on inviting subscription from the public:* No venture capital fund shall issue any document or advertisement inviting offers from the public for the subscription or purchase of any of its units.
2. *Private placement*: A venture capital fund may receive monies for investment in the venture capital fund only through private placement of its units.
3. *Placement memorandum or subscription agreement:* The venture capital fund shall issue a placement memorandum which shall contain details of the terms and conditions subject to which monies are proposed to be raised from investors or enter into contribution or subscription agreement with the investors which shall specify the terms and conditions subject to which monies are proposed to be raised. The Venture Capital Fund shall file with the Board for information, the copy of the placement

memorandum or the copy of the contribution or subscription agreement entered with the investors along with a report of money actually collected from the investor.

4. *Contents of placement memorandum:* The placement memorandum or the subscription agreement with investors shall contain information such as:
   - The details of the trustees or Trustee Company and the directors or chief executives of the venture capital fund.
   - The proposed corpus of the fund and the minimum amount to be raised for the fund to be operational.
   - The minimum amount to be raised for each scheme and the provision for refund of monies to investor in the event of non-receipt of minimum amount, details of entitlements on the units of venture capital fund for which subscription is being sought.
   - Tax implications that are likely to apply to investors.
   - Manner of subscription to the units of the venture capital fund, the period of maturity, if any, of the fund.
   - The manner in which the fund shall be wound up.
   - Manner in which the benefits accruing to investors in the units of the trust are to be distributed, details of the fund manager or asset Management Company, if any, and the fees to be paid to such manager.
   - The details about performance of the fund, if any, managed by the Fund Manager, investment strategy of the fund.
5. *Maintenance of books and records:* Every venture capital fund shall maintain for a period of eight years books of accounts, records and documents which shall give a true and fair picture of the state of affairs of the venture capital fund. And intimate the Board, in

writing, the place where the books, records and documents are being maintained.

6. *Power to call for information*: SEBI may at any time call for any information from a venture capital fund with respect to any matter relating to its activity as a venture capital fund and it shall be furnished within the time specified it.
7. *Submissions of reports to the Board*: The SEBI may at any time call upon the venture capital fund to file such reports as the Board may desire with regard to the activities carried on by the venture capital fund.
8. *Winding up*: A scheme of a venture capital fund set-up as a trust shall be wound up, when the period of the scheme, if any, mentioned in the placement memorandum is over or if it is the opinion of the trustees or the trustee company, as the case may be, that the scheme shall be wound up in the interests of investors in the units or if seventy five percent of the investors in the scheme pass a resolution at a meeting of unit holders that the scheme be wound up or if the Board so directs in the interests of investors.
9. *Effect of winding up:* On and from the date of intimation no further investments shall be made on behalf of the scheme so wound up. Within three months from the date of intimation the assets of the scheme shall be liquidated, and the proceeds accruing to investors in the scheme distributed to them after satisfying all liabilities.
10. *Placement memorandum*: The venture capital fund established as a trust shall, before issuing any units file with the SEBI, a placement memorandum which shall give details of the terms subject to which monies are proposed to be raised from investors. A venture capital fund established as a company shall, before making an offer inviting any subscription to its securities, file with the Board a placement memorandum which shall give details of the terms subject to which monies are proposed to be raised from the investors. The placement memorandum shall contain the following, namely:

(a) Details of the securities that are being offered.
(b) Details of investments that are proposed to be made.
(c) Details of directors of the company.
(d) Tax implications that are likely to apply to investors.
(e) Manner of subscription to the securities that are to be issued.
(f) Manner in which the benefits accruing to investors in the securities are to be distributed.
(g) Details of the asset management company, if any, and of fees to be paid to such a company.

11. *Circulation of placement memorandum*: The placement memorandum may be issued for private circulation only after the expiry of twenty-one days of its submission to the Board. If, within twenty-one days of submission of the placement memorandum, the Board communicates any amendments to the placement memorandum, the venture capital fund shall carry out such amendments in the placement memorandum before such memorandum is circulated to the investors.
12. *Changes in the placement memorandum to be intimated to the Board*: Amendments or changes to any placement memorandum already filed with the Board can be made only if : (a) a copy of the placement memorandum indicating the changes is filed with the Board, and (b) within twenty-one days of such filing, the Board has not communicated any objections or observations on the said amendments or changes.

INSPECTION AND INVESTIGATION

1. *Board's right to inspect or investigate*: The Board may *suo moto* or upon receipt of information or complaint appoint one or more persons as inspecting or investigating officer to undertake inspection or investigation of the books of accounts, records and documents relating to a venture capital fund for any of the following reasons, namely:

- to ensure that the books of account, records and documents are being maintained by the venture capital fund,
- to inspect or investigate into complaints received from investors, clients or any other person, on any matter having a bearing on the activities of the venture capital fund,
- to ascertain whether the provisions of the Act and these regulations are being complied with by the venture capital fund, and
- to inspect or investigate suomoto into the affairs of a venture capital fund, in the interest of the securities market or in the interest of investors.

2. *Notice before inspection or investigation*: Before ordering an inspection or investigation the Board shall give not less than ten days notice to the venture capital fund. Where the Board is satisfied that in the interest of the investors no such notice should be given, it may by an order in writing direct that the inspection or investigation of the affairs of the venture capital fund be taken up without such notice. During the course of an inspection or investigation, the venture capital fund against whom the inspection or investigation is being carried out shall be bound to discharge its obligations.
3. *Obligation of venture capital fund on inspection or investigation*: Every officer of the Venture Capital Fund in respect of whom an inspection or investigation has been ordered and any other associate person who is in possession of relevant information pertaining to conduct and affairs of such Venture Capital Fund including fund manager or asset management company, has to produce to the Investigating or Inspecting Officer such books, accounts and other documents in his custody or control and furnish him with such statements and information as the said Officer may require for the purposes of the investigation or inspection. The Investigating or Inspecting Officer shall, for the purposes of inspection or investigation, have power

to examine on oath and record the statement of any employees, directors or person responsible for or connected with the activities of venture capital fund or any other associate person having relevant information pertaining to such Venture Capital Fund. The Inspecting or Investigating Officer shall, for the purposes of inspection or investigation, have power to obtain authenticated copies of documents, books, accounts of Venture Capital Fund, from any person having control or custody of such documents, books or accounts.

4. *Submission of Report to the Board*: The inspecting or investigating officer shall, as soon as possible, on completion of the inspection or investigation submit an inspection or investigation report to the Board.
5. *Communication of findings, etc. to the venture capital fund:* SEBI may after consideration of the investigation or inspection report and after giving reasonable opportunity of hearing to the venture capital fund or its trustees, directors issue such direction as it deems fit in the interest of securities market or the investors including directors in the nature of:
   - (i) Requiring a venture capital fund not to launch new schemes or raise money from investors for a particular period.
   - (ii) Prohibiting the person concerned from disposing of any of the properties of the fund or scheme acquired in violation.
   - (iii) Requiring the person connected to dispose of the assets of the fund or scheme in a manner as may be specified in the directions.
   - (iv) Requiring the person concerned to refund any money or the assets to the concerned investors along with the requisite interest or otherwise, collected under the scheme.
   - (v) Prohibiting the person concerned from operating in the capital market or from accessing the capital market for a specified period.

6. *Obligations of venture capital fund on inspection or investigation by the Board:* Every director, officer and employee of the venture capital fund whose affairs are being inspected or investigated, has to produce before the inspecting or investigating officer such books, securities, accounts, records and other documents in its custody or control and furnish him with such statements and information relating to the venture capital fund, as the inspecting or investigating officer may require, within such reasonable period as the inspecting officer may specify. The venture capital fund shall allow the inspecting or investigating officer to have reasonable access to the premises occupied by such venture capital fund or by any other person on his behalf and also extend reasonable facility for examining any books, records, documents and computer data in the possession of the venture capital fund or such other person and also provide copies of documents or other materials which, in the opinion of the inspecting or investigating officer are relevant for the purposes of the inspection or investigation, as the case may be. The inspecting or investigating officer, in the course of inspection or investigation shall be entitled to examine or to record the statements of any director, officer or employee of the venture capital fund.

PROCEDURE FOR ACTION IN CASE OF DEFAULT

Liability for action (such as suspension of certificate) in case of default shall be taken in the following circumstances:

(a) Contravenes any of the provisions of the Act or these regulations;
(b) Fails to furnish an information relating to its activity as venture capital fund as required by the Board;
(c) Furnishes to the Board information which is false or misleading in any material particular;

(d) Does not submit periodic returns or reports as required by the Board;
(e) Does not co-operate in any enquiry, inspection or investigation conducted by the Board; and
(f) Fails to resolve the complaints of investors or fails to give a satisfactory reply to the Board in this behalf.

Cancellation of certificate: The Board may cancel the certificate granted to a venture capital fund when the venture capital fund is guilty of fraud or has been convicted of an offence involving moral turpitude or the venture capital fund has been guilty of repeated defaults of the nature.

Manner of making order of cancellation or suspension: No order of suspension or cancellation of certificate shall be made by the Board, except after holding an enquiry in accordance with the procedure.

Manner of Holding Enquiry before Suspension or Cancellation

- The Board may appoint one or more enquiry officers.
- The enquiry officer shall issue to the venture capital fund, at its registered office or its principal place of business, a notice setting out the grounds on which action is proposed to be taken against it and calling upon it to show cause against such action within a period of fourteen days from the date of receipt of the notice.
- The venture capital fund may, within fourteen days from the date of receipt of such notice, furnish to the enquiry officer a written reply, together with copies of documentary or other evidence relied on by it or sought by the Board from the venture capital fund.
- The enquiry officer shall give a reasonable opportunity of hearing to the venture capital fund to enable him to make submissions in support of its reply made.
- Before the enquiry officer, the venture capital fund may appear through any person duly authorized by the venture capital fund.

- The enquiry officer may, if he considers it necessary, ask the Board to appoint a presenting officer to present its case.
- The enquiry officer shall, after taking into account all relevant facts and submissions made by the venture capital fund, submit a report to the Board and recommend the penal action, if any, to be taken against the venture capital fund as also the grounds on which the proposed action is justified.

Show-cause notice and order: On receipt of the report from the enquiry officer, the Board shall consider the same and may issue to the venture capital fund a show-cause notice as to why the penal action as proposed by the enquiry officer or such appropriate action should not be taken against it. The venture capital fund shall, within fourteen days of the date of the receipt of the show-cause notice, send a reply to the Board. The Board, after considering the reply, if any, of the venture capital fund, shall, as soon as possible pass such order as it deems fit.

Effect of suspension and cancellation of certificate: On and from the date of the suspension of the certificate, the venture capital fund shall cease to carry on any activity as a venture capital fund during the period of suspension, and shall be subject to such directions of the Board with regard to any records, documents or securities that may be in its custody or control, relating to its activities as venture capital fund, as the Board may specify. On and from the date of cancellation of the certificate, the venture capital fund shall, with immediate effect, cease to carry on any activity as a venture capital fund, and shall be subject to such directions of the Board with regard to the transfer of records, documents or securities that may be in its custody or control, relating to its activities as venture capital fund, as the Board may specify.

Publication of order of suspension or cancellation: The order of suspension or cancellation of certificate passed may be published by the Board in two newspapers.

Action against intermediaries: The Board may initiate action for suspension or cancellation of registration of an intermediary holding a certificate of registration who fails to exercise due diligence in the performance of its functions or fails to comply with its obligations under these regulations.

NEGATIVE LIST FOR VENTURE CAPITAL BUSINESS

1. Non-banking financial services excluding those Non-Banking Financial Companies which are registered with Reserve Bank of India and have been categorized as Equipment Leasing or Hire Purchase companies.
2. Gold financing excluding those companies which are engaged in gold financing for jewellery.
3. Activities not permitted under industrial policy of Government of India.
4. Any other activity which may be specified by the Board in consultation with Government of India from time to time.

18

Credit Rating Services

CONCEPT AND EVOLUTION

Credit Rating is a symbolic indication of the current opinion regarding the relative capability of a corporate entity to service its debt obligations in time with reference to the instruments rated. It enables the investor to differentiate between debt instruments on the basis of their underlying credit quality. To facilitate simple and easy understanding, credit rating is expressed in alphabetical or alphanumerical symbols. A rating is specific to a debt instrument and is intended to grade different such instruments in terms of credit risk and ability of the company to service the debt obligations as per terms of contract namely, principal as well as interest. A rating is neither a general purpose evaluation of a corporate entity, nor an over all assessment of the credit risk likely to be involved in all the debts contracted or to be contracted by such entity.

Credit rating, in general sense, is the evaluation of the credit worthiness of an individual or of a business concern or of an instrument of a business based on relevant factors indicating ability and willingness to PB:Y obligations as well as net worth. Financial ratings are used as a guide to the investment quality of bonds and stocks, based on security of principal and interest (or dividends), earning power, mortgage position, market history and marketability. Credit ratings establish a link between risk and return. An investor or any other interested person uses the rating to assess the risk-level and compares the offered rate of return with his expected rate of return.

Credit rating is extremely important as it not only plays a role in investor protection but also benefits industry as a whole in terms of direct mobilization of savings from individuals. Rating also provide a marketing tool to the company and its investment bankers in placing company's debt obligations with a investor base that is aware of, and comfortable with, the level of risk. Ratings also encourage discipline amongst corporate borrowers to improve their financial structure and operating risks to obtain a better rating for their debt obligations and thereby lower the cost of borrowing. Companies those get a lower rating are forewarned, as it were and have the freedom, if they desire, to take steps on their financial or business risks and thereby improve their standing in the market.

The need for reliable information in channelisation of the resources to the most productive uses can hardly be overemphasized. Relevant and reliable information helps the investors to arrive at their investment decisions. These include offer documents of the issuers, research reports of market intermediaries and media reports. In the developed markets, credit rating agencies have also come to occupy a leading position as information providers along with rating of financial instruments. Particularly for the credit-related opinions in respect of debt-related instruments. Such agencies offer Independent opinions which are objective, well research and credible.

During the great American depression year, high levels of default triggered the growth of credit rating as an essential input for the investors. The recognition for credit rating received a new impetus when Government Pension Funds, Insurance Companies, etc. were directed not to invest in securities rated below a particular grade by credit rating agencies. This led to the growth in the awareness of credit rating as a primary of risk assessment.

The first Mercantile Credit Agency was established in New York in 1841 rating guide was published in 1859 by Robert Dun. Another similar agency was set up by John Bradstreet which published its rating guide in 1857. These two agencies got merged to form Dun and Bradstreet in 1933 which acquired Moody's Investor Service in 1962. Moody's was founded by Moody in 1900. The other world renowned rating agency namely Standard and Poor was created in 1941 by merging the Standard Statistics Company and Poor's Publishing Company which had their origin earlier.

Developing nations are short of financial resource. Scarce funds available at their disposal are to be deployed sagaciously to earn better return. Savings of the public in general are to be mobilized for investment in trade and industry. Therefore, to motivate savers to invest in industry and trade it is necessary that their funds should be invested in safe enterprises where financial risk is least. It is only when the savers have developed confidence in enterprises, they would invest their savings. Safety of their investment can be pre-assessed if the company's ability and capacity to pay-off the principal and other accruing dues is indicated in advance through a reliable agency. This role is played by the credit rating agencies. Investors rely upon their indications and release their savings for investment in the corporate sector enterprises. A well-rated enterprise can get funds from the credit lending institutions. Even the lower risk profile company can obtain easily funds at lower rate of interest, as low risk profile investors would put their monies therein.

INDIAN EXPERIENCE OF CREDIT RATING

Credit rating emerged in India with the birth of Credit Rating Information Services of India Ltd. (CRISIL) in 1988 January. ICRA's (Investment Information and Credit Rating Agency of India Limited) was set-up in 1991 and CARE (Credit Analyses and Research Limited) in 1994 and Duff and Phelps (India) Pvt. Limited in 1997. Onida Individual Credit Rating

Agency of India Ltd. (ONICRA) is functioning from 25th Nov. 1993 to evaluate the credit worthiness of an individual who is buying a product on loan or seeking Trade Credit or other type of financing.

Corporate sector enterprises have depended in India for funds to finance their projects or expansion of existing projects upon the financial institutions and banks and it was the name of these institutions and banks associated with the company that enhanced the image in public estimation of the company and of the public issues too. The need for Credit Rating Agency has been felt much more now when the capital market is growing, to attain efficiency and the corporate enterprises are raising funds is growing, to attain efficiency and the corporate enterprises are raising funds from the issue of securities depending on the capital market. A move in the corporate sector from debt-age to free-market finance-age has further increased the chances for more Credit Rating Agencies.

A time has come for investors to measure risk as well as prospects of the corporate units to use credit rating as a marketing tool. The growth of the capital market is discernible from the fact that there are now stock exchanges operating in India with increasing trend of investible funds and increasing demand for funds from the industry. Investors have to rely upon rated instruments, rather than following the advices of the financial intermediaries. Rating has not been made compulsory in India for companies going public. It is only debt instruments, i.e., debentures, certificate of deposit or money market instruments like commercial paper for which rating is obligatory under the recent guidelines issued in this regard.

CREDIT RATING APPLICATIONS

Though "credit rating is considered" more relevant for gradation of debt securities. It can be applied for other purposes also. The various purposes for which credit rating is applied are:

1. Long-term/Medium-term debt obligations (debentures, bonds, preference shares or project finance debts are considered long-term and debts

ranging from 1 to 3 years like fixed deposits are considered medium-term.

2. Short-term debt obligations—the period involved is one year or less and cover money market instruments such as commercial paper, credit notes, cash certificates, etc.
3. Equity Grading and Assessment, structured obligations, municipal bonds, mutual fund schemes, plantation schemes, real estate projects, infrastructure-related debts, ADR, GDR issues, bank securities, etc.

Credit rating does not amount to a hold or sell an instrument as it does not take into consideration factors such as market prices, personal risk preferences and other consideration which may influence an investment decision. It does not create any fiduciary relationship between the rating agency and the user of the rating. A credit rating agency does not perform an audit but relies on information provided by the issuer and collected by the analysis from different sources hence it does not guarantee the completeness or accuracy of the information on which the rating is based.

In determining a rating, both qualitative and quantitative analyses are employed. The judgement is qualitative in nature and the role of the quantitative analysis is to help make the best possible over all qualitative judgment or opinion. The reliability of the rating depends on the validity of the criteria and the quality of analysis. The quality of credit rating mainly depends upon Quality of the rating agency and Rating elements. The agency should have good reputation, personal competence, independence, qualified and experienced staff.

Credit Rating Agencies should not confine their operation to investigation of the companies bringing debt instruments to public for subscription, but their activities and scope of information should have a wider coverage to include the work of credit investigation of companies so that, not only investors or creditors but others dealing with the company are also benefited. For example, the factoring services companies, suppliers of raw materials, etc. Kalyansundaram study group on factoring services set-up Reserve Bank of India had also suggested the need for setting-up specialized agencies for credit investigation of companies for making a success of factoring services.

FACTORS FOR SUCCESS OF A RATING SYSTEM

- Credible and independent structure and procedures;
- Objectivity and impartiality of opinions;
- Analytical research, integrity and consistency;
- Professionalism and industry-related expertise;
- Confidentiality;
- Timeliness of rating review and announcement of changes; and
- Ability to reach wide range of investors by means of Press reports, print or electronic media and investor oriented research services.

Importance of Credit Rating

(a) *Surveillance:* The rating published by credit rating agencies is subjected to a continuous surveillance during the life of the instrument or so long as any amount is outstanding against the specific instrument. The frequency of surveillance may range between quarterly or yearly. A formal and extensive written review is taken at least once in an year but where some specific concern arises about the industry or the issuing entity, the review is taken up immediately. When justified, the rating agency may change the rating by up-gradation or down-gradation depending on the likely impact of changing circumstances on the debt servicing capability of the issuer. In other cases, the rating is retained at the same level.

(b) *Credit Watch:* When a major deviation from the expected trends of the issuers business occurs, or when an event has taken place, it creates an impact on the debt servicing capability of the issuer and warrants a rating change, the rating agency may put such ratings under credit watch till the exact impact of such unanticipated development is analyzed and decision is taken regarding the rating change. The credit watch listing may also specify positive or negative outlooks. It should be noted that being under credit watch does not necessarily mean that there would be a rating change.

(c) *Sovereign Ceiling:* International credit rating agencies while rating an issue outside the issuer's country of domicile impose an equal to the sovereign rating assigned to the country of domicile. This implies that the rating of any instrument of any issuer domicile in that country would be above the sovereign rating of the country of domicile. This concept may not however be applicable when domicile of the issuer in a country is wholly incidental or otherwise internationally disbursed business operations.

(d) *Ownership as a rating consideration:* Ownership by a strong concern may enhance the credit rating of an entity, unless there exists a strong barrier separating the activities of the parent and the subsidiary. The important issues involved in deciding the relationship are the mutual dependence on each other, legal relationship, to what extent one entity has the desire and ability to influence the business of the other and how important is the operation of the subsidiary to the owner. Rating agency keeps the information provided by the issuer confidential and completes the rating within 2 to 4 weeks. Once the rating is assigned, it is communicated to the issuer, who is given an opportunity to make one request for a review, only in case fresh facts or clarifications become relevant. After these considered, the final rating is assigned. In India, the issuer has the option of accepting the assigned rate in which case the rating is not disclosed by the rating agency. However, if the rating is accepted, it comes under the surveillance process of the concerned agency.

METHODOLOGY

1. *Industry Risk:* It is defined as the strength of the

industry within the economy and relativity to the economic trends. It is evaluated on the basis of factors like business cyclicality, earnings volatility, growth prospects, demand-supply projections, entry barriers and extent of competition and nature and extent of regulation.

2. *Company's industry and market position:* The Company's sales position in its major fields and its historical background of its market position is analyzed along with ability to sustain/increase market shares; brand strengths and position; price leadership and distribution and marketing strengths/ weaknesses.
3. *Operating efficiencies:* Ability to control costs, productivity efficiencies relative to others, labour relationship, extent of forward and backward integration, access to raw materials/markets, and technology.
4. *Accounting Quality:* Financial statements are adjusted for non-standard accounting treatments. Overall evaluation of the accounting policies employed and the extent to which they understate or overstate financial performance and position. These include analysis of auditor's qualifications, revenue recognition, depreciation policy, inventory evaluation, funding for pension liabilities, undervalued assets, etc.
5. *Financial flexibility:* Evaluation of the company's financing needs, plans and alternatives, its flexibility to accomplish its financing programmes under stress without damaging creditworthiness.
6. *Earnings protection:* The key measurements which indicate the basic long-term earnings power of the company including return on capital, profit margins, earnings from various business segments, sources of future earnings growth, coverage ratios, etc.
7. *Financial leverage:* Relative usage of debt and levels of debt appropriate to different types of businesses, utilization of long and short-term sources of funds, management of working capital.

8. *Cash flow adequacy:* It is the relationship of cash flows to leverage and the ability to internally meet all cash needs of the business. It measures the magnitude and variability of future cash flows relative to debt servicing obligations and other commitments such as group company funding, BIFR packages and contingent liabilities. This analysis goes into the inherent protective factors for expected cash flows of the company and the sensitivity of these cash flows to changes in variables like raw material costs and selling prices.
9. *Management evaluation:* The record of achievement in operations and financial results, strategic and financial planning, commitment, consistency and credibility, overall quality of management, line of succession, strength of middle management and organization structure and its linkage with the operating environment and management strategies.
10. *Rating methodology:* for non-banking financial services companies is based on CAMEL model encompassing, Capital adequacy, Asset quality, Management, Earnings and liquidity. The nature and accessibility of funding sources is also considered.

RATING OF STRUCTURED OBLIGATIONS/ ASSET SECURITIZATION

Structured borrowing arrangements are entered into by companies for various reasons. However, the most important one is that less credit worthy instruments or corporates are able to tap sources of funds at a more advantageous borrowing rate by offering a variety of credit enhancements. The process of converting loans or receivables into negotiable instruments is known as securitization. These negotiable instruments are then sold to investors; they are secured by the underlying assets and have other credit enhancements. Securitization transforms illiquid assets like the renewable portfolio on the balance sheet of a lender into a marketable security.

The principal credit risk in asset backed financing is potential impairment of cash flows due to the assets becoming defaulting on repayments or turning into a loss. The main factors considered for credit rating are :

- The overall risk profile and monitoring and collection procedures of the issuer.
- The quality of the assets being securitized.
- The process of selection of the asset pool to be securitized.
- The characteristics of the pool.
- The cash flows from it based on the past record of its behaviour.
- The possible credit loss and other deficiencies of the pool in terms of timing and quantum of cash flows are analyzed and the extent and nature of credit enhancement is then determined.

Other important considerations in a securitization transaction are the legal and tax structure and the ability and willingness of the services and trustee to manage and maintain control on assets and payment streams from them.

RATING PROCESS

Rating process refers to the typical practices and procedures which a rating agency follows to gather information for evaluating the credit risk of specific issuers and issues, to analyze and conclude on the appropriate rating to monitor the credit quality of the rated issuer or security over time, deciding on timely changes in ratings, as and when companies' fundamentals change and to keep investors and the market place informed. All these are interrelated and ongoing processes. The general principals followed all over the world are the same. The rating agencies in India have adopted the methodology of the major international credit rating agencies.

Every credit rating agency shall:

- Specify the rating process.
- File a copy of the same with the Board (SEBI) for record; and file with the Board any modifications or additions made therein from time to time.

- Follow a proper rating process.
- Have professional rating committees, comprising members who are adequately qualified and knowledgeable to assign a rating.
- All rating decisions, including the decisions regarding changes in rating, shall be taken by the rating committee.
- Staffed by analysts qualified to carry out a rating assignment.
- Inform the Board about new rating instruments or symbols introduced by it.
- Exercise due diligence in order to ensure that the rating given by the credit rating agency is fair and appropriate.
- A credit rating agency shall not rate securities issued by it.
- Rating definition, as well as the structure for a particular rating product, shall not be changed by a credit rating agency, without prior information to the Board (SEBI).
- A credit rating agency shall disclose to the concerned stock exchange through press release and websites for general investors, the rating assigned to the securities of a client, after periodic review, including changes in rating, if any.

BENEFITS OF CREDIT RATING

For different class of persons different benefits accrue from use of rated instruments. Such benefits particularly accruing to investors, the rated company and the financial intermediaries or brokers are noted below.

Benefits to Investors

Investors are benefited in very many ways if the corporate security in which they intend to invest their saving has been rated by credit rating agency. Some of the benefits directly accruing to investors through and rated instruments are precisely narrated below:

- *Safeguards against Bankruptcy:* Credit rating of an instrument done by Credit Rating Agency gives an idea to the investors about the degree of financial strength of the issuer company which enables him to decide about investment. Highly rated instrument of a company gives an assurance to the investors of safety of instrument and minimum risk of bankruptcy.
- *Credibility of Issuer:* Rating symbol assigned to a credit instrument gives a clue to the credibility of the issuer company. The rating agency is quite independent of the issuer company and has no business connections or otherwise any relationship with it or its Board of Directors, etc. Absence of business likes between the rater and the rated firms establish a ground for credibility and attract investors.
- *Independence of Investment Decision:* For making investment decisions, investors have to seek advice of financial intermediaries, the stock brokers, merchant bankers, the portfolio managers, or financial consultants about good investment proposals, but for rated instrument, investors need not depend upon the advice of these financial intermediaries as the rating symbol assigned to particular instrument suggests the creditworthiness of the instrument and indicates the degree of risk involved in it. Thus, investors can make direct investment decisions.
- *Easy Understandability of the Investment Proposal:* Rating symbols, can be understood by an investor which needs no analytical knowledge on his part. Investor can take quick decisions about the investment to be made in any particularly rated security of a company.
- *Saving of Resources, i.e. Energy and Time:* Investor relies upon credit rating. This relieves investor from the necessity of knowing about the fundamentals of a company, its actual strength, financial standing, management details, etc. The quality of credit rating done by the professional experts of the credit rating

agency reposes confidence in him to rely upon the rating for taking investment decisions.

- *Recognition of Risk:* Credit rating provides investors with rating symbols which carry information in easily recognizable manner for the benefit of investors to perceive risk involved in investment. It becomes easier for the investors by looking at the symbol to understand the worth of the issuer company because the instrument is backed by the financial strength of the company which in detail cannot be provided at minimum cost to each and everyone and at the same time they cannot also analyze or understand such information for taking any investment decisions. Rating symbol gives them the idea about the risk involved or the expected advantages from the investment.
- *Choice of Investments:* Several alternative credit rated instruments are available at a particular point of time for making investment in the capital market and the investors can make choice depending upon their own risk profile and diversification plan.
- *Goodbye to Thumb Rules:* Investors can make own risk evaluation on the basis of the rating done by credit rating agency without depending upon the name of the Group or the reputation of persons who have promoted the company. The well known or a prominent group's companies often go sick and investors' funds deposited with them are rendered unsafe. This has happened with many reputed companies where investors, ignorant of their latest developments and in the absence of availability of any rating, had made investments and the companies went sick.
- *Benefits of Rating Surveillance:* Investors get the benefit of credit rating agency's on-going surveillance of the rating and rated instruments of different companies. The Credit Rating Agency downgrades the rating of any instrument if subsequently the company's financial strength declines or any event takes place

which necessitates consequent dissemination of information on its position to the investors.

- In addition to above, investors have other advantages like—(a) quick understanding of the credit instruments and weigh the ratings with advantages from instruments; (b) quick decision-making for investment and also selling or buying securities to take advantage of market conditions (c) payment of reasonable price due i.e., representative pricing of securities *vis-a-vis* creditworthiness of the company indicated by the rated instruments, and (d) perceiving of default risk by the company.

Benefits of Ratings on Companies: A company which had its credit instrument or security rated by a credit rating agency is benefited in many ways as summarized below:

- *Lower Cost of Borrowing:* A company with highly rated instrument has the opportunity to reduce the cost of borrowing from the public by quoting lesser interest rate on fixed deposits or debentures or bonds as the investors with low risk preferences would come forward to invest in safe securities though yielding marginal rate of return.
- *Wider Audience for Borrowing:* A company with a highly rated instrument can approach the investors extensively for resource mobilization using the press media. Investors in different strata of the society could be attracted by higher rated instruments as the investors understand the degree of certainty about timely payment of interest and principal on a debt instrument with better rating.
- *Rating as Marketing Tool:* Companies with rated instruments improve their own image and avail of the rating as a marketing tool to create better image in dealings with its customers and constituents, lenders and creditors. Even consumers feel confident in the utility products manufactured by the companies carrying higher rating for their credit instruments.

- *Self-discipline by Companies:* Rating encourages the companies to come out with more disclosure about their accounting system, financial reporting and management pattern, etc. The company gets opportunity and motivation to improve upon its existing practices to match to the competitive standard and maintain the standard of rating attained by it or make improvement upon the rating.
- *Reduction of Cost in Public Issues:* A company with higher rated instrument is able to attract the investors and with least efforts can raise funds. Thus, the rated company can economies and minimize cost of public issues by controlling expenses on media coverage, conferences and other publicity stunts and gimmicks.
- *Motivation for Growth:* Rating provides motivation to the company for growth as the promoters of the company feel confident in their own efforts and are encouraged to undertake expansion of their operations or new projects. With better image created through higher credit rating the company can mobilize funds from the public and institutions or banks. The most important benefit which accrues to a company with rated instrument is the self-assessment of its own status which is subject to self-discipline and self-improvement. Once it shows its own status, it can perceive and avoid sickness.

Benefits to Brokers and Financial Intermediaries

Highly credit rated instruments put the brokers at an advantage to make less efforts in studying the company's credit position to convince their clients to select a particular investment proposal. Rated instruments speak themselves about the soundness of the company and the strength of the instrument rated by the credit rating agency. This enables brokers and other financial intermediaries to save their time, costs, energy and manpower in convincing their clients about investments in any particular instrument. They utilize their resources in expanding their clientele and intensifying their business activities.

General Benefits of Credit Rating

- *Grading Debt Instruments:* Credit rating helps in grading the debt securities through rating symbols to suit the requirements of different investor groups depending upon their risk preferences.
- *Source of Reliable Information:* Rating in specified grade provide needed information to persons dealing with the company whose debt instruments have been rated by the credit rating agency.
- *Identification of Strength and Weakness:* A company having obtained the rating for its security understands its own strength and weakness in all spheres of corporate environment and can take corrective steps to improve upon its position and also remain guided by the surveillance efforts of the Credit Rating Agency. Particularly, companies with low rating make efforts to improve upon their performance. Thus, rating creates a tendency amongst rated corporate units to remain healthy and maintain higher corporate standard which also create better image of the business class of the country as a whole in the international market.
- *Liquidity and Marketability of Debt Securities:* Rated debt securities become easily marketable and thus attain the status of more liquid instrument. Rating grade sets the market price range for the rated securities. The virtues of easy marketability and more liquidity of the instrument make it popular with the investors and the issuer company can sell the rated security with least cost.
- *Impact on Capital Market:* Rated securities bring improvement in capital market and reflect upon its efficient functioning. Trading of rated securities both in primary market as well as in secondary market becomes smooth and frequent with easy marketability and liquidity as stated above which benefits all the constituents of the capital market.

Disadvantage of Credit Rating

Despite the benefits which credit rating provides to investors, financial intermediaries, the rated companies and the country as a whole, credit rating carries certain negative aspects also which are stated below:

- *Biased Rating and Misrepresentations:* In the absence of quality rating, credit rating is a curse for the capital market industry. To avoid biased rating, the experts in Rating Agency, carrying out detailed analysis of the company, should have no links with the company or the persons interested in the company so that they can make in their report impartial and judicious recommendations for rating committee. Again, rating committee members should also be impartial and judicious in their decision-making. The companies having lower grade rating do not advertise or use the rating while raising funds from the public. In such cases, the Credit Rating Agencies should themselves in the public interest, advertise the rating symbols assigned to such companies for public information and make the public aware of the weak position of the company. The person dealing with the company shall have a note of the rated grade and have to take precautions in dealing with the company.
- *Static Study:* Rating is done on the present and historical data of the company and this is only a static study. Prediction of the company's health through rating is momentary and anything can happen after assignment of rating symbols to the company. Dependence for future results on the rating, therefore defeats the very purpose of risk indicativeness of rating. Many changes take place in the economic environment, political situation, government policy framework which directly affect the working of a company. With such changes the rating serves no fruitful purpose.
- *Concealment of Material Information:* Rating a company might conceal material information from the investigating team of the credit rating company. In

such cases quality of rating suffers and renders the rating unreliable.

- *Rating is no Guarantee for Soundness of the Company:* Rating is done for a particular instrument to assess the credit risk but it should be construed as a certificate for the matching quality of the company or its management. Independent views should be informed by the user public of the rating symbol.
- *Human Bias:* Findings of the investigation team, at times, may suffer with human bias for unavoidable personal weaknesses of the staff and might affect the rating.
- *Reflection of Temporary Adverse Conditions:* Time factor affects rating. Sometimes, misleading conclusions are derived.
- *Down Grade:* Once a company has been rated and if it is not able to maintain its working results and performance, credit rating agency would review the grade and down grade the rating resulting into impairing the image of the company. Shortcomings associated with rating as pointed out above are more or less of verbal nature standing up from the psychological layers of human thinking frame and can be improved upon by taking precautions.

Credit Rating Symbols

Rating symbols are insignia to distinguish credit quality of the issuer of credit instruments. These symbols enable the viewers to understand the purpose of investment, the risk involved in such investment, and take investment decision on decoding the message hidden behind the symbol. Symbols represent the opinion of the experts based on the findings of the detailed investigation about the functioning of the issuer company. These symbols are just like code numbers which convey a particular message to be understood by investors who have no such specialized knowledge but only prudence of ordinary person. Different symbols are used for different instruments for rating to distinguish them with each other and also the purpose of their issue.

CRISIL'S SYMBOLS

Rating symbols are used in terms of alphabets. For preference shares the letters 'pt' are prefixed to the debenture rating symbols and 'f' prefixed for fixed deposits while 'pt' (prime) is prefixed to short-term instruments. CRISIL may apply + (plus) or - (minus) signs for ratings from AA to D to reflect comparative standing on a better or worse scale within the category.

CRISIL Debenture Rating Symbols

High Investment Grades		
AAA (triple A)	-	Highest Safety
AA (double A	-	High Safety
Investment Grades		
A	-	Adequate safety
BBB (triple B)	-	Moderate safety
Speculative Grades		
BB (double B)	-	Inadequate safety
B	-	High risk
C	-	Substantial risk
D	-	Default

CRISIL Fixed Deposit Rating Symbols

FAAA (F triple A)	-	Highest safety
FAA (F double A)	-	High safety
FA	-	Adequate safety
FB	-	Inadequate safety
FC	-	High risk
FD	-	Default

CRISIL's Rating for Short-term Instruments

P-1	-	VERY STRONG
P-2	-	STRONG
P-3	-	ADEQUATE
P-4	-	LESS FAVOURABLE
P-5	-	DEFAULT

CRISIL's Rating Symbols for Structured Obligations (SO)

Structured obligations ratings are based on the same scale (AAA to D) as CRISIL ratings for long-term instruments. However, reflecting the distinction of structured obligations from a debt instrument, structured obligations rating symbols are defined differently:

(1) High, Investment Grades:

AAA (SO) (Triple A)	-	Highest Safety
AA (SO) (Double A)	-	High safety

(2) Investment Grades

A (SO)	-	Adequate Safety
BBB (SO) (Triple B)	-	Moderate Safety

(3) Speculative Grades

BB (SO) (Double B)	-	Inadequate Safety
B (SO)	-	High Risk
C (SO)	-	Substantial Risk
D (SO)	-	Default

CRISIL's Rating Symbols for Real Estate Developers' Projects

Highest Ability	: PA-1
High Ability	: PA-2
Adequate Ability	: PA-3
Inadequate Ability	: PA-4
Inability	: PA-5

Rating Symbols of Icra (Investment Information and Credit Rating Agency of India Ltd.)

(a) Long-term including debentures, bonds and preference shares

LAAA	-	Highest Safety
LAA	-	High Safety
LA	-	Adequate Safety
LBBB	-	Moderate Safety
LBB	-	Inadequate Safety
LB	-	Risk Prone
LC	-	Substantial Risk
LD	-	Default

(b) Medium-term including fixed deposits

MAAA	-	High Safety
MAA	-	High Safety
MA	-	Adequate Safety
MB	-	Inadequate Safety
MC	-	Risk Prone
MD	-	Default

Short-term Debt including Commercial Paper

A-1	-	Highest Safety
A-2	-	High Safety
A-3	-	Adequate Safety
A-4	-	Risk Prone
A-5	-	Defaut

ICRA's Equity Grades Under Epra Scheme

ERA 1	-	Excellent Earnings prospects—Low Risk
ERA 2	-	Excellent Earnings—Moderate Risk
ERA 3	-	Excellent Earnings—High Risk
ERB 1	-	Good Earnings prospects—Low Risk
ERB 2	-	Good Earnings prospects—Moderate Risk
ERB 3	-	Good Earnings prospects High Risk
ERC 1	-	Moderate Earnings prospects—Low Risk
ERC2	-	Moderate Earnings prospects Moderate Risk
ERC 3	-	Moderate Earnings prospects—High Risk
ERD 1	-	Poor Earnings prospects—Low Risk
ERD 2	-	Poor Earnings prospects—Moderate Risk
ERD 3	-	Poor Earnings prospects—High Risk

'P' Rating : The letter 'P' in parenthesis after the rating symbol shall indicate that the debt instrument is being issued to raise resources by a new company for financing a new project and the rating assumes successful completion of the

project. During 1992, ICRA also launched two schemes of credit assessment and general assessment.

Credit Rating Agencies Regulations, 2003

Code of Conduct

1. A credit rating agency shall make all efforts to protect the interests of investors.
2. A credit rating agency, in the conduct of its business, shall observe high standards of integrity, dignity, and fairness in the conduct of its business.
3. A credit rating agency shall fulfil its obligations in a prompt, ethical and professional manner.
4. A credit rating agency shall at all times exercise due diligence, ensure proper care and exercise independent professional judgment in order to achieve and maintain objectivity and independence in the rating process.
5. A credit rating agency shall have a reasonable and adequate basis for performing rating evaluations, with the support of appropriate and in-depth rating researches. It shall also maintain records to support its decisions.
6. A credit rating agency shall have in place a rating process that reflects consistent and international rating standards.
7. A credit rating agency shall not indulge in any unfair competition nor shall it wean away the clients of any other rating agency on assurance of higher rating.
8. A credit rating agency shall keep track of all important changes relating to the client companies and shall develop efficient and responsive system to yield timely and accurate ratings. Further a credit rating agency shall also monitor closely all relevant factors that might affect the creditworthiness of the issuers.
9. A credit rating agency shall disclose its rating methodology to clients, users and the public.

10. A credit rating agency shall, wherever necessary, disclose to the clients, possible sources of conflict of duties and interest, which could impair its ability to make fair objective and unbiased ratings. Further it shall ensure that no conflict of interest exists between any member of its rating committee participating in the rating analysis, and that of its client.
11. A credit rating agency shall not make any exaggerated statement, whether oral or written, to the client either about its qualification or its capability to render certain services or its achievements with regard to the services rendered to other clients.
12. A credit rating agency shall not make any untrue statement, suppress any material fact or make any misrepresentation in any documents, reports, papers or information furnished to the Board, Stock exchange or public at large.
13. A credit rating agency shall ensure that the Board is promptly informed about any action, legal proceedings, etc., initiated against it alleging any material breach or non-compliance by it, of any law, rules, regulations and directions of the Board or of any other regulatory body.
14. A credit rating agency shall maintain an appropriate level of knowledge and competence and abide by the provisions of the Act, regulations and circulars, which may be applicable and relevant to the activities carried on by the credit rating agency. The credit rating agency shall also comply with award of the Ombudsman passed under Securities and Exchange Board of India (Ombudsman) Regulations, 2003.
15. A credit rating agency shall ensure that there is no misuse of any privileged information including prior knowledge of rating decisions or changes.
16. (a) A credit rating agency or any of his employees shall not render, directly or indirectly any investment advice about any security in the publicly accessible media.

(b) A credit rating agency shall not offer fee-based services to the rated entities, beyond credit ratings and research.

17. A credit rating agency shall ensure that any change in registration status/any penal action taken by board or any material change in financials which may adversely affect the interests of clients/investors is promptly informed to the clients and any business remaining outstanding is transferred to another registered person in accordance with any instructions of the affected clients/investors.

18. A credit rating agency shall maintain an arm's length relationship between its credit rating activity and any other activity.

19. A credit rating agency shall develop its own internal code of conduct for governing its internal operations and laying down its standards of appropriate conduct for its employees and officers in the carrying out of their duties within the credit rating agency and as a part of the industry. Such a code may extend to the maintenance of professional excellence and standards, integrity, confidentiality, objectivity avoidance of conflict of interests, disclosure of shareholdings and interests, etc. Such a code shall also provide for procedures and guidelines in relation to the establishment and conduct of Rating Committees and duties of the officers and employees serving on such committees.

20. A credit rating agency shall provide adequate freedom and powers to its compliance officer for the effective discharge of his duties.

21. A credit rating agency shall ensure that the senior management, particularly decision-makers have access to all relevant information about the business on a timely basis.

22. A credit rating agency shall ensure that good corporate policies and corporate governance are in place.

23. A credit rating agency shall not, generally and particularly in respect of issue of securities rated by it, be party to or instrumental for :
    (a) Creation of false market;
    (b) Price rigging or manipulation; or
    (c) Dissemination of any unpublished price sensitive information in respect of securities which are listed and proposed to be listed in any stock exchange, unless required, as part of rationale for the rating accorded.

REGISTRATION OF CREDIT RATING AGENCIES

Promoter of credit rating agency: The Board shall not consider an application unless the applicant is promoted by a person belonging to any of the following categories, namely:

1. A public financial institution.
2. A scheduled commercial bank.
3. A foreign bank operating in India with the approval of the Reserve Bank of India.
4. A foreign credit rating agency recognized by or under any law for the time being in force in the country of its incorporation, having at least five years experience in rating securities.
5. Any company or a body corporate, having continuous net worth of minimum rupees one hundred crores as per its audited annual accounts for the previous five years prior to filing of the application with the Board for the grant of certificate under these regulations.
6. The applicant is set-up and registered as a company under the Companies Act, 1956.
7. The applicant has, in its Memorandum of Association, specified rating activity as one of its main objects.
8. The applicant has a minimum net worth of rupees five crores.
9. The applicant and the promoters of the applicant, have professional competence, financial soundness

and general reputation of fairness and integrity in business transactions, to the satisfaction of the Board.

10. Neither the applicant, nor its promoter, nor any director of the applicant or its promoter, is involved in any legal proceeding connected with the securities market, which may have an adverse impact on the interests of the investors.
11. Neither the applicant, nor its promoters, nor any director, of its promoter has at any time in the past been convicted of any offence involving moral turpitude or any economic offence.
12. The applicant has, in its employment, persons having adequate professional and other relevant experience to the satisfaction of the Board.
13. Neither the applicant, nor any person directly or indirectly connected with the applicant has in the past been : (i) refused by the Board a certificate, and (ii) subjected to any proceedings for a contravention of the Act or of any rules or regulations made under the Act.

GENERAL OBLIGATIONS OF CREDIT RATING AGENCIES

Agreement with the Client

Every credit rating agency shall enter into a written agreement with each client whose securities it proposes to rate, and every such agreement shall include the following provisions, namely:

- The rights and liabilities of each party in respect of the rating of securities shall be defined;
- The fee to be charged by the credit rating agency shall be specified;
- The client shall agree to a periodic review of the rating by the credit rating agency during the tenure of the rated instrument;
- The client shall agree to co-operate with the credit rating agency in order to enable the latter to arrive at, and maintain, a true and accurate rating of the clients

securities and shall in particular provide to the latter, true, adequate and timely information for the purpose.

- The credit rating agency shall disclose to the client the rating assigned to the securities of the latter through regular methods of dissemination, irrespective of whether the rating is or is not accepted by the client.
- The rating assigned to the client's listed securities by any credit rating agency during the last three years.
- Any rating given in respect of the client's securities by any other credit rating agency, which has not been accepted by the client.
- The client shall agree to obtain a rating from at least two different rating agencies for any issue of debt securities whose size is equal to or exceeds rupees one hundred crores.

Monitoring of ratings: Credit rating agency has to monitor during the life time, securities rated by it. Every credit rating agency shall disseminate information regarding newly assigned ratings, and changes in earlier rating promptly through press releases and websites, and, in the case of securities issued by listed companies, such information shall also be provided simultaneously to the concerned regional stock exchange and to all the stock exchanges where the said securities are listed.

Procedure for review of rating: Every credit rating agency shall carry out periodic reviews of all published ratings during the lifetime of the securities. If the client does not co-operate with the credit rating agency so as to enable the credit rating agency to comply with its obligations, the credit rating agency shall carry out the review on the basis of the best available information. Provided that if owing to such lack of co-operation, a rating has been based on the best available information, the credit rating agency shall disclose to the investors the fact that the rating is so based. A credit rating agency shall not withdraw a rating so long as the obligations under the security rated by it are outstanding, except where the company whose security is rated is wound up or merged or amalgamated with another company.

Disclosure of Rating Definitions and Rationale: Every credit rating agency : (a) shall make public the definitions of the concerned rating, along with the symbol and, shall also state that the ratings do not constitute recommendations to buy, hold or sell any securities. Every credit rating agency shall make available to the general public information relating to the rationale of the ratings, which shall cover an analysis of the various factors justifying a favourable assessment, as well as factors constituting a risk.

Maintenance of Books of Accounts records, etc.: Every credit rating agency shall keep and maintain, for a minimum period of five years, the following books of accounts, records and documents, namely, a copy of its profit and loss account for each accounting period:

- a copy of the auditor's report on its accounts for each accounting period;
- copy of its balance sheet, as on the end of each accounting period;
- a copy of the agreement entered into with each client;
- information supplied by each of the clients;
- correspondence with each client;
- ratings assigned to various securities including up-gradation and down-gradation (if any) of the ratings so assigned.
- rating notes considered by the rating committee;
- record of decisions of the rating committee;
- letter assigning rating; and
- particulars of fees charged for rating and such other records as the Board may specify from time to time.

19

Mutual Funds

A mutual fund pools the savings of the community and invests the corpus subject to the terms and conditions of the scheme, after careful research and analysis in various types of securities. It offers the individual the advantages of reasonable dividend and capital appreciation coupled with safety and liquidity. The origin of Mutual Funds can be traced to the U.K. in the 19th century, which spread to the United States in the beginning of the 20th Century. Subsequently, hundreds of mutual funds have been developed and expanded in Latin America, Far East and Europe. In India at present there are about 38 registered mutual funds functioning. A list is given at the end of this chapter.

A mutual fund is simply a financial intermediary that allows a group of investors to pool their money together with a predetermined investment objective. The mutual fund will have a fund manager who is responsible for investing the pooled money into specific securities such as stocks or bonds. When a person invests in a mutual fund, he/she buy units (shares) of the mutual fund and become a shareholder of the fund. Mutual funds are one of the best investments ever created because they are very cost efficient and very easy to invest in. By pooling money together in a mutual fund, investors can purchase stocks or bonds with much lower trading costs than if they tried to do it on their own in the secondary or primary market.

Small investors generally lack expertise in investing of securities. The cooperative principle of 'mutual fund' is the best vehicle for small investors who lack knowledge of financial market. The investors benefit in terms of reduced risk and higher returns arising from the professionalism of mutual funds. The mutual fund industry was opened up to the private sector during the beginning of the 90s of the last century.

RETURNS TO INVESTORS FROM MUTUAL FUNDS

Investors in mutual funds obtain return in the form of dividends, capital gains and appreciation in NAV.

- *Dividends:* The dividend income of a mutual fund company from its investments in shares, both equity and preference is passed on to the unit holders. All income received by investors from mutual funds is exempt from tax.
- *Capital Gains:* Mutual fund unit holders or owners also got benefits of capital gains which are realized and distributed to them in cash or kind.
- *Increase or Decrease in NAV:* The increase or decrease in the NAV (Net Asset Value) is the result of unrealized gains or losses on the portfolio holdings of the mutual fund. Although mutual funds do not earn high rates of return, they are able to reduce risk to the systematic level of market fluctuations. Most mutual funds earn in long-run, an average rate of return that exceeds the return on bank term deposits.

Advantages of Mutual Funds

1. *Diversified portfolio of securities optimizes return and minimizes risk*: According to the nature of the fund, the Mutual funds diversify the portfolio of holding, which make them to get diversified returns and at

the same time the risk in investing in few portfolios avoided. A small investor is highly benefited by this advantage. Diversification is the idea of spreading out money across many different types of investments. When one investment is down another might be up. Choosing to diversify investment holdings reduces risk tremendously. The most basic level of diversification is to buy multiple stocks rather than just one stock. Mutual funds are set-up to buy many stocks—sometimes hundreds many a times. Beyond that, it can diversify even more by purchasing different kinds of stocks, then adding bonds, and so on. It could take even weeks to buy all these investments, but purchase from mutual funds could be done in a few hours because mutual funds automatically diversify in a predetermined category of investments.

2. *Good market rate and very less rate of brokerage by way of redemption load, etc.*: The large corpus of funds is the strength of the Mutual funds and because of that they are able get good rate while buying and pass the benefit to unit holders.
3. *Professional management team*: Every mutual funds are managed by the AMCs. Since they have highly qualified research and management team the funds in their hands are parked at high earning portfolios.
4. *Return on investment is high*: Apart from ensuring that the shareholders get return as in the case of share and debentures they also ensure long-term capital appreciation.
5. *Accessibility*: Mutual funds have grater accessibility compared to single investors.
6. *Direct access*: Due to the greater corpus amount and ability park huge amounts in specified sectors, they are able to attract private placements and invest through book-building process at cheaper rates.
7. *Low cost of investment*: The investment cost is low compared to the investors' normal expenses in the stock market route. Mutual funds cannot charge more than the load prescribed by SEBI.

8. *Convenient for small investors*: Small investors become smart when they choose the MF route. Because they share the expertise of the mutual funds. So it is convenient for them to invest and gain without much effort on their part.
9. *Offers tax benefits*: Mutual funds return are exempted from income tax
10. *Mobilizes savings*: It is a sort of savings mobilization. Investors all around the country contribute to the fund, which is invested in specific sectors. This indirectly contributes to the growth of economy.
11. *Liquidity is ensured*: liquidity is ensured for units of mutual fund, either by quoting the close-end fund or by offering the redemption rate by publishing the NAV by the concerned mutual fund.
12. *Increased shareholder value*: The funds are ultimately invested in corporate securities and so they get shareholders' value that may be available for shareholders go invest directly on company shares.

Disadvantages of Mutual Funds

1. Fund managers are not accountable for poor performance of the fund.
2. Poor planning of investment in portfolios of companies will result in poor returns.
3. Concentration of mutual funds to invest in blue chip companies may not yield higher return on investment.
4. Too much diversification of portfolios will result in loss lesser concentration in high earning segments.
5. Efforts of mutual funds to offer higher turnover of securities through liquidation of portfolios might result in large payment of transaction costs and reduce return to unit-holders.
6. Risk of the schemes offered by mutual funds may not always be same with risk of the market.

Types of Accounts

There are three types of accounts offered by most of the

mutual funds. The investors select the type that matches their objectives. The various accounts are:

Regular Account: An investor is permitted to purchase any number of shares of the mutual fund, at any time he chooses. An investor is paid the dividend either monthly, quarterly or half as he chooses as per the scheme. This income can be reinvested to acquire additional units by the investors.

Accumulation Account: An investor is allowed to open an account, with a very small initial investment and continue adding to the fund, periodically. Accumulation account may be voluntary or contractual. In the voluntary accumulation plan, an investor has flexibility to make periodic investment at his choice. But in the contractual plan, the investor has to make investments at regular, intervals.

Withdrawal Account: Under this plan, the individual investor can withdraw the amount of funds on a regular basis which suits elderly people to supplement their pension benefits.

Points to Considered before Investing in Mutual Fund

- *Take note of advertisements:* Mutual funds normally come out with an advertisement in newspapers publishing the date of launch of the new schemes. Investors can also contact the agents and distributors of mutual funds who are spread all over the country for necessary information and application forms, filled application forms can be deposited with mutual funds through these agents/distributors, etc. Nowadays post offices and banks also distribute the units of .mutual fund. However, an investor must note that the mutual funds schemes being marketed by banks and post offices should not be taken as their own schemes and no assurance of returns is given by them.
- *Application particulars:* The application must contain clearly name, address, number of units applied for and such other information as required in the application form. Bank account details are also required so as to avoid any fraudulent encashment of

any cheque/draft issued by the mutual fund at a later date for the purpose of dividend or repurchase. Any changes in the address, bank account details, etc. at a later date should be informed to the mutual fund immediately.

- *Eligibility of non-residents:* Even non-resident Indians can also invest in mutual funds. Necessary details in this respect are given in the offer documents of the schemes.
- *Quantum of investment:* An investor must decide how much to invest depending on the available savings but precautions should be taken on the aspects relating to risk taking capacity, age, financial position, etc., before making any investment.
- *Read the offer document carefully:* An abridged offer document, which contains very useful information, is required to be given to the prospective investor by the mutual fund. Before investing the whole offer document should be read very carefully. The application form for subscription to a scheme is an integral part of the offer document. SEBI has prescribed minimum disclosures in the offer document. They may also look into the past track record of performance of the scheme or other schemes of the same mutual fund. They may also compare the performance with other schemes having similar investment objectives.
- *Look for main features of the scheme:* Due care must be given to portions relating to main features of the scheme, risk factors, initial issue expenses and recurring expenses to be charged to the scheme, entry or exit loads, sponsor's track record, educational qualification and work experience of key personnel including fund managers, performance of other schemes launched by the mutual fund in the past, pending litigations and penalties imposed.
- *Certificate of investment*: Mutual funds are required to despatch certificates or statements of accounts within six weeks from the date of closure of the initial subscription of the scheme. In case of close-ended

schemes, the investors would get either a demat account statement or unit certificates as these are traded in the stock exchanges. In case of open-ended schemes, a statement of account is issued by the mutual fund within 30 days from the date of closure of initial public offer of the scheme. The procedure of repurchase is mentioned in the offer document.

- *Purchase price:* The price or NAV a unit holder is charged while investing in an open-ended scheme is called sales price. It may include sales load (charge/ expense), if any. Repurchase or redemption price is the price or NAV at which an open-ended scheme purchases or redeems its units from the unit holders. It may include exit load, if any.
- *NAV and its relevance:* The performance of a scheme is reflected in its net asset value (NAV) which is disclosed on daily basis in case of open-ended schemes and on weekly basis in case of close-ended schemes. NAV of mutual funds are required to be published in newspapers. The NAVs are also available on the web sites of mutual funds. All mutual funds are also required to put their NAVs on the web site of Association of Mutual Funds in India (AMFI) www.amfiindia.com and thus the investors can access NAVs of all mutual funds at one place.
- *Analyze the NAV:* The mutual funds are also required to publish their performance in the form of half-yearly results which also include their returns/yields over a period of time, i.e. last six months, 1 year, 3 years, 5 years and since inception of schemes. Investors can also look into other details like percentage of expenses of total assets as these have an affect on the yield and other useful information in the same half-yearly format.
- *Study the reports:* Investors should study the reports of mutual funds and keep themselves informed about the performance of various schemes of different mutual funds. Investors can compare the performance of their schemes with those of other mutual funds under the same category. They can also

compare the performance of equity oriented schemes with the benchmarks like BSE Sensitive Index, S and P CNX Nifty, etc. On the basis of performance of the mutual funds, the investors should decide when to enter or exit from a mutual fund scheme.

- *Lower price doesn't mean good:* Some of the investors have the tendency to prefer a scheme that is available at lower NAV compared to the one available at higher NAV. Sometimes, they prefer a new scheme which is issuing units at Rs. 10 whereas the existing schemes in the same category are available at much higher NAVs. Investors may please note that in case of mutual funds schemes, lower or higher NAVs of similar type schemes of different mutual funds have no relevance. On the other hand, investors should choose a scheme based on its merit considering performance track record of the mutual fund, service standards, professional management, etc.
- *Price of mutual fund units do not fluctuate much:* IPOs (initial public offerings) of companies may open at lower or higher price than the issue price depending on market sentiment and perception of investors. However, in the case of mutual funds, the par value of the units may not rise or fall immediately after allotment. A mutual fund scheme takes some time to make investment in securities. NAV of the scheme depends on the value of securities in which the funds have been deployed.
- *Past performance:* Though past performance of a scheme is not an indicator of its future performance and good performance in the past may or may not be sustained in the future, this is one of the important factors for making investment decision. In case of debt-oriented schemes, apart from looking into past returns, the investors should also see the quality of debt instruments which is reflected in their rating. A scheme with lower rate of return but having investments in better rated instruments may be safer. Similarly, in equities schemes also, investors may

look for quality of portfolio. They may also seek advice of experts.

- *Mutual benefit means not mutual fund:* Some companies having the name "mutual benefit" should not be confused and meant as mutual funds. These companies do not come under the purview of SEBI. On the other hand, mutual funds can mobilize funds from the investors by launching schemes only after getting registered with SEBI as mutual funds.
- *Sponsor's track record:* In the offer document of any mutual fund scheme, financial performance including the net worth of the sponsor for a period of three years is required to be given. The only purpose is that the investors should know the track record of the company which has sponsored the mutual fund. However, higher net worth of the sponsor does not mean that the scheme would give better returns or the sponsor would compensate in case the NAV falls.

Mutual Fund Costs

- *Operating Costs:* Costs that are incurred for management of the funds, such as advisory fees paid to investment consultants, custodial services, audit services, transfer agents, trustees, etc. These expenses are calculated on annual basis and are charged to schemes of the fund on prò-rate basis.
- *Sales costs:* These costs are charged to the investor directly. This is technically called as sales load. There are two types of loads. Front end load, which is a one time payment paid by investor at the time of purchase. Sometime these costs are waived by the mutual funds. The other type of sales cost is back-end load, which also called a redemption load. It is charged while a investor decides to exit the scheme.
- *Transactions costs:* There is also a fee charged by some funds when investors switch over from one scheme to another scheme of the same mutual fund. It can be called as transaction cost.

WORKING OF MUTUAL FUNDS

Considering the market trends, any prudent fund managers can change the asset allocation, i.e. it can invest higher or lower percentage of the fund in equity or debt instruments compared to what is disclosed in the offer document. It can be done on a short term basis on defensive considerations, i.e. to protect the NAV. Hence, the fund managers are allowed certain flexibility in altering the asset allocation considering the interest of the investors. In case the mutual fund wants to change the asset allocation on a permanent basis, they are required to inform the unit holders and giving them option to exit the scheme at prevailing NAV without any load.

The mutual funds are required to disclose full portfolios of all of their schemes on half-yearly basis which are published in the newspapers. Some mutual funds send the portfolios to their unit-holders. The scheme portfolio shows investment made in each security, i.e. equity, debentures, money market instruments, government securities, etc. and their quantity, market value and percent to NAV. These portfolio statements also required to disclose illiquid securities in the portfolio, investment made in rated and unrated debt securities, non-performing assets (NPAs), etc. Some of the mutual funds send newsletters to the unit holders on quarterly basis which also contain portfolios of the schemes.

However, no change in the nature or terms of the scheme, known as fundamental attributes of the scheme, e.g. structure, investment pattern, etc. can be carried out unless a written communication is sent to each unit-holder and an advertisement is given in one English daily having nationwide circulation and in a newspaper published in the language of the region where the head office of the mutual fund is situated. The unit-holders have the right to exit the scheme at the prevailing NAV without any exit load if they do not want to continue with the scheme. The mutual funds are also required to follow similar procedure while converting the scheme from close-ended to open-ended scheme and in case of change in sponsor.

According to SEBI Regulations, transfer of units is required to be done within thirty days from the date of lodgment of certificates with the mutual fund. The mutual funds are required to inform about any material changes to their unit-holders. At present, offer documents are required to be revised and updated at least once in two years. In the meantime, new investors are informed about the material changes by way of addendum to the offer document till the time offer document is revised and reprinted.

The mutual funds are also required to send annual report or abridged annual report to the unit-holders at the end of the year. Various studies on mutual fund schemes including yields of different schemes are being published by the financial newspapers on a weekly basis. Apart from these, many research agencies also publish research reports on performance of mutual funds including the ranking of various schemes in terms of their performance.

A mutual fund is required to despatch to the unit-holders the dividend warrants within 30 days of the declaration of the dividend and the redemption or repurchase proceeds within 10 working days from the date of redemption or repurchase request made by the unit-holder. In case of failures to despatch the redemption/repurchase proceeds within the stipulated time period, Asset Management Company is liable to pay interest as specified by SEBI from time to time (15% at present).

Incase a scheme of a mutual fund is wound up, the concerned mutual fund pays back the sum based on the NAV after adjustment of necessary expenses. The mutual fund will give a report on the scheme and why it was wound up. Incase of complaints, the contact person named in the offer document has to be contacted. The Trustees of mutual fund monitor the activities of the fund. SEBI can also be approached for redressal of grievances.

SEBI REGULATION ON MUTUAL FUNDS

The mutual fund is regulated by the SEBI guidelines which include the following major points:

1. A sponsor who have sound track record—having

financial services business of not less than 5 years, a positive net worth and having profits in the last five years.

2. Every mutual fund should be registered as a trust.
3. The mutual fund should appoint a Asset Management Company (AMC) to manage the funds of the trust.
4. The sponsor should contribute at least 40% of net worth of Asset Management Company.
5. No person appointed to the trust or AMC shall be involved in any fraud or convicted for any offence.
6. A custodian has to be appointed by the mutual fund to take custody of securities and carry out the custodian activities prescribed by the trustees.

Trust Deed and its Contents

1. A trust deed has to be executed by the sponsor that creates a trust in the form of a trust. Such trust deed has to be made in favour of the trustees of the trust. No person shall be eligible as a trustee if such a person is already a trustee of any other mutual fund. And two-third of the should be independent persons.
2. Number of trustees should be mentioned and the minimum number also to be mentioned in the deed. The deed should provide for minimum of four trustees.
3. No trustee shall attend or vote in the meeting in which he is interested. The interest of the trustees should be clearly made known to the trust.
4. The deed must provide for trustees taking up the control over the property of the schemes of the mutual fund.
5. It should also provide for the beneficial interest of unit holders.
6. Deed should also contain the duties of the trustees
7. It should provide for appointment of AMC.
8. The trustees have to enter into an investment management agreement with the AMC and the deed should provide for it.

9. The trustees should have power to cancel the contact of agreement with the AMC.
10. It should provide for appointment of custodian.
11. An auditor has to be appointed for the trust and the AMC, but they are to be different persons.
12. Broad policies on the allocation of payments on income should be mentioned in the deed.
13. The mutual fund should be forbidden to make any guarantee of loans or grant loans against the rules made by SEBI for mutual funds.
14. The liability of unit holders cannot be made unlimited by the mutual fund at any circumstance.
15. The fee payable to trustees shall also be mentioned in the deed.
16. It should provide for quorum for meeting and at least four meetings should be held in a year at every three months.
17. Rules regarding the removal of trustees should also be mentioned in the deed.

Contents of Investment Management Agreement

1. AMC appointed by the trustees with the prior approval of SEBI is responsible for floating schemes for the mutual fund after approval of the same by the trustees and managing the funds mobilized under various schemes.
2. AMC should not undertake any other business activity other than activities agreed. It may carry out such other activities as financial services consultancy, exchange of research and analysis on commercial basis as long as they are not in conflict with the fund management.
3. Trustees have the power to dismiss the AMC.
4. The investment of the funds raised under various schemes shall be made by AMC as per the deed.
5. It shall not acquire any of the assets out of the scheme property which involves the assumption of any liability which will make the unit holders' liability unlimited.

6. AMC should ensure that no offer document of a scheme, key information memorandum, results published without the trustees' approval.
7. The basis of calculating the repurchase price and NAV of the various schemes of the fund shall be disclosed to investors.
8. Trustees may obtain from the AMC all information concerning the operations of the various schemes of the mutual fund managed by the AMC to ensure that the AMC is carrying out the activities as agreed.
9. Loss or damage or expenses incurred by the AMC or officers of AMC or any person delegated by the AMC should not be met out of its property.
10. Quarterly report on the functioning of the schemes of the mutual fund to be submitted to trustees.

Duties of Trustees

- To ask for information from AMC as they may deem fit.
- Trustees should see that the Asset management company has office and accounting system and appointed fund manager and other important persons for conduct of business, and auditors, compliance officer, registrars, brokers and agents.
- The asset management company (AMC) should be diligent in empanelling the brokers in monitoring the securities transactions with brokers and avoid concentration of business with any broker and the trustees should over see it.
- The trustees shall ensure that no change in the fundamental attributes of any scheme or the trust or fees and expenses payable is made which would affects the interest of unit holders.
- No person shall take unfair advantage to any associate or dealt with any of the associates of the AMC in a manner detrimental to the interest of the beneficiaries.
- Transaction entered into by the AMC has to be in

accordance with these regulations for the mutual fund scheme.

- Adequate steps have to be taken to protect the interest of investors and the investors of one scheme are not to be compromised with that of other schemes.
- On quarterly basis the activities of the mutual fund should be reviewed including service contracts custodial services
- The trustees shall be responsible for the calculation of any income to be paid mutual fund and also of any income received in the mutual fund for the holders' unit of any scheme.
- On the requisition of 3/4 of the unit holders of any scheme or when the majority of the trustees decide to wind up or pre-maturely redeem the units the trustees should get the consent of the unit holders.
- Trustees shall be accountable for as per the deed and they have to file the details of his transactions of dealing in securities with a mutual fund on a quarterly basis In case the conduct of business *of* the mutual fund is not in accordance with these regulations and the scheme, the same may be informed SEBI and remedial actions has to be taken.

Advertisement Code for Mutual Funds

- It shall be true, fair and clear and not to contain misleading statement or promise or forecast. Representations made about the performance or activities of the mutual fund in the absence of necessary qualifying statements or exaggerated performance or activities, or inaccurate portrayal of a past performance or statements promising the benefits of owning units or investing in the schemes of the mutual funds without simultaneous mention of material risks associated with such investments will all mean as misleading advertisements.
- It should not be designed in content and format

likely to be misunderstood and not to have statements which may mislead the investor.

- Advertisements so framed as to exploit the lack of experience or knowledge of the Investors are prohibited. As the investors may not be sophisticated in legal or financial matters, care should be taken that the advertisement is set forth in a clear, concise, and understandable manner.
- It should not contain information, the accuracy of which is to any extent dependent on assumptions. Any advertisement that makes claims about the performance of the fund shall be supported by relevant figures.
- The advertisement shall not compare one fund with another, implicitly or explicitly, unless the comparison is fair and all information relevant to the comparison is included in the advertisement.
- The funds which advertises yield must use standardized computations.
- Mutual funds shall indicate in all advertisements, the names of the trustee, manager, financial advisor to the fund.
- While giving details of yield, return or any scheme detail or inviting subscription to the scheme shall contain disclosures of all the risk factors associated with the scheme.
- If minimum rate of return or yield to prospective investors are guaranteed, resources to back such a guarantee shall also be indicated.
- Since investments in mutual funds and securities are subject to market risks . The NAV of schemes may go up or down depending on various factors, hence such risk should also be mentioned.
- All advertisement launched in connection with the scheme should also mention prominently the risks factors as stated in the offer document along warning statement that "is only the name of the scheme and does not in any manner indicate either the quality of the scheme, its future prospects or returns; and please read the offer document before investing".

- Any Information contained in a offer document if reproduce such information shall be in full and disclose all relevant facts and not be restricted to select extracts relating to that item which could be misleading
- Celebrities cannot form part of the advertisement.
- No name can be given to a scheme with a view to subtly indicate any assurance of return, except in the cases of guaranteed return scheme.
- No advertisement shall be issued stating that the scheme has been subscribed or over-subscribed during the period the scheme is open for subscription.
- During the subscription period, no reference shall be made to the scheme of the mutual fund or mutual fund itself, if an advertisement is issued by the sponsor or by group companies or an associate company of the sponsor.
- Advertisement on the performance of a mutual fund or its AMC shall compare the past performances only on the basis of per unit of statistics.
- Advertisements for NAVs must indicate the past and the latest NAV of a scheme.
- In case of close ended scheme shall be listed in recognized stock exchange with in 6 months from the date of closure of the subscription.
- The AMC at its option may repurchase a close ended scheme at stated intervals as disclosed in the offer document. It may permit conversion of close ended scheme into open ended scheme.
- No scheme of mutual fund other than an initial offer of equity linked savings scheme shall be open for subscription for more than 45 days.
- Unit certificates are freely transferable except where it is specially restricted or prohibited under the scheme.

Types of Investing Pattern of Mutual Funds

Bottom-up investing: In this process, the fundamental factors that contribute to a stock performance are considered before taking note of the economical factors which affect the industry are considered.

Top-down investing: This is just opposite to the above model, where, the investment strategy is based on the economical factors that contribute to the success of the industry are considered first before looking at the individual company performance.

Classification of Mutual Funds

Based on advantages and services offered to various sections of the society, Mutual Funds are classified into three broad categories:

- ❖ Functional classification of Mutual Fund.
- ❖ Portfolio classification of Mutual Fund.
- ❖ Geographical classification of Mutual Fund.

Two major fund categories of mutual funds are closed-end funds and the open-end funds. Open-end funds are commonly referred to as the mutual funds. Mutual funds can be further classified into equity funds, growth funds, income funds, real estate funds, offshore funds, leveraged funds and hedge funds. Such schemes are listed on the stock exchanges for dealings in the secondary market.

FUNCTIONAL CLASSIFICATION OF MUTUAL FUNDS

Closed-end Funds

Closed-end mutual funds have the following characteristics. Firstly, closed-end fund Investment Company cannot sell share units after its initial offering. Its growth in terms of the number of shares is limited. The shares are issued like the new issues of any other company; listed and quoted on a stock exchange. Secondly, the shares of the closed-end funds are not redeemable at their NAV as in the case of open-end funds. On the other hand, these shares are traded in the secondary market on a stock change, at market prices that may be above or below their Net Asset Value (NAV). Thirdly, the objectives of the closed-end funds may differ from that of the open-end funds. Fourthly, closed-end funds are channelized into the secondary market, for the acquisition of corporate securities. Finally, the prices of closed-end mutual funds' shares are determined by demand and supply and not by NAV as in the case of open-end mutual fund shares. Redemption is after a specified period (4 to 7 years).

Open-end Funds

The open-end mutual funds are characterized by the continual selling and redeeming of shares. In other words, mutual funds do not have a fixed capitalization and tenure for redemption. The MF sells its shares to the intending investors and stands ready to repurchase the same, directly from the investing public, at the net asset value per share.

Portfolio Classification of Mutual Fund

Portfolio Classification of Mutual Fund Mutual Funds differs with reference to the type of instruments in which the money can be invested. These are specified in the offer document prospectus and accordingly the fund is structured for a particular purpose.

Bond Funds: They provide fixed return for those who desire safety and steady income, The fund is invested in government securities and bonds. It is a more liquid, diversified and conservative investment with regular income and moderate capital gains. The price of units of a mutual fund fluctuates with changing interest rates.

Stock Funds: They are mainly for those who are willing to accept risks in the hope of high return. These are called common stock fund. There are two types i.e., Growth fund and Go-Go fund. The former consists of investments in Blue chips and the latter in high-risk stocks.

Income Funds: They are mainly to maximize the current income of investors. There are two types of funds: (i) Low investment risk with steady income, and (ii) High-risk investment with maximum income. Investments would typically be in fixed income securities, to a greater extent and in shares to a small extent. Capital appreciation in such schemes may be limited.

Hybrid Funds: Funds that cater to the income as well as growth needs of the investor. These funds adopt balance investment approach to stabilize the earning prospects and the growth prospects.

Money Market Mutual Funds: Investments are predominantly in money market instruments like certificate of deposits, commercial paper, treasury bills, etc. They are short term in tenor, highly liquid with high safety. This fund is an alternative to savings account for high bracket savers. The fund cannot invest the corpus in shares, debentures and such other papers. Return on these schemes may fluctuate, depending upon the interest rates prevailing in the market. This is ideal for Corporate and Individual Investors as a means to park their surplus funds for short period or awaiting a more favourable investment alternative.

Leverage Funds: These funds are raised to increase the size and value of portfolio and offer benefits to members from out of the excess of gains over the cost of borrowed funds. These are tending to be speculative in nature of trading. Unit holders benefit out of the comparative cost of investment made by mutual funds. The funds borrow money in order to increase the size of the corpus and thereby increase the benefit to the shareholders by operating with a larger corpus than the money collected.

Specialized Funds: These funds invest in securities of certain industries/specific sector or specific income producing securities. They carry more risks due to lack of diversification.

Hedge Funds: Investment based on speculative trading are called hedge funds. The mutual funds invest in share whose prices are likely to go up and sell shares likely to slide down.

Balanced Funds: Here, assets are made up of a judicious mixture of industries stocks and bonds. To secure reasonable rate of return, the funds are employed in high-grade common stock and conservative fixed income securities like debentures, bonds and preference shares. In a rising stock market, the NAV of these schemes may not normally keep phase, or fall equally when the market falls. This is ideal for Investors looking for a combination of income and moderate growth.

Fund for Funds: money collected for investment in other mutual fund are called fund for funds. But such types of funds are operating in some of the foreign countries and not in India.

Growth Funds: The principle objective of these funds is capital appreciation of investment over a period of time. Investment would be mostly in equity shares. These schemes are not for investors seeking regular income or needing their money back in the short-term. This is ideal for Investors in their prime earning years and for Investor seeking growth over the long-term.

Special Funds: The funds are invested in equity share of top rated companies, which offer long-term capital growth and provide large dividend income.

Dual Purpose Funds: Here, funds are invested according to investor's preference, i.e. those who prefer income and those who prefer growth separately.

Real Estate Funds: The fund is named so because of primary investment in real estate ventures.

Pension Funds: These funds provide for long-term investment out of individual investor's superannuation savings. They take advantages of tax breaks available for such investments.

Asset Allocation Funds: These funds aim at profit maximization by allocating investments to areas where growth is perceived to be high.

Country Funds: These are overseas funds (off-shore) where investments are made in a particular country (example India fund) or a group of countries (example emerging market fund).

Index Funds: Investments are made in the index scrips with the same proportion and weightage as that of the index. The performances of fund will be in line with the index.

New Direction Funds: Mutual funds that deploy their funds in some of the scientific and technological research activity based companies such as pollution control, etc are called new direction funds.

Tax Savings Schemes: These schemes offer tax rebate to the investors under tax laws as prescribed from time to time. This is made possible because the government offers tax incentives for investments in specified avenues.

Assured Return Schemes: These are those schemes that assure a specific return to the unit holders irrespective of performance of the scheme. A scheme cannot promise returns unless such returns are fully guaranteed by the sponsor or AMC and this is required to be disclosed in the offer document.

Investors should carefully read the offer document whether return is assured for the entire period of the scheme or only for a certain period. Some schemes assure returns one year at a time and they review and change it at the beginning of the next year.

Off-shore Funds: companies that invest in companies of other countries are called off-shore funds. However, due clearance form RBI is necessary for this.

Geographical Classification of Mutual Fund

Domestic Mutual Funds: These are savings schemes, which are opened for mobilizing savings of the residents within the country and also non-residents of the country.

Off-shore Mutual Funds: The offshore fund is meant to attract foreign capital for investment in the country.

ASSETS UNDER MANAGEMENT WITH AMC

The term asset management is often used to refer to the investment management of collective investments, while the more generic fund management may refer to all forms of institutional investment as well as investment management for private investors. Investment managers who specialize in advisory or discretionary management on behalf of private investors may often refer to their services as wealth management or portfolio management. The provision of 'investment management services' includes elements of financial statement analysis, asset selection, stock selection, plan implementation and ongoing monitoring of investments. Fund manager or known as investment adviser refers to both a firm that provides investment management services and an individual who directs fund management decisions.

Mutual funds collect the pool of investment from various people/groups/individuals. The money thus collected is then invested by the fund manager in different types of securities. These could range from shares to debentures to money market instruments, depending upon the scheme's stated objectives. The income earned through these investments and the capital appreciation realized by the scheme is shared by its unit-holders in proportion to the number of units owned by them.

Thus a Mutual Fund is the most suitable investment for the common man as it offers an opportunity to invest in a diversified, professionally managed basket of securities at a relatively low cost. Worldwide, Mutual Fund or Unit Trust as it is referred to in some parts of the world, has a long and successful history. The popularity of Mutual Funds has increased manifold in developed financial markets, like the United States.

The Indian capital market has been increasing tremendously during last few years. With the reforms of economy, reforms of industrial policy, reforms of public sector and reforms of financial sector, the economy has been opened up and many developments have been taking place in the Indian money market and capital market. In order to help the small investors, mutual fund industry has come to occupy an important place. As mutual fund has entered into the Indian Capital market, growing profitable enough to attract competitors into this cherished territory encouraging competition among all the mutual fund operators, there is need to take some strategy to bring more confidence among investors for which mutual fund would be able to project the image successfully. With the structural liberalization policies no doubt Indian economy is likely to return to a high grow path in few years. Hence mutual fund organizations are needed to upgrade their skills and technology.

To invest in mutual funds, one need to first understand what they are, and how they work. Mutual funds act as intermediaries and facilitate investments in various securities (stocks and bonds). Investing in a mutual fund allows to minimize risk and maximize returns, because it acts as a middle man for a group of investors with a shared and predefined investment objective. SEBI-approved Asset Management Companies (AMC) manage the funds by making investments in various types of securities. This means that all recognized AMCs are monitored by higher authorities and stringent regulations, and funds are managed by professionals who have the necessary expertise. Typically, investing in a mutual fund means investing in more than one stock. Some fund managers will diversify and spread your investment further by buying a mosaic of stocks and bonds. Investing in a large number of assets, or diversification, means that a loss incurred on one investment is minimized by gains in others. Since the AMC buys and sells large amounts of securities at a time, transaction costs are reduced, and the benefit is extended to the investor, because the average cost of the unit is lowered.

ASSOCIATION OF MUTUAL FUNDS IN INDIA

With the increase in mutual fund players in India, a need for mutual fund association in India was generated to function as a non-profit organisation. Association of Mutual Funds in India (AMFI) was incorporated on 22nd August, 1995. AMFI is an apex body of all Asset Management Companies (AMC) which has been registered with SEBI. Till date all the AMCs are that have launched mutual fund schemes are its members. It functions under the supervision and guidelines of its Board of Directors. Association of Mutual Funds India has brought down the Indian Mutual Fund Industry to a professional and healthy market with ethical lines enhancing and maintaining standards. It follows the principle of both protecting and promoting the interests of mutual funds as well as their unit holders.

The Association of Mutual Funds of India works with 30 registered AMCs of the country. It has certain defined objectives which juxtaposes the guidelines of its Board of Directors. The objectives are as follows:

- This mutual fund association of India maintains a high professional and ethical standards in all areas of operation of the industry.
- It also recommends and promotes the top class business practices and code of conduct which is followed by members and related people engaged in the activities of mutual fund and asset management. The agencies who are by any means connected or involved in the field of capital markets and financial services also involved in this code of conduct of the association.
- AMFI interacts with SEBI and works according to SEBIs guidelines in the mutual fund industry.

- Association of Mutual Fund of India do represent the Government of India, the Reserve Bank of India and other related bodies on matters relating to the Mutual Fund Industry.
- It develops a team of well qualified and trained Agent distributors. It implements a programme of training and certification for all intermediaries and other engaged in the mutual fund industry.
- AMFI undertakes all India awarness programme for investors inorder to promote proper understanding of the concept and working of mutual funds.
- At last but not the least association of mutual fund of India also disseminate informations on Mutual Fund Industry and undertakes studies and research either directly or in association with other bodies.

GROWTH OF MUTUAL FUND INDUSTRY

Over the past decades mutual funds have grown intensely in popularity and have experienced a considerable growth rate. Mutual funds are popular because they make it easy for small investors to invest their money in a diversified pool of securities. There are about 52 mutual fund companies in India. The growth in the number of MFs in India in recent years in very surprising and phenomenal. Although the MF market in India is not comparable and significant to the growth of MF in some of the developed countries, yet the pace of growth of MF market is very much encouraging.

TABLE 19.1
Growth of Assets and Schemes Over the Years

(Rs. in Crores)

Year	*1989*	*1994*	*1999*	*2004*	*2005*	*2006*	*2007*	*2008*
Growth of assets in (Rs. crore)	13455	61028	68472	139616	149554	231862	326388	505152
No. of schemes	21	756	167	277	403	451	592	956

www.amfiindia.com.

Mutual funds have been a significant source of investment in both government and corporate securities. It has been for decades the monopoly of the state with UTI being the key player, with invested funds exceeding Rs. 300 bn. (US $ 10 bn.). The state-owned insurance companies also hold a portfolio of stocks. Presently, numerous mutual funds exist, including private and foreign companies. Banks—mainly state-owned too have established Mutual Funds (MFs). Foreign participation in mutual funds and asset management companies is permitted on a case by case basis. UTI, the largest mutual fund in the country was set-up by the government in 1964, to encourage small investors in the equity market. UTI has an extensive marketing network of over 35,000 agents spread over the country. The UTI scrips have performed relatively well in the market, as compared to the Sensex trend. However, the same cannot be said of all mutual funds.

All MFs are allowed to apply for firm allotment in public issues. SEBI regulates the functioning of mutual funds, and it requires that all MFs should be established as trusts under the Indian Trusts Act. The actual fund management activity shall be conducted from a separate asset management company (AMC). The minimum net worth of an AMC or its affiliate must be Rs. 50 million to act as a manager in any other fund. MFs can be penalized for defaults including non-registration and failure to observe rules set by their AMCs. MFs dealing exclusively with money market instruments have to be registered with RBI. All other schemes floated by MFs are required to be registered with SEBI. In 1995, the RBI permitted private sector institutions to set-up Money Market Mutual Funds (MMMFs). They can invest in treasury bills, call and notice money, commercial paper, commercial bills accepted/co-accepted by banks, certificates of deposit and dated government securities.

MF GROWTH WORLD OVER

One of the most interesting financial phenomena of the 1990s was the explosive growth of mutual funds. This was particularly true in the United States where total net assets of mutual funds grew from USD 1.6 trillion in 1992 to 5.5 trillion in 1998, equivalent to an average annual rate of growth of 22.4 percent. With the exception of some East Asian countries (including Japan), it was also true of most other countries around the world. The global growth of mutual funds was fuelled by the increasing globalization of finance and expanding presence of large multinational financial groups in a large number of countries and by the strong performance of equity and bond markets throughout most of the 1990s. A third factor was probably the demographic aging that characterizes the populations of most high and middle-income countries and the search of financial instruments that are safe and liquid but also promise high long-term returns by growing numbers of investors. It is also important to note that this growth occurred contemporaneously with a period of high growth in market capitalizations around the world, fueled in part by the technology/internet boom.

Conventional assets under management of the global fund management industry increased by 14% in 2009, to $ 71.3 trillion. Pension assets accounted for $ 28.0 trillion of the total, with $ 22.9 trillion invested in mutual funds and $ 20.4 trillion in insurance funds. Together with alternative assets (sovereign wealth funds, hedge funds, private equity funds and exchange traded funds) and funds of wealthy individuals, assets of the global fund management industry accounted for over $105 trillion, a increase of 15% on the previous year. The increase in 2009 followed 18% decline in the previous year and was largely a result of the recovery in equity markets during the year. The US remained by far the biggest source of funds, accounting for around a half of conventional assets under management or some $ 36 trillion. The UK was the second largest centre in the world and by far the largest in Europe with around 9% of the global total. The latest available data shows that assets under management of the world's largest 500 fund managers declined 23% in 2008 to $ 53.4 trillion. Funds under management of the top 500 are likely to have staged a recovery in 2009 in parallel with the increase in global assets under management of the fund management industry.

The mutual fund industry is larger in countries with stronger rules, laws, and regulations, and specifically where mutual fund investors' rights are better protected. The industry is also larger in countries with wealthier and more educated populations, where the industry is older, trading costs are lower and in which defined contribution pension plans are more prevalent. The industry is smaller in countries where barriers to entry are higher. Laws and regulations, supply-side and demand-side factors affect the size of the fund industry.

ASSET MANAGEMENT COMPANY (AMC)

Asset management companies are responsible for the financial, administrative and accounting management of products under management in collective investment schemes and under discretionary mandates. They manage their assets independently and exclusively in the investor's interest. An asset management company is always liable for its business activities, even if it out sources some of them. In law, their liability is based on the notion of a management mandate. Under the terms of the mandate, the manager is responsible for making management decisions by buying and selling securities on behalf of investors (or customers).

Asset management companies must act solely in the investors' interest. The company is bound by the terms of regulations to fair dealing and ethical principles that the industry has set out officially in various rules and regulations. Asset management companies are subject to transparency requirements with regard to their customers. Official recognition of the asset management business and the segregation of this function from the custody function, and from businesses that are likely to cause conflicts of interest, such as investment banking, market activities and proprietary trading, are preventive measures taken to protect investors.

The asset management company must have sufficient financial resources such as, capital, technical capabilities, accounting system, analytical resources, performance monitoring, and personnel for the business type and volume.

The fund management takes over all responsibility for the fund from an investment perspective. Fund managers are responsible for 'beating' their bench mark. The fund manager will also often be responsible for ensuring that the fund has cash available when required to meet obligations of the fund.

Fund management responsibility is usually carried out by senior investment staff with other, often related, roles, Generally the larger the client, the more senior the fund manger. Fund managers also take responsibility that orders are executed accurately, ie that the correct line of stock has been ordered, that sufficient cash will be available for settlement and sold responsible for stock certificates. They are also responsible for ensuring that all clients receive equal treatment, i.e., stock are to be bought simultaneously across all similar funds.

LAW ON AMC

Registration

No asset management company can commence business without registration. A company proposing to commence business as an asset management company shall be eligible for registration if—

- It is registered as a public limited company under the Companies Ordinance, 1984;
- It has a paid up capital of not less than thirty million rupees;
- No director, officer or employee of such company has been convicted of fraud or breach of trust;
- No director, officer or employee of such company has been adjudicated as insolvent or has suspended payment or has compounded with his creditors; and
- The promoters and directors of such company are, in the opinion of SEBI, persons of means and integrity and have special knowledge and experience of matters which the company may have to deal with as an asset management company.

A company eligible for registration may make an application with processing fee of fifty thousand rupees in the form of bank draft payable to the Commission. The SEBI may, after satisfying itself that the applicant is eligible for registration and that it would be in the interest of the capital market so to do, grant a certificate of registration to such company.

Restrictions—No asset management company shall—

(a) Merge with, acquire or take over any other asset management company or a scheme, unless it has obtained the prior approval of the SEBI in writing to the scheme of such merger, acquisition or takeover;
(b) Pledge any of the securities held or beneficially owned by a scheme except for the benefit of the scheme;
(c) Accept deposits from a scheme;
(d) Make a loan or advance money to any person except in connection with the normal business of the scheme;
(e) Participate in a joint account with others in any transaction;
(f) Apply any part of its assets to real estate except property for its own use;
(g) Make any investment with the purpose of having the effect of vesting the management, or control, in the scheme; and
(h) Employ as a broker, directly or indirectly, any of its director, officer or employee or a member of a family of such person which shall include spouse, parents, children, brothers and sisters.

Obligations of AMC.—An asset management company shall—

(a) Be obliged to manage the assets of the scheme in the interest of the unit holders in good faith and to the best of its ability and without gaining any undue advantage for itself or any of its related parties or its officers;
(b) Account to the trustee for any loss in value of the assets of the scheme where such loss has been caused by its negligence, reckless or wilful act or omission;
(c) Be responsible for the acts and omissions of all persons to whom it may delegate any of its functions as manager as if they were its own acts and omission;

(d) Maintain at its principal office, proper accounts and records to enable a complete and accurate view to be formed of the assets and liabilities and the income and expenditure of the scheme, all transactions for the account of the scheme and amounts received by the scheme in respect of issues of units and paid out by the scheme on redemption of units and by way of distributions;

(e) Prepare and transmit the annual report, together with a copy of the balance sheet and income and expenditure account and the auditor's report of a scheme within four months of closing of the accounting period to the unit holders, and the balance sheet and income and expenditure account shall comply with requirements prescribed

(f) Within two months of the close of the first half of its year of account, prepare and transmit to the unit holders and the Authority a profit and loss account for, and balance sheet as at the end of that half year, whether audited or otherwise;

(g) Maintain a register of unit holders of a scheme and inform the Authority of the address where the register is kept;

(h) Appoint, at the establishment of a scheme and upon any vacancy, an auditor who shall be a Chartered Accountant and independent of the auditor of the management company and the trustees.

(i) Furnish a copy of the annual report together with copies of the balance sheet, income and expenditure account and the auditor's report of a scheme to the Authority within four months of the close of the accounting period together with a statement containing the following information, namely:
   (i) Total number of unit holders; and
   (ii) Particulars of the personnel (executive, research and other) of the asset management company; and

(j) Furnish a copy of the company's annual report together with copies of the balance sheet, income and expenditure account and the auditors' report within four months of the close of the accounting period.

Remuneration payable to asset management company: An asset management company shall be entitled to a remuneration. During the first five years of the scheme, of an amount not exceeding three per cent of the net assets of the scheme as at the end of its year of accounts and thereafter of an amount equal to two per cent of such assets; and of an amount not exceeding one-half of the amount by which the dividend distributed by the scheme exceeds twenty per cent.

Authorization of Scheme

- No scheme shall be offered to the public unless the same is authorized by the Authority—SEBI.
- An application for authorization of a scheme shall contain information as specified in Form III and shall be accompanied by the following information and documents, namely :
    - The scheme's constitutive documents contents of which have been set out in Schedule III;
    - The management company's latest audited accounts, if applicable, and resumes of its directors;
    - The trustee's latest audited accounts, if available;
    - Letter of consent to the appointment from the trustee;
    - an undertaking from the management company that it will invest or arrange the investment of two hundred fifty million rupees for a minimum period of two years provided that the Commission may reduce this requirement to fifty million rupees, where the management company has good performance record of average seventeen and half per cent total annual return or average twelve and half per cent dividend payment in respect of schemes under its management for previous three years and for

the purpose of this clause "total annual return" shall mean pay out and appreciation in the value of units on the date of preparation of accounts. Provided that an undertaking may not be given in case a scheme has been established prior to the commencement of these Rules; and

- Application fee of twenty thousand rupees in the form of bank draft payable to the Authority.

Investment Policy and Diversification

(1) Investment policy with respect to a scheme shall be clearly and concisely stated in public offering document for the sale of securities of such scheme.

(2) A scheme shall invest not less than fifty per cent of its assets in listed securities or in securities for the listing of which an application has been approved by a stock exchange.

(3) Investment of a scheme in any company shall not, at any time, exceed an amount equal to ten per cent of the total net asset value of the scheme at the time of investment or ten per cent of the issued capital of the company.

(4) No scheme shall invest more than twenty-five per cent of its net asset value in securities of any one sector as per classification of stock exchanges. Provided that the Commission may, on application by the asset management company, relax any, or all the requirements of this rule in case of any scheme established for a specific investment objective where the intention to that effect was expressed in the offer document; and in case a scheme has been in operation prior to the commencement of these Rules and has been subsequently authorized under these Rules, the Investments made prior to the grant of authorization shall be exempt from restrictions mentioned for such a period as may be specified by the Commission.

20

Depository System

Under the physical movement of securities transfer of ownership happens by sending securities to broker and through him the transferee gets his title from the company after necessary formalities are completed by the company. It has become due to the complexity of capital market system an inefficient system. In many cases, the process of transfer takes much longer than the two months stipulated in the Companies Act, and a significant proportion of transactions end up as bad delivery due to faulty compliance of paper work or defective titles caused by forgery, mutilation of certificates and other irregularities which are rampant in the physical transfer of securities. In these circumstances a genuine transferee may not get good title of the securities after parting with the money. Besides, it also costs much and delays settlement, restricts liquidity and makes investor grievance redressal time-consuming. These are some of the defects the physical movement of securities suffers.

The Depositories Act, 1996 was one piece of legislation that has got the appreciation of all concerned due to the benefits it carried to the capital market activity. It provided for establishment of depositories in securities for ensuring free transferability of securities with speed, accuracy and security by making securities of public limited companies freely transferable subject to certain exceptions. Dematerialization of securities in the depository mode and for maintenance of ownership records of securities in a book entry form were others objectives of the Act.

In order to streamline both the stages of settlement process, the Depositories Act envisages transfer of ownership of securities electronically by book entry without making the securities move from person to person. The Act has made the securities of all public limited companies freely transferable by restricting the company right to use discretion in effecting the transfer, of securities, and dispensing with the transfer deed and other procedural requirements under the Companies Act. A depository holds securities in dematerialized form. It maintains ownership record of securities and effects transfer of ownership through book entry. The name of the depository appears in the records of the issuer as registered owner of securities. The name of actual owner appears in the records of the depository as beneficial owner. The beneficial owner of securities still holds all the rights.

A depository is an organization which holds securities of investors in electronic form at the request of the investors through a registered Depository Participant. It also provides services related to transactions in securities. It can be compared with a bank, which holds the funds for depositors. The depository system involves conversion of securities from physical to electronic form, settlement of trades in electronic segment, electronic transfer of ownership and electronic custody of securities. If an investor wants to keep the securities, he exercises the option to hold them in physical form but if he wants to sell he has to offer the securities for dematerialization through a depository participant. An investor who has dematerialized his securities can again opt for rematerialization and the depository will have to do the rematerialization within 30 days from the date of receipt of physical demat request. A depository holds securities in safe custody just like a Bank which keeps custody of cash. As we issue a cheque for drawing cash from the Bank, we issue a debit instruction for delivery of securities from our account. All these are done in a secured environment.

STAMP DUTY ON SECURITIES

To give effect to the Depositories Act, 1996, the following has been inserted as in the Indian Stamp Act, 1899 and accordingly the following securities are not liable to Stamp duty:

- Issue of securities to depositories.
- Transfer of registered ownership of shares from a person to a depository or from a depository to a beneficial owner shall not be liable to any stamp duty.
- Transfer of beneficial ownership of shares, such shares being shares of a company formed and registered under the Companies Act, 1956 (1 of 1956), or a body corporate established by a Central Act dealt with by a depository, shall not be liable to duty.
- Transfer of beneficial ownership of units, such units being units of a mutual fund including units of the Unit Trust of India and dealt with by a depository.

DEPOSITORIES

At present two Depositories, viz. National Securities Depository Limited (NSDL) and Central Depository Services (I) Limited (CDSL) are registered with SEBI. A Depository Participant (DP) is an agent of the depository through which it interfaces with the investor. A DP can offer depository services only after it gets proper registration from SEBI. Banking services can be availed through a branch whereas depository services can be availed through a DP. The minimum net worth stipulated by SEBI for a depository is Rs. 100 crore. As on 31.03.2006, total of 538 DPs are registered with SEBI.

According to Depositories Act, 1996, a depository can be set-up by getting a certificate of commencement of business from SEBI. Normally, it shall not grant certificate unless it is satisfied that the depository has adequate system safeguards to prevent manipulation of records and transactions. There are at present two depository services in India. There name and addresses are given at the end of the discussion.

All securities held by depository shall be dematerialized and kept in a fungible form. And it shall be deemed to be the registered owner for the purposes of effecting transfer of ownership of a security on behalf of a beneficial owner. The depository as registered owner shall not have any voting rights or any other rights in respect of securities held by it. The beneficial owner only shall be entitled to all the rights and benefits and be subject to all the liabilities in respect of his securities held by a depository.

Depository shall maintain a register and an index of beneficial owners. Every depository has to furnish to the issuer information about the transfer of securities in the name of beneficial owners at frequent intervals. Beneficial owner can opt out of a depository in respect of any security by informing the depository. And it has to make appropriate entries in its records and inform the issuer. Every issuer shall, within 30 days of the receipt of the intimation and on payment of such fees as may be specified by the regulations, issue the certificate of securities to the beneficial owner or the transferee.

Monitoring of Depositories

1. *Inspection on depository*: SEBI, may by order call upon any issuer, depository, participant or beneficial owner to furnish in writing such information relating to the securities held in a depository as it may require, or authorize any person to make an inquiry or inspection in relation to the affairs of the issuer, beneficial owner, depository or participant, who shall submit a report of such inquiry or inspection to it within such period as may be specified in the order. Every director, manager, partner, secretary, officer or employee of the depository or issuer or the participant or beneficial owner shall on demand, produce before the person making the inquiry or inspection of information or such records and other

documents in his custody which have bearing on the subject matter of such inquiry or inspection.

2. *Issue directions:* SEBI may in the interest of investor, or orderly development of securities market; or to prevent the affairs of any depository or participant being conducted in a manner detrimental to the interests of investors or securities market. It may issue such directions to any depository or participant or any person associated securities market or to any issuer, as may be appropriate in the interest of investors or the securities market.

Advantages of Depository System of Trading

- A safe, convenient way to holding of securities.
- Immediate transfer of securities can be made.
- Physical transfer of securities attract stamp duty on transfer of securities, such costs are not involved here.
- Elimination of risks associated with physical certificates such as bad delivery, fake securities, delays, thefts, etc.
- Reduction in paperwork involved in transfer of securities.
- Reduction in transaction cost.
- No odd lot problem, even one share can be sold. In physical form of securities trading only a particular (minimum lot) number of shares could be traded.
- Nomination facility is available like that of holding and operating a bank account.
- Change in address recorded with DP gets registered with all companies in which investor holds securities electronically eliminating the need to correspond with each of them separately.
- Transmission of securities is done by DP eliminating correspondence with companies.
- Automatic credit into demat account of shares, arising out of bonus, split, consolidation and merger.

OPENING DEMAT ACCOUNT

1. *Opening an Account:* To avail the services of a depository an account with any of the depository participant of any depository has to be opened. For this one has to approach a DP and fill up an account opening form and follow the account opening procedure. The account opening form must be supported by Proof of Identity on whose name the account has to be opened. Signature and photograph of investor must be authenticated by an existing demat account holder or by investor's bank.
2. *Proof of Identity*: Any one of the following document can also be produced for proof of identity, such as Passport, Voters Id Card, or Driving License. The Ministry of Finance has made it compulsory from April 2006 to furnish PAN for all persons trading in demat form.
3. *Proof of Address:* A copy of ration card or passport or voter ID or driving license or bank passbook as proof of address. Investor should carry original documents for verification by an authorized official of the depository participant, under his signature. Further, investor has to sign an agreement with DP in a depository prescribed standard format, which details investor's and DPs rights and duties. DP should provide investor with a copy of the agreement and schedule of charges for future reference.
4. *Multiple Accounts:* The DP will open investors' account in the system and give an account number, which is also called BOID (Beneficiary Owner Identification Number). Holding of multiple accounts is possible but since the adoption of PAN there is no possibility of evading tax but for other conveniences a person may hold more than one account in the same name with the same DP and also with different DPs.
5. *Minimum Balance:* There is no minimum balance of securities that has to be maintained in demat my account.

6. *Accounts in Joint Name, etc:* The demat account must be opened in the same ownership pattern in which the securities are held in the physical form. If one share certificate is in individual name and another certificate is jointly with some other, two different accounts would have to be opened.
7. *Choosing a DP:* Depository/DP can be chosen by investor as per convenient irrespective of the DP of the broker.
8. *Freezing the Account:* The account can be frozen. That is the investor can lock accounts for any given period of time. Accounts can be frozen for debits (preventing transfer of securities out of accounts) or for credits (preventing any movements of hindrances into accounts) or for both.

ACCOUNT OPERATIONS

- To avail the services of a depository an investor is required to open an account with a depository participant of any depository.
- First an investor has to approach a DP and fill-up an account opening form. The account opening form must be supported by copies of anyone of the approved documents to serve as proof of identity (POI) and proof of address (POA) as specified by SEBI.
- Besides, production of PAN card in original at the time of opening of account has been made mandatory effective from April 1, 2006.
- All applicants should carry original documents for verification by an authorized official of the depository participant under his signature.
- Further, the investor has to sign an agreement with DP in a depository prescribed standard format, which details rights and duties of investor and DP. DP should provide the investor with a copy of the agreement and schedule of charges for their future reference. The DP will open the account in the system

and give an account number, which is also called BO 10 (Beneficiary Owner Identification number).

- The DP may revise the charges by giving 30 days notice in advance.
- SEBI has rationalized the cost structure for dematerialization by removing account opening charges, transaction charges for credit of securities, and custody charges.
- No charges can be levied by a depository on DP and consequently, by a DP on a Beneficiary Owner (BO) when a BO transfers all the securities lying in his account to another branch of the same DP or to another DP of the same depository or another depository, provided the BO Account/s at transferee DP and at transferor DP are one and the same.
- In case the BO Account at transferor DP is a joint account, the BO Account at transferee DP should also be a joint account in the same sequence of ownership.
- The bank account number will be mentioned on the interest or dividend warrant, so that such warrant cannot be encashed by anyone else.
- Further, cash corporate benefits such as dividend, interest will be credited to the investors' account directly through the ECS (Electronic Clearing Service) facility, wherever available, by the company.
- Since in the depository system monetary benefits on the security balances are paid as per the bank account details provided by the investor at the time of account opening, the investor must ensure that any subsequent change in bank account details is informed to the DP.
- Investor should immediately inform his/her DP, who in turn will update the records. This will obviate the need of informing different companies.
- An investor can open more than one account in the same name with the same DP and also with different DPs.
- The investor need not keep any minimum balance of securities in his/her accounts.

- Depository/DP can be chosen by investor as per convenience irrespective of the DP of the broker.
- An investor cannot open a single account for securities owned in different ownership patterns such as securities owned individually and securities owned jointly with others.
- In this case the investor may open only one account with A and B as the account holders and lodge the security certificates with different order of names for dematerialisation in the same account. An additional form called "Transposition-*cum*-Demat" form will have to be filled in. This would help you to effect change in the order of names as well as dematerialize the securities.
- The demat account cannot be operated on "either or survivor" basis like the bank account.
- If the BO authorizes any person to operate the account by executing a power of attorney and submit it to the DP, that person can operate the account on behalf of the BO.
- The names of the account holders of a BO account cannot be changed. If any change has to be effected by addition or deletion, a new account has to be opened in the desired holding pattern (names) and then transfer the securities to the newly opened account. The old account may be closed.
- The investor can submit account closure request to his DP in the prescribed form. The DP will transfer all the securities lying in the account, as per the instruction, and close the demat account.
- No charges shall be levied by a depository on DP and consequently, by a DP on a Beneficiary Owner (BO) when a BO transfers all the securities lying in his account to another branch of the same DP or to another DP of the same depository or another depository, provided the BO Accounts at transferee DP and at transferor DP are one and the same, i.e. identical in all respects. In case the BO Account at transferor DP is a joint account, the BO Account at transferee DP should also be a joint account in the

same sequence of ownership. All other transfer of securities consequent to closure of account, not fulfilling the above-stated criteria, would be treated like any other transaction and charged as per the schedule of charges agreed upon between the BO and the DP.

- Investors can freeze or lock their accounts for any given period of time, if so desired. Accounts can be frozen for debits (preventing transfer of securities out of accounts) or for credits (preventing any movements of hindrances into accounts) or for both.

The Process of Dematerialization and Rematerialization

The beneficial owner, who has entered into an agreement with a participant, should inform the participant of the details the certificate of security which is to be dematerialized and shall surrender such certificate to the participant. If such beneficial owner has appointed a custodian of securities, then he may surrender the certificate of security to the participant through his custodian of securities. The participant shall, on receipt of the above forward such details of the certificate of security to the depository and intimate about the agreement entered with the beneficial owner. For dematerialization of the physical securities, one has to fill in a DRF (Demat Request Form) which would be available with the DP and submit the same along with physical certificates one wishes to dematerialize. Even odd lot share certificates can also be dematerialized.

- Separate DRF has to be filled for each ISIN No. ISIN (International Securities Identification Number) is a unique identification number for a security.
- Surrender of certificates for dematerialization to depository participant.
- Depository participant intimates Depository of the request through the system.
- Depository participant submits the certificates to the Registrar.
- Registrar confirms the dematerialization request from depository.

- After dematerializing certificates, Registrar updates accounts and informs depository of the completion of dematerializations.
- Depository updates its accounts and informs the depository participant.
- Depository participant updates the account and informs the investor

For getting back your securities in the physical form RRF (Remat Request Form) has to be filled and request the DP for re-materialization of the balances in your securities account.

- Making request for rematerialization of shares/ securities in demat form.
- Depository participant intimates depository of the request through the system.
- Depository confirms rematerialization request to the registrar.
- Registrar updates accounts and prints certificates.
- Depository updates accounts and downloads details to depository participant.
- Registrar dispatches certificates to investor.

The issuer of demat securities shall maintain a record of certificate of securities which have been dematerialized. The issuer or its agent shall also reconcile the records of dematerialized with all the securities issued by the issuer on a daily basis. Every issuer whose securities have been declared as eligible for dematerialization in a depository, to give information to depository about book closures, record dates, dates for the payment of interest or dividend, dates for annual general meetings and other meetings, dates for redemption debentures, dates for conversion of debentures and warrants, call money dates and such other information as specified by the depository.

Dematerialized shares do not have any distinctive numbers. These shares are fungible, which means that all the holdings of a particular security will be identical and interchangeable. After the company/registrar have transferred the shares in ones name they will request one to let them know whether one wishes to receive them in electronic mode. In case one opts to receive in electronic mode one should inform the company/registrar through ones DP within 30 days of the date of option letter failing which company or registrar can despatch the certificates and the securities shall be credited to ones account. This facility is offered only for those scrips for which the issuer company has agreed to provide this facility.

Sale and Purchase of Demat Securities

The procedure for buying and selling dematerialized shares is similar to the procedure for buying and selling physical shares. The difference lies in the process of delivery and receipt of securities. For purchase, the broker will receive the securities in his account on the payout day. The broker will give instruction to its DP to debit his account and credit to the buying investor account and the investor will give 'Receipt Instruction' to DP for receiving credit by filling appropriates form. However, the investor can give standing instruction for credit into his account that will obviate the need of giving Receipt Instruction every time. For selling of securities under demat, the investor has to give delivery instruction to DP to debit your account and credit your broker's account. Such instruction should reach to your DP's office at least 24 hours before the pay-in other wise DP will accept the instruction only at your risk.

Importance of Delivery Instruction Slips (DIS)

To give the delivery instruction to DP filling up of Delivery Instruction Slip (DIS) is necessary. This DIS may be compared to cheque book of a bank account. The following precautions are to be taken in respect of DIS:

- Ensure and insist with DP to issue DIS book; do not use *loose* slips.
- Ensure that DIS numbers are pre-printed and DP takes acknowledgment for the DI$ booklet issued to investor.
- Ensure that the account number i.e., client id, is pre-stamped.

- If the account is a joint account, all the joint holders have to sign the instruction slips. Instruction cannot be executed if all joint holders have not signed.
- Avoid using loose slips
- Do not leave signed blank DIS with anyone viz., broker/sub-broker.
- Keep the DIS book under lock and key when not in use.
- If only one entry is made in the DIS book, strike out remaining space to prevent misuse by anyone.
- Investor should personally fill in target account ID and all details in the DIS.

CORPORATE BENEFITS

- It is possible to get securities allotted to in Public Offerings directly in the electronic form. In the public issue application form there is a provision to indicate the manner in which an investor wants the securities allotted. He has to mention the BO (Beneficial Owner) ID and the name and ID of the DP on the application form. Any allotment made will be credited into the BO account.
- The concerned company obtains the details of beneficiary holders and their holdings as on the date of the book closure/record date from Depositories. The payment to the investors will be made by the company through the ECS (Electronic Clearing Service) facility, wherever available. Thus, the dividend/interest will be credited to your bank account directly. Where ECS facility is not available dividend/interest will be given by issuing warrants on which your bank account details are printed. The bank account details will be those which you would have mentioned in your account opening form or changed thereafter.
- The concerned company obtains the details of beneficiary holders and their holdings as on the date of the book closure/record date from depositories.

The entitlement will be credited by the company directly into the BO account.

- In case of discrepancies in corporate benefits, one can approach the company fits RandT Agent.

Transaction Statement from DP: The DP gives a Transaction Statement periodically, which details current balances and various transactions made through the depository account. If so desired, DP may provide the Transaction Statement at intervals shorter than the stipulated ones, may be at a cost. Otherwise, Transaction Statement is received DP once in a quarter. If a transaction has been carried out during the quarter, the statement is received within fifteen days of the transaction. In case of any discrepancy in the transaction statement, the DP should be contacted. If the discrepancy cannot be resolved by the DP then Depository should, approached. In case of any complaint or problem or query also first DP contacted. If DP is unable to solve complaint or problem or query then concerned depository should be approached. Even after that the problem is not redressed SEBI approached. One may also approach SEBI directly.

Pledge of Dematerialized Securities: The beneficial owner may, with the previous approval of the depository create a pledge or hypothecation in respect of security owned by him through a depository. Every beneficial owner shall give intimation of such pledge or hypothecation to the depository and such depository shall hereupon make entries in the records accordingly. Pledging dematerialized securities is easier and more advantageous as compared to pledging physical securities. Both investor (pledgor) as well as the lender (pledgee) must have depository accounts. Investor has to initiate the pledge by submitting to DP the details of the securities to be pledged in a standard format. The pledgee has to confirm the request through his/her DP. Once this is done, securities are pledged.

All financial transactions between the pledgor and the pledgee are handled as per usual practice outside the depository system. After repayment of the loan, closure of pledge can be made by instructing the DP in a prescribed format. The pledgee on receiving the repayment will instruct his DP accordingly for the closure of the pledge. It may be noted that if the pledgee [lender] agrees, the securities offered in a pledge may be changed. It may also be noted that securities pledged are only blocked in the account of pledgor in favor of the pledgee. The pledgor would continue to receive all the corporate benefits.

Lending and Borrowing of Demat Securities

1. If any person required to deliver a security in the market does not readily have that security, he can borrow the same from another person who is willing to lend as per the Securities Lending and Borrowing Scheme.
2. Lending and borrowing has to be done through an 'Approved Intermediary' registered with SEBI. The approved intermediary would borrow the securities for further lending to borrowers. Lenders of the securities and borrowers of the securities enter into separate agreements with the approved intermediary for lending and borrowing the securities. Lending and borrowing is effected through the depository system.
3. A person can lend securities through Approved Intermediaries registered with SEBI.
4. An agreement may enter into with the approved intermediary to be a lender under this scheme. After that, lending of securities may be made at any time by submitting lending instruction to DP.
5. Intermediary may return the securities at any time or at the end of the agreed period of lending. Intermediary has to repay the securities together with any benefits received during the period of the loan.
6. The benefits will be given to the Intermediary/ borrower.

Nomination and Transmission of Demat Securities

Nomination can be made only by individuals holding beneficiary accounts either singly or jointly. Non-individuals including society, trust, body corporate, Karta of Hindu

Undivided Family, holder of power of attorney cannot nominate. Only an individual can be a nominee. A nominee shall not be a society, trust, body corporate, partnership firm, Karta of Hindu Undivided Family or a power of attorney holder.

Transmission is the process by which securities of a deceased account holder are transferred to the account of his legal heirs/nominee. Process of transmission in case of dematerialized holdings is more convenient as the transmission formalities for all securities held in a demat account can be completed by submitting documents to the DP, whereas in case of physical securities the legal heirs/nominee/surviving joint holder has to independently correspond with each company in which securities are held. The DP, after ensuring that the application is genuine, will transfer securities to the account of the claimant. The major advantage in case of dematerialized holdings is that the transmission formalities for all securities held with a DP can be completed by interaction with the DP alone, unlike in the case of physical share certificates, where the claimant will have to interact with each Issuing company or its Registrar separately. The claimant should submit to the concerned DP an application Transmission Request Form (TRF) along with the following supporting documents.

- Succession certificate
- Copy of probated will
- Letter of Administration

Custodian: A custodian is basically an organization which helps register and safeguard the securities of its clients. Besides safeguarding securities, a custodian also keeps track of corporate actions, i.e. collecting dividends, rights shares, bonus shares and other activities on behalf of its clients.

Power of SEBI on Demat

SEBI may by notification, can make rules relating to:

- Manner of maintenance of record.
- Manner in which the certificate of security shall be surrendered.

- Manner of creating a pledge or hypothecation in respect of security under demat.
- Conditions and fees payable with respect to the issue of certificate of securities to beneficial owners opting out of depository.
- Rights and obligations of the depositories, participants and the issuers.
- Eligibility criteria for admission of securities in the depository.

Procedure for Registration of Depository Participant

1. The certificate of registration as a depository participant shall be valid for five years and may be renewed by submitting an application for renewal within stipulated time period. An application has to be made to SEBI through a depository. The depository has to forward to SEBI such application not later than 30 days of its receipt, along with recommendations and a certificate that the participant complies with the eligibility criteria. The applicant shall be accompanied by a fee of Rs. 5000. SEBI may reject the application and communicate same in writing within 30 days of such decision along with the grounds for rejection.
2. SEBI may call from the applicant further information and clarification needed and permit the applicant or his authorized representative to appear before SEBI to make personal representation. SEBI has to ensure all matters relevant for the efficient and orderly functioning of a participant are possible. It must be a public financial institution, scheduled bank, foreign bank, state financial corporation, financial services institutions, custodian of securities, clearing corporation or clearing house of a Stock Exchange or a stock broker.
3. In the case of stock broker, he shall have a minimum net worth of Rs. 50 lakh and the aggregate value of portfolio securities of the beneficial owners held in

demat form in a depository through him shall not exceed the limit, i.e. 100 times of the net worth of the stock broker. If a stock broker seeks to act as a participant in more than one depository, he shall comply with the criteria specified above for each such depository.

4. Certificate of registration may be granted also to a non-banking finance company having net worth of not less than Rs. 50 lakh. Such an NBFC shall act as a participant only on behalf of itself and not on behalf of any other person. However, such a company may act as participant on behalf of any other person if it has a net worth of Rs. 50 crores in addition to the net worth specified by any other authority.
5. A registrar to an issue or a share transfer agent who has a minimum net worth of Rs. 50 lakh and has received a certificate of registration from SEBI to operate as share transfer agent/registrar to an issue can also be recognized as depository participant. SEBI should be satisfied that the applicant is eligible to be admitted as a participant the depository, it has adequate infrastructure, systems safeguards and trained staff carry on the activity as a participant, the applicant is a fit and proper person and grant of certificate of registration is in the interest of investors in the securities market.

Securities Eligible Under Demat

- Shares, scrips, stocks, bonds, debentures, debenture stock or other marketable securities of a like nature in or of any incorporated company or other body corporate.
- Units of mutual funds, rights under collective investment schemes and venture capital funds, commercial paper, certificates of deposit, securitized debt, money market instruments, government securities and unlisted securities.

Document to be Maintained by a Depository

1. Securities declared to be eligible for dematerialization in the depositary mode.
2. Records of securities dematerialized and rematerialized.
3. In respect of transfer of securities the names of the transferor, transferee and the dates.
4. A register and an index showing names of beneficial owners.
5. Details of the holdings of the securities of the beneficial owners on a daily basis.
6. Records of instructions to and fro of participants, issuers, their agents and beneficial owners.
7. Records pertaining to approval, notice, entry and cancellation of pledge or hypothecation.

Duties of Intermediaries of Dematerialization

- When an issuer or the investor exercises an option to hold his securities with a depository in dematerialized form, the issuer shall enter into an agreement with the depository to enable the investor to dematerialize the securities. Such agreement shall not however be required where the depository itself is an issuer of securities or where the Government is the issuer of securities. Where the issuer has appointed a registrar to the issue or a Share Transfer Agent, the depository shall enter into tripartite agreement with the issuer and the Registrar to the Issue/Share Transfer Agent, in respect of the securities to be declared by the depository as eligible.
- Shares or debentures or any interest therein of a company are freely transferable and every depository that has to maintain continuous electronic means of communication with all participants, issuers, issuer agents.
- The depository shall have systems and to coordinate with the issuer or its agent and the participants to reconcile the procedures of ownership of securities

with the issuer as its agent and the participants on a daily basis.

- It has to maintain continuous electronic mode of communication with all its participants, issuers, agents, clearing houses, clearing corporations and the stack exchanges and with other depositories.
- A depository shall register the transfer of a security in the name of the transferee only after ensuring that payments for such transfer have been made. SEBI to ensure that a depository has a mechanism in place to ensure that the interest of the persons buying and selling securities held in the depository are adequately protected.
- Inter-depository transfer of beneficial ownership of securities should be made by the depositories only after the change in registered ownership in favour of the transferee-depository has been effected by the issuer-company or the registrar and share transfer agent. The issuer Company or the Registrar to an issue and share transfer agent, may effect the necessary changes of the registered ownership of securities in their records and communicate the same to the depositories within twó hours.
- A participant may withdraw or transfer its account from a depository provided it is in accordance with conditions stipulated in the bye-laws of the depository.
- Every depository shall have adequate mechanisms for the purposes of reviewing, monitoring and evaluating the depository's controls, systems, procedures and safeguards.
- Every depository to take adequate measures including insurance of the interests of the beneficial owners against risks likely to be incurred an account of its activities as a depository.
- Where records are kept electronically by the depository, it shall ensure that the integrity of the automatic data processing systems is maintained at all times and take necessary precautions to ensure that the records are not last, destroyed or tampered

with and in the event of loss or destruction, ensure that sufficient back-up of records is available at all times at a different place.

- Depository has to mention where the documents and records are maintained and preserve them for 5 year.
- The depository has to extend cooperation to all the intermediaries of the demat system.
- It does not have the power to delegate any other person its functions as a depositary, without the prior approval of SEBI.

The Depository Agreement and its Contents

Every participant should execute an agreement with a beneficial owner before acting as a participant on his behalf in the lanner specified by the depository in its bye-laws and should provide for:

- For each beneficial owner separate account shall be maintained and it shall not be mixed up with the securities of other beneficial owners or with the participant's own securities.
- A participant shall register the transfer of securities to or from the beneficial owner's account, only on receipt of instructions from the beneficial owner and thereafter confirm the same to the beneficial owner.
- Every entry in the beneficial owner's account shall be supported by electronic instructions or any other mode of instruction received from the beneficial owner.
- Statement of accounts to the beneficial owner to be given in such form, manner and time as provided in the agreement with the beneficial owner.
- Participant shall allow a beneficial owner to withdraw or transfer from his account in such manner as specified in the agreement
- Participant to have adequate mechanism for the purpose of reviewing, maintaining and evaluating the participant's internal accounting.
- Every participant shall make available for the inspection of the depository in which it is a

participant, all the above mentioned records. It shall allow persons authorized by such depository to enter its premises during normal office hours and inspect its records.

- Participant shall intimate SEBI the place where the records and documents are maintained and also arrange to preserve them for a minimum period of five years.
- If records are kept electronically by the participant, it shall ensure that the integrity of the data processing system is maintained at all times and take necessary precautions to ensure that the records are not lost, destroyed or tampered with and in the event of loss or destruction, ensure that sufficient back-up of records is available at all times at a different place.
- If a participant enters into an agreement with more than one depository, it shall maintain all relevant records in respect of each depository. No participant shall assign or delegate its function as participant to any other person without the prior approval of the depository.

Securities Appellate Tribunal

An aggrieved person against the order of SEBI may within a period of 45 days from the date on which a copy of the order made by SEBI apply to SAT. A memorandum of appeal shall be presented in the prescribed form by any aggrieved person in the registry of the Securities Appellate Tribunal (SAT) within whose jurisdiction his case falls or shall be sent by registered post addressed to the Registrar of the Tribunal. A memorandum of appeal sent by post shall be deemed to have been presented in the registry on the day it was received in the registry. The Tribunal shall hold its sitting either at a place where its office is situated or at such other place.

21

Functioning of Stock Exchanges

STOCK EXCHANGE

The Securities Contracts (Regulation) Act of 1956 defines a "Stock Exchange" as "An association, organization or body of individuals, whether incorporated or not, established for the purpose of assisting, regulating and controlling, business in buying, selling and dealing in securities". In simple words, a stock exchange is an organized market for the purchase and sale of second-hand, listed industrial and financial securities. The stock exchange is otherwise known as "Secondary Market". The securities dealt within the stock exchange include the shares and debentures of public companies already issued by them. Government securities and bonds and debentures issued by municipal bodies or port trusts.

The stock exchanges should provide a well developed efficiently administered and properly regulated market system for the efficient mobilization of resources for the corporate sector and to provide liquidity on investments, by providing a fair and orderly market. The stock exchanges have a wide responsibility towards investors, corporate sector, government and the society at large.

Today stock exchanges have become part and parcel of the economic system. Without a stock exchange, the saving of the community economic progress and productive efficiency would remain underutilized. The task of mobilization and allocation of savings could be attempted in the old days by a much less specialized institution than the stock exchange. But as business and industry expanded, the economy assumed more complex nature, the need for permanent finance arose. Entrepreneurs needed money for long-term whereas investors demanded liquidity—the facility to convert their investments into cash at any given time. The answer was a ready market for investments and this was how the stock exchange came into being. Stock exchange means anybody of individuals, whether incorporated or not, constituted for the purpose of regulating or controlling the business of buying, selling or dealing in securities. These securities include shares, scrip, stocks, bonds, debentures stock or other marketable securities of a like nature in or of any incorporated company or other body corporate; the government securities and rights or interest in securities.

NATURE AND IMPORTANCE OF STOCK EXCHANGE

1. Channeling Savings

There is an extraordinary amount of ignorance and of prejudice born out of ignorance with regard to the nature and functions of stock exchange. As economic development proceeds, the scope for acquisition and ownership of capital by private individuals also grows. Along with it, the opportunity for stock exchange to render the service of stimulating private savings and channeling such savings into productive investment exists on a vast scale. These are services which the stock exchange alone can render efficiently. It is no exaggeration to say that in a modern industrialist society, which recognizes the rights of private ownership of capital, stock exchanges are not simply a convenience, they are essential. In fact, they are the markets which exist to facilitate purchase and sale of securities of companies and the securities or bonds issued by the government in the course of its borrowing operation. As our country moves towards liberalization, this tendency is certain to be strengthened. The task facing the stock exchanges is to devise the means to reach down to the masses, to draw the savings of the man in the street into productive investment, to create conditions in which many millions of little investors in cities, towns and villages will find it possible to make use of the facilities, which have so far been limited to the privileged few. This calls for far-reaching changes, institutional as well as operational.

2. Creating Stokeholders

The stock exchanges in, India, thus, have an important role to play in the building of a real shareholders democracy. Aim of the stock exchange authorities is to make it as nearly perfect in the social and ethical sense as it is in the economic. To protect the interests of the investing public, the authorities of the stock exchanges have been increasingly subjecting not only its members to a high degree of discipline, but also those who use its facilities joint stock companies and other bodies in whose stocks and shares it deals. There are stringent regulations to ensure that directors of joint stock companies keep their shareholders fully informed of the affairs of the company. In fact, some of the conditions that the stock exchange imposes upon companies before their shares are listed, are more rigorous and wholesome than the statutory provisions such as those contained in the Companies Act.

3. Free Market on Securities

Apart from providing a market that mobilizes and distributes the nation's savings, the stock exchange ensures that the flow of savings is utilized for the best purpose from the community's point of view. Free markets are not simply a matter of many buyers and sellers. If the prices at which stocks and shares change hands are to be 'fair' prices, many important conditions must be satisfied. It is the whole vast company of investors, competing with one another as buyers and sellers, which decide what the level of security prices shall be. But the public is prone to sudden swings of hope and fear. If left entirely to itself, it would produce needlessly violent and often quite irrational fluctuations. The professional dealers inside the stock exchange, and those outside who depend upon them, absorb a large part of the stock of these movements. These are valuable activities. So as to ensure that the investors reap the full benefit of them, they (dealers as well as investors) need to be regulated by a recognized code of conduct. Fair prices and free markets require, above all things, clean dealings both by professionals and by the investors and dealings based upon up-to-date and reliable information, easily accessible to all.

4. Ensures a Regulated Market

In case the investment markets are not active and free or adequate information were not available promptly and widely, the unscrupulous people would be able to manipulate particular prices for their own ends. In any of these contingencies, the relative values of securities would no longer be 'true' values, so that the relative yields obtainable from them would be mutually distorted. The signposts which, in a well regulated market show the way along which savings ought to move, would point in the wrong directions. Good businesses would get less, and indifferent or bad businesses more finance than they deserved. The savings of the community would be misdirected and wasted. In addition, some investors would incur losses which they might otherwise have avoided, and others might reap profits which not otherwise could have been made.

5. Fair Market Dealing

Any such unfairness as between one investor and another is obviously undesirable. Not for a moment, however, should it be supposed that this is the most important evil that may flow from distortion of the security markets. Much more far reaching is the fact that any misdirection of savings forces the whole society to accept a lower standard of living than it could have enjoyed had its resources been rightly used.

6. Updated Security Information

Thus a free and active market in stock and shares has become a pre-requisite for the mobilization and distribution of the nation's savings on the scale needed the support modern business. The stock exchange by a process of prolonged trial and error, which is by no means complete, has been continuously streamlining its structure to meet these wide and ever growing responsibilities to the public. The activities of the stock exchange are governed by a recognized code of conduct apart from statutory regulations. Investors, both actual and potential, are provided, through the daily stock exchange price quotations, with an up-to-the minute approval of the present worth of their holdings, in the light of all the influences that affect the position and prospectus of the companies in question. But the stock market does not determine the health of one company, it merely reflects it. It is thermometer, not the fever.

7. Helps for Assessment of True Value

The prices are sometimes distorted by excessive speculation but, by and large, they provide a continuous assessment of the current value of assets, not available to those who invest in houses or land, or other assets, not traded on the stock exchange. In fact, whether the demand for a stock is motivated by income or profits, so long as it is related to a corporation, the prices of the securities markets will play a realistic part in determining the corporation's ability to raise funds. For those enterprises that must finance externally, the receptivity of the market to their offerings establishes both the volume and cost of capital raised. For those companies that finance the bulk of their requirements through reinvested earnings, the willingness of stock holders to defer dividends in the expectation of a higher return through capital gains, establishes both the volume and cost of the capital raised. If a company's outlook is very promising and buyers bid up the security's market value, new financing becomes easier whether through external or internal sources—the earnings price ratio is reduced, and the cost of capital becomes correspondingly low.

8. Helps in Judging the Value of Securities

However, the capacity of a business to raise fresh capital for approved purposes by selling shares to the public, and the cost of capital to the borrower, do not depend mainly upon the intrinsic merits of the business. They depend upon the public's estimate of the investment merits of its shares in comparison with those of other comparable securities. But these relative investment merits are measured very largely by the prices at which the new securities are offered and the comparable existing securities quoted in the market. More precisely, they are determined by the relative yields, actual or prospective, that can be obtained in interest or dividends on the capital sum that these market prices represent. The cost of a company of raising new capital is not the price at which the new shares are sold to investors, but the effective rate of interest that investors obtain by buying at that. The 'price' of new capital is the interest yield that has to be offered in order to secure it. Other things being equal, investors will readily accept a lower interest yield for a progressive and promising company than they will demand from a slow moving and inefficient one.

9. Used as a Security for Borrowings

Sometimes, to secure the working capital from the banks, individual businessmen, partnerships and corporations provide the stocks and shares of companies as collateral. Securities which are listed and for which published quotations are readily available make the satisfactory collateral for such short-term loan taken by the industries to serve the purpose of working capital. Industries are therefore, particularly appreciative of the usefulness of collateral value of listed securities. In this respect the stock exchange indirectly helps the industries to secure working capital from the banks.

10. Creates Liquidity

Expanded business needed permanent finance and could not expand without it. Investors needed 'liquidity'—the ability to turn their investment into cash at any time and would not invest without it. It was this dilemma that brought the stock exchange into being. As business (and governments, too, for that matter) could not ordinarily return invested capital, an investor could not get cash for his investment unless he found somebody else who was ready to buy it from him to take over his share in the company's 'Joint Stock', or his holdings of government securities. What was needed was a market for investments. The job of the stock exchange and its members is to satisfy that need—to bring the buyers and sellers of investments together, and to make the 'exchange' of stock between them as simple and fair a process as possible.

11. Ensures Flow of Funds to Industry

The tremendous important and socially useful service that the stock exchange renders to the industries is with regard to the shifting of the burden of financing from the management to those of the investors. It will be realized more so from the fact that there is always a conflict of motives between the industries and the investors. Industries require long-term finance with the end in view of locking it up in land, buildings, plants, etc. Investors, on the other hand, have liquidity preference, that is to say they want to get back the money as and when they would need it. In other words, while the industries require permanent finance, the investors can lend it only for a while because the money that they lend to the industries comes from their savings (part of the income not spent presently) which are made for future spending over contingencies. It is not merely the individual investors alone who suffer from the 'liquidity preference' complex, institutional investors too have the same motive.

12. Benefits the Society in General

It is generally thought that a stock exchange serves only those who have money to invest and securities to sell. But a stock benefits the whole community in a variety of ways. By enabling producers to raise capital, it indirectly gives employment to millions of people and helps consumers to get the goods needed by them. Again, all those who save and put their money either in banks or in life insurance, invest in buying shares and securities, are also helped by stock exchanges, because the institutions with which they place their savings avail themselves of the services of the exchanges to invest the money collected by them.

13. Inducement for Saving and Investment

It is evident from the foregoing analysis that the ready liquidity and constant evaluation of assets, together with the wide range of available investments act as a powerful inducement to save and invest and draw the savings of the community into the channels which are expected to be most productive. It would be difficult to find a more effective method of doing this. In addition, the overall trend of prices and volume of business on the stock exchange serve as an economic barometer which faithfully registers the changing events and opinion about the investment outlook. Even allowing for the aberrations of speculation, this mirror of the investment scene is one that neither economists nor businessmen nor the government, charged with the formulation of economic policy, can afford to ignore.

ORGANISATIONAL STRUCTURE OF THE SECONDARY MARKET

1. Non-profit Organizations

The stock exchanges are the exclusive centers for trading of securities. At present, there are 23 operative stock exchanges in India. Most of the stock exchanges in the country are incorporated as 'Association of Persons' as Section 25 companies under the Companies Act. These are organized as 'mutual companies' and are considered beneficial in terms of tax benefits and matters of compliance. The trading members, who provide broking services also own, control and manage the stock exchanges. They elect their representatives to regulate the functioning of the exchange, including their own activities. Until recently, the area of operation/jurisdiction of an exchange was specified at the time of its recognition, which in effect precluded competition among the exchanges. These are called regional exchanges. In order to provide an opportunity to investors to invest/trade in the securities of local companies, it is mandatory for the companies, wishing to list their securities, to list on the regional stock exchange nearest to their registered office. If they so wish, they can seek listing on other exchanges as well. Monopoly of the exchanges within their allocated area, regional aspirations of the people and mandatory listing on the regional stock exchange resulted in multiplicity of exchanges. As a result, we have 24 exchanges in the country recognized over a period of time to enable investors across the length and breadth of the country to access the market.

2. Network-based Trading

The three newly set-up exchanges—Over the Counter Exchange of India (OTCEI), National Stock Exchange of India

(NSE) and Inter-connected Stock Exchange of India (ICSE) were permitted since their inception to have nation-wide trading. Listing on these exchanges was considered adequate compliance with the requirement of listing on the regional exchange. SEBI recently allowed all exchanges to set up trading terminals anywhere in the country. Many of them have already expanded trading operations to different parts of the country. The trading platforms of a few exchanges are now accessible from many locations. Further, with extensive use of information technology, the trading platforms of a few exchanges are also accessible from anywhere through the internet and mobile devices. This made a huge difference in a geographically vast country like India. It significantly expanded the reach of the exchange to the homes of ordinary investors and assuaged the aspirations of people to have exchanges in their vicinity. The issuers/investors now prefer to list/trade on exchanges providing nationwide network rather than on regional exchanges. Consequently, territorial jurisdiction of an exchange, opportunity to invest in securities of local companies through listing on regional exchanges, and convenience of trading from a nearby exchange lost relevance.

3. Membership

The trading platform of a stock exchange is accessible only to brokers. The broker enters into trades in exchanges either on his own account or on behalf of clients. The clients may place their orders with them directly or through a sub-broker indirectly. A broker is admitted to membership of an exchange in terms of the provisions of the Security Contracts (Regulation) Act, 1956 (SCRA), the Securities and Exchange Board of India (SEBI) Act, 1992, the rules, circulars, notifications, guidelines, etc. prescribed thereunder and the byelaws, rules and regulations of the concerned exchange. No stock broker or sub-broker is allowed to buy, sell or deal in securities, unless he or she holds a certificate of registration granted by SEBI. A broker/sub-broker complies with the code of conduct prescribed by SEBI. The stock exchanges are free to stipulate stricter requirements for its members than/those stipulated by SEBI. The minimum standards stipulated by NSE for membership are in excess of the minimum norms laid down by SEBI. The standards for admission of members laid down by NSE stress on factors, such as, corporate structure, capital adequacy, track record, education, experience, etc. and reflect a conscious endeavour to ensure quality broking services.

4. Corporate Brokers

The authorities have been encouraging corporatization of the broking industry. Over time, a number of brokers - proprietor firms and partnership firms—have converted themselves into corporates. As at end-March 2001, there were 9,782 brokers (including multiple registrations) registered with SEBI as compared to 9,192 brokers as at end-March 2000. Of these, 3,808 brokers, accounting for, nearly 39% of total, were corporate entities. It may be noted that around 88% of brokers on NSE were corporatised as at end-March 2001, followed by OTCEI with 77% corporate brokers. Some of the brokers hold multiple memberships of exchanges, i.e., they trade on more than one exchange.

5. Legislations

Regulatory Framework of Stock Exchanges

The four main legislations governing the securities market are:

- The SEBI Act, 1992 which establishes SEBI to protect investors and develop and regulate securities market;
- The Companies Act, 1956, which sets out the code of conduct for the corporate sector in relation to issue, allotment and transfer of securities, and disclosures to be made in public issues;
- The Securities Contracts (Regulation) Act, 1956, which provides for regulation of transactions in securities through control over stock exchanges; and
- The Depositories Act, 1996 which provides for electronic maintenance and transfer of ownership of demat securities.
- *Securities Contracts (Regulation) Act, 1956*: It provides for direct and indirect control of virtually all aspects

of securities trading and the running of stock exchanges and aims to prevent undesirable transactions in securities. It gives Central Government regulatory jurisdiction over (a) stock exchanges, through a process of recognition and continued supervision, (b) contracts in securities, and (c) listing of securities on stock exchanges. As a condition of recognition, a stock exchange complies with conditions prescribed by Central Government. Organized trading activity in securities takes place on a specified recognized stock exchange. The stock exchanges determine their own listing regulations, which have to conform to the minimum listing criteria set out in the Rules.

- *Companies Act, 1956:* It deals with issue, allotment and transfer of securities and various aspects relating to company management. It provides for standards of disclosure in public issues of capital, particularly in the fields of company management and projects, information about other listed companies under the same management, and management perception of risk factors. It also regulates underwriting, the use of premium and discounts on issues, rights and bonus issues, payment of interest and dividends, supply of annual report and other information.
- *SEBI Act, 1992:* The SEBI Act, 1992 was enacted to empower SEBI with statutory powers for:
  - (a) Protecting the interests of investors in securities.
  - (b) Promoting the development of the securities market.
  - (c) Regulating the securities market.

Its regulatory jurisdiction extends over corporates in the issuance of capital and transfer of securities, in addition to all intermediaries and persons associated with securities market. It can conduct enquiries, audits and inspection of all concerned and adjudicate offences under the Act. It has powers to register and regulate all market intermediaries and to penalise them in case of violations of the provisions of the Act, Rules and

Regulations made thereunder. SEBI has full autonomy and authority to regulate and develop an orderly securities market.

- *Depositories Act, 1996:* The Depositories Act, 1996 provides for the establishment of depositories V1 securities with the objective of ensuring free transferability of securities with speed, accuracy and security by:
  - (a) Making securities of public limited companies freely transferable subject to certain exceptions.
  - (b) Dematerializing the securities in the depository mode.
  - (c) Providing for maintenance of ownership records in a book entry form. In order to streamline the settlement process, the Act envisages transfer of ownership of securities electronically by book entry without making the securities move from person to person. The Act has made the securities of all public limited companies freely transferable, restricting the company's right to use discretion in effecting the transfer of securities, and the transfer deed and other procedural requirements under the Companies Act have been dispensed with.

6. Rules and Regulations

The Government has framed rules under the SCRA, SEBI Act and the Depositories Act. SEBI has framed regulations under the SEBI Act and the Depositories Act for registration and regulation of all market intermediaries, and for prevention of unfair trade practices, insider trading, etc. Under these Acts, Government and SEBI issue notifications, guidelines, and circulars, which need to be complied with by market participants. The self-regulatory organisations (SROs) like stock exchanges have also laid down their rules of game.

7. Regulators

The absence of conditions of perfect competition in the securities market makes the role of regulator extremely important. The regulator ensures that the market participants behave in a desired manner so that securities market continue to be a major source of finance for corporates and government and the interest of investors are protected. The responsibility for regulating the securities market is shared by Department of Economic Affairs (DBA), Department of Company Affairs (DCA), Reserve Bank of India (RBI) and SEBI. The activities of these agencies are co-ordinated by a High Level Committee on Capital Markets. The orders of SEBI under the securities laws are appealable before a Securities Appellate Tribunal (SAT).

Most of the powers under the SCRA are exercisable by DBA, while a few others by SEBI. The powers of the DEA under the SCRA are also concurrently exercised by SEBI. The powers in respect of the contracts for sale and purchase of securities, gold-related securities, money market securities and securities derived from these securities and ready forward contracts in debt securities are exercised concurrently by RBI. The SEBI Act and the Depositories Act are mostly administered by SEBI. The rules under the securities laws are framed by government and regulations by SEBI. All these are administered by SEBI. The powers under the Companies Act relating to issue and transfer of securities and non-payment of dividend are administered by SEBI in case of listed public companies and public companies proposing to get their securities listed. The SROs ensure compliance with their own rules as well as with the rules relevant for them under the securities laws.

STOCK MARKETS AND FINANCIAL DEVELOPMENT IN INDIA

1. *Stock markets enhance economic development:* The role of stock markets as a source of economic growth has been widely debated. It is well recognized that stock markets influence economic activity through the creation of liquidity. Liquid financial market was an important enabling factor behind most of the early innovations that characterized the early phases of the Industrial Revolution. Recent advances in this area reveal that stock markets remain an important conduit for enhancing development. Many profitable

investments necessitate a long-term commitment of capital, but investors might be reluctant to relinquish control of their savings for long periods. Liquid equity markets make investments less risky and more attractive. At the same time, companies enjoy permanent access to capital raised through equity issues. By facilitating longer-term and more profitable investments, liquid markets improve the allocation of capital and enhance the prospects for long-term economic growth. Furthermore, by making investments relatively less risky, stock market liquidity can also lead to more savings and investments.

2. *Increased market capitalization:* Over the years, the stock market in India has become strong. The number of stock exchanges increased from 8 in 1971 to 9 in 1980 to 21 in 1993 and further to 23 as at end-March 2000. The number of listed companies also moved up over the same period from 1,599 to 2,265 and thereafter to 5,968 in 1990 and 9.871 in March 2000. The market capitalization at BSE as a percentage of GDP at current market prices also improved considerably from around 28 per cent in the early nineties to over 45 per cent at the end of the nineties, after witnessing a fall in certain intervening years. In 1998, India ranked twenty-first in the world in terms of market capitalization, nineteenth in terms of total value traded and second in terms of number of listed domestic companies. Though the Indian stock market was founded more than a century ago, it remained quite dormant from independence in 1947 up to the early eighties, with a capitalization ratio (market capitalization to GDP) of only 4 per cent. However, the patterns of demand for capital have undergone significant changes during the last two decades and improved stock market activity.

3. *Capital market reforms led to development:* It may be recalled that till the nineties, institutional term-lending acted as the primary source of Industrial finance in India. Financial Institutions raised money

through Government guaranteed bonds at low rates of interest, which, in turn, lent funds at concessional rates of interest. This system provided corporates a cushion to absorb the relatively high risk of implementing new projects. This, in turn, discouraged the corporates to raise risk capital from equity markets. On this account, the debt market segment, which is sensitive to 'economic information' also remained underdeveloped and illiquid. With the onset of the reforms process in the nineties, institutions had to raise resources at market related rates. At the same time, the market has witnessed the Introduction of several new customized bonds at maturities tailored to suit investor needs and with market-driven coupons. Along with this development, a number of measures were initiated to reform the stock markets, which helped to improve the overall activity in the stock market significantly. The turnover ratio increased from a low of 6.7 per cent at the beginning of the nineties, to reach 35.1 per cent in 1999-2000, excepting certain years of relative inactivity.

4. *Control through Capital market regulator*: The Indian capital market has experienced a significant structural transformation over the years. It now compares well with those in developed markets. This was deemed necessary because of the gradual opening of the economy and the need to promote transparency in alternative sources of financing. The regulatory and supervisory structure has been overhauled with most of the powers for regulating the capital market having been vested with the Securities and Exchange Board of India (SEBI). Apart from changes in the fundamental factors, information asymmetries and the associated constraints to efficient price discovery remain at the heart of the volatile movements in stock prices. The extent of stock price volatility is also influenced by the extent of integration between the domestic and international capital markets as well as the regulatory framework

governing the stock market. In India, two most important factors which had a significant bearing on the behaviour of stock prices during the nineties were net investments by FIIs and trends in the international stock exchanges, especially NASDAQ.

LISTING OF SECURITIES

The official listing denotes inclusion of the securities of a company in the list of stock exchange stocks. Section 73(1) of the Companies Act, 1956, insists company intending to offer shares or debentures to the public for listing. A company should make an application for listing to one or more recognized exchanges. Every recognized stock exchange, has the power to make bye-laws for listing of securities on the stock exchange, the inclusion of any security for the purpose of dealings and the suspension or withdrawal of any such from trading. The Power to make bye-laws is subject to the previous approval of he central Government. Further, the Central Government has the power to make or amend bye-laws of recognized stock exchanges.

Listing Requirements: The Securities Contracts (Regulation) Rules, 1957, provides for requirements with respect to the listing of securities on recognized stock exchanges. This rule is very exhaustive and comprehensive. The same is reproduced below:

> A public company as defined under the Companies Act, 1956, desirous of getting its securities listed on a recognized stock exchange, shall apply for the purpose to the stock exchange and forward along with its application the following documents and particulars:
>
> 1. Memorandum and Articles of Association and, in the case of debentures issue, a copy of the trust deed.
> 2. Copies of all prospectuses or statements in lieu of prospectuses issued by the company at any time.
> 3. Copies of offers for sale and circulars or advertisements offering any securities for subscription of sale during the last five years.

4. Copies of balance sheets and audited accounts for the last five years, or in the case of new companies, for such shorter period for which accounts have been made up.
5. A statement showing: (i) dividends and cash bonuses, if any, during the last ten years (or such shorter period as the company has in existence, whether as a private or public company); and (ii) dividends or interest in arrears, if any.
6. Certified copies of agreements or other documents relating to arrangements with or between: (i) vendors and/or promoters, (ii) underwriters and sub-underwriters; and (iii) brokers and sub-brokers.
7. Certified copies of agreements with: (i) managing agents and secretaries and treasures; (ii) selling agents; and (iii) managing directors and technical directors; (iv) general manager, salesman, manager or secretary.
8. Certified copy of every letter, report, balance sheet, value of contract, court order or other document, part of which is reproduced or referred to in any prospectus, offer for sale, circulated advertisement offering securities for subscription or sale, during the last five years.
9. A statement containing particulars of the dates of, and parties to all material contracts, agreements (including agreements or technical advice and collaboration), concessions and similar other documents.
10. A brief history of the company since its incorporation giving details of its activities including any reorganization, reconstruction or amalgamation, changes in its capital structure (authorized issued and subscribed) and debenture borrowings, if any.
11. Particulars of shares and debentures issued: (i) for consideration other than cash, whether in whole or in part; (ii) at a premium or discount; or (iii) in pursuance of an option.
12. A statement containing particulars of any commission, brokerage, discount or other special

terms including an option for the issue of any kind of the securities granted to any person.

13. Certified copies of: (i) letters of consent of the Controller of Capital Issues; and (ii) agreements, if any, with the Industrial Finance Corporation, Industrial Credit and Investment Corporation and similar bodies.
14. Particulars of shares forfeited.
15. A list of highest ten holders of each class or kind of securities of the company.
16. Particulars of shares or debentures for which permission to deal is applied for.

OBLIGATIONS UNDER A LISTING AGREEMENT

An applicant company shall satisfy the stock exchange that:

1. Its Articles of Association provide for the following among others:
   - that the company shall use a common form of transfer;
   - the fully paid shares will be free from all lien, while in the case partly paid shares, the company's lien, if any, will be restricted to moneys called or payable at a fixed time in respect of such shares;
   - that any among paid-up in advance of calls on any share carry interest but shall not entitle the holder of the share participate in respect thereof, in a dividend subsequently declare;
   - there will be no forfeiture of unclaimed dividends before the claim becomes barred by law; and
   - That option or right to call or shares shall not be given to any person except with the sanction of the company in general meeting.
2. At least sixty percent of each class or kind of securities issued by the company was offered to the

public for subscription through advertisement in newspapers for a period not less than two days.

3. A company applying for listing shall, as a condition precedent, undertake *inter alia:*
   - that letters of allotment will be issued simultaneously;
   - that letters of right will be issued simultaneously;
   - that letters of allotment, acceptance or rights will be serially numbered, printed on good quality paper and examined and signed by a responsible officer of the company;
   - that letters of allotment and renunciable letters of right will contain a provision for splitting; and
   - That letters of allotment and letters of right will state how the next payment of interest or dividend on the securities will be calculated.
4. To issue, when so required, receipts for all securities deposited with it whether for registration, sub-division, exchange or for other purposes.
5. To issue, when so required, consolidation and renewal certificates in denominations of the market unit of trading to split certificates, letters of allotment, letters of right, and transfer, renewal, consolidation and split receipts into smaller units, to split call notices issue. duplicates thereof and not require any discharge on call receipts, and to accept the discharge of members of stock exchange on split, consolidation and renewal receipts as good and sufficient without insisting on the discharge of the registered holders.
6. When documents are lodged for sub-division or consolidation or renewal through the clearing house of the exchanges:
   - to accept the discharge of an official of the stock exchange clearing house on the company's split receipts and consolidation receipts and renewal receipts as good as sufficient discharge without insisting on the discharge of the registered holders;

- to verify when the company is unable to issue certificates or split receipt or consolidation receipts or renewal receipt immediately on lodgement whether the discharge of the registered holders, on the documents lodged for sub-division or consolidation or renewal and their signatures on the relative transfers are in order.
- On production of the necessary documents by shareholders or by members of the exchange, to make on transfers an endorsement to the effect that the power of attorney or letters of a administration or death certificate or certificate of the Controller of Estate or similar other document has been duly exhibited to and register by the company.
- To issue certificates in respect of shares or debentures lodged for transfer within a period of one month of the date of lodgement or transfer and to issue balance certificates to the same person of whom the transfer is accompanied by a certificate.

7. Other obligations :
   - To advise the stock exchange of the date of the board meeting which the declaration or recommendation of a dividend or the issue of right or bonus share will be considered.
   - To recommend or declare all dividends and or cash bonuses at least five days before the commencement of the closure of its transfer books.
   - To notify the stock exchange of any material change in the general character or nature of the company's business.
   - To notify the stock exchange of any change: (i) in the company's directorate by death, resignation, removal or otherwise; (ii) of managing director, managing agent or secretaries and treasurers; and (iii) of auditors

appointed to audit the books of accounts of the company.

- To forward to the stock exchange copies of statutory and annual reports and audited accounts as soon as issued, including director's report.
- To forward to the stock exchange as soon as they are issued copies of all other notices and circulars sent to the shareholder including proceedings of ordinary and extraordinary genera meetings of the company and to fill with the stock exchange certified copies of resolutions of the company as soon as sue resolutions become effective.
- To notify the stock exchange prior to intimating the shares new issue of securities whether by way of, offer bonus or otherwise and the manner in which it is proposed to or allot the same.
- To notify the stock exchange in the event for reissue or forfeited securities or the issue of securities held in reserve future issue.
- To notify the stock exchange of any other alteration including calls.
- To close the transfer books only for the purpose of declaration of dividend or issue of right or bonus shares or for other purposes.
- To forward to the stock exchange an annual return immediately or after each annual general meeting.
- To grant to shareholders the right or renunciation in all cases of issue of rights, privileges and benefits.
- To promptly notify the stock exchange: (i) of any action which will result in the redemption, cancellation or retirement in whole or in part of any securities listed on the exchange; (ii) of the intention to make a drawing of such securities, intimating at the same time the date of the drawing and the period of the closing of the

transfer books (or the date of the striking of the balance) for the drawing; and (iii) of the amount of securities outstanding after any drawing has been made.

- To intimate the stock exchange any other information necessary to enable the shareholders to appraise the position of the company and to avoid the establishment of a false market in the shares of the company.
- That in the event of the application of listing being granted, such listing shall be subject to the rules and bye-laws of the exchange in force time to time and that the company will comply within a reasonable time, with such further listing requirements as may be promulgated by the exchange as a condition for new listings.
- A fresh application for listing will be necessary in respect of all new issues desired to be dealt in, provided that, where such new securities are identical in all respects with those already listed, admission to dealings will granted on the company intimating to the stock exchange particulars of new issues.
- A recognized stock exchange may suspend or withdraw admission of dealing in the securities of a company or body corporate for non-compliance with, any of the conditions of admission or for any other reason to be recorded in writing, by the stock exchange, Provided, where a recognized stock exchange has withdrawn to dealings in any security or where suspension of admission to has continued for a period exceeding three months, the company concerned may appeal to the Central Government and the Government may, after giving the stock exchange an opportunity of heard vary or set aside the decision of the stock exchange and the orders of the Central Government shall be carried out by the exchange.

- A recognized stock exchange may, either at its own discretion in accordance with the orders of the Central Government, shall restore or re-admit to dealings in securities. The Central Government may, at its own discretion or the recommendation of a recognized stock exchange, waive or relax the enforcement of any or all of the requirements with respect to listing prescribed.

INTERMEDIARIES IN STOCK EXCHANGE ACTIVITIES

Functional specialization of members at the stock exchanges helps a lot in making it a free, active and continuous market. It is, therefore, common at the leading foreign stock exchanges. In India, the stock exchange rules, by-laws and regulations do not prescribe any functional distinction between members. However, as' a matter of fact, there is a fairly well-established specialization under the following main categories:

Brokers: They act as intermediaries between buyers and sellers of securities. The main job is to bring the buyers and sellers together and help them in making a deal. They charge commission from both the parties and therefore they are known as commission agents. Selection of a broker through the investor or seller's Bank for purchase or sale to be made. The bankers approach their brokers at exchange for dealings on behalf of their customers. The broker on the recommendation of the bank opens the client's account. Assurance is given by the banker about the financial condition of the client. Brokers in order to succeed in their business must provide an office with adequate financial information sources, current quotation facilities and sales representative—advisers to enable investors to make the decisions. They must know when to find, where to find the best unlisted markets for their customers and how to obtain new securities currently being offered by underwriters and distributors. And they must arrange memberships in or contacts with the principal stock exchange of the country, for a very large percentage of all securities buying and selling is done on the stock exchanges. They must also offer their customers incidental services in the financing of their transactions and in the storage of their securities.

Commission broker: Almost all members act as commission brokers. The commission broker executes buying and selling orders on the floor of the exchange. For that, he charges a commission not exceeding the official scale of brokerage.

Floor broker: The floor brokers are not officially attached to other members. The floor broker executes orders for any members and receives as his compensation a share of the brokerage charged by the commission broker to his constituent. Such brokers are not found on Indian stock exchanges.

Dealers in non-cleared securities: The dealer in non-cleared securities specializes in buying and selling on his own account shares which are not in the active list. He is generally prepared to buy what is on offer and sell what is required but the price at which he deals varies with the activity of the particular stock.

Odd-lot dealer: The odd-lot dealer specializes in buying and selling in amount less than the prescribed trading units or lots. He buys odd lots and makes them up into marketable trading units. He likewise sells odd-lots obtained by buying or by splitting up round lots. The odd-lot dealer does not rely on commission but earns his profit on the difference between the prices at which he buys and sells.

Financier: The budliwalla or financier lends money to the market by taking up delivery on the due date at the end of the clearing for those who wish to carryover their purchases; or loans securities to the market when it is short by giving delivery on the due date at the end of the clearing for those who wish to carry over their sales. His purchases or sales on the last date of the current clearing are matched by corresponding concurrent sales to or purchase from the same party for the ensuing clearing. The difference between the two is contango or the backwardation charge for the continuation facility offered to the market, i.e. for loaning money or stock for a short period of two to three weeks. The loan is fully secured and the return is governed by the technical position of the market and the ruling rate of interest.

Arbitrageur: The arbitrageur specializes in making purchases and sales in different markets at the same time and profits by the differences in prices between the two centers. Arbitrage depends on the number of securities dealt in the common on more than one stock exchange and the existence of ready means of communication.

Security dealer: The security dealer specializes in buying and selling gilt-edged securities, that is, securities issued by the Central and State Governments and by statutory public bodies such as Municipal Corporation, Improvement Trusts and Electricity Boards. He acts mainly as jobber and is prepared to take risks inherent in the ready purchase and sale of securities to meet current requirements. The gilt-edged market is over-the-counter market, and each purchase and sale has to be separately negotiated. The market, therefore, tends to be restricted. Moreover, as a result of their active touch with RBI as well as with commercial banks, the LIC and other institutional investors, gilt-edged securities enjoy the benefit of extremely fine quotes.

Jobbers: They are security merchants dealing in shares, debentures as independent operators. They deal with securities on their own behalf and earn through price changes. They cannot deal on behalf of public. Generally two prices are quoted by the Jobbers one at which they want to sell and the other at which they want to purchase the security. The difference between the prices is the jobber's profit which is known as Jobber's turn. For example a jobber may quote equity shares of ABC Ltd., at Rs. 55 to Rs. 57. This indicates that a Jobber is prepared to purchase these shares at Rs. 55 each and sells Rs. 57 each. The difference between these two prices is the Jobber's return. The taravniwalla or jobber may be a jobber or specialist who specializes in stocks located at the same trading post. He trades in and out of the market for a small difference in price and as such is an important factor in "making a market", i.e. maintaining a continuous and liquid market in stock in which he specializes.

Stag: A stag is a speculator who applies for shares in new companies to sell it at a premium if the shares are allotted to him. He selects those companies shares that are more in demand and are likely to be issued at a premium. These speculators apply for shares in large numbers so that he gets some allotment in case there are over subscription.

TRADING MECHANISM

The rules and procedures for buying and selling securities are the same in all the recognized stock exchanges in India. The procedures are listed below:

Purchase of Shares: Purchasing of shares can be divided into two parts, namely purchase of existing shares from the market (i.e., secondary market) and purchase of shares of companies issuing fresh shares (i.e. primary market).
Purchase of existing shares from the market: Placing the order with the broker: In the case of purchasing shares of existing companies, the order must be placed with the broker. The broker will require certain sum of money as margin money to be given along with the order.

- *Receipt of Contract Note*: When the shares are purchased a contract note is sent to the client as to the number, rate and date of purchase. Many brokers require their clients to pay the balance amount (Purchase Price less Margin Money) on receipt of contract.
- *Intimation of delivery*: When the broker receives the share certificate(s) and transfer deed(s) from the seller he intimates the client to take those shares and make payment in case it has been made. In case of outstation clients, the broker will call for balance payment and then send the share certificate(s) and transfer deed(s) through registered post.
- *Sending shares for transfer*: The last stage is the transfer of shares in the name of the purchaser. The buyer signs in the transferee(s) column of the transfer deed(s). The transfer deed is filled up if not already done. Share transfer stamps have to be affixed on the back of the transfer deed(s). Thus the share certificate(s) and complete transfer deed(s) are now ready which are sent at the share transfer department of the company concerned. The share certificates are received duly transferred within three months.

Purchase of Shares being Issued by a Company

- *Filling application form with application money*: The company issuing the shares circulates printed application forms on which the intending purchaser has to fill-in the details like Name, Address, Occupation, Age, Specimen signatures, etc. Application money per share multiplied by the number of shares applied for has to be paid along with this application.
- *Receipt of allotment letter/refund order*: Depending on response the company announces an allotment procedure. If the shares are allotted on investor's application, he will receive the allotment letter otherwise a refund order of the amount applied for will be received. Some companies send share certificates with the allotment letter.
- *Payment of allotment money and call money*: In most companies the face value of the share is not asked for with application. The company fixes allotment money and call money per share which it asks the shareholders to pay at certain intervals decided by the board of directors of that company.
- *Endorsement of payment on share certificate*: In companies where share certificates are issued before call money on those shares is received, the company makes an endorsement on the share to show that how many calls have been paid by the shareholders.

Sale of Shares

- *Placing the order with the broker*: The order of the sale of shares has to be placed with the broker, as an individual cannot sell or purchase shares at the stock exchange directly. Only members of that particular stock exchange can transact business at that stock exchange either for themselves or on behalf of their clients. Usually along with the order the broker will ask investor to submit the share certificate(s) and transfer deed(s). The seller must sign at the transferor(s) column on the transfer deed(s).

- *Receipt of contract note*: On the sale of Shares the broker issues a Contract Note. A contract indicates the number of shares sold, the rate per share, the date of sale and the terms and conditions governing the sale. A contract note binds the broker and his client. In case the client is not satisfied he must notify his broker immediately on receipt of the contract.
- *Delivery of share certificate(s) and transfer deed(s)* : The share certificate(s) and transfer deed(s) have to be delivered by the broker to the broker of the same stock exchange, member of another stock exchange or another of his clients, to whom he had sold the shares. The stock exchanges have fixed delivery days. On this day, the members deliver to each other the shares they have sold and purchased. The delivery day avoids the confusion that would arise if members could deliver on any day of their choice.
- *Receipt of payment*: Payment is made by the broker usually after 10 to 15 days from the day the shares have been sold and the share certificate(s) along with valid transfer(s) for the same are given to the broker. The payment is made according to the rate appearing on the contract as the rate is calculated after deducting the commission payable to the broker.

Placing Orders : The client places the order for purchase and sale of securities after the selection of the broker. The broker guides the client regarding the purchase and sale of securities and the favourable time for purchase and sale, etc. The client then informs the broker regarding the purchase of shares, number of shares to be purchased, the price to be paid, etc. The prices contracted are paid or received as agreed. The broker then tries to purchase the securities as far as to the nearest price offered by the client. The broker is given the choice for bargaining for the purchase or sale of securities.

Making the Contract: There are different trading posts for different types of securities in the trading floor of the stock exchange. The clerk of the broker goes to the concerned post and expresses his intention to buy or sell the security. A deal is struck when the other party also agrees for the sale. The parties note the bargain in their notebooks.

SETTLEMENT

The selling broker after receiving the price, hands over the transfer form and share certificates to the Buying broker. Different procedure is adopted for settlement of ready delivery and forward contracts. The members of recognized Stock Exchanges are permitted to enter into transactions in securities in different modes of settlement.

Settlement of Ready Delivery Contracts: If the settlement is done by giving actual delivery of securities after receiving the price is called liquidation in full.

Settlement of Forward Delivery Contracts: These contracts are done for speculative purposes. Only active market securities are traded in forward contracts. The settlement of these contracts can be done in anyone of the following ways.

Liquidation in Full: After crossing all intermediary purchases and sales the payment is received and securities are delivered.

Liquidation by payment of differences: The purchase or sale of securities is finalized at the ruling price. Here the securities are not delivered but only the current prices and the difference in prices is noted.

Carry over to the next settlement: If the contract is not settled but carried over to a future date by the buyer is called carryover. For this concession the buyer has to pay a certain amount to the seller, which is known as Badla or Contango charge.

Spot delivery: Delivery and payment takes place on the same day as the date of the contract or on the next day.

Hand delivery: Delivery and payment takes place within the time or on the date stipulated when entering into the bargain, which time or date shall not be more than 14 days following the date of the Contract.

Special delivery: Delivery and payment takes place within any time exceeding 14 days following the date of contract as may be stipulated when entering into the bargain and permitted by the Governing Board or the President.

TYPES OF MARKETS

Bull market: A Bull is an operator who expects a rise in the price of securities in the near future. He purchases the securities with the intention of selling them at a higher price in the future. He as a speculator deal with the differences of prices and does not take the delivery of the securities. He is called a Bull because a bull throws his victims up in the air. A Speculator by placing huge orders tries to raise the prices of the securities. Action can be taken against a speculator, however, that no such action shall be taken by exchange without affording to the company or body corporate reasonable opportunity by a notice in writing, stating the reasons for the proposed action.

Bear market: Bear is a speculator who anticipates the prices to fall. Bear speculator purchases shares during bearish trend and sell them at future date for a good price. He will earn profits out of these transactions if the prices as per the expectation of the Bear move up. He is called a Bear because he makes the victims fall down to the ground. Bear takes the differences, if price falls down but does not take of securities. In case if there is a rise in prices then he will have to difference between the prevailing prices and the price at which he bought the security. A Market is said to be bearish when there is a strong tendency of fall in prices. In case if there is no fall in prices of the securities then they shall start spreading rumours to pressurize price downwards.

ISSUES CONNECTED WITH TRANSFER OF SECURITIES

1. *Transfer of securities by procedure established:* To effect a transfer in the physical mode the securities should be sent to the company along with a valid, duly executed and stamped transfer deed duly signed by or on behalf of the transferor (seller) and transferee (buyer). It would be a good idea to retain photo-copies of the securities and the transfer deed when they are sent to the company for transfer. It is essential that you send them by registered post with

acknowledgement due and watch out for the receipt of the acknowledgement card. If you do not receive the confirmation of receipt within a reasonable period, you should immediately approach the postal authorities for confirmation. Sometimes, for your own convenience, you may choose not to transfer the securities immediately. This may facilitate easy and quick selling of the securities. In that case you should take care that the transfer deed remains valid. However, in order to avail the corporate benefits like the dividends, bonus or rights from the company, it is essential that you get the securities transferred in your name.

2. *Company procedure:* On receipt of your request for transfer, the company proceeds to transfer the securities as per provisions of the law. In case they cannot effect the transfer, the company returns back the securities giving details of the grounds under which the transfer could not be effected. This is known as company objection.
3. *Objection for transfer:* When you happen to receive a company objection for transfer, you should proceed to get the errors/discrepancies corrected. You may have to contact the transferor (the seller) either directly or through your broker for rectification or replacement with good securities. Then you can resubmit the securities and the transfer deed to the company for affecting the transfer. In case you are unable to get the errors rectified or get them replaced, you have recourse to the seller and his broker through the Stock Exchange to get back your money. However, if you had transacted directly with the seller originally, you have to settle the matter with the seller directly.
4. *Loss of securities etc:* Sometimes, your securities in physical form may be lost misplaced. You should immediately request the company to record a stop transfer of the securities and simultaneously apply for issue of duplicate securities. For effecting stop transfer, the company may require you to produce a

court order or the copy of the FIR filed by you with the Police. Further, to issue duplicate securities to you, the company may require you to submit, indemnity bonds, affidavit, sureties, etc. besides issue of a public notice. You . . . have to comply with these requirements in order to protect your own interest.

22

Important Stock Exchanges in India

BOMBAY STOCK EXCHANGE LIMITED

Bombay Stock Exchange Limited is the oldest stock exchange in Asia with a rich heritage. Popularly known as "BSE", it was established as "The Native Share and Stock Brokers' Association" in 1875. It is the first stock exchange in the country to obtain permanent recognition in 1956 from the Government of India under the Securities Contracts (Regulation) Act, 1956. The Exchange's pivotal and pre-eminent role in the development of the Indian capital market is widely recognized and its index, SENSEX, is tracked worldwide. Earlier an Association of Persons (AOP), the Exchange is now a demutualized and corporatized entity incorporated under the provisions of the Companies Act, 1956, pursuant to the BSE (Corporatization and Demutualization) Scheme, 2005 notified by the Securities and Exchange Board of India (SEBI).

Demutualization

With demutualization, the trading rights and ownership

rights have been de-linked effectively addressing concerns regarding perceived and real conflicts of interest. The Exchange is professionally managed under the overall direction of the Board of Directors. The Board comprises eminent professionals, representatives of Trading Members and the Managing Director of the Exchange. The Board is inclusive and is designed to benefit from the participation of market intermediaries. In terms of organization structure, the Board formulates larger policy issues and exercises over-all control. The committees constituted by the Board are broad-based. The day-to-day operations of the Exchange are managed by the Managing Director and a management team of professionals.

Nationwide Transparent Trading

The Exchange has a nation-wide reach with a presence in 417 cities and towns of India. The systems and processes of the Exchange are designed to safeguard market integrity and enhance transparency in operations. During the year 2004-05, the trading volumes on the Exchange showed robust growth. The Exchange provides an efficient and transparent market for trading in equity, debt instruments and derivatives. The BSE's On Line Trading System (BOLT) is a proprietary system of the Exchange and is BS 7799-2-2002 certified. The surveillance and clearing and settlement functions of the Exchange are ISO 9001:2000 certified.

BSE's Book Building System

- BSE offers the book building services through the Book Building software that runs on the BSE Private network.
- This system is one of the largest electronic book building networks anywhere spanning over 350 Indian cities through over 7000 Trader Work Stations via eased lines, VSATs and Campus LANS.
- The software is operated through book-runners of the issue and by the syndicate member brokers. Through this book, the syndicate member brokers on behalf of themselves or their clients' place orders.

- Bids are placed electronically through syndicate members and the information is collected on line real-time until the bid date ends.
- In order to maintain transparency, the software gives visual graphs displaying price v/s quantity on the terminals.

New Direct Listing Norms

The Governing Board of the Exchange at its meeting held on 6th August, 2002 amended the direct listing norms for companies listed on other Stock Exchange(s) and seeking listing at BSE. These norms are:

1. The company should have minimum issued and paid up equity capital of Rs. 3 crores.
2. The Company should have profit making track record for last three years. The revenues/profits arising out of extra ordinary items or income from any source of non-recurring nature should be excluded while calculating distributable profits.
3. Minimum networth of Rs. 20 crores (networth includes Equity capital and free reserves excluding revaluation reserves).
4. Minimum market capitalization of the listed capital should be at least two times of the paid up capital.
5. The company should have a dividend paying track record for the last 3 consecutive years and the minimum dividend should be at least 10%.
6. Minimum 25% of the company's issued capital should be with Non-Promoters' shareholders as per Clause 35 of the Listing Agreement. Out of above Non-Promoter holding no single shareholder should hold more than 0.5% of the paid-up capital of the company individually or jointly with others except in case of Banks/Financial Institutions/Foreign Institutional Investors/Overseas Corporate Bodies and Non-Resident Indians.
7. The company should have at least two years listing record with any of the Regional Stock Exchange.

8. The company should sign an agreement with CDSL and NSDL for demat trading.

Cash Management Services (CMS)—Collection of Listing Fees

As a further step towards simplifying the system of payment of listing fees, the Exchange has entered into an arrangement with HDFC Bank for collection of listing fees, from 141 locations, situated all over India. Details of the HDFC Bank branches are available on BSE website site as well as on the HDFC Bank website. The above facility is being provided free of cost to the Companies. Companies intending to utilize the above facility for payment of listing fee would be required to furnish the information (mentioned below) in the Cash Management Cash Deposit Slip. These slips would be available at all the HDFC Bank centers. The Cheque should be drawn in favour of Bombay Stock Exchange Limited, and should be payable, locally. Companies should to mention in the deposit slip, the financial year(s) for which listing fee is being paid. Payment made through any other slips would not be considered. The above slips will have to be filled in quadruplicate. One acknowledged copy would be provided to the depositor by the HDFC Bank.

THE NATIONAL STOCK EXCHANGE OF INDIA LIMITED

The National Stock Exchange of India Limited has genesis in the report of the High Powered Study Group on Establishment of New Stock Exchanges, which recommended promotion of a National Stock Exchange by financial institutions (FIs) to provide access to investors from all across the country on an equal footing. Based on the recommendations, NSE was promoted by leading Financial Institutions at the behest of the Government of India and was incorporated in November 1992 as a tax-paying company unlike other stock exchanges in the country. On its recognition as a stock exchange under the Securities Contracts (Regulation) Act, 1956 in April 1993, NSE commenced operations in the Wholesale Debt Market (WDM) segment in June 1994. The

Capital Market (Equities) segment commenced operations in November 1994 and operations in Derivatives segment commenced in June 2000.

Capital Market Segment

The CM segment of NSEIL provides a fully automated screen based trading system for trading of equity and preference shares, debentures, warrants and coupons. The trading system, known as the National Exchange for Automated Trading (NEAT) system. It is an anonymous order-driven system and operates on a strict price/time priority. It enables members from across the country to trade simultaneously with enormous ease and efficiency. It provides tremendous flexibility to the users in terms of kinds of orders that can be placed on the system. Several time-related (Good-till-Cancelled, Good-till-Day, Immediate-or-Cancel), price-related (buy/sell limit and stop-loss orders) or volume-related (All-or-None, Minimum Fill, etc.) conditions can be easily built into an order. Orders are sorted and matched automatically by the computer keeping the system transparent, objective and fair. The trading system also provides complete market information on-line, which is updated on real time basis.

Wholesale Debt Market Segment

The WDM segment provides the only formal trading platform for trading of a wide range of debt securities. Initially, government securities, treasury bills and bonds issued by public sector undertakings (PSUs) were made available for trading. This range has been widened to include non-traditional instruments like floating rate bonds, zero coupon bonds, index bonds, commercial papers, certificates of deposit, corporate debentures, state government loans, SLA and non-SLA bonds issued by financial institutions, units of mutual funds and securitized debt. The WDM trading system, known as NEAT (National Exchange for Automated Trading), is a fully automated screen-based trading system that enables members across the country to trade simultaneously with enormous ease and efficiency. The trading system is an order driven system, which matches best buy and sell orders on a price/time priority.

Trading system provides two market sub-types: continuous market and negotiated market. In continuous market, the buyer and seller do not know each other and they put their best buy/sell orders, which are stored in order book with price/time priority. If orders match, it results into a trade. The trades in WDM segment are settled directly between the participants, who take an exposure to the settlement risk attached to any unknown counter-party. In the NEAT-WDM system, all participants can set-up their counter-party exposure limits against all probable counter-parties. This enables the trading member/participant to reduce/minimize the counter-party risk associated with the counter-party to trade. A trade does not take place if both the buy/sell participants do not invoke the counter-party exposure limit in the trading system. In the negotiated market, the trades are normally decided by the seller and the buyer, and reported to the Exchange through the broker. Thus deals negotiated or structured outside the exchange are disclosed to the market through NEAT-WDM system. In negotiated market, as buyers and sellers know each other and have agreed to trade, no counter-party exposure limit needs to be invoked.

The trades on the WDM segment could be either outright trades or repo transactions with flexibility for varying days of settlement (T + 0. to T + 5) and repo periods (3 to 14 days). For every trade, it is necessary to specify the number of settlement days and the trade type (repo or non-repo) and in the event of a repo trade, the repo term. The NEAT-FandO trading system is accessed by two types of users. The Trading Member (TM) has access to functions such as, order entry, order matching, or trade management. The Clearing Member (CM) uses the trader workstation for the purpose of monitoring the trading member(s) for whom he clears the trades. Additionally, he can enter and set limits to position, which a trading member can take.

Contracts: Futures contract on the NSEIL is based on SandP CNX Nifty Index. Currently, it has a maximum of 3-month expiration cycle. Three contracts are available for trading with t month, 2 months and 3 months expiry. A new contract is introduced on the next trading day following the expiry of the near month contract. Various conditions like,

Good-till-Day, Good-till-Cancelled; Good-till-Date, Immediate or Cancel, Stop loss, etc. can be built into an order.

Clearing and Settlement: NSCCL undertakes clearing and settlement of all deals executed on the NSEIL's Derivatives segment. It acts as legal counterparty to all deals on the Derivatives segment and guarantees settlement.

Derivatives Segment: In the Derivatives segment, NSCCL has admitted Clearing Members (CMs) distinct from Trading Members (TMs) in line with the 2-tier members/lip structure stipulated by SEBI to enable wider participation in the Derivatives segment. All trades on the Derivatives segment are cleared through a CM of NSCCL. Nifty index futures contracts are cash settled, i.e., through exchange of cash differences in value. Settlement is done on a daily basis by marking to market all open positions on the basis of the daily settlement price. The contracts are finally settled on expiry of the Nifty index futures contract when NSCCL marks the open positions of a CM to the closing price of the underlying index and resulting profit/loss is settled in cash.

Securities Lending

This method is regulated by SEBI which introduced guidelines in 1997 for this purpose. Under the scheme, a person with idle shares can lend them to another who If does not have the shares to fulfill his obligation under a trade finalized by him. There will be no direct contacts between the borrower and lender of securities. An intermediary who can guarantee the scheme and make good the loss in the borrower who fails to honour his obligations can alone provide substance to the scheme. The borrower has to put up collateral for his borrowings and pay cash margin levied on the securities by the authorities. Income from securities lending is exempt from Capital Gains Tax.

Automated Lending and Borrowing Mechanism: NSCCL commenced securities lending and borrowing called Automated Lending and Borrowing Mechanism (ALBM) on February 10, 1999. ALBM provides a facility to members to lend/borrow securities/funds for weekly market as well as for rolling market, at market determined rates. The ALBM mechanism is unique in as much as it provides investors/

members across the length and breadth of the country an opportunity to participate through participants in lending and borrowing of securities. It is designed essentially to facilitate the members to meet the settlement obligations by borrowing the securities from the members willing to lend securities. The investor is able to lend/borrow at market determined rates.

In order to allow members to borrow seamlessly for discharge of settlement obligations and in line with international practices in this regard. ALBM settlement is integrated with normal settlements. In the interest of market efficiency and risk management, it is meaningful for a clearing corporation to net all liabilities, falling due on any auction, rolling, etc. In such situations, as long as the clearing corporation is a centralized legal counter-party, risk management would dictate that it nets all obligations *vis-a-vis* each counter-party to itself.

Features of ALBM

1. The basic purpose of ALBM is to provide a mechanism for borrowing of securities. Securities may be borrowed for any purpose to completion of settlements on NSEIL or on exchange to any other purpose.
2. As the basic objective of ALBM is securities borrowing, securities are necessarily given to the borrower against cash collateral and are not withheld by the Clearing Corporation. The cash collateral is given to the lender as it forms a part of the returns to the lender; this is a common practice internationally where a discount on lending is offered on deposit of cash collateral.
3. As the Clearing Corporation as an Approved Intermediary is required to return the securities the lender, an obligation is created at the end of the ALBM session to return the securities borrowed.
4. Transactions are done on a separate, distinct and transparent electronic book. This facilitates members to ascertain what can be lent/what needs to be

borrowed, since the members' offices are spread at various locations across the country.

5. NSCCL provides securities lending services backed by an efficient and transparent lending system and sophisticated, risk management to enable investors to find new ways to enhance their revenues.

Benefits of ALBM: The participants acting as lenders in ALBM have the following advantages:

- Extensive range of securities available for lending.
- Nation-wide reach through NEAT trading system.
- Lending of securities on an ongoing basis.
- Facility of offsetting custody fee.
- Use of idle stocks to generate income.
- Retention of the right to receive all accrued corporate benefits during the loan period.
- Market determined lending rate.
- Minimum risk for the lenders.
- all loan transactions are fully collateralized; loans are marked to market on daily basis, and
- NSCCL ensures return of equivalent securities.

Similarly, the participants acting as borrowers in the ALBM scheme have the following advantages:

- Extensive range of securities available for borrowing.
- Borrowing of securities on an ongoing basis.
- Discharge of settlement obligations.
- No auction/close out loss.
- Market determined borrowing rates.
- Availability of borrowed securities in demat form.
- No extra transaction cost for moving borrowed securities towards fulfilling settlement obligations.

Mechanism

The NEAT trading system of the NSEIL, which has a nationwide reach, is used for the purpose of lending and borrowing under ALBM. A participant who wishes to borrow security/lend funds for a particular security executes borrow transaction/buy order. Similarly, the participant who wishes to lend security/borrow funds executes a lend transaction/sale order.

The net obligations of a participant in a particular security at the end of each ALBM session determine the net intention to lend or borrow. A net buy position for a security implies a firm and irrevocable intention to borrow, whereas a net sale position for a security implies a firm and irrevocable intention to lend. Based on this, NSCCL gives effect to lending or borrowing transactions by selling these along with the obligations of the relevant settlement at the transacted price. The net obligations of these lending or borrowing transactions and obligations of relevant settlement are honoured on the settlement date of respective settlement by making pay-in of required securities to the NSCCL.

TRADE VERIFICATION MODULE

Investors are provided with a facility to verify trades on the NSE website. Using this facility, an investor who has received a contract note from a trading member of the Exchange, can check whether the trade has been executed on the Exchange. This facility is available on the NSE website for the Capital Market, Derivatives (FandO) and Retail Debt Market segments.

Working of Trade Verification Module

- Trade details are available for verification on the same day (i.e. T itself) after 19:00 hours IST.
- The investor needs to input minimum details of the trade, viz. client code (provided by the trading member), security details (symbol and series), order number, trade number, trade quantity and price (excluding brokerage). All the above details are mandatory.
- If an identical match is found for the details provided, a confirmation along with the details of the trade is displayed to the investor. If no match is found, a message is displayed to that effect.

- Where no match is found, investors are advised to contact their trading member for clarification. For further assistance, please contact the Investor Grievance Cell of the Exchange.
- Trade details for the last 5 trading days will be available on the website. That is, trades executed on 'T' day, can be verified till the T+4th day.
- All trades can be verified.

Listing: Listing means admission of securities of an issuer to trading privileges on a stock exchange through a formal agreement. The prime objective of admission to dealings on the Exchange is to provide liquidity and marketability to securities, as also to provide a mechanism for effective management of trading. Listing on NSE provides qualifying companies with the broadest access to investors, the greatest market depth and liquidity, cost-effective access to capital, the highest visibility, the fairest pricing, and investor benefits. NSE trading terminals are now situated in various cities and towns across the length and breath of India. Securities listed on the Exchange are required to fulfill the eligibility criteria for listing. Various types of securities of a company are traded under a unique symbol and different series.

NSE plays an important role in helping an Indian companies access equity capital, by providing a liquid and well-regulated market. NSE has about 1016 companies listed representing the length, breadth and diversity of the Indian economy which includes from hi-tech to heavy industry, software, refinery, public sector units, infrastructure, and financial services. Listing on NSE raises a company's profile among investors in India and abroad. Trade data is distributed worldwide through various news-vending agencies. More importantly, each and every NSE listed company is required to satisfy stringent financial, public distribution and management requirements. High listing standards foster investor confidence and also bring credibility into the markets. NSE lists securities in its Capital Market (Equities) segment and its Wholesale Debt Market segment.

Trading: NSE introduced for the first time in India, fully automated screen-based trading. It uses a modern, fully computerised trading system designed to offer investors across the length and breadth of the country a safe and easy way to invest. The NSE trading system called 'National Exchange for Automated Trading' (NEAT) is a fully automated screen-based trading system, which adopts the principle of an order driven market.

Clearing and Settlement (Equities): NSCCL carries out clearing and settlement functions as per the settlement cycles of different sub-segments in the Equities segment. The clearing function of the clearing corporation is designed to work out : (a) what counter-parties owe, and (b) what counter-parties are due to receive on the settlement date. Settlement is a two way process which involves legal transfer of title to funds and securities or other assets on the settlement date. NSCCL has also devised mechanism to handle various exceptional situations like security shortages, bad delivery, company objections, auction settlement, etc.

Risk Management: A sound risk management system is integral to an efficient clearing and settlement system. NSE introduced for the first time in India, risk containment measures that were common internationally but were absent from the Indian securities markets. NSCCL has put in place a comprehensive risk management system, which is constantly upgraded to preempt market failures. The Clearing Corporation ensures that trading member obligations are commensurate with their net-worth. Risk containment measures include capital adequacy requirements of members, monitoring of member performance and track record, stringent margin requirements, position limits based on capital, online monitoring of member positions and automatic disablement from trading when limits are breached, etc.

NSCCL: The National Securities Clearing Corporation Ltd. (NSCCL), a wholly owned subsidiary of NSE, was incorporated in August 1995. It was the first clearing corporation to be established in the country and also the first clearing corporation in the country to introduce settlement guarantee. NSCCL commenced clearing operations in April 1996. It has since completed more than 1150 settlements (equities segment) without delays or disruptions. It was set-up with the following objectives:

- To bring and sustain confidence in clearing and settlement of securities;
- To promote and maintain, short and consistent settlement cycles;
- To provide counter-party risk guarantee; and
- To operate a tight risk containment system.

OVER THE COUNTER EXCHANGE OF INDIA (OTCEI)

OTCEI was incorporated in 1990 as a Section 25 company under the Companies Act 1956 and is recognized as a stock exchange under Section 4 of the Securities Contracts Regulation Act, 1956. The Exchange was set-up to aid enterprising promoters in raising finance for new projects in a cost effective manner and to provide investors with a transparent and efficient mode of trading. Modeled along the lines of the NASDAQ market of USA, OTCEI introduced many novel concepts to the Indian capital markets such as screen-based nationwide trading, sponsorship of companies, market making and scripless trading. As a measure of success of these efforts, the Exchange today has 115 listings and has assisted in providing capital for enterprises that have gone on to build successful brands for themselves like VIP Advanta, Sonora Tiles and Brilliant mineral water, etc.

Specialized Exchange for Technology and Growth Companies

Studies by NASSCOM, Software Technology Parks of India, the venture capital funds and the government's IT Task Force, as well as the rising interest in information technology, pharmaceutical, biotechnology and media shares have repeatedly emphasized the need for a national stock market for innovative and high growth companies. Innovative companies are critical to developing economies like India, which is undergoing a major technological revolution. With their abilities to generate employment opportunities and contribute to the economy, it is essential that these companies not only expand existing operations but also set-up new units. The key issue for these companies is raising timely, cost effective and long term capital to sustain their operations and enhance growth. Such companies, particularly those that have been in operation for a short time, are unable to raise funds through the traditional financing methods, because they have not yet been evaluated by the financial world.

Useful Exchange

- High-technology enterprises.
- Companies with high growth potential.
- Companies focused on new product development.
- Entrepreneurs seeking finance for specific business projects.
- OTCEI offers an exit route for venture capital and private equity funds.
- Threshold listing requirements on OTCEI are ideally suited for VCF disinvestments.
- Provide greater visibility for companies through the Exchange.
- Enhance portfolio liquidity through the Unlisted Securities segment.

The Indian economy is demonstrating signs of recovery and it is essential that these companies have suitable financing alternatives to fund their growth and maintain competitiveness. OTCEI, with its entry guidelines and eligibility requirements tailored for such innovative and growth oriented companies, is ideally positioned as the preferred route for raising funds through Initial Public Offer (IPOs) or primary issues, in this country. Just what is the connection between these products and the OTC Exchange, you may ask. The answer is that these are popular products made by companies listed on the OTC Exchange of India (OTCEI). OTCEI is the primary Stock Exchange for these securities. The Company issuing the security enters into an agreement to comply with all the regulations of the Stock Exchange. The securities can be bought or sold through our brokers (Members/Dealers) all over India.

OTCEI offers an exit opportunity: With its advanced trading systems and market-friendly trading procedures, OTCEI presents an excellent opportunity to venture capitalists and private equity funds to generate appreciable returns by offloading their holdings. This provides these institutions an assured exit for their investments. With new opportunities opening up in sectors such as information technology, it assumes greater significance for OTCEI and the venture capital industry to join forces and promote a common objective i.e. to encourage and promote listings of innovative and high growth enterprises. Although the preferred route for an exit can be through the IPO mechanism on OTCEI, the Exchange would soon be launching the unlisted securities market. The market structure would be such that venture capitalists would have an attractive alternative market to offload their holdings to a wide range of financial intermediaries. This segment can act as a prelude to a full listing on the Exchange thereby ensuring higher subscription in the IPO. With a professional team and offices at the major metros, OTCEI can deliver quality and efficient services.

Benefits of OTCEI Listing

- OTCEI is the only stock exchange in the country with a specific mandate to service small and medium innovative and high growth enterprises, in raising resources efficiently through the capital markets.
- The only exchange to offer listing to companies with paid-up capital below Rs. 3 crores.
- Is ideally suited for start-up enterprises as 3-year track record is not mandatory.
- Does not require companies to have 10% equity/debt participation by banks/financial institutions.
- Offers support functions critical for start-up/venture capital backed companies.
- Competitive issue cost through OTCEI (less than 10%).
- Enhanced visibility through national reach.
- Sponsorship and Market Making ensures liquidity and better valuation for the securities.

Highlights of OTCEI

1. The first screen based nationwide stock exchange in India.
2. The first exchange to introduce Market-making in India.
3. The first exchange to introduce Sponsorship of companies in India.
4. The only exchange to allow listing of companies with paid-up below Rs. 3 crores.
5. The only exchange to allow companies with less than 3 year track record to tap capital market.
6. Has shifted trading from counter receipts to share certificates.
7. Has introduced Weekly Settlement Cycle.
8. Allows short selling.
9. Allows demat trading through NSDL.
10. Has tied-up with NSCCL for Clearing.

As part of the Dave Committee report in 1996, it was suggested that equity shares of unlisted companies should be allowed to be traded on OTCEI. In this context, the exchange has designed the trading rules and the market guidelines for the initiation of Trading in Unlisted Securities and the same has been submitted to SEBI for approval. This market is quite active and robust in the financial sector abroad (PORTAL market in the U.S.) and is expected to receive a positive response from investors in the Indian markets. OTCEI proposes to introduce a vibrant and a well regulated market structure for trading in unlisted securities thereby giving an exit option for venture capital/Private equity, offshore funds and other institutions and corporates. This provides improved investment opportunities in start-up enterprises, especially in the growth sectors.

The Business Objectives of OTCEI

- To promote organized trading in Unlisted Securities.
- To broad-base the existing informal market in order to make it more liquid.

- To provide a source of valuation for securities.
- To act as a launch pad to an IPO.

Benefits to the Participants

- Act as a benchmark to value
- Creating an exit option for illiquid stocks/venture capitalists.
- Introducing transparency for trading in Unlisted Securities.
- Platform for issuers and first level investors (QPs) like financial institutions, State level Financial corporations, Foreign Institutional Investors to trade
- System for defining benchmark for securities.
- Organizing and broad-basing trading in the existing market.
- Shuffling portfolios for the investors.
- Increasing business for the market constituents.
- Easier launch pad for an IPO.

Investor Grievance Cells

OTCEI in 1993 became the first Exchange in the country to open Investor Grievance Cells (IGCs) at four Metros—Chennai, Delhi, Kolkata and Mumbai. The IGCs handle complaints/ queries from investors against brokers and/or companies listed on the OTCEI.

Common Grievances: Investor grievances can be largely classified as:

Company-related

- Non-receipt of securities sent for transfer,
- Non-receipt of corporate benefits, e.g., dividends/ interest/bonus/rights, etc.
- Non-receipt of share certificates in exchange for counter receipts.

Broker-related

- Non-rectification of documents returned as bad delivery by the broker.

- Non-receipt of funds/securities on sale/purchase

Procedure for Grievance Redressal

- OTCEI tries to resolve complaints received from investors at the earliest. We have devised a format for lodging complaints in order to get the required details from the investor.
- Complaint given a unique reference number, investor is sent an acknowledgment.
- Complaint forwarded to Company/Registrar/Broker, who are asked to reply within 21 days.
- If complaint unresolved within 30 days from date of acknowledgment, investor may again approach OTCEI with reference number.

Investor Compensation Fund: OTCEI set-up the Investor Compensation Fund in 1995 to address and compensate the claims of investors and protect them in case of default or loss of security. The Investor Compensation Committee of OTCEI decides on the claims filed by the investors. Claims can be lodged by any class of investors for any pecuniary loss suffered on account of default or non-performance by any constituent of OTCEI. OTCEI must be notified of any claim substantiated with evidence within one month from the date of first discovery of the loss by the investor, failure to do this would affect the investor's right to claim any compensation from the Investor Compensation Fund.

INTERMEDIATION IN OTCEI

The Exchange has three types of intermediaries called Members, Dealers and Sponsors, who contribute to the Exchange's activities by trading and enabling listing of companies on the Exchange. Members and Dealers may carry out the activities of trading, underwriting, market making and participation in bought out deals, but Dealers cannot sponsor an issue for listing. Sponsors can perform the function of sponsorship of issues, but are not permitted to participate in secondary market activities.

Base Minimum Capital deposited with the Exchange: The Base Minimum Capital is taken as security for due performance and fulfilment by the member of his operations and obligations towards the Exchange. The minimum base capital is Rs. 4 lakhs. All members have to comply with the Base Minimum Capital requirements before their activation. The members may opt for Base Minimum Capital by way of Cash, FDRs, Bank Guarantee or Securities.

- Cash to be deposited with the Exchange—minimum 25% i.e. Rs. 1 lakh.
- Deposit of Fixed Deposit Receipts (FDRs)—(25%) issued by approved banks.
- Deposit/lodgement of Securities—(maximum 50%) with approved custodian (HDFC Bank Ltd.) with 20% margin.
- Irrevocable Bank guarantees (in lieu of securities—maximum 50%) from approved banks.
- Members can also deposit additional base capital with the Exchange. The cash component of the additional base capital to be deposited should be a minimum 30%.

Turnover Limit: Members are subject to intra-day trading limits. Gross Turnover (buy + sell) for the day shall not exceed twenty five times (25) the base capital deposited by the members. Members desirous of increasing their limits will have to submit additional deposits by way of cash, bank guarantees, fixed deposit receipts and securities. Trading Members violating the intra-day gross turnover limit at any time on any trading day shall not be permitted to trade forthwith.

Gross Exposure Limit: Members are subject to gross exposure limits. Gross exposure, being the aggregate of the cumulative net outstanding positions (purchase or sales) in each security shall not exceed eight and half times (8.5) the base capital deposited by the members. Gross Exposure at any point of time shall also include net outstanding positions of the previous settlement till the securities pay-in for the previous settlement. Members desirous of increasing their limits will have to submit additional deposits by way of cash, bank guarantees, fixed deposit receipts and securities.

Margins: All margins imposed by the Exchange are payable on T+1 day. The Exchange collects the following margins from brokers depending on their positions/exposures and market volatility, in line with SEBI requirements:

(a) *Daily Margin:* Daily margin payable by the member consists of value at Risk Margin and Mark to Mark Margin.

(b) *Mark to Market Margin*: Mark to market margin is computed on the basis of mark to market loss of a member. Mark to market loss is potential loss, in case the cumulative net outstanding position of the member in all securities at the end of day is closed out. Mark to Market margin is calculated by marking each transaction in a scrip to the closing price of the scrip at the end of trading. MTM Profit/loss across different securities within the same settlement is set-off to determine the MTM loss for a settlement. Such MTM losses for settlements are computed at client level.

(c) *Value at Risk Margin*: Value at Risk Margin is computed for all securities in the rolling settlement. All securities are classified into three groups for purpose of this margin.

Settlement Schedule for the Rolling Settlement

Sl. No.	*Day*	*Description*
1.	T	Trade Day
2.	T+1 10.30 a.m.	Custodial Confirmation.
3.	T+2 11.30 a.m.	Securities and Funds pay-in
4.	T+2	Securities and Funds pay-out
5.	T+3	Auction for shortages
6.	T+4	Auction pay-in and pay-out

Working days do not include Saturdays, Sundays and any other holidays. Securities are paid-in by the Delivering Member to the clearing house/Depository on morning of T+2. Funds are paid-in to the clearing bank by the Receiving Member on morning of T+2. The pay-out for both funds and securities takes place evening of T+2.

Auction Settlement: In a typical settlement cycle, auctions are usually held on T+3. The auction pay-in for both funds and securities is on T+4.

CERTAIN CONCEPTS ASSOCIATED WITH TRADING IN STOCK EXCHANGES

Badla Trading

Badla is the price payable by the buyer to carry over his speculative purchases to the next settlement. This system helps a trader to carry forward his settlement without taking deliveries of stocks purchased. This help to build large volumes on the exchanges and impart liquidity in securities. In this system, a position is carried forward. In the event of a long purchase the investor may want to carry forward the transaction to the next settlement cycle and for doing so, he has to compensate the seller. The 'seedha badla' financier enters the market to lend money to the investor for a return. This is measured as interest on the funds made available for one settlement cycle, i.e. one week or a longer period in case of a book closure badla system. Similarly, 'undha badla' or a 'contango' charge is a return paid by the stock borrower to the stock lender. In a short sale, when the investor wants to carry forward the transaction to the next settlement cycle, he has to borrow the stocks to compensate the other party in the contract. The charge paid on the borrowed stock is called a 'contango' charge or 'share badla'.

The Badla session is held every Saturday in Mumbai, Delhi and Ahmedabad and on Thursday at the Calcutta Stock Exchange. The outstanding positions of various stocks are listed along with the quantities outstanding. Depending on the demand and supply of money, the carry forward rates are determined. If the market is over bought, i.e. there is more demand for funds, it results in Vyaj badla. However, when the market is oversold, or when in a particular stock the short position is more, the Undha badla applies.

Vyaj badla: In many a times the lender lends money to the borrower through the clearinghouse. This transaction is called Vyaj Badla. The lender takes up the delivery of the shares from the original buyer at a standard rate (average or hawala rate) and sells the same in the next settlement back to him at a standard rate plus finance charge, to pay for the stock for that particular period. Vyaj Badla is not speculation since the financier or the investor is not taking any investment position in the market. His role is that of a financier and he steps into the shoes of the buyer only for funding the delivery at a pre-determined rate.

Hawala and badla rates: The hawala rate is the price at which buyers and sellers settle their speculative transactions at the end of the settlement on any exchange. It becomes the basis for buy and sell for the investor opting for carry forward during the next settlement. This price is fixed by taking the weighted average of trades in the last half-an-hour of trading on the settlement day for securities in the carry forward list, also known as a group or specified group. This price is significant because for a speculative buyer or a seller, the hawala rate is the standard rate for settling his trade and for carrying forward business to the next settlement.

CLEARING HOUSE

It is where the securities are settled through a consortium of banks. A clearing house was established in 1921.it receives delivery and payment on behalf the customers. All the banks of the country are members. It guarantees payments for trades. It returns shares to the concerned bank if a member defaults. Clearing houses cost huge sums of money to the exchanges. The services tendered in the interest of the investing public. The clearing house operations were in introduced in Calcutta in 1944 and in Chennai in 1957.

MARGIN TRADING

Most security purchases do not have to be made on a cash

basis; borrowed funds can be used instead. This activity is referred to as margin trading, and is used for one basic reason to magnify returns. This is possible because the use of borrowed funds reduce the amount of capital that must be put up by the investor. As peculiar as it may sound, the term margin itself refers to the amount of equity in an investment, or the amount that is not borrowed. If an investor uses 75 percent margin, for example, it means that 75 percent of the investment position is being financed with the person's own capital and the balance (25 percent) with borrowed money.

Essentials of Margin Trading

Margin trading can be used with most kinds of securities. It normally leads to increased returns, but there are also some substantial risks. One of the biggest is that the issue may not perform as expected. If this in fact occurs, no amount of margin trading can correct matters. Margin trading can only magnify returns, not produce them. Because the security being margined is always the ultimate source of return, the security selection process is critical to this trading strategy. Using an investor's equity as a base, the idea of margin trading is to employ financial leverage, or debt, to magnify returns.

Margin Transactions

To execute a margin transaction, it is necessary to establish a margin account. It is opened either in the form of cash or securities. Margin credit can be obtained from a broker or a banker, although nearly all margin trading is done through brokers. The broker will retain any securities purchased on margin as collateral for the loan. There are basically two types of margin requirements.

Initial Margin: Initial margin stipulates the minimum amount of equity that must be provided by the investor at the time of purchase. It is used to prevent overtrading and excessive speculation. Generally, it is this margin requirement that investors refer to when discussing margin trading. Any security that can be margined has a specific initial requirement, although these can be changed by the authorities from time to time. As long as the margin in an account remains at a level equal to or greater than prevailing initial requirements, the investor is free to use the account in any way he or she sees fit. H the value of the investor's holdings declines, the margin in his or her account will also drop. This situation can lead to what is known as a restricted account, one whose equity is less than the initial margin requirement. It does not mean that the investor must put up additional cash or equity, but it does require the investor to bring the margin back to the initial level when securities are sold while the account is restricted.

Maintenance Margin: Maintenance margin is the absolute minimum amount of margin (equity) that an investor must maintain in the margin account at all times. The margin falls below the maintenance margin; the broker is authorized to sell enough of the securities to bring the account back up to standard. When an insufficient amount of maintenance margin exists, an investor will receive a margin call to remedy the situation. This call gives the investor a short period of time to find some means to bringing the equity up to the required level. If this is not done, the broker has no alternative but to sell enough of the investor's margined holdings to bring the equity in the account up to this level. The maintenance margin protects both the brokerage house and investors. Brokers avoid having to absorb excessive investor losses, and investors avoid being wiped out. The maintenance margin on equity securities rarely changes, although it is often set slightly higher by brokerage houses for the added protection of both brokers and their customers. For straight debt securities, generally there is no official maintenance margin except that set by the brokerage houses themselves.

Uses of Margin Trading

Margin trading is most often used in one of two ways. One of its uses is to magnify transaction returns. Another major margin tactic is called pyramiding, which takes the concept of magnified returns to its limits. The principle of pyramiding is to use the excess margin in the account to purchase additional securities. The only constraint, and the key to pyramiding, is that when the additional securities are purchased, the investor's margin account must be at or above the prevailing required initial margin level. Remember that it is the account, and not the individual transactions, that must meet the minimum standards. If the account has excess margin, the investor can use it to build up security holdings.

Pyramiding uses the paper profits in margin accounts, to partly or fully finance the acquisition of additional securities. This allows such transactions to be made at margins below prevailing initial margin levels, and sometimes substantially so. In fact, with this technique, it is even possible to buy securities with no new cash at all; rather, they can all be financed entirely with margin loans. The reason is that the paper profits in the account lead to excess margin, more equity in the account than necessary.

Pyramiding can continue as long as there are additional paper profits in the margin account and as long as the margin level exceeds the prevailing initial requirement when purchases are made. The tactic is somewhat complex but also profitable, especially because it minimize the amount of new capital required in the investor's account. In general, margin trading is simple, but it is also risky. It should therefore be used only by investors who fully understand its operation and appreciate its pitfalls.

Short Selling

Short selling is used when a decline in security prices is anticipated. The technique enables investors to profit from falling security prices. However, it can also be used to protect investors from falling security prices. Almost any type of security can be shorted, the short-selling activities of most investors are limited almost exclusively to equity shares and to put and call options.

Uses of Short Selling: Investors short sell for one of two reasons to seeks pecu1ative profits when the price of a security is expected to drop, or to protect a profit and defer taxes by "hedging" their position. The first use is the standard short-sale transaction. The hedge tactic, in contrast, is a conservative use of short selling, employed to lock in a given profit level. All shorts are executed on margin, so it seems appropriate to begin our discussion of uses of short selling by looking at how margin fits into a short sale and affects returns.

Shorting on margin: There are no borrowed funds with margined short sales. With short selling, the term 'margin' simply indicates the size of the equity deposit the investor must make an order to initiate the transaction. Margined short sales are executed in the same margin account as margined long transactions. They are subject to initial margin requirements and have maintenance margin levels. In fact, the only thing that we do not have to be concerned about with a margined short sale is the account's debit balance. Margining a short sale, then, is much like margining a long transaction. Many of the investment principles, margin features, and behavioral characteristics we discussed previously apply equally here. Of course, if the price of the security being shorted goes up, the investor loses money. If the price of the security being shorted goes up too much, the account can become restricted or subject to a margin call.

23

Investors' Protection

Investors in general decide to enter into securities market buying on the basis of information provided to them by the brokers, analysts, news papers, specialized TV channels and the like. If the information is incomplete or contained misrepresentation or is fraudulent, the investor stands to lose. Under these circumstances, it is almost impossible to sustain investor confidence for the healthy growth and development of the capital market in a country. It is thus essential to ensure providing adequate, accurate and authentic information to the investors and to safeguard them against unscrupulous promoters trying to deceive them. Besides, the investors need to be protected from delays in listing of securities with the stock exchanges, dispatch of allotment letters and refund orders, transfer of securities, non-payment of interest and dividend, issue of notices regarding meetings and issue of copies of the audited accounts, director's report and other relevant information which help them to take prompt decisions in keeping or disposing of their shares.

The basic financial system that exists in India has enabled the public to have comparatively higher rate of saving in the among world countries. The investment of this savings in productive channels and in corporate sector is encouraging. Moreover, the ability of the investors to look for an appropriate profitable investment avenue is very low. This is due to the poor investor education and awareness. This malady can be cured by providing information on risks involved and view points on the merits and demerits of the investment. Hence, adequate, accurate, relevant and authentic information is required by the investors for proper decision-making. Such information should be available on a continuous basis so that the investor is able to make sale decisions at the right time.

The intermediaries serving the investors should not only be honest but should also be efficient having sufficient expertise. The legislative framework that operates in any financial market is master minded with the twin objectives of investors' protection and regulation of stock exchanges and the intermediaries. Hence, a strong and effective system of regulation of financial market will ensure in the long-run better information to investors and protect them from unscrupulous intermediaries and persons, tapping the capital market.

GRIEVANCES OF INVESTORS

Grievances of the investors are many that arise while they deal with the securities, not only with the company but also with intermediaries of shares. Right from bankers to the issue and up to the company that receives the money of the investor they face different sort of problems. The following are some of the grievances faced investors of the primary or secondary market. In respect of each of the grievances listed below complaint can be preferred with the Registrar of Companies, stock exchanges or SEBI as the case may be and in certain cases, they can be pursued with the Company Law Board too.

- Non-listing of securities with the appropriate stock exchanges as mentioned in the offer documents.
- Allowing the publication of and being a party to inadequate information or false information misrepresentation in prospectus, applications, advertisements.

- Not replying to the letters of investors by companies relating to refund orders, allotment letters and non-receipt of share certificates.
- Delay in execution of transfer dealings after fulfilling of necessary formalities in that regard.
- Non-receipt of share certificates after sub division or consolidation.
- Non-receipt of notice of general meeting and annual report.
- Non-declaration of dividend and non-receipt of dividend.
- Company not communicating of rights issue/bonus issue.
- Unable to market the odd lots of shares held by investors.
- Obtaining undue benefits by company insiders.
- Default in payment of interest and repayment of deposits.

RIGHTS AND RESPONSIBILITIES OF INVESTOR

Rights of Investor as a Shareholder

- To receive the share certificates, on allotment or transfer (if opted for transaction in physical mode) as the case may be, in due time.
- To receive copies of the Annual Report containing the Balance Sheet, the Profit and Loss account and the Auditor's Report.
- To participate and vote in general meetings either personally or through proxy.
- To receive dividends in due time once approved in general meetings.
- To receive corporate benefits like rights, bonus, etc. once approved.
- To apply to Company Law Board (CLB) to call or direct the Annual General Meeting.
- To inspect the minute books of the general meetings and to receive copies thereof.

- To proceed against the company by way of civil or criminal proceedings.
- To apply for the winding up of the company.
- To receive the residual proceeds.

Besides the above rights, which shareholders you enjoy as an individual, the shareholders also enjoy the following rights as a group:

- To requisite an Extra-ordinary General meeting.
- To demand a poll on any resolution.
- To apply to Company Law Board/Tribunal to investigate the affairs of the company.
- To apply to Company Law Board/Tribunal for relief in cases of oppression and/or mismanagement.

Rights of Investors as a Debenture Holder

The shareholder/investor may note that the below mentioned rights may not necessarily be absolute. For example, the right to transfer securities (in physical mode) is subject to the company's right to refuse transfer as per statutory provisions.

- To receive interest/redemption in due time.
- To receive a copy of the trust deed on request.
- To apply for winding up of the company if the company fails to pay its debt.
- To approach the Debenture Trustee with your grievance.

Responsibilities of an Investor as a Security Holder

While an investor may be happy to note that he/she have so many rights as a stakeholder in the company that should not lead him/her to complacency; because the shareholders have also certain responsibilities to discharge.

- To be specific about where to invest and how to invest.
- To remain informed what happens in the capital

market, what are the duties of investors and the extent of liability of the company to the shareholder.
- ❖ To be vigilant of the market forces and be cheated by sentiments of the market.
- ❖ To participate and vote in general meetings and discharge the liability as a shareholder.
- ❖ To exercise your rights on your own or as a group.

Friendly Measures of SEBI for Investor Protection

1. Grievance cells have been set-up in stock exchanges for expeditious settlements of complaints of investors. These cells are required to monitor and remedy the complaints and also furnish monthly progress report to the governing bodies of the stock exchanges.
2. The stock markets have been made broad based with more exchanges to get integrated into the system and so the system of trading has been improved and settlement period shortened.
3. Registration of brokers has been tightened by prescribing norms for capital adequacy and eligibility and brokers and sub-brokers are better regulated to offer prompt services. Further, greater transparency has been brought out in the trading activities of the brokers and their associates.
4. Insider trading is prohibited through regulations special on insider trading and in the past several insiders have been punished.
5. The presidents of stock exchanges have been advised to hold open house session or arrange investor service week periodically with the investors and redress their grievances.

Regulatory Measures

Major changes have been introduced in legislations dealing with company administration, stock market, rules and procedures to ensure adequate protection to the investors. The legislations that have been amended to this effect are the Companies Act, Securities Contract (Regulation) Act,

Consumer Protection Act, and Depositories Act. Besides, the Listing Agreement of Stock Exchanges has been amended. The circulars and press notes are issued by the Ministry of Finance, Ministry of Law, Justice and Company Affairs and SEBI from time to time. SEBI was set-up with following primary objectives of protecting the interest of the investors in securities and to promote the development of and to regulate the securities market and other matters connected therewith or incidental thereto. SEBI Act seeks to achieve through the following investor protection:

1. Prohibition of Fraudulent Practices Relating to Securities Markets and Bans Insider Trading in Securities

Fraud means any act committed by a party to a contract or by his agent, with intent to deceive another party thereto or his agent, or induce him to enter into contract:

- The suggestion as to a fact of that which is not true, by one who does not believe it to be true.
- The active concealment of a fact by one having knowledge or belief of the fact.
- A promise made without intention of performing it.
- Any other act done to deceive.
- Any such act or omission as the law specially declares to be fraudulent.

2. Prohibits Misleading Statements to Induce Sale or Purchase of Securities

It lays down that no person shall make any statement or disseminate any information which is:

- is misleading in a material particular, and
- is likely to induce the sale or purchase of securities by any other person or is likely to have the effect of increasing or depressing the market price of securities, if and when he makes the statement or disseminates the information, (a) he does not care whether the statement or information is true or false, or (b) he knows or ought reasonably to have known

that the statement or information is misleading in any material particular.

3. *Prohibits Unfair Trade Practice Relating to Securities*

The regulation lays down that no person shall:

- In the course of his business knowingly engage in act or practice which would operate as a fraud upon any other person in connection with the purchase, sale or any other dealing in securities.
- On his own behalf or on behalf of any other person, knowingly buy, sell or otherwise deal in securities, pending the execution of any order of his client relating to the same security for purchase, sale or other dealings in respect of securities. However, this clause shall not apply where according to the clients' instructions the transaction for the client is to be effected only under specified conditions or in specified circumstances.
- Intentionally or in contravention of any law for the time being in force, delays the transfer of securities in the name of the transferee or the despatch of securities or connected documents to any transferee.
- Indulge in falsification of the books, accounts and records, whether maintained manually or in computer or in any other form.
- When acting as an agent, execute a transaction with a client at a price other than the price at which the transaction was executed by him, whether on a stock exchange or otherwise or at a price other than that at which it was offset against the transaction of another client.

4. *Investigations into Alleged Contraventions and Powers of SEBI in this Regard*

SEBI either on *suo motu* (on self) or upon information received from affected parties may order investigation to be caused on the buying and selling of securities. No such investigation shall be made except for the following purposes, to ascertain whether there are any circumstances which would render any person guilty of having contravened any of these regulations or any directions issued and to investigate into any complaint of any contravention of the regulation, received from any investor, intermediary or any other person.

- SEBI shall give notice to concerned parties. No notice, if SEBI is satisfied that in the interest of the investors no such notice should be given.
- It shall be duty of every person in respect of whom an investigation has been ordered under for investigation to produce to the investigating officer such books, accounts and other documents in his custody or control and furnish him with such statements and information as the said officer may reasonably be required for the purposes of the investigation.
- Allow the investigating officer to have access to the premises at all reasonable premises for the purpose of investigation.
- Extend to the investigation officer reasonable facilities for examining any books, accounts and other documents in his custody or control whether kept manually or in electronic form as may reasonably be required for the purposes of investigation
- Provide to such investigating officer copies of any such books, accounts and records which in the opinion of the investigating officer, are relevant to the investigation or, as the case may be, allow him to take out computer print-outs thereof.
- The investigating officer shall have power to examine orally and to record the statement of the person concerned, any director, partner, member or employee of such person. It shall be the duty of every such person to give to the investigating officer all such assistance and otherwise extend all such cooperation as may reasonably be required in connection with the investigation and to furnish relevant information as may be sought from him.
- The investigating officer shall submit a report to the

Board, on completion of the investigation taking into account all relevant facts.

- The SEBI may direct the person concerned not to deal in securities in any particular manner in the interest of investors.
- Require the person concerned to call upon any of its officers, other employees or representatives to refrain from dealing in securities in any particular manner
- It may prohibit the person concerned from disposing of any of the securities acquired in contravention of these regulations.
- Direct the person concerned to dispose of any such securities acquired in contravention of these regulations, in such manner as the Board may deem fit, for restoring the *status quo.*
- The Board may initiate action for suspension or cancellation of registration of an intermediary who holds a certificate of registration for proved contraventions.

SEBI GUIDELINES ON DISCLOSURE AND INVESTOR PROTECTION (DIP)

The SEBI Guidelines on disclosure and investors protection provide for working procedures for different intermediaries, also have the basic purpose of protecting the investors. SEBI has been emphasizing the importance of disclosure standards for corporates and disseminating relevant and correct information to the investors. The committee under the Chairmanship of Shri C.B. Bhave suggested measures for improving the continuing disclosure standards by corporates and timely dissemination of price sensitive information to the public. It recommended for a change in the listing agreement of stock exchanges. Some these changes are:

- *Un-audited financial results:* As per existing Clause 41 of the Listing Agreement, the company is required to furnish to the Stock Exchange and to publish un-audited financial results on half yearly basis. The clause has been modified to make these requirements quarterly.

- *Explanation on deployment of funds:* Clause 43 of the Listing Agreement has to provide for companies which mobilize funds from the public through public/rights issues to publish the details of deployment of such funds on an half yearly basis instead of yearly basis.
- *Change of accounting policies, if any:* The un-audited results has to be sent to the Stock Exchange and published in newspapers should be based on the same set of accounting policies as those followed in the previous year. In case, there are changes in the accounting policies, the results of previous year will be recast as per the present accounting policies, to make it comparable with current year results.
- *Event having bearing an impact on operations of the company:* Clause 36 of the Listing Agreement requires the company to inform immediately to the Stock Exchange of events such as strike, power cuts, etc. This should be applicable for all events which will have bearing on performance/operations of the company as well as price sensitive information. The material events may be events such as: change in the general character or nature of business, etc.
- *Change in the general character of its business*: The issuer has to promptly notify the Exchange of any material change in the general character or nature of its business where such change is brought about by the issuer entering into or proposing to enter into any agreement for technical, manufacturing, marketing or financial tie-up or by reason of the issuer, selling or disposing of or agreeing to sell or dispose of any unit or division by the issuer, enlarging, restricting or closing the operations of any unit or division or proposing to enlarge, restrict or close the operations of any unit or division or otherwise.
- *Information about natural disturbances*: The issuer will, soon after the occurrence of any natural calamity like earthquake, flood or fire disrupting the operation of

anyone or more units of the issuer, keep the Exchange informed of the details of the damage caused to the unit thereby and whether the loss/ damage has been covered by insurance, and without delay furnish to the Exchange an estimate of the loss in revenue or production arising there from and the steps taken to restore normalcy, in order to enable the security holders and the public to appraise the position of the issue and to avoid the establishment of a false market in its securities.

- *Information on new division's commercial operation:* The issuer will promptly notify the Exchange the commencement of commercial production or the commencement, of commercial operations of any division where revenue from the division for a full year of production or operations is estimated to be not less than ten per cent of the revenues of the issuer for the year.
- *Information relating to Government policy affecting operations of the company:* The issuer will promptly inform the Exchange of the developments with respect to pricing or in realization on its goods or services arising out of modification or change in Government's or other authority's policies provided the change can reasonably be expected to have a material impact on its present or future operations or its profitability.
- *Information about litigations, etc:* The issuer will promptly after the event inform the Exchange of the development; with respect to any dispute in conciliation proceedings, litigation which can reasonably expected to have a material impact on its present or future operations or its profitability or its financials.
- *Change in credit rating:* The issuer will promptly notify the Exchange, the details of any rating or revision n rating assigned to any debt or equity instrument of the issuer or to any fixed deposit, programme or to any scheme or proposal of the issuer involving mobilization of funds whether in India or abroad

provided the rating so assigned has been quoted, referred to, reported, relied upon or otherwise used by or on behalf *of* the issuer.

- *Merger and amalgamation:* Any other information having bearing on the operation/performance of the company as well as price sensitive information which includes but not restricted to issue of any class of securities, acquisition, merger, demerger, amalgamation, restructuring, scheme of arrangement, spin off of setting divisions of the company, etc., change in market lot of the companies shares, sub-division of equity shares of company and voluntary delisting by the company from the stock-exchange.
- *Redemption of securities:* Any action which will result in alteration in the terms regarding redemption/ cancellation/retirement in whole or in part of any securities issued by the company.
- *Global issues:* Information regarding opening, closing or status of ADR, GDR or any other class of securities to be issued abroad.
- *Cancellation of dividend/rights/bonus issue:* Cancellation of dividend/rights/bonus, etc. The above information should be made public immediately.
- *Buy back of shares:* For buy back by companies, in order to provide equal opportunities to the investors and protecting their interest. Explanatory statement to be annexed to the notice of the general meeting. It should also prescribe the contents of the public announcement and disclosures to be made in the letter of offer respectively by the companies resorting to buy back of securities.

Investor Education

The Department of Company affairs is taking several initiatives for investors' education. The Investor Protection and Education Fund administered by the Department is effectively used for investor education. Investor education forms an important part of the efforts of SEBI to protect the interest of the investors in securities markets. A series of information brochures and pamphlets have been issued in the past for the benefit of the investor. These publications indicate the various risks associated with capital market investment, the rights of the investors, the responsibilities and details of the grievance redressal machinery available to them in respect of various grievances and the remedy and relief to be obtained from different agencies like SEBI, Department of Company Affairs, Stock Exchanges, Reserve Bank of India and Registrars to the Issue, apart from seeking relief through consumers disputes redressal forums, Company Law Board and Courts of Law. The brochures/pamphlets contain tips and clarifications on trading of securities on the stock exchange and ensure proper transfer of securities to the transferee.

Associations of investors registered with SEBI, the stock exchanges and professional bodies like ICSI, ICAI, etc., also conduct investor education programmes from time to time to appraise the investors of the changes in the law and regulations and the methods of protecting themselves against malpractices and delays cropping up in the market. Information about the depository system of trading in securities has been disseminated to the investors explaining the advantages and benefits available in the system that eliminates unnecessary paper work and loss and delays in postal delivery. An active investor can get more knowledge from the journals and magazines in the field of corporate investment as well as news paper that carry articles which highlight the general market trends and the initiatives of government in preventing investor from being cheated in the market.

Points to be noted by an Investor before Investing in Securities

- One has to keep in mind the basic aspects of safety, liquidity and profitability of the security.
- The investors who choose to layout their money on securities must necessarily educate themselves continuously on the developments in the law, regulations of different instruments and different players in the market.
- Investors have to keep themselves abreast of the new developments in the market and make a proper assessment of the type of instrument, organizations

and intermediaries they are dealing with before venturing into investment.

- Promoters' track record and experience in the chosen field, their reputation and integrity should be noted.
- The sector in which the money is going to deployed has to be analyzed.
- Risk factors as pronounced in the offer documents has to be given effect and pending litigations against the company should be noted to judge whether unfavourable decision would lead to change in management, technology, location, profitability of the company.
- Whether statutory clearances have been obtained and registered in the recognized stock exchanges.

Remedies Available to Investors under the Companies Act

- *Problems of transfers and transmissions*: For transfer and transmission of securities necessary provisions are available in Section 111 and 113. As regards listed companies, the listing agreement contains provisions for prompt issue of certificates after effecting transfers. Failure to comply with the provisions of Companies Act can be brought before the Company Law Board through an appeal under Section 111. After hearing the parties Company Law Board may by order direct the company to register the transfer.
- *Violation of listing agreement:* As regards violation of provisions in the listing agreement, investors can forward their complaints to the stock exchanges with whom the company is listed to initiate action. The Investors are also at liberty to file complaints before the District Forum State Commission or National Commission. In the case of listed companies investors are entitled to forward their complaints to the company and SEBI. It has the power to take action including criminal proceeding where necessary against persons responsible for delay.
- *Offences committed*: Section 621 of the Companies Act, 1956 permits the shareholder to proceed against the

company and its officers in a court of law generally for offences committed under the Companies Act including prospectus, abridged prospectus, allotment, listing, transfer of shares, dividend payment, etc., committed by the company as well as its officers under various provisions in the Act.

- *Non-payment of dividend:* SEBI has been delegated powers to take action against listed companies under 45 Sections of the Companies Act in relation to issue and transfer of securities and non-payment of dividend. It has been given teeth to deal with violations and defaults under Sections 55 to 84, 108 to 122, 206 and 206A and 207, committed by listed companies as well as public companies which intend to make public issues and get their securities listed on any recognized stock exchange.
- *Inspection of books*: The Officers of SEBI can undertake inspection of books of the company and SEBI need not give previous notice to the company in this regard.
- *Protection to small depositors:* Section 58AA has been inserted in the Companies (Amendment) Act, 2000 affording special protection to small depositors and prescribing punishments for violations. Small depositor means a depositor who has deposited in a financial year a sum not exceeding Rs. 50,000.
- *Protection of debenture holders:* Section 117A to 117C has been inserted in the Act to protect the debenture holders, and the new sections contains stringent punishments for default.
- *Interim dividend also meant as dividend:* Section 205 has been amended to include interim dividend under the term dividend. The provisions applicable to dividend are also applicable to interim dividend.

Some of the areas which need to be tuned up for investors' protection are:

- *Accountability for growth:* Suitable legislative provision to be made to fix accountability and responsibility on the Executive Directors to bring about growth in the organization. If such directors manage the show for protecting their vested interest rather than the shareholders' interest, such persons should not be allowed to continue in listed companies.

- *Accountability of Management Personnel:* Some directors manipulate the resources of the company with the connivance of the management personnel. Such people forget about the larger interest of the shareholders and act supporting the vested interest of directors. To overcome this, the Board of every public company should name the personnel who are coming under senior cadre management for protecting the larger interest of the shareholders.
- *Whistle Blowers to be recognized*: There should be provision in the Act to stipulate that the Board of every public company should approve a whistle blowing and ethic policy every year. It is seen that those who pinpoint the misdeeds of the WDs are shown the door. This should be checked.
- *Disclosure of the directors' interested transactions*: Proper disclosure mechanism to be adopted to disclose—the interested party-related transactions and its effect on the profitability. All monetary values and pecuniary loss arising by way of these transactions of the directors must be disclosed. The negative effect on the bottom line by these transactions should be commented by the Auditors.
- *Duties and Responsibilities of Directors:* The duties and responsibilities of Directors and Whole-time Directors should be listed in the Act as a guide only. It is not possible to list all the duties and responsibilities exhaustively. But, this will help alert and make it known to the Directors on the spot when they are going to do any act against these duties.
- *Dual Positions to be discouraged*: No person shall be permitted to hold more than one post simultaneously.
- *Auditors and Secretaries to play their role effectively*: The Auditors who fail to disclose the interested party

related transactions of the Directors should be slapped heavy penalty on a per day basis. Auditors should not certify the closing stocks of inventories merely on a certificate from the MD. They should conduct the physical verification by using their own staff and the Company's staff. Similarly, Secretaries should not issue Compliance Certificate based on a declaration signed by the MD or Chief Executive Officer stating that the provisions of sections 297, 299 and 300 have been complied with.

- *Compliance Certificate:* The Compliance Certificate by Practising Secretary should be made applicable to all listed Companies and all unlisted Companies having a paid up share capital of more than a certain limit such as Rs. 5 Crores and above.
- *Listing of unlisted Companies*: Certain unlisted companies having a threshold limit of over a particular limit and shareholders strength of over a limit should be made to compulsorily list in stock exchanges. However certain relaxation on the norms for dividend paying capacity may be granted.

INVESTORS' PROTECTION AND INSIDER TRADING

1. *Corporate Disclosure Policy:* To ensure timely and adequate disclosure of price sensitive information, the following norms shall be followed by listed companies:
   - Prompt disclosure of price sensitive information.
   - Price sensitive information shall be given by listed companies to stock exchanges and disseminated on a continuous and immediate basis.
   - Listed companies may also consider ways of supplementing information released to stock exchanges by improving investor access to their public announcements.
   - Disclosure of shareholdings/ownership by major shareholders and disclosure of changes in ownership as provided under any Regulations

made under the Act and the listing agreement shall be made in a timely and adequate manner.

2. *Overseeing and co-ordinating disclosure:* Listed companies shall designate a senior official—such as compliance officer to oversee corporate disclosure. This official shall be responsible for ensuring that the company complies with continuous disclosure requirements, overseeing and co-ordinating disclosure of price sensitive information to stock exchanges, analysts, shareholders and media, and educating staff on disclosure policies and procedure. Information disclosure/dissemination may normally be approved in advance by the official designated for the purpose. If information is accidentally disclosed without prior approval, the person responsible may inform the designated officer immediately, even if the information is not considered price sensitive.
3. *Responding to market rumours:* Listed companies shall have clearly laid down procedures for responding to any queries or requests for verification of market rumours by exchanges. The official designated for corporate disclosure shall be responsible for deciding whether a public announcement is necessary for verifying or denying rumours and then making the disclosure.
4. Disclosure/dissemination of Price Sensitive Information with special reference to Analysts, Institutional Investors. Listed companies should follow the guidelines given hereunder while dealing with analysts and institutional investors:
   - Only Public information to be provided.
   - Listed companies shall provide only public information to the analyst/research persons/ large investors like institutions. Alternatively, the information given to the analyst should be simultaneously made public at the earliest.
   - *Recording of discussion*: In order to avoid misquoting or misrepresentation, it is desirable that at least two-company representative be present at meetings with Analysts, brokers or

Institutional Investors and discussion should preferably be recorded.

- *Handling of unanticipated questions*: A listed company should be careful when dealing with analysts' questions that raise issues outside the intended scope of discussion. Unanticipated questions may be taken on notice and a considered response given later. If the answer includes price sensitive information, a public announcement should be made before responding.
- *Simultaneous release of Information*: When a company organises meetings with analysts, the company shall make a press release or post-relevant information on its website after every such meet. The company may also consider live webcasting of analyst meets.

5. Medium of disclosure/dissemination :
   - Disclosure/dissemination of information may be done through various media so as to achieve maximum reach and quick dissemination.
   - Corporates shall ensure that disclosure to stock exchanges is made promptly.
   - Corporates may also facilitate disclosure through the use of their dedicated Internet website.
   - Company websites may provide a means of giving investors a direct access to analyst briefing material, significant background information and questions and answers.
   - The information filed by corporates with exchanges under continuous disclosure requirement may be made available on the company website.

Dissemination by Stock Exchanges

- The disclosures made to stock exchanges may be disseminated by the exchanges to investors in a quick and efficient manner through the stock exchange network as well as through stock exchange websites.

- Information furnished by the companies under continuous disclosure requirements, should be published on the web site of the exchange instantly.
- Stock exchanges should make immediate arrangement for display of the information furnished by the companies instantly on the stock exchange web site.

CODE OF CONDUCT FOR PREVENTION OF INSIDER TRADING IN OTHER CASES

- Employees/directors/partners shall maintain the confidentiality of all Price Sensitive Information. Employees/directors/partners must not pass on such information directly or indirectly by way of making a recommendation for the purchase or sale of securities.
- Price Sensitive Information is to be handled on a "need to know" basis, i.e. Price Sensitive Information should be disclosed only to those within the organization/firm who need the information to discharge their duty and whose possession of such information will not give rise to a conflict of interest or appearance of misuse of the information.
- Files containing confidential information shall be kept secure. Computer files must have adequate security of login and pass word, etc.

1. Chinese Wall

To prevent the misuse of confidential information the organization/firm shall adopt a "Chinese Wall" policy which separates those areas of the organization/firm which routinely have access to confidential information, considered "inside areas" from those areas which deal with sale/marketing/investment advise or other departments providing support services, considered "public areas".

- The employees in the inside area shall not

communicate any Price Sensitive Information to anyone in public area.

- The employees in inside area may be physically segregated from employees in public area.
- Demarcation of the various departments as inside area may be implemented by the organization/firm.
- In exceptional circumstances employees from the public areas may be brought "over the wall" and given confidential information on the basis of "need to know" criteria, under intimation to the compliance officer.

2. Misuse of Price Sensitive Information

Employees/directors/partners shall not use Price Sensitive Information to buy or sell securities of any sort, whether for their own account, their relative's account, organization/firm's account or a client's account. The following trading restrictions shall apply for trading in securities:

- All directors/officers/designated employees of the organization/firm who intend to deal in the securities of the client company (above a minimum threshold limit to be determined by the organization/firm) shall pre-clear the transactions as per the pre-dealing procedure as described hereunder.
- An application may be made in such form as the organization/firm may specify in this regard, to the Compliance officer indicating the name and estimated number of securities that the designated employee/director/partner intends to deal in, the details as to the depository with which he has a security account, the details as to the securities in such depository mode and such other details as may be required by any rule made by the organization/firm in this behalf.
- An undertaking shall be executed in favour of the organization/firm by such designated employee/partners/directors incorporating, *inter alia*, the following clauses, as may be applicable:

- That the designated employee/director/partner does not have any access or has not received any " Price Sensitive Information" up to the time of signing the undertaking.
- That in case the designated employee/director/partner has access to or receives "Price Sensitive Information" after the signing of the undertaking but before the execution of the transaction he/she shall inform the Compliance officer of the change in his position and that he/she would completely refrain from dealing in the securities of the client company till the time such information becomes public.
- That he/she has not contravened the code of conduct for prevention of insider trading as specified by the organization/firm from time to time.
- That he/she has made a full and true disclosure in the matter.

3. Restricted/Grey List

In order to monitor chinese wall procedures and trading in client securities based on inside information, the organization/firm shall restrict trading in certain securities and designate such list as restricted/grey list. Security of a listed company shall be put on the restricted/grey list if the organization/firm is handling any assignment for the listed company or is preparing appraisal report or is handling credit rating assignments and is privy to Price Sensitive Information. Any security which is being purchased or sold or is being considered for purchase or sale by the organization/firm on behalf of its clients/schemes of mutual funds, etc. shall be put on the restricted/grey list. As the restricted list itself is a highly confidential information it shall not be communicated directly, or indirectly to anyone outside the organization/firm. The Restricted List shall be maintained by Compliance Officer. When any securities are on the Restricted List, trading in these securities by designated employees/directors/partners may be blocked or may be disallowed at the time of pre-clearance.

4. Other Restrictions

- All directors/designated employees/partners shall execute their order within one week after the approval of pre-clearance is given. If the order is not executed within one week after approval is given, the employee/director/partners must pre-clear the transaction again.
- All directors/officers/designated employees/partners shall hold their investments for a minimum period of 30 days in order to be considered as being held for investment purposes.
- The holding period shall also apply to purchases in the primary market (IPOs). In the case of IPOs, the holding period would commence when the securities are actually allotted.
- In case the sale of securities is necessitated by personal emergency, the holding period may be waived by the compliance officer after recording in writing his/her reasons in this regard.
- Analysts, if any, employed with the organization/firm while preparing research reports of a client company(s) shall disclose their share holdings/interest in such company(s) to the compliance officer.
- Analysts who prepare research report of a listed company shall not trade in securities of that company for thirty days from preparation of such report.

5. Reporting Requirements for Transactions in Securities

- All directors/designated employees/partners of the organization/firm shall be required to forward following details of their Securities transactions including the statement of dependent family members (as defined by the organization/firm) to the Compliance officer.
- All holdings in securities by directors/officers/designated employees/partners at the time of joining the organization.

- Periodic statement of any transactions in securities (the periodicity of reporting may be defined by the firm or organization. The organization/firm may also be free to decide whether reporting is required for trades where pre-clearance is also required.
- Annual statement of all holdings in securities
- The Compliance officer shall maintain records of all the declarations given by the directors/designated employees/partners in the appropriate form for a minimum period of three years.
- The Compliance officer shall place before the Chief Executive Officer/Partner or a committee notified by the organization/firm, on a monthly basis all the details of the dealing in the securities by designated employees/directors/partners of the organization/firm and the accompanying documents that such persons had executed under the pre-dealing procedure as envisaged in this code.
- Any employee/partner/director who trades in securities or communicates any information or counsels any person trading in securities, in contravention of the code of conduct may be penalized and appropriate action may be taken by the organization/firm.

24

Securitization

INTRODUCTION

The recent past has seen financial innovation in the international and the domestic market. Products and techniques like factoring, securitization of debt, etc. are becoming common in view of the changing needs of borrowers and lenders. In the US and some European countries the word 'securitization' was common in bankers vocabulary in the late 1980's. The securitization process in India has come a long way since the widely reported first deal in 1990 when Citibank securitised auto loans and placed a paper with GIC mutual fund. Since then, a variety of deals have been undertaken.

According to John Henderson and Jonathon Scott, securitization is defined as the process which takes place when a lending institution's assets are removed in one way or the other from its balance sheet and are funded instead by the investors who purchase a negotiable financial instrument evidencing this indebtness, without recourse to the original lender.

Securitization of debt, or asset securitization as is more often referred to, is a process by which identified pools of receivables, which are usually illiquid on their own, are transformed into marketable securities through suitable repackaging of cash flows that they generate. Securitization, in effect, is a credit arbitrage transaction that permits for more efficient management of risks by isolating a specific pool of assets from the originator's balance sheet. Further, unlike the case of conventional debt financing, where the interest and principal obligations of a borrowing entity are serviced out of its own general cash flows, debt servicing with asset-backed securities (ABS) is from the cash flows originating from its underlying assets.

The securitization of debt originated as a response to the twin problems of liquidity crunch and concentration of risks faced by financial institutions. Asset securitization is a product of financial engineering which enables the structuring and selling of negotiable instrument in order to spread risk over a large group of investors, a risk which would normally have been taken by a lender or a consortium and thereby make funds available to borrowers which would otherwise not have been possible. This is the risk management aspect of banking which securitization deals with.

Securitization can also be used as a tool for fund management. In case of financial institutions large funds are locked up in loans and advances given for development projects. The cash flows from these assets come over an extended period and in small quantum. By resorting to securitization, financial institutions can convert these illiquid assets into cash and use these funds for making further investments thus increasing the profitability of the organisation as a whole.

Securitization is a process by which financial assets are pooled and the cash flows are used to guarantee and service a security. Virtually any kind of asset, which can generate a stream of cash flows, can be securitised. These securities are subsequently subscribed to and traded among the investors. These financial assets can be residential mortgages, auto loans, credit card receivables, leases, consumer loans, trade credits, corporate bonds, etc. If the asset is a mortgage, the instruments are called mortgage-backed securities and the other instruments are known as non-mortgage asset backed securities.

Though the Indian capital market is over 100 years old, it continues mainly as a market for equity related products. Debt is more or less financed through banks and financial institutions, although in the recent past, financial markets are playing an increasingly significant role. Even the Government securities market essentially consists of primary issues and inter-institutional trades. This is also mainly influenced by 'demand management' by the Government through SLR (statutory liquidity ratios) and PLR (Prime lending rate) ratios which inhibit true price discovery. World over, the size and scope of debt markets is at least five to ten times larger than the equity markets—both in cash and in derivatives markets. This is because while equity related products originate primarily from the corporate sector, debt instruments could originate from various areas including corporate and governments sectors. Moreover, the scope of product development, by way of securitization of debt etc., also enlarges the potential for the market for debt instruments. In fact, the debt financing route takes precedence over equity finance to meet the current demands of the infrastructure sector. However, due to a variety of institutional and regulatory reasons, the Indian debt market has not been able to achieve its true potential.

GLOBAL SECURITIZATION MARKETS

Several factors have led to the development of global ABS markets. Principal factors that have spurred the development of ABS markets in the OECD world include:

1. Competitive pressures released due to deregulation, forcing sharp declines in bank lending margins.
2. Successive financial sector leading to sectoral level credit deterioration.
3. Universal adoption of capital adequacy standards, with efficiency of capital usage increasingly becoming the basis of evaluating banks and financial institutions.

4. Increasing functional specialisation leading to large scale outsourcing.
5. Giant strides in information technology.
6. Global trend towards making all debt issuances in tradable form.
7. The patronage of national governments by enacting supportive legislation, setting up specialized agencies to provide credit enhancement, etc.

NEED FOR SECURITIZATION IN INDIA

In developed countries there have been successful attempts to issue securitised instruments based on future income streams—also known as future flow securitization—that arise from the use of physical assets income arising due to regulations, income from sale of natural resources. Furthermore, a wide variety of receivables have been securitised like, residential mortgages, credit card receivables, auto loans, swap contracts, trade receivables, unsecured term loans, collateralized bond/loan obligation, export receivables, finance leases, aircraft leases, finance leases, aircraft leases, insurance premia, firm and music album receivables, etc. However, considering the stage of maturity that the Indian financial markets are in apart from the category of assets that are presently being securitised, there is a possibility that the securitization of the following kinds of receivables could gain popularity in the near future:

- Collateralized Loan/Bond Obligations
- Housing Mortgage Loans
- Credit Card Receivables
- Two Wheeler Receivables
- Consumer Durable Receivables
- Trade Receivables
- Aircraft Hire Purchase/Lease Receivables

Securitization is the only ray of hope for funding resource starved infrastructure sectors like power in India. For power utilities burdened with delinquent receivables from state electricity boards, securitization seems to be the only hope of meeting resource requirements. Securitization can help Indian borrowers with international assets in pricing the sovereign rating and placing an investment grade structure. An example, albeit failed, is that of Air India's aborted attempt to securitise its North American ticket receivables. Such structured transactions can help premier corporates to obtain a superior pricing than a borrowing based on their non-investment grade corporate rating. A market for Mortgage backed Securities (MBS) in India can help large Indian housing finance companies (HFCs) in churning their portfolios and focus on what they know best—fresh asset origination. Indian HFCs have traditionally relied on bond finance and loans from the National Housing Bank (NHB). MBS can provide a vital source of funds for the HFCs. After the merger of India's largest financial institution ICICI with ICICI Bank, ICICI, faced with SLR and other requirements, is actively seeking to launch a CLO to reduce its overall asset exposure. It appears to be only a matter of time before other Public Financial Institutions merge with other banks. Such mergers would result in the need for more CLOs in the foreseeable future.

Securitization effort will call for considerable investments in time and resources. Hence, on a comparative cost scale it can even be somewhat more expensive than other types of debt financing that may be available to a borrower, at least in the initial stages. However, it has been demonstrated that a continuing securitization program rather than a single deal often goes to reduce the costs, as economies of scale and expertise pick up over a period of time. Bearing this in mind, many securitization programs are run with a long-term strategic perspective. Growing importance of securitization is perhaps best illustrated by the volume through-put in the non-OECD world over the past few years.

Indian institutional investors also have a preference for liquidity in the ABS instrument. This preference exists more in the nature of a liquidity backstop rather than a demand for an active secondary market. A liquidity backstop facility is ideally provided by a credible entity working on a transparent benchmark. The facility also needs to be formalised through appropriate documentation. Support from a Government agency or an institution of repute would be of considerable value in this regard. In addition to such preferences, institutional investors such as mutual funds also require reliable valuation benchmarks on ABS in order to evaluate their portfolio performance. Until the ABS market reaches a certain critical volume and level of activity, market maker quotations would be hard to come by.

SECURITIZATION SCENARIO

Securitization began in India in the early nineties. CRISIL rated the first securitization programme in 1991-92 when Citibank securitised a pool from its auto-loan portfolio and placed the paper with GIC Mutual Fund. The market for ABS has been stagnant largely for want of a suitable enabling regulatory framework. In the Indian context, the benefits that securitization can bring about can be quite significant. The following merit consideration in this regard. In a capital-short economy, an opportunity that permits effective use of available capital hardly requires any major emphasis. In addition, the ability to diversify one's funding base by reaching out to new investor markets, without increasing the financial leverage, which may otherwise have regulatory implications in some cases, is also of definite value. Obtaining matched funding leading to effective balance sheet management is particularly significant from commercial banks' perspective. Reallocating risks in a planned and transparent manner helps in managing them better. Originators would also stand to benefit on account of possible gains that would accrue in the form of improvements in their credit and operating processes, as these come under detailed scrutiny.

Credit history of the Indian banking system indicates that substantial volumes of ABS of credit quality consistent with the rating required are available. This would ensure continuous supply of assets that can be tailored to meet the credit appetites of investors. Institutional investors may not only benefit from such customized issuances, but also may have access to invest into otherwise illiquid assets at superior yields without compromising on their credit standards.

The securitization process would upgrade the level of sophistication of banking and finance in the country in the long-run. This, combined with an appropriate regulatory framework, can make securitization an important catalyst in mobilising domestic savings as well as attracting foreign capital, which can be of immense value, particularly in the context of capital requirements to develop the country's infrastructure sector. Securitizing project finance, telecom, toll road and other similar receivables could well become reality in the medium term future.

FUNDING STRATEGY

The assets of financial institutions include loans, bills receivables, trade receivables, etc. These assets are financed through debt and equity. Securitization is a funding strategy that involves funding based on asset value and cash flow characteristics of the asset pool which are not supported by the firm's equity.

Raising funds through debt or equity is termed as the left hand side of the balance sheet approach. Securitization is a right hand side of the balance sheet approach of raising funds based on the specific asset pool's cash flow and values. Usually funding is from new creditors whose recourse is restricted to the assets being financed. Securitization is a funding technique that combines pure asset sales and secured financing. In securitization the financial institution raises funds by selling a portion of its asset portfolio to a Trustee or Special Purpose Vehicle (SPV).

Firms can improve their liquidity position and improve certain key ratios through securitization. Securitization enables banks and institutions to borrow at a lower cost. An improvement in the liquidity position will lower working capital requirements and thus reduce the interest burden. The proceeds from securitization can also be invested in projects that give a higher rate of return, thus improving the overall performance of the institution.

SECURITIZATION PROCESS

The process of securitization primarily involves three parties, namely, the originator, the special purpose vehicle

(SPV) and the investor. The originator is the one who owns the financial asset and who wants to offload the same in the market. The originator could be a banking, industrial or finance company. The SPV or in other words the issuer is the one who issues mortgage-backed securities to investor in the market. Generally merchant bankers function as SPV's. The investor is the one who buys securities from the SPV. Essential features of a securitization transaction comprise the following:

Creation of asset pool and its sale: The originator/seller (of assets) creates a pool of assets and executes a legal true sale of the same to a special purpose vehicle (SPV). An SPV in such cases is either a trust or a company, as may be appropriate under applicable law, setup to carry out a restricted set of activities, management of which would usually rest with an independent board of directors.

Issuance of the securitised paper: This activity is usually performed by the SPV. Design of the instrument however would be based on the nature of interest that investors would have on the asset pool. In the case of pass-through issuances, the investors will have a direct ownership interest in the underlying assets, while 'pay-through' is a debt issued by the SPV secured by the assets and their cash flows.

Credit Risk: It must be made abundantly clear at the very outset that the accretions on the asset-backed security, i.e., interest, amortization and redemption payments, are entirely dependent on the performance of the pooled assets, and will have nothing to do with the credit of the originator. By the same argument, such cash flows would also be not influenced by events affecting the condition of the originator, including insolvency.

Pool Selection: The process of selecting assets to build a securitization pool would take into careful consideration, loan characteristics that are important from a cash flow, legal, and credit points of view, such as type of asset, minimum and maximum loan size, vintage, rate, maturity and concentration limits such as, geographic, single-borrower, etc. 'Cherry-picking' to include only the highest quality assets in the pool should be consciously avoided. Ideal selection would be a random choice among assets conforming only to cash flow or legal criteria. Often, substitution of eligible assets in the place of original assets that mature/prepay in order to maintain the level of asset cover would also be required.

Administration: Formal delineation of duties and responsibilities relating to administration of securitised assets, including payment servicing and managing relationship with the final obligors must be spelt out clearly through a contractual agreement with the entity that would perform those functions.

Stages in Securitization

Identification of Assets: The 'originator', first identifies the asset or a pool of assets that have to be securitised. There must be some basic conditions that must be satisfied by an asset, which is to be securitised. The cash flows from the reference asset should be reliable and payments should be periodically obtained. This means that the asset portfolio should have a documented history showing default and delinquency experience. This record should be credible. The assets have to be of good quality that in turn facilitates the marketability to be quick and easy. This could be either on assets own strength or with some sort of credit enhancement. This is to ensure that default risks are brought down considerably. The pool of assets should carry identical dates of interest payment and maturities. To make the transaction meaningful, the total quantity of assets to be securitised should be huge enough to spread over the securitization costs. Assets that stand a chance of being sold to investors with only the minimum layer of additional credit enhancement should ideally have the following characteristics:

- Be well diversified.
- Have a statistical history of loss experience.
- Be homogenous in nature.
- Be broadly similar in repayment and final maturity structures.
- Be to some extent liquid.

Structuring of Asset Backed Securities (ABS)

These are fundamental to every securitization deal, as they determine the specifics relating to the ABS instrument, the issuer, the relevant tax and accounting treatment, and other key factors. Every ABS issuance may have to be structured differently in order to take the best advantage of the various environmental factors.

Structuring decisions would concern the manner in which the pool of assets will be sold or transferred. This would be followed by the design of the ABS instrument, as either a pass through or a pay through security. Pass-throughs represent direct ownership interests in the underlying assets, which are typically held in trust for the investors, so that payments on the assets are passed through to the investors directly from the assets (after payment of all fees and expenses, including excess servicing). Pay throughs, on the other hand, are general obligations or preferred stock of the issuer (SPV), substantially all the assets of which consist of a pool of receivables and the related credit enhancement or other structural support.

In a typical deal, the asset originator creates a SPV and sells reference assets to the same. The SPV is a legal entity designed to isolate receivables and associated cash flows from the risk of the originators bankruptcy. The SPV then structures the ABS based on the preferences of the originator and the investors. The type of ABS is decided by the nature of the reference asset and the nature of payments to the investors. To make the ABS attractive to the investors, issuers follow some credit enhancement procedures. Securities are credit enhanced through an insurance or a third party assurance. Sometimes the security is over-collateralized to improve the credit rating of the issue. After structuring the ABS, they are offered to the investor public through a merchant banker. The issuer takes up the responsibility of creating a market in the securities that are created. As they are negotiable instruments and are listed, they can be traded in the secondary market and hence liquidity for the investor is not a problem.

Tax and accounting treatments constitute other important dimensions of structuring. Typical tax issues that need to be addressed relate to transfer charges (stamp duty), capital gains taxation as applicable to the originator on sale of assets, taxation of the issuer, and withholding tax or taxes deducted at source as applicable to the issuer and the investors. Accounting treatment of securitization could fall into one of the following three categories, viz., full derecognition, partial derecognition where only transferred assets receive derecognition, and full on-balance sheet recognition. Specialist opinion must be obtained on both tax and accounting aspects. These would be environment specific.

Credit enhancement of the ABS would also be an important structuring consideration, as it strives to strike a balance between the investor and the issuer needs on the credit quality of the instrument. Typical forms of credit enhancement include: Spread Account or Reserve Account, Over-collateralization, Letters of credit, Insurance company guarantees, Senior/subordinated structure, etc. Other structuring issues that need to be addressed relate to extraction of excess servicing, identification of payment and loss priorities, etc.

Investor Servicing

The investor is serviced by periodic payments depending on the nature of the ABS. According to the terms of the issue, the investor may be paid interest periodically and the principal at the end of the maturity as a bullet payment. Or they may be paid both interest and principal periodically over the period of maturity.

Documentation

A set of documentation as per the applicable legal framework is fundamental to structuring transactions. While the system of documentation may vary from one jurisdiction to another, there is a generic body of documentation that is normally applicable in most cases. Legal opinions constitute the very foundations. These must provide clear affirmation on all things fundamental, such as the legality of the transaction, the bankruptcy remoteness of the issuer from the originator, the issuer's authority to enter into such transactions, the legal true sale of receivables to the issuer, the creation of security over the receivable pool, etc.

Receivable documentation should first establish the existence and nature of underlying obligations, such as payment schedules, the conditions under which the obligors may either renege or repudiate payments, and terms of sale of such receivables. It must also confirm that the receivables have been originated in compliance with the applicable statutes. When receivables are sold, documentation specifying the items sold, the mechanics of sale and the representations and warranties made by the seller on their characteristics would be drawn up. Further, the claims of investors in ABS over such flows need to be established clearly through the security documentation.

Service documentation specifying the duties and responsibilities of the servicer or servicing agent would also be a key one. In practice, originators often double up as servicers. Related documentation in addition to the above would typically comprise those relating to credit enhancement, liquidity and market-making, listing agreements with stock exchanges, as well as transaction prospectus or information memoranda, as may be appropriate.

PLAYERS IN SECURITIZATION

Securitization programs usually involve several participants, each carrying out a specialist function, such as, creating and analyzing the asset pool, administration, credit rating, accounting, legal negotiation, etc. The participants who involve in the issuance of asset-backed securities are:

- Originator
- Special Purpose Vehicle
- Servicer
- Issuer
- Merchant Bankers
- Credit Enhancer
- Rater
- Trustee
- Regulators
- Specialists
- Investors.

Originators: Originator also interchangeably referred to as the Seller, is the entity whose receivable portfolio forms the basis for ABS issuance. It creates the underlying assets that are sold or used as collateral, the merchant banker and the originator establish the structure and the issuing vehicle, the rating agencies set the rating, credit enhancer improve the credit quality, and the trustees create the trust and issue certificates. Originators create the assets that are sold or used as collateral for asset-backed securities. Originators include finance companies, financial institutions, commercial banks, and insurance companies, thrift institutions and securities firms.

Benefits to the Originator

- *Funding alternative*: Being distinct and different from the originator's own obligations, a well structured ABS stands on its own credit rating and thus generates genuine incremental funding. This is so as the originator's existing creditors may invest in the ABS in addition to providing lines of credit to the originator. Further, there may also be other investors in the ABS who do not have a lending relationship with the originator. It is also possible to achieve a superior credit rating for the ABS than the originator's own through appropriate structuring and credit enhancement. This could mean accessing an investor base focusing on high grades, which otherwise may not be possible for an originator. Also, where the originator is not permitted to issue capital market instruments on its own ABS could help overcome such constraints.
- *Balance sheet management*: Fundamental benefit of a true sale, i.e., freeing up the capital of the originator would apply in the case of all securitization transactions. In response, the balance sheet gets compressed and becomes more robust. Its ratios improve. Alternately, reduction in leverage post-securitised sale can be restored by adding on new assets to the balance sheet. Thus the asset through-put of the originator's balance sheet increases. Securitization can also generate matched funding for balance sheet assets. Further, it may also enable the

disposal of non-core assets through suitable structuring.

- *Re-allocation of risks*: Securitization transfers much of the credit risk in the portfolio to the ABS investors and helps to quantify the residual credit risk that the originator is exposed to. These are very useful because, the originator can then take larger exposure to individual obligors and provide a higher degree of comfort to his creditors. Securitization also transfers the originator's market risks, i.e., liquidity, interest rate and prepayment risks, to ABS investors and reduces risk capital requirement. This can lead to more competitive pricing of the underlying asset products.
- *Operating process efficiency*: The extent of portfolio analysis and information demanded by securitization programs often lead to serious re-examination and consequent reengineering of operating processes within the originator organisation. Further, specialist handling of various functional components, such as origination, funding, risk management and administration, often achieved through outsourcing, promotes efficiency across operating processes.
- *Securitization improves operating leverage*: The originator usually assumes the function of the servicer, the issuing and paying agent, and sometimes that of the credit enhancer. Fees accrue on account of all of these. Excess servicing, i.e., the difference between the asset yield and the cost of funds, is also normally extracted by the originator. These income streams can push up the operating leverage of the originator generating income from a larger asset base than what may be otherwise possible for a given capital structure.

Special Purpose Vehicle (SPV): This as the issuer of the ABS ensures adequate distancing of the instrument from the originator.

Servicer: Servicers who are usually the originators or affiliates of the originators of the assets, are responsible for collecting principal and interest payments on the assets when due and for pursuing the collection of delinquent accounts. They also provide the trustee and the certificate holders with monthly and annual reports about the portfolio of assets sold or used as collateral. The reports details the sources collected and the distributed funds, the remaining principal balance, the remaining insurance amount, the amount of fees payable out of the trust and information necessary for certificate holders to prepare their financial statements and to assess their tax liability.

Issuers: The originator does not usually sell assets to third-party investors directly as asset-backed securities. Instead, they are sold first to either a conduit or a "bankruptcy—remote" finance company. Such companies, known as limited purpose corporations, are subsidiaries or affiliates of the originator or the merchant banker that were separately incorporated to facilitate the sale of assets or to issue collateralized debt instruments. Issuers become bankruptcy remote by limiting their activities to issue asset-backed securities and using the proceeds to buy the assets that back the securities. Conduits are issuers of asset-backed securities that do not originate or necessarily service the assets that underlie the securities. They buy assets from different originators or sellers, pool the assets and then sell them to investors. Conduits are particularly useful for firms that do not have enough assets to package as asset-backed securities themselves.

Merchant Bankers: As asset-backed securities issue involves a merchant banker, who either underwrites the securities for public offering or privately places them. As an underwriter, the merchant banker purchases the securities from the issuer for resale. In a private placement, the merchant banker does not purchase the securities and resell them, rather the merchant banker acts as an agent for the issuer, matching the seller with a handful of buyers. The issuers and merchant bankers work together to see that the structure of the issue meets all the legal, regulatory, accounting and tax objectives. The merchant banker also works with the credit enhancers, rating agencies and trustees.

Credit Enhancers: Credit enhancement is a vehicle that reduces the overall credit risk of a security issue. The purpose of the credit enhancement is to improve the rating, and therefore the pricing and marketability of an asset-backed security. Most asset-backed securities are credit enhanced. Credit enhancement can be provided by the issuer or by a third party. Sometimes more than one type of enhancement supports the issue. Credit enhancement provided by a third party has taken the form of either a letter of credit from a bank with a high credit rating or an issuance bond from a firm with a high credit rating. The issuer has enhanced credit by providing recourse through senior-subordinated structure, over-collateralization or a spread account.

Rating agencies: Credit rating agencies assign rating to asset-backed securities issues just as they do for corporate bonds. Credit rating is based on three criteria: the probability of the issuer defaulting on the obligation, the nature and provisions of the obligation and the relative position of the obligation in the event of bankruptcy.

Trustees: A Trustee in asset-backed security is the intermediary between the servicer and the investors and between the credit enhancer and the investors. A trustee is used whether the issue is a sale of assets by the issuer or a collateralized debt obligation of the issuer. The responsibilities of the trustee include buying the assets from the issuer on behalf of the trust and issuing certificates to the investors. As the obligors make principal and interest payments on the assets, the servicer deposits the proceeds in a trust account, and the trustees passes them on the investors. The trustee should be willing to take over the servicer's role if the servicer withdraws or is unable to perform.

Regulators: It principal concerns relate to capital adequacy, liquidity, and credit quality of the ABS, and balance sheet treatment of the transaction,

Specialists: These are those functionaries such as legal and tax counsels, accounting firms, pool auditors, *et. al.*

Investors: More important than all the aforementioned are the investors in the securitised paper. Investors are the ultimate judges of any securitization effort. Originators should therefore interact actively with the investor community to get to know investor preferences and concerns for effective structuring and distribution of ABS. Such knowledge would also make the origination process more efficient. Further, it shall always be remembered that investors have their constraints in the form of legal restrictions, complexity of credit analysis, house name limits, long response time for in-house approvals, etc., all of which can block a deal, and more so in the case of ABS, which, on account of their uniqueness and complexity, present a host of issues which are not normally encountered, say in a straightforward bond investment.

Benefits to Investors

Low event risk: The pool of assets representing the obligations of a number of entities is usually more resilient to event risks than the obligations of a single borrower—i.e. the risk that the credit rating of the security will deteriorate due to circumstances usually beyond the obligor's control is much higher in the latter case. The diversity that the securitization pool represents makes the ABS largely immune to event risks.

Higher yields for lower/similar risk: ABS usually offers higher yields over securities of comparable credit and maturities. The yield spread typically represents the premium paid to compensate for prepayment risk, amortizing cash-flows and the uniqueness of the instrument. In some cases, ABS also provides an opportunity to invest into a pool of otherwise illiquid and inaccessible assets.

Structured issuances: Through appropriate structuring, an ABS can be tailored to meet investor standards on credit quality, yield and maturity. Working with a pool of receivables gives the originator the needed flexibility to be able to offer investors a menu of options around which issuances could be made.

Secondary Market Liquidity: Investment decisions of institutional investors accord a sizeable weightage to instrument liquidity. ABS does fit the requirement in this regard. While the ideal scenario would be to have an active secondary market trading in ABS, institutional investors are often willing to settle for credible liquidity backstops provided by well-rated institutions.

COLLATERAL ENHANCEMENT

The collateral is enhanced to reduce the following risks to the investors:

- Credit risk that the borrowers will default on their obligations.
- Liquidity risk that the borrowers will not make timely repayment of interest and principal.
- Reinvestment risk, where usually there is a delay between payment made by borrower and payment of interest to investors in securities. During this period the funds will be invested. If the interest rate falls, there could be a shortfall in the amount required to meet the obligations to the investors.

Credit Enhancement

There are a number of ways in which credit enhancement can be achieved. The most widely used methods are as follows:

- *Letter of credit*: Obtained usually from a bank, whereby the bank agrees to guarantee a set of percentage of the receivables from arrears and defaults
- *Pool insurance*: For a fee, an insurer will agree to underwrite any defaults over a certain percentage on the underlying assets.
- *Over-collateralization*: The cash flows provided by the collateral are considerably in excess of what is required to fund the cash flows on the securities issued to the investors. Over-collateralization is typically achieved by the use of senior/subordinated issue structure.
- *Spread account*: A part or all of the spread between the average rate of interest paid on the assets and the coupon on the securities issued to the investors after servicing fees charged is placed in an escrow, to be used in the event of default and sometimes delayed payment by the borrowers. Once the securities have been redeemed, the balance remaining on the spread

account will usually revert to the issuer or the originator. Providers of insurance will often require the establishment of a spread account to reduce their exposure.

- Liquidity insurance: In this case an insurance company will guarantee timely payment in the event of a delay.
- Guaranteed investment contract: A bank or an insurance company will guarantee that funds invested with it will earn a stated rate of interest.

FORMS OF CREDIT ENHANCEMENT

Cash collateral: Where a specified amount of cash collateral is kept reserved with the sole purpose of meeting shortfalls in making contractual payouts to investors if and when the need arises. About 38% of the credit enhancement in securitization transactions issued in India has been in the form of cash collateral.

Guarantee by a highly rated corporate or a bank: The rating assigned to the securitised instrument cannot be higher that that of the guarantor in this form of credit enhancement.

Over-collateralization or the issue of subordinate securities: The subordinate securities are typically unrated and invested in by the originators themselves. The payouts on these securities are subordinate to the meeting of all obligations on the senior class of securities, which are rated.

INSTRUMENTS

In concept, all assets generating stable and predictable cash flows can be taken up for securitization. In practice however, much of the securitized paper issued have underlying periodic cash flows secured through contracts defining cash flow volumes, yield and timing. In this respect, securitization of auto loans, credit card receivables, computer leases, unsecured consumer loans, residential and commercial mortgages, franchise/royalty payments, and other receivables relating to telecom, trade, toll road and future export have gained prominence. Typically, asset portfolios that are relatively homogeneous with regard to credit, maturity and interest rate risk could be pooled together to create a securitization structure. However, to make reasonable estimates of the credit quality and payment speed of the securitised paper, it would be essential to analyse the historical data on portfolio performance over some reasonable length of time. Some of the types of instruments for securitization are discussed below.

Pass-through certificates: A pass-through certificate is an instrument that gives the investor a direct undivided ownership interest in the underlying pool of mortgages. These securities are not the debt obligations of the originator. Accordingly, the mortgages are removed from the balance sheet of the originator. Under a pass-through structure, interest and principal payments made by the mortgagors are specifically dedicated to interest and principal payments to the investors after deducting the service fee and the same are passed through to the investors on a pro-rata basis.

Some of the characteristics of pass-through securities are listed below:

- Security represents ownership in underlying pool of assets.
- Assets are removed from the originators balance sheet.
- Payments of principal and interest are passed through to the investors.

Enhancement Loans: The originator sells the assets to a trust. The trustee, then, on behalf of the trust, issues certificates to the investors. Each certificate represents an undivided interest in the entire portfolio of loans. Along with the loans, the originator conveys to the trust for the benefit of the investors, all rights, title, and interest in the assets and rights to receive payments due under the credit enhancements (e.g. insurance policies covering the loan contract). The credit enhancement, an insurance bond purchased by the originator covers some portion of the amount of the underlying assets at the date of the issue. Defaulted contracts are, in effect, purchased by the credit enhancer, and all rights under those contracts are assigned to the credit enhancer. Any payments made on defaulted contracts are reimbursed to the credit enhancer. The investors, trustee, and credit enhancer have no recourse to the originator unless the originator breaches its warranty that each loan contract complies with all the requirements of law or breaches its warranties relating to validity, subsistence, perfection, and priority of the interest in the collateral securing each loan contract.

Asset-backed bonds: The oldest type asset-backed security is the asset-backed bond (ABB). Patterned after the mortgage-backed bond (MBB), the ABB is a debt obligation of the issuer collateralized by a portfolio of loans or sometimes by a portfolio of pass-through securities. The portfolio of loans used as collateral remains on the issuer's books as assets and the ABB's are reported a liabilities. The cash flows from the collateral are not dedicated to the payment of principal and interest on ABB's. Interest is usually paid semi-annually and principal is paid at maturity.

Important characteristic of ABBs is that they are usually over-collateralized. The collateral is evaluated quarterly, and if it falls below the level stated in the bond indenture, more loans or securities must be added to the collateral. There are three reasons for over-collateralization of ABBs. First, because the cash flows accrue to the issuer rather than to the loan pool or to the bondholders, the outstanding balance of any pool of loans may decline faster over time than the principal on the ABBs. Second, the excess collateral provides additional protection to the bondholder against default on individual loans in the pool. Third, the excess collateral protects bondholders from declines in the market value of collateral between the valuation dates. The main characteristics of asset-backed bond are given below:

- Securities are collateralized debt obligations of issuers.
- Assets remain on the originators balance sheet.
- Payments of principal and interest are passed through to the investors.

The issuer segregates a pool of loans and pledges them to a trustee as collateral for the notes it issues via a merchant banker that privately places those securities with investors. Usually, at issuance, the value of the collateral will exceed the value of the notes. In lieu of over-collateralization, the issuer may purchase a credit enhancement from a third party in the form of insurance bond or a letter of credit.

Pay-through Security

A pay-through security is essentially a hybrid between a pass-through certificate and a mortgage-backed bond. A pay-through security is a general obligation of the issuer secured on a pool of mortgages. To this extent, it is like a mortgage-backed bond. Further, like a mortgage-backed bond, the issuer owns the underlying pool and the loans in the pool remain on his balance sheet. The main characteristics of a pay-through are listed below:

- Securities are collateralized debt obligations of issuers.
- Assets remain on the originator's balance sheet.
- Payments of principal and interest are passed through to the investor.
- Collateralized Mortgage Obligation (CMO).

A collateralized mortgage bond obligation (CMO) is a pay-through that consists of more than one maturity class. Generally each CMO is divided into three maturity classes, each class receives semiannual interest payments, and the classes are retired sequentially. Class 1 bondholders receive the first instalments on principal payments and any prepayments, until they were paid off. Class 2 bondholders, in turn, received principal payments and prepayments before Class 3 bondholders received any principal payments. Generally Class 1 bonds are repaid within 5 years of the offering date, Class 2 bonds within 12 years and Class 3 bonds within twenty years.

ASSETS SECURITISED IN INDIA

Existing Assets v. Future Flow

Future flow securitization is different from the traditional asset-backed securitization wherein the securities issued are backed by cash flows generated by an existing pool of assets like hire purchase receivables of cars and commercial vehicles and residential mortgage receivables. In these types of assets the originator has already earned the receivables and they do not depend on the performance of the originator. In other words such types of assets do not involve "generation risk". On the other hand future flow securitization involves receivables which involve "generation risk", i.e., the receivables would come into being only if the originator performs (i.e., it continues to exist, operate, deliver products or services and generate the receivables) like airline ticket receivables, export receivables and remittances from abroad. In future flow securitizations, the securities issued are backed by cash flows from assets that must be generated in the future.

Asset Class Distribution involving receivables backed: Delinquencies in auto-loans in general are the main reasons for this asset category being popular. Because of the inherent higher yields in auto-loans, the originators could offer attractive yields to the investor and still book profits on securitization.

Future Flow Backed Securitization transactions: Presently, there is considerable interest and activity in this area in terms of raising funds by the securitization of future flow receivables especially in industries like construction, media and road development. It is expected that going forward, as the market for securitization, in general, gains maturity in India, the market for future flow securitization would also be impacted favourably.

THE SECURITIZATION AND RECONSTRUCTION OF FINANCIAL ASSETS AND ENFORCEMENT OF SECURITY INTEREST ACT, 2002

Definitions

Appellate Tribunal: A Debts Recovery Appellate Tribunal established under sub-section (1) of section 8 of the Recovery of Debts Due to Banks and Financial Institutions Act, 1993 (51 of 1993).

Asset reconstruction: It means acquisition by any securitization company or reconstruction company of any right or interest of any bank or financial institution in any financial assistance for the purpose of realisation of such financial assistance.

Bank: A bank means—(i) a banking company; or (ii) a corresponding new bank; or (iii) the State Bank of India; or (iv) a subsidiary bank; or (v) such other bank which the Central Government may, by notification, specify for the purposes of this Act.

Banking company: As assigned to it in clause (c) of section 5 of the Banking Regulation Act, 1949 (10 of 1949).

Board: It means the Securities and Exchange Board of India established under section 3 of the Securities and Exchange Board of India Act, 1992 (15 of 1992).

Borrower: Any person who has been granted financial assistance by any bank or financial institution or who has given any guarantee or created any mortgage or pledge as security for the financial assistance granted by any bank or financial institution and includes a person who becomes borrower of a securitization company or reconstruction company consequent upon acquisition by it of any rights or interest of any bank or financial institution in relation to such financial assistance.

Debts Recovery Tribunal: The Tribunal established under sub-section (1) of section 3 of the Recovery of Debts due to Banks and Financial Institutions Act, 1993 (51 of 1993).

Default: Non-payment of any principal debt or interest thereon or any other amount payable by a borrower to any secured creditor consequent upon which the account of such borrower is classified as non-performing asset in the books of account o the secured creditor in accordance with the directions or guidelines issued by the Reserve Bank.

Financial assistance: Any loan or advance granted or any debentures or bonds subscribed or any guarantees given or letters of credit established or any other credit facility extended by any bank or financial institution.

Financial asset: Debt or receivables and includes—(i) a claim to any debt or receivables or part thereof, whether secured or unsecured; or (ii) any debt or receivables secured by, mortgage of, or charge on, immovable property; or (iii) a mortgage, charge, hypothecation or pledge of movable property; or (iv) any right or interest in the security, whether full or part underlying such debt or receivables; or (v) any beneficial interest in property, whether movable or immovable, or in such debt, receivables, whether such interest is existing, future, accruing, conditional or contingent; or (vi) any financial assistance.

Financial institution: (i) a public financial institution within the meaning of section 4A of the Companies Act, 1956 (1 of 1956); (ii) any institution specified by the Central Government under sub-clause (ii) of clause (h) of section 2 of the Recovery of Debts Due to Banks and Financial Institutions Act, 1993 (51 of 1993); (iii) the International Finance Corporation established under the International Finance Corporation (Status, Immunities and Privileges) Act, 1958 (42 of 1958); (iv) any other institution or non-banking financial company as defined in clause (f) of section 45-I of the Reserve Bank of India Act, 1934 (2 of 1934), which the Central Government may, by notification, specify as financial institution for the purposes of this Act.

Hypothecation: A charge in or upon any movable property, existing or future, created by a borrower in favour of a secured creditor without delivery of possession of the movable property to such creditor, as a security for financial assistance and includes floating charge and crystallization of such charge into fixed charge on movable property.

Non-performing asset: An asset or account of a borrower, which has been classified by a bank or financial institution as sub-standard, doubtful or loss asset, in accordance with the directions or under guidelines relating to asset classifications issued by the Reserve Bank.

Obligor: A person liable to the originator, whether under a contract or otherwise, to pay a financial asset or to discharge any obligation in respect of a financial asset, whether existing, future, conditional or contingent and includes the borrower.

Originator: The owner of a financial asset which is acquired by a securitization company or reconstruction company for the purpose of securitization or asset reconstruction.

Property: (i) immovable property; (ii) movable property; (iii) any debt or any right to receive payment of money, whether secured or unsecured; (iv) receivables, whether existing or future; (v) intangible assets, being know-how, patent, copyright, trade mark, licence, franchise or any other business or commercial right of similar nature.

Qualified Institutional Buyer: A financial institution, insurance company, bank, state financial corporation, state industrial development corporation, trustee or any asset management company making investment on behalf of mutual fund or provident fund or gratuity fund or pension fund or a foreign institutional investor registered under the Securities and Exchange Board of India Act, 1992 (15 of 1992) or regulations made there-under, or any other body corporate as may be specified by the Board.

Securitization: Acquisition of financial assets by any securitization company or reconstruction company from any originator, whether by raising of funds by such securitization company or reconstruction company from qualified institutional buyers by issue of security receipts representing undivided interest in such financial assets or otherwise.

Securitization company: Any company formed and registered under the Companies Act, 1956 (1 of 1956) for the purpose of securitization.

Security agreement: An agreement, instrument or any other document or arrangement under which security interest is created in favour of the secured creditor including the creation of mortgage by deposit of title deeds with the secured credit.

Secured creditor: Any bank or financial institution or any consortium or group of banks or financial institutions and includes—(i) debenture trustee appointed by any bank or financial institution; or (ii) securitization company or reconstruction company; or (iii) any other trustee holding securities on behalf of a bank or financial institution, in whose favour security interest is created for due repayment by any borrower of any financial assistance.

Security interest: Right, title and interest of any kind whatsoever upon property, created in favour of any secured creditor and includes any mortgage, charge, hypothecation, assignment other than those specified in section 31.

Security receipt: A receipt or other security, issued by a securitization company or reconstruction company to any qualified institutional buyer pursuant to a scheme, evidencing the purchase or interest in the financial asset involved in securitization; acquisition by the holder thereof, of an undivided right, or title.

Sponsor: Any person holding not less than ten per cent. of the paid-up equity capital of a securitization company or reconstruction company.

Registration of securitization companies or reconstruction companies:

- No securitization company or reconstruction company shall commence or carry on the business of securitization or asset reconstruction without— (a) obtaining a certificate of registration granted under this section; and (b) having the owned fund of not less than two crore rupees or such other amount not exceeding fifteen per cent of total financial assets acquired or to be acquired by the securitization company or reconstruction company, as the Reserve Bank may, by notification, specify: Provided that the Reserve Bank may, by notification, specify different amounts of owned fund for different class or classes of securitization companies or reconstruction companies: Provided further that a securitization company or reconstruction company, existing on the commencement of this Act, shall make an application for registration to the Reserve Bank before the expiry of six months from such commencement and notwithstanding anything contained in this sub-section may continue to carry on the business of securitization or asset reconstruction until a certificate of registration is granted to it or, as the case may be, rejection of application for registration is communicated to it.
- Every securitization company or reconstruction company shall make an application for registration to the Reserve Bank in such form and manner as it may specify.
- The Reserve Bank may, for the purpose of considering the application for registration of a securitization company or reconstruction company to

commence or carry on the business of securitization or asset reconstruction, as the case may be, require to be satisfied, by an inspection of records or books of such securitization company or reconstruction company, or otherwise, that the following conditions are fulfilled, namely:- (a) that the securitization company or reconstruction company has not incurred losses in any of the three preceding financial years; (b) that such securitization company or reconstruction company has made adequate arrangements for realisation of the financial assets acquired for the purpose of securitization or asset reconstruction and shall be able to pay periodical returns and redee on respective due dates on the investments made in the company by the qualified institutional buyers or other persons; (c) that the directors of securitization company or reconstruction company have adequate professional experience in matters related to finance, securitization and reconstruction; (d) that the board of directors of such securitization company or reconstruction company does not consist of more than half of its total number of directors who are either nominees of any sponsor or associated in any manner with the sponsor or any of its subsidiaries; (e) that any of its directors has not been convicted of any offence involving moral turpitude; (f) that a sponsor is not a holding company of the securitization company or reconstruction company, as the case may be, or, does not otherwise hold any controlling interest in such securitization company or reconstruction company; (g) that securitization company or reconstruction company has complied with or is in a position to comply with prudential norms specified by the Reserve Bank.

- The Reserve Bank may, after being satisfied that the conditions specified in sub-section (3) are fulfilled, grant a certificate of registration to the securitization company or the reconstruction company to commence or carry on business of securitization or asset reconstruction, subject to such conditions, which it may consider, fit to impose.

- The Reserve Bank may reject the application made under sub-section (2) if it is satisfied that the conditions specified in sub-section (3) are not fulfilled: Provided that before rejecting the application, the applicant shall be given a reasonable opportunity of being heard.
- Every securitization company or reconstruction company, shall obtain prior approval of the Reserve Bank for any substantial change in its management or change of location of its registered office or change in its name: Provided that the decision of the Reserve Bank, whether the change in management of a securitization company or a reconstruction company is a substantial change in its management or not, shall be final.
- *Explanation*—For the purposes of this, the expression "substantial change in management" means the change in the management by way of transfer of shares or amalgamation or transfer of the business of the company.

Questions at a Glance

SHORT ANSWER QUESTIONS

1. What are the functions of financial market?
2. What are the elements of financial service sector?
3. What are financial services?
4. Briefly explain about regulatory system on financial services.
5. What are the functions of financial service industry?
6. Write a note on the component of the Indian financial services sector.
7. State the powers of central government to call for periodical returns or direct inquiries?
8. What are the powers of recognized stock exchanges?
9. Explain the role of securities and exchange board of India in recognition of stock exchanges.
10. What are the powers of central government regarding amendment of rules of stock exchanges?
11. State the powers of central government to supersede governing body of a recognized stock exchange.
12. Can the central government to suspend business of recognized stock exchanges?
13. What do you mean by exclusion of spot delivery contracts?
14. State the remedy available for refusal of stock exchanges to list securities.
15. Write a note on Title to dividends.

16. Explain the composition of the management of SEBI.
17. Explain the requirements as to registration of intermediaries.
18. Write a note on the role of Securities Appellate Tribunal.
19. How does SEBI prohibit manipulative and deceptive devices, insider trading and substantial acquisition of securities and control?
20. What are the general responsibilities of a portfolio manager?
21. What are the functions of SEBI?
22. Explain the conditions for grant or renewal of certificate to underwriter.
23. How Underwriters are granted certificate by SEBI.
24. Explain the Capital adequacy requirements of Underwriters.
25. How trading and clearing members are registered with SEBI?
26. State the conditions for registration of Registrars to an issue and Share Transfer Agents.
27. What are the obligations of Stock-brokers *vis-a-vis* other stock-brokers?
28. State the SEBI rules on bankers to an issue.
29. Explain the SEBI rules on debenture trustees.
30. What do you mean by foreign exchange market?
31. Write short notes on capital account convertibility.
32. Explain the settlement system in financial intermediation.
33. What do you mean by transformation function?
34. Write a brief note on financial intermediaries.
35. Explain the conditions for grant or renewal of certificate to underwriter.
36. How Underwriters are granted certificate by SEBI.
37. Explain the Capital adequacy requirements of Underwriters.
38. How trading and clearing members are registered with SEBI.?
39. State the conditions for registration of Registrars to an issue and Share Transfer Agents.

40. What are the obligations of Stock-brokers *vis-a-vis* other stock-brokers?
41. State the SEBI rules on bankers to an issue.
42. Explain the SEBI rules on debenture trustees.
43. What is money market?
44. What are the features of Repos?
45. State the features of money market.
46. State the importance of developed money market for an economy.
47. What are the components of money market?
48. Explain Treasury bills as a money market instrument.
49. Explain the types of commercial papers.
50. What are the features of bills of exchange?
51. What are the features of euro market?
52. What are the exchange rates applied in international financial market?
53. State the factors determining interest rates on Eurocurrency.
54. Write a note on the international capital markets.
55. Explain briefly about Eurocurrency deposits. Explain the characteristics of FCCB/GDR.
56. Write a note on Global depository receipt.
57. What are the advantages of raising money through FCCB/GDRS?
58. Briefly explain the documentation required for issue for GDR/FCCB.
59. Explain the factors to be considered by borrowers for availing of foreign currency loan.
60. What you mean by external commercial borrowings?
61. Who can act as Merchant Bankers?
62. Write a brief note on Indian history of merchant banking.
63. State the Procedure for inspection on merchant bankers.
64. Explain briefly about primary market intermediaries.
65. Explain the conditions under which cancellation or suspension of Registration will be done by SEBI.
66. What are the Post-issue obligations of merchant bankers?
67. Explain about the deposits not considered as deposits

68. What are powers of central government to grant extension of time/exemption?
69. Write a note the penalties for contravention of deposit rules.
70. What do you mean by free reserves?
71. Briefly explain about the acceptance of deposits and the restrictions and limits on it.
72. What is maintenance of liquid assets?
73. State the restrictions and conditions on powers of investment.
74. Loans to companies under 'same management'.
75. Write a note on Register of investment.
76. What do you mean by pricing by companies issuing securities.
77. What is the basis for issue price?
78. What do you mean by lease?
79. Write a note on lease rentals.
80. Merits and demerits of leasing
81. Explain what is accounting for lease?
82. What do you mean by the accounting standard on lease?
83. Explain the disclosures on lease.
84. What is fixation of lease rentals?
85. What is lease evaluation?
86. What is hire purchase?
87. State the contents of hire purchase agreement.
88. Differentiate between Hire purchase vs. leasing.
89. Explain how Lease and hire purchase differ based on accounting?
90. State the importance of Factoring.
91. What are the characteristic features of factoring services?
92. How does factoring work?
93. How do banks facilitate Factors?
94. Distinguish between Bills discounting and factoring.
95. What is International factoring?
96. Write a note on the changing consumer attitudes in India.
97. State the benefits of credit cards.

98. What do you know about the security features in debit or credit cards?
99. What are the considerations made for issue of credit or debit card?
100. What are the costs associated with credit card?
101. What is venture capital?
102. Explain the origin of venture financing.
103. What are the forms of venture financing?
104. Explain the features of venture capital financing.
105. What are the conditions to be fulfilled for availing of venture capital?
106. Explain the stages in venture capital financing.
107. How venture capital funds are registered?
108. Explain the concept of credit rating and its evolution.
109. State the Indian experience of credit rating.
110. What are the Credit rating applications and the factors for success of a rating system?
111. Explain the importance of credit rating.
112. Explain the Rating process?
113. What do you mean by Mutual Funds?
114. Write a note on open-ended Mutual Fund?
115. What do you mean by geographical classification of Mutual Funds?
116. Explain any three types of mutual fund schemes.
117. Explain the types of mutual fund costs.
118. What are duties of trustees?
119. What are the disadvantages of mutual funds?
120. What does the trust deed contain?
121. Write a note on SEBI regulation on mutual funds.
122. Explain the type/types of accounts offered by most of the mutual funds.
123. Write on the Depositories system of trading.
124. What are procedures for registration of depository participant?
125. How monitoring is done on depositories?
126. State the advantages of depository system of trading.
127. Write a note about sale and purchase of demat securities.
128. State the importance of delivery instruction slips.
129. What are the corporate benefits due to demat?

130. Briefly explain pledge and lending and borrowing of demat securities.
131. How nomination and transmission of demat securities take place?
132. Explain the regulatory framework of stock exchanges.
133. Explain the contributions of stock markets for financial development in India.
134. What are the aspects to be considered while buying securities?
135. Write a note on the settlement system of securities trading.
136. Explain the listing requirements of companies.
137. What do you mean by bull and bear markets?
138. Explain the issues connected with transfer of securities.
139. Briefly explain about Badla Trading.
140. What is Margin Trading
141. What do you mean by Capital Market Segment.
142. Write a note on The National Securities Clearing Corporation Ltd. (NSCCL).
143. What is trade verification module?
144. Explain the mechanism of Wholesale Debt Market Segment.
145. State the highlights and features of OTCEI market.
146. Write a note on the importance of Investor Education.
147. What are the remedies available to investors under the Companies Act?
148. State the points to be noted by an investor before investing in securities.
149. What are the friendly measures undertaken by SEBI for investor protection?
150. What are the classifications of issues?
151. State the eligibility norms for making issues?
152. What is the role of SEBI's in an issue?
153. Write a note on 'issue documents.
154. Book building and normal public issue.
155. Explain the types of book-building process?
156. Explain some of the new terms and concepts in securities issue.
157. Write a note on derivatives in Indian capital market.

158. Differentiate forward from futures.
159. Explain the types of futures.
160. Who are the players in futures market and options market?
161. Explain the forward contracts on foreign exchange

ESSAY TYPE QUESTIONS

1. Discuss the categories of financial services available in India.
2. Trace the origin and growth of financial services sector in India.
3. Explain the contributions of financial intermediation in the process of economic development.
4. Discuss about macroeconomic aggregates. What role do they play in the development of the economy?
5. Illustrate the various factors that contribute to a conducive economic situation.
6. Discuss the procedure for recognition of stock exchanges.
7. What are the activities prohibited under the Securities Contract Act?
8. What are the powers of central government regarding making rules for stock exchanges?
9. Discuss the penalty provisions of the SCR Act.
10. Explain the powers of recognized stock exchanges to make bye-laws.
11. Explain the contents of agreement between the portfolio manager and his clients.
12. Discuss briefly the code of conduct of portfolio manager.
13. List the contents of the contract with clients and disclosure requirements.
14. Discuss the Powers of SEBI.
15. Explain the SEBI intermediation in the functioning of portfolio manager and investment of clients' moneys.
16. Explain the penalty imposable under SEBI Act for various offences.
17. What are the powers of Central Government under SEBI Act?

18. Discuss the general obligations and responsibilities of Underwriters.
19. Describe the code of conduct for underwriters.
20. Discuss the code of conduct for stock brokers.
21. Illustrate the inspection and disciplinary proceedings on Underwriters.
22. Describe the procedure for registration and renewal of Underwriters.
23. Describe the advantages of fixed rate exchange system.
24. Describe the advantages of flexible rate exchange system.
25. Explain the various foreign exchange participants.
26. Discuss the concept of convertibility of rupee.
27. What are the factors determining spot exchange rates?
28. What are the factors determining forward margin?
29. Explain the characteristics of foreign exchange market.
30. Discuss the general obligations and responsibilities of Underwriters.
31. Describe the code of conduct for underwriters.
32. Discuss the code of conduct for stock brokers.
33. Illustrate the inspection and disciplinary proceedings on Underwriters.
34. Describe the procedure for registration and renewal of Underwriters.
35. Trace the growth of money market in India.
36. Explain the characteristics of a developed money market.
37. What are the characteristics of Indian money market.
38. Explain in detail the features and benefits of certificate of deposits.
39. Explain the role of various money market players.
40. Explain the working, features and benefits of call money market.
41. Commercial Papers provide greater liquidity of funds to corporate—comment.
42. Trace the growth of international financial market.

43. Explain what is Eurocredit? And the types of euro-credits available
44. Explain the types of Certificates of deposit.
45. Eurobonds a sound of international finance—Illustrate.
46. Describe how funds can be accessed through Euronotes in international market?
47. Discuss the concept of offshore banking and prospects and problems of offshore unit in India.
48. Explain the procedure for issue of FCCBS/GDR
49. Narrate the steps to be taken for issue of FCCBS/GDR.
50. Discuss the features of ECB policy.
51. Describe the procedure for issue of FCCBS/GDRs.
52. Illustrate the schemes of ECB available to Indian borrowers.
53. What are the latest developments in Merchant Banking?
54. Discuss the SEBI guidelines on Lead Merchant Banker and the responsibilities of Lead Managers.
55. Describe clearly the various functions of a Merchant Banker.
56. Discuss the Obligations of Merchant Bankers.
57. Explain the Code of conduct of Merchant Banker.
58. What are the regulations on public deposits?
59. Discuss about the Companies (Acceptance of Deposits) Rules, 1975.
60. Describe the procedure for acceptance of deposits.
61. Explain the Procedure for investment under sec. 372.
62. How does pricing done on different issues?
63. Trace the origin and growth of leasing in India.
64. Discuss the types of leases.
65. Describe the accounting treatment by the lessee and lessor for lease.
66. What are the methods of lease evaluation?
67. Explain the role played by hire purchase business in transport industry.
68. Discuss the policy measures on hire purchase.
69. What are the financial aspects to be considered on hire purchase?

70. Illustrate the types of hire purchase.
71. Describe the origin and growth of hire purchase business in India.
72. Explain the accounting practices for hire purchase.
73. What are the regulations on public deposits?
74. Discuss the merits and demerits of factoring.
75. Describe the types of domestic factoring.
76. Explain the types of international factoring?
77. Explain in detail what is export factoring and its merits and demerits.
78. Describe the factoring services origin and development in India.
79. What are the functions of factors and services of factors?
80. Explain the working of debit and credit cards.
81. Discuss the features of consumer finance.
82. What are the points to be considered while applying for cards?
83. Explain the factors that contributed to the increased uses of credit cards in India.
84. Discuss the different types of cards.
85. Explain in detail the growth of consumer financing in India.
86. Detail the application procedure and issue of certificate for VCFs.
87. Discuss the investment conditions and restrictions on VCFs.
88. What are the General obligations and responsibilities venture funds?
89. What are the powers of Inspection and investigation by SEBI?
90. What are the consequences in case of default/ violation on VCFs?
91. Discuss the benefits and disadvantage of credit rating.
92. Discuss about the rating symbols of CARE and CRISIL.
93. Explain the Code of conduct of rating agencies.
94. Explain the Rating of companies and structured obligations.

95. Explain the procedure for Registration and the general obligations of credit rating agencies.
96. Describe are the advantages of Mutual Funds.
97. Explain the working of mutual funds.
98. What are the points to be considered by an investor before investing in mutual fund?
99. Explain in detail the various types of Mutual Funds.
100. Explain the advertisement code for Mutual Funds.
101. Discuss the Contents of investment Management Agreement:
102. Illustrate the organization and management of Mutual Funds.
103. Discuss the services offered by Mutual Funds.
104. Describe the demat account operation and precautions necessary for its opening.
105. Explain the process of dematerialization and rematerialisation.
106. What are the powers of SEBI under Depositories Act?
107. What are the documents to be maintained by a depository?
108. What are the duties of intermediaries of dematerialization?
109. What are the contents of the depository agreement?
110. Discuss the nature of stock exchange.
111. Who are all associated with trading of securities in the secondary market and explain their role?
112. Discuss the obligations under a listing agreement.
113. Illustrate the organizational structure of the secondary market.
114. Describe the trading mechanism of stock exchanges.
115. Narrate the working of Bombay Stock Exchange Limited.
116. Discuss the features and benefits of Automated Lending and Borrowing Mechanism.
117. The National Stock Exchange of India Limited.
118. Comment on the working of Over the Counter Exchange of India small companies.
119. Discuss the SEBI guidelines on disclosure and investor protection.

120. What are the Regulatory measures taken by government for investor protection?
121. Explain the areas which need to be tuned up for investors' protection.
122. Describe the rights and responsibilities of investors.
123. What are the measures taken by SEBI for curbing insider trading for investors' protection?
124. Describe the code of conduct for prevention of insider trading.
125. Describe the SEBI's disclosure and investor protection guidelines for new issues.
126. Discuss the contents of offer document.
127. What is role of intermediaries in securities issue?
128. Explain the book-building guidelines of SEBI.
129. What are the points to be kept in mind by investors entering primary market?
130. Discuss the Book building process in India and steps involved in it.
131. Discuss the system of working of futures contracts.
132. What are the margin requirements in derivatives trading?
133. Discuss whether futures transactions are speculative?
134. Describe options trading and its kinds?
135. Write detail note on hedging and swaps.

Index